International Internet Law

This book discusses the international legal issues underlying Internet governance and proposes an international solution to its problems. The book encompasses a wide spectrum of current debate surrounding the governance of the Internet. It focuses on the areas and issues which urgently require attention from the international community in order to sustain the proper functioning of a global network which forms the foundation of our information-fuelled society. Among the topics discussed are international copyright protection, state responsibility for cyberattacks (cyber-terrorism), and international online privacy protection.

Taking a comparative approach by examining how different jurisdictions such as the United States, the European Union, China and Singapore have attempted various solutions to the problem of Internet governance, the author offers a practical solution to the problem and is a proponent of 'International Internet Law'. Kulesza suggests that, just as in the case of international environmental law, an Internet Framework Convention could shape the starting point for international cooperation and lead to a clear, contractual division of state jurisdictional competences.

International Internet Law is of particular interest to legal scholars engaged with the current challenges in international law and international relations, as well as students of law, international relations and political science. The issues discussed in the book are also relevant to journalists and other media professionals facing the challenges of analyzing current international developments in cyberspace.

Joanna Kulesza is an assistant professor of international public law at the Faculty of Law and Administration, University of Lodz, Poland. Her research interests include limits of state competence in cyberspace, international co-operation on Internet governance and the future of the World Wide Web.

Routledge Research in IT and E-Commerce Law

Titles in this series include:

Law of Electronic Commercial Transactions
Contemporary Issues in the EU, US and China
Faye Fangfei Wang

Online Dispute Resolution for Consumers in the European Union
Pablo Cortés

The Current State of Domain Name Regulation
Domain Names as Second Class Citizens in a Mark-Dominated World
Konstantinos Komaitis

International Internet law
Joanna Kulesza

International Internet Law

Joanna Kulesza

Translated by Magdalena Arent and WojciechWołoszyk

Translation funded by the Foundation for Polish Science

LONDON AND NEW YORK

First published 2012
by Routledge
2 Park Square, Milton Park, Abingdon, Oxfordshire OX14 4RN

Simultaneously published in the USA and Canada
by Routledge
711 Third Avenue, New York, NY 10017

Routledge is an imprint of the Taylor & Francis Group, an informa business

First issued in paperback 2013

This translation was funded by the Foundation for Polish Science.

British Library Cataloguing in Publication Data
A catalogue record for this book is available from the British Library

Library of Congress Cataloging-in-Publication Data
Kulesza, Joanna.
International internet law / Joanna Kulesza.
p. cm.
ISBN 978–0–415–67468–3 (hardback)—ISBN 978–0–203–12325–6 (e-book)
1. Conflict of laws—Jurisdiction. 2. Internet—Management—International cooperation. 3. Internet—Law and legislation. 4. International law. I. Title.
K7625.K85 2012
343.09'944—dc23
2011040533

ISBN 978–0–415–67468–3(hbk)
ISBN 978-0-415-73057-0 (pbk)
ISBN978–0–203–12325–6(ebk)

Typeset in Garamond
by Swales & Willis Ltd, Exeter, Devon

The translation was funded by the Foundation for Polish Science.

To my Husband

Contents

Preface

In only a few years, the Internet has revolutionized trade, health, education, and, indeed, the very fabric of human communication and exchange. Moreover, its potential is far greater than what we have seen in the relatively short time since its creation. In managing, promoting, and protecting its presence in our lives, we need to be no less creative than those who invented it. Clearly, there is a need for governance, but that does not necessarily mean that it has to be done in the traditional way, for something that is so very different.[1]

K. Annan

The Internet has, in a relatively short time, become an essential instrument of modern social functioning. As of late 2011 the global network includes an estimated 2.5 billion users[2] which means that every third resident of the world uses the Internet. The growing awareness of the social, economic, and political impact of the Internet on society has brought the question of governing the Internet as a whole into sharper focus. However, the process of regulating legal and social consequences of technological solutions always falls behind technological innovations and their implementation. This applies to the Internet as well, if not most of all. It has become apparent that the Internet requires a comprehensive regulation to prevent the loss of its functionality (which may be an unavoidable consequence of gradual fragmentation) and to maintain its efficiency and interoperability. Moreover, laying down common legal principles governing the Internet as a whole would facilitate the protection of users' rights and formulate straightforward and uniform responsibilities of their relevant groups. Currently, the international community conducts negotiations on Internet governance. The World Summit on the Information Society (WSIS), held in Geneva in December 2003, officially placed the issue of Internet governance on agendas of diplomatic meetings and discussions. The *Declaration of Principles* and *Action Plan* adopted at WSIS provided for the implementation of a number of initiatives in

1 The United Nations Secretary-General, K. Annan, during the Global Internet Governance Forum, New York, March 2004; see E. Gelbstein and J. Kurbalija (2005), *Internet Governance, Issues, Actor and Divides*, Msida: Diplo Foundation, p. 7.

2 All statistical data as per Miniwatts Marketing Group, *Internet World Stats*. <http://www.internetworldstats.com/stats.htm> (accessed 17 February 2009 based on statistics last updated 9 February 2009).

the field of Internet governance, including the establishment of a Working Group on Internet Governance (WGIG).[3] WSIS and WGIG comprised the first phase of the process of establishing international mechanisms to govern the Internet, which should result in the clarification of Internet governance issues, as well as introduce new related procedures and mechanisms. The international forum which is expected to produce solutions to the burning issues could be the Internet Governance Forum (IGF), under the auspices of the Secretary-General of the United Nations.[4]

All abovementioned efforts have contributed to the establishment of the foundations of a new, international and interdisciplinary branch of law, which may be referred to as the 'International Internet Law'. This is the area combining both national and supranational efforts overlapping all branches of law, closely related to issues of the technical structure of the global network. The basic notion requiring clarification (which underlies the entire debate on the form of the new branch of law) is the concept of Internet governance. Until now, the only attempt at establishing international definition of this quite difficult idea has been made by the World Summit on the Information Society. The final document of the WSIS in Tunis in 2005 comprised the definition of "Internet governance" as "more than Internet naming and addressing". It also includes "other significant public policy issues such as, *inter alia*, critical Internet resources, the security and safety of the Internet, and developmental aspects and issues pertaining to the use of the Internet".[5] Moreover, the document includes a call on all members of the Internet community to extend and modify the proposed definition so that "Internet governance" is democratic and transparent with the involvement of governments, the private sector, civil society and international organizations. Internet governance should "ensure a stable and secure functioning of the Internet, taking into account multilingualism".[6] It seems that the essence of the problem lies in the lack of consensus as to the scope of the notion itself: whether Internet governance should take account of network technical administration and related competence of state authorities only or, more reasonably (due to practical impossibility of separating strictly technical issues), look far ahead in directions specified by WSIS ("development-oriented aspects"). What is more, in this context, even the very definition of the term "Internet", which usually includes only the physical elements of the global network, proves disputable: the definition definitely does not reflect the

3 Article 50 of the (2003) *Declaration of Principles* (WSIS-03/GENEVA/DOC/4-E <http://www.itu.int/wsis/docs/geneva/official/dop.html> (accessed 14 January 2009) reads as follows: "International Internet governance issues should be addressed in a coordinated manner. We ask the Secretary-General of the United Nations to set up a working group on Internet governance, in an open and inclusive process that ensures a mechanism for the full and active participation of governments, the private sector and civil society from both developing and developed countries, involving relevant intergovernmental and international organizations and forums, to investigate and make proposals for action, as appropriate, on the governance of Internet by 2005".

4 More about all entities involved in the debate on global network governance, their role and achievements can be found in chapter 4.

5 United Nations (2005) *World Summit on the Information Society Tunis Agenda for the Information Society*, Geneva: ITU. <http://www.itu.int/wsis/docs2/tunis/off/6rev1.html> (accessed 4 January 2011), para. 77.

6 Ibid., item 29.

current nature of this phenomenon.[7] For the purposes hereof, the term "Internet governance" – being essential to considerations on the form of international Internet law – includes issues directly related to the technical administration of electronic resources, including private entities, as well as any and all actions performed by state authorities using legal instruments and international organizations exerting a direct impact on activities performed using the electronic medium, including those outside a regulating state. This definition enables us to focus on the priority goal of the international community, namely to establish common international standards as to the freedoms and obligations of all categories of entities involved in electronic activities and set limits of their mutual influences, particularly by using instruments specifying the distribution of jurisdictional competence at international level. Apart from state authorities developing national regulations, other entities that affect Internet governance include private-law entities (with particular regard to ICANN, but also all other entities involved in Internet governance), international organizations such as ITU[8] or WTO (acting mainly as consultants and experts rendering their forum available for initiating and stimulating international debate) as well as end users – natural persons who have *de facto* become the object and not the subject of national and international regulations on the electronic network. Actions of state authorities are intended to produce effects at national level, even though, in reality, they often produce effects at international level. The actions of other entities, such as international and social organizations which most often unite network users, are of an international nature, though without legally binding force.

As a result of the foregoing discussions, an obvious and still unresolved dispute has arisen between the supporters of new "cyberlaw" (gathered around non-governmental organizations and universities), and those who believe that issues, including those relating to the Internet, are sufficiently regulated by "old" legal provisions if these are applied appropriately (such a position may be proved, for instance, by the practice of applying national law provisions to cyberspace related situations).[9] Supporters of the latter argue that the Internet does not constitute a new object: the Internet is just another new device, no different from the telegraph, the telephone, or radio. Representatives of this approach argue that existing laws can be successfully applied to the Internet with only minor adjustments for, as long as it involves communication between people, the Internet is no different from the telephone or the telegraph, and it can be regulated like other telecommunications media. Proponents of the approach that promotes the need for new regulations on electronic activities, on the other hand, argue that the Internet is a fundamentally different device from all previous devices to which it is compared by cyber-law opponents, and thus that it requires new regulation. This approach was particularly popular in the early days of the Internet;[10] today,

7 For more about the definition of the Internet, please refer to chapter 2.
8 International Telecommunication Union.
9 See chapter 3.
10 See Barlow, J. P. (1996) 'A Declaration of the Independence of Cyberspace', paper published online. <https://projects.eff.org/~barlow/Declaration-Final.html>. The declaration was made on 8 February 1996 in Davos.

the main assumption is that the Internet has detached social and political reality from the world of sovereign states.[11] Cyberspace is different from real space and it requires a different form of governance. (The influence of this approach is noticeable in the creation of ICANN and the manner in which this organization functions.) Supporters of cyberlaw argue that existing laws on jurisdiction, cybercrime and contracts cannot be properly applied to the Internet and that new laws must be established. There are still no convincing counterarguments to those allegations – there are more and more instances in which traditional norms have proven inadequate or insufficient.[12] The assessment that the current infrastructure management of the Internet is a public good still remains disputable.[13] Currently most of the infrastructure on which the Internet is based is owned by (private and state) companies, typically telecommunication operators. One might point here to the analogy of shipping of goods by sea which requires the use of sea areas free from individual ownership title. However, sea routes are open and regulated by the Law of the Sea, based on the concept of *res communis omnium* (open sea), while the backbones of the Internet are owned by private entities. This raises a number of questions which still remain unanswered. Existing legal frameworks do not allow private companies to be required to use their private property in the public interest, for they do not necessarily consent to the notion that the Internet, or parts of it, is to be considered a public good. There is also no final position on whether the concept of *res communis omnium* may be applied to the Internet, as was the case with regulating the Law of the Sea. The current state of affairs is the effect of Internet evolution (or revolution). However, it is not the consequence of deliberate decisions on the part of the international community or the entities using the network themselves. The exclusive reason is the genesis of the development and success of the Internet itself; what once constituted the property of the United States became the grounds for development of a global network. The issue of ownership of the components thereof was not subject to debate. It seems, however, that without such debate it will be difficult to maintain the current Internet development level. The main challenge of the discussion (on the superiority of private over public ownership) is whether there can be a guarantee of further development of the Internet as a public good, combining elements of state power and civil rights (including protection for private ownership).

The aspect which has exerted the strongest impact on the need to reform the way state jurisdiction has been perceived and understood so far, is that the world perceived through the prism of the Internet is opposed to traditional geography. One of the first assumptions regarding the Internet was that it crossed national borders and

11 The premise is especially noticeable assuming the concept of cyberspace "independence" as an area beyond the powers of state authorities, international authorities and legal systems as such. Contrasting the traditional territoriality with the Internet's aterritoriality enables one to show that the consequences of actions in "free" cyberspace are not subject to any authority. Notwithstanding that this radical view is supported only by a few, even from among the most ardent cyber-liberals, the idea on which the assumption was based is still attractive – cyberspace is, *de facto*, a new area of human activities of different quality, which requires relevant legal regulation.

12 See chapter 3.

13 See chapter 4, where the proposal of recognizing cyberspace as international space is discussed.

was independent of a mistakenly understood idea of state sovereignty. The "Declaration of the Independence of Cyberspace" by J. P. Barlow sent an explicit message to all state authorities.[14] This declaration is an example of the predominant techno-optimism typical of the early 1990s – since the declaration, the concept of independence on the Internet has considerably changed, including as a result of significant modifications to the software, now allowing geo-location of users.[15] It is obvious that the more the user-identifying software is efficient, the less is the need for separate regulations pertaining especially to the Internet, and the existing conflict of laws rules prove useful.[16] Nowadays, however, there are still insufficient technical facilities to fully disregard the issue of the aterritoriality of the Internet and the consequences of this fact for users at each level of community organization. Furthermore, arguments against the development of mechanisms precisely identifying all users of the network have been enunciated, resulting from the need to protect privacy and counteract the gathering of personal data by state authorities against the will of the persons concerned.[17]

Notwithstanding that the technologies of Internet regulation and administration are at a level satisfying the international community's expectations and thus allow sustainable use of the global network, the legal and commercial mechanisms of Internet governance are at least at an inadequate technical level of their evolution, for there is no international organization which would decide about the form and manner of the distribution of resources and represent all entities active in cyberspace.[18] Experience of regulating other areas of law shows that regimes regulating areas common for all entities of the international community (for instance environment protection law, air transport or control of armaments) are based on frameworks of legal references; that is, specific values, common understanding of causation, comprehension or terminology. Such a mechanism is yet to be developed with respect to the Internet. What is more, it is still difficult to even talk about a common international forum competent to initiate works aiming at similar goals. Each possible international Internet governance

14 "You are not welcome among us. You have no sovereignty where we gather. You have no moral right to rule us nor do you possess any methods of enforcement we have true reason to fear. Cyberspace does not lie within your borders": J. P. Barlow, op. cit.

15 Although, today, it is still difficult to identify exactly the entity using a particular computer connected to the network, it is relatively easy to identify the Internet service provider. The latest national laws require Internet service providers to identify their users and, if requested by the authorities, to provide necessary information about them (see chapter 3).

16 This concept of reinforcing the geo-location of Internet users is supported by M. Geist, in (2001) 'Is There a There There? Toward Greater Certainty for Internet Jurisdiction', Ottawa: University of Ottawa. <http://arxiv.org/ftp/cs/ papers/0109/0109012.pdf> (accessed 6 February 2007), pp. 50ff. and J. Zittrain (2003) 'Be Careful What You Ask For: Reconciling a Global Internet and Local Law', 60 *Harvard Law School Public Law Research Papers*. <http://ssrn.com/abstract_id395300> (accessed 28 December 2006). The chance for the implementation of the intention may be the "integrated identity" (Identity 2.0) – see: M. Strzelecka (2007) Nadchodzi Epoka Internetu z Otwartą Przyłbicą?' *Gazeta Wyborcza*. <http://gospodarka.gazeta.pl/gospodarka/1,52981,3937067.html> (accessed 6 March 2009). For more information see OpenID <http://openid.net/>.

17 See chapter 2.

18 IGF has no mandate to regulate electronic activities, and in any case, its incomplete representativeness and the voluntary nature of participation therein is an issue, whereas ICANN still has little international legitimacy.

regime will certainly be a complex structure involving a large number of participants, mechanisms, procedures and instruments. Nevertheless all these elements will have a common ground – international agreement allowing for the opinions of all parties concerned.

Despite the abovementioned difficulties, fundamental principles, which should be followed by decision-makers on key global network issues,[19] have already been successfully developed. Some of these principles have been explicitly provided for in instruments of the WSIS, whereas others have been introduced, mainly impliedly, through the application of various regulations onto the Internet. Any initiative in the field of Internet governance should result from existing regulations, which can be divided into three groups: 1) those provided specifically for the Internet (e.g. relating to ICANN) 2) those that require considerable adjustments in order to address Internet (e.g. trademark protection, taxation) and 3) those that can be applied to the Internet without significant adjustments (e.g., to a large extent, the protection of human rights). It is obvious that adjustment of existing principles would significantly increase stability and reduce the complexity of the Internet governance regime. This, however, is not always possible. Internet governance must, above all, meet one condition: it must maintain the current functionality and dynamics of Internet development, being at the same time flexible enough to effectively adopt occurring changes. Only such mechanism would allow increased functionality and higher efficiency. It is the need for stability and resilience of the Internet that should underlie Internet governance reform. The stability of the Internet should be preserved through, *inter alia*, the practice developed at an early stage of Internet development, that is, the gradual introduction of new solutions and their careful testing.

Given the absence of international consensus and co-ordinated debate, the Internet has become one of main objects of state authorities' interest, even though prevention of crime is not the exclusive reason for which governments want to exercise control over the Internet. Financial aspects are of considerable importance (such as taxes, intellectual property rights, commerce and gambling). States' willingness to effectively enforce due benefits grows along with their willingness to regulate Internet-related issues. The consequence of the absence of an international agreement as to the area and manner of regulating Internet actions is the fact that states' national or local regulations to the Internet are often in conflict with one another. It is essential to determine the manner of regulating cyberspace, and more accurately, identify the entity or entities authorized to implement such regulation. May one state enforce its laws so that they affect the entire world? How far may particular states go in regulating cyberspace? Is one document of international extent, which regulates the scope of national powers, a possible and sufficient solution? Should we vest an international organization, possibly established on the basis of a treaty, with competence to regulate the Internet and to set limits for national regulations, and would such an organization be legitimate?

The purpose of this study is to juxtapose basic principles of international law governing jurisdiction (deriving from the principle of the sovereignty of states) with new

19 See chapter 4.

factual circumstances, namely the effects of actions taken in cyberspace. As a result of this analysis, an attempt will be made to identify criteria which enable states to regulate behaviors in cyberspace, prosecute those violating the standards and enforce their own laws conclusively. At the same time, it is also necessary to specify the scope of actions which are admissible without interference in the exclusive sphere of competence of other states. Such an analysis requires the juxtaposition of the current national practices of sovereigns which play key roles in the electronic arena.[20] It seems necessary to verify not only practices of particular states, but also all areas of legal regulation which have proved to be inadequate with respect to the actual circumstances arising from the "Internet revolution". It seems to be of key significance in determining the source and scope of competence of states in cyberspace to establish the limits of state jurisdiction and the possibility of applying its traditional principles to the "space" of new quality. It is only when based on such an analysis that one may provide a legal assessment of the behaviors of states and international organizations and the scope of their competence. To this end, it is necessary to present traditional principles governing states when exercising their cross-border competence (chapter 1). Then one should examine how the Internet has revolutionized the existing legal system and point to major problems to be faced by the national, and most of all, international law makers (chapter 2). To show discrepancies present in national regulations, the author will analyze the most multifarious and at the same time representative approaches of national law makers (users subject to their laws constitute in excess of half the total number of Internet recipients – chapter 3). Finally, the author will sum up the efforts of international negotiators and organizations so far in developing a uniform regulation, at least of a framework nature, on Internet-related legal issues and will analyse these against other existing international law regimes (chapter 4). In the course of these considerations, the author will prove the need to develop an international framework treaty which will serve as the basis for national law makers to implement local legal solutions concerning the global Internet in a correlated manner.

20 Based on the number of users in a given state. These include states mentioned in chapter 3: the United States, China (including the regulation of another fast-developing Asian country, Singapore, as an example of a completely different approach to controlling content of the Internet) and European Community member states.

Abbreviations

APEC	Asia-Pacific Economic Co-Operation Forum
ASIL	American Society of International Law
ccTLDs	Country Code Top-Level Domains
CoE	Council of Europe
DoC	United States Department of Commerce
ECHR	European Court of Human Rights
ECJ	European Court of Justice
ECSG	Electronic Commerce Steering Group of APEC
EJIL	European Journal of International Law
ETS	European Treaty Series
GNSO	Generic Names Supporting Organisation
gTLDs	Generic Top-Level Domains
IANA	Internet Assigned Names Authority
ICANN	Internet Corporation for Assigned Names and Numbers
IESG	Internet Engineering Steering Group
IETF	Internet Engineering Task Force
IGF	Internet Governance Forum
ILI	International Law Institute
ILO	International Labor Organisation
ISOC	Internet Society
IT-UT	International Telecommunications Union Standardization Sector
NATO	North Atlantic Treaty Organisation
OECD	Organisation for Economic Co-operation and Development
RIAA	Recording Industry Association of America
TGI	Tribunal de Grande Instance
UIIPA	Uniform Interstate and International Procedure Act (United States model law)
UNCITRAL	United Nations Commission on International Trade Law
UNDP	United Nations Development Programme
UNTS	United National Treaty Series
UST	United States Treaties
WGIG	Working Group on Internet Governance
WIPO	World Intellectual Property Organization
WSIS	World Summit on the Information Society
WTO	World Trade Organization

Table of cases and statutes

Cases

Domestic constitutions, legislation and legislative codes

International legal and quasi-legal documents

Protocol on Environmental Protection to the Antarctic Treaty, Madrid, 1991 ('Madrid Protocol') 21, 23 n. 111
Rome Statute of the International Criminal Court, Rome, 17 July 1988, 2187 UNTS 90 10, 10 n. 46
Treaty Banning Nuclear Weapon Tests in the Atmosphere, in Outer Space and Under Water, Moscow, 1963 24, 24 n. 117
Treaty on Principles Governing the Activities of States in the Exploration and Use of Outer Space, including the Moon and Other Celestial Bodies, New York, 1967 21, 21 n. 101, 24, 27 n. 139
United Nations
UNESCO Charter on the Preservation of Digital Heritage, Paris, 2003 137 n. 64
UNESCO Universal Declaration on Cultural Diversity, Paris, 2001 76, 138 n. 75, 139
United Nations Commission on International Trade Law (UNCITRAL)
Model Law on Electronic Commerce, 1997 31 n. 5, 71, 71 n. 215, 137 n. 64
Draft Uniform Rules on Electronic Signatures, New York, 2000 31 n. 5
Model Law on Electronic Commerce, New York, 1996. 31 n. 5, 71 n. 101, 137 n. 64
United Nations Draft Code Against the Peace and Security of Mankind, 1991 9 n. 44
United Nations Economic and Social Council (ECOSOC) Resolution 2010/2 on the Assessment of the Progress Made in the Implementation of and Follow-Up to the outcomes of the World Summit on the Information Society. 139 n. 80
United Nations International Covenant on Civil and Political Rights, 1966 47, 48 n. 100, 123 n. 175, 142. n. 97
United Nations International Covenant on Economic, Social and Cultural Rights, 1966 123 n. 175, 142 n. 97
United Nations Resolution on Developments in the Field of Information and Telecommunications in the Context of International Security
53/70 (1998) 137 n. 63
54/49 (1999) 137 n. 63
55/28 (2000) 137 n. 63
56/19 (2001) 137 n. 63
United Nations Resolution 57/239 on Creation of a Global Culture of Cybersecurity, 2002 137 n. 63
United Nations Resolution 58/199 on Creation of a Global Culture of Cybersecurity and the Protection of Critical Information Infrastructures (2003) 137 n. 63
United Nations Resolution of the 12th session of the Human Rights Council, 'Freedom of Opinion and Expression' (2009) 48 n. 101
Universal Copyright Convention, Geneva (1952) 34, 34 n. 15
Universal Declaration of Human Rights (1948) 123, 123 n. 174, 142 n. 97
WIPO Copyright Treaty (1996) 34, 137 n. 64
WIPO Draft Revised Trademark Law Treaty (2004) 42 n. 62
WIPO Performances and Phonograms Treaty, 1996) 34, 137 n. 64

1 The limits of state competence

Traditional notions of jurisdiction

Statehood, sovereignty and jurisdiction in cyberspace

The Internet has revolutionized not only everyday life, but also shown the need to redefine many key legal terms which have been so far considered as well formulated and sufficient to describe and explain international relations. It has become clear that many well-established definitions require amending to better adapt to this new phenomenon.

One of the key categories that demand alteration is the concept of statehood and territorial links between international relations which follow from the fact of the existence of states. In contrast to relations hitherto defined "territorially" cyberspace is perceived by S. Rosenne as elusive, indefinite and straying from the natural characteristics of states.[1] The limitlessness of the Internet, its aterritoriality and its common presence, require that statehood in its traditional sense, or, more precisely, the competence of states to regulate social and international relations in terms of territoriality, be redefined and supplemented as far as the new, electronic dominium is concerned. In order to consider how this might be achieved, we must first consider the competence or jurisdictional activities[2] of the state.

In legal terms, the state is defined as an original entity, i.e. its legal and international subjectivity originates from the fact of its sole existence.[3] According to the most general definition, the "state" is a conglomerate of three features: territory, population and state authority.[4] A condition precedent to be met by an entity aspiring to statehood is the

1 S. Rosenne (2001) 'The Perplexities of Modern International Law: General Course on Public International Law', 291 *Recueil des Cours*, p. 9 at p. 349.

2 The terms variously used herein, "jurisdictional competence" "powers" "activities" of the state refer to the execution by state authorities of their powers to regulate interpersonal relations (including at international level) for which the state is authorised solely through its attribution of statehood (the term falls within the concept of acta de iure Imperii, yet it is not exhaustive). Powers to make and safeguard the law using coercive measures are of essence here, and not any and all indications of activity of the state at international level.

3 See e.g. H. Kelsen (2002) *Principles of International Law*, New Jersey: The Lawbook Exchange, Ltd., pp. 207ff.

4 In the opinion of the Arbitration Committee for Yugoslavia, a state is defined as a community which consists of a territory and a population subject to an organized political authority and characterized by sovereignty (opinion 1, 29 November 1991), see A. Pellet (1992) 'The Opinions of the Badinter

condition of effectiveness of governance;[5] that is its independence from any external authorities or forces: in other words, its sovereignty.[6] One may point to a wide range of indicators of state sovereignty. The most representative and uncontroversial are the exclusiveness of power over state territory and citizens, execution of foreign policy, the ability to make decisions on engaging in war or keeping peace, free recognition of states and governments, decisions concerning the creation of diplomatic relations and participation in military alliances and international organizations.[7] Sovereignty therefore manifests itself in a number of activities performed by states at international level under competence vested by international law. State competence has two dimensions. In a material dimension it means the regulation of social relations by organizing social life within the state – commonly described as the state power towards persons, items and events. In a formal dimension, on the other hand, state competence includes the ability to establish legal norms necessary for the organization of a particular social sphere, as well as the ability to safeguard their execution (the execution of norms). This aspect of state activities is referred to as the execution of jurisdiction.[8]

The execution of jurisdictional competence is, above all, a territorial phenomenon. State competence is, as a rule, exercised in a particular physical space and remains bound thereto. The analysis of state competence is made, therefore, *ratione loci*, and the basic area within which it is exercised is the territory of the state.[9] The presence

Arbitration Committee: a Second Breath for the Self-Determination of Peoples', 3 *EJIL*, pp. 178–185. <http://www.ejil.org/article.php?article=1175&issue=68> (accessed on 14 January 2011). Cf. also M. N. Shaw (2003) *International Law*, 5th edn., Cambridge: Cambridge University Press, pp. 183ff., A. Aust (2005) *Handbook of International Law*, 2nd edn., Cambridge: Cambridge University Press, pp. 16ff., and L. Oppenheim (2006) *International law: A Treatise*, vol. I, New Jersey: The Lawbook Exchange, Ltd, p. 126, paras. 64ff.

5 See L. Oppenheim, op. cit., p. 384 para. 222 and Shaw, op. cit., p. 180 and pp. 183ff.

6 Sovereignty is a concept variously defined in numerous studies within the ambit of law and political sciences, cf. Kelsen, op. cit., p. 438, G. M. Bard (1984) *State Immunity: An Analytical and Prognostic View*, The Hague: Martinus Nijhoff Publishers, pp. 9ff., K. Bartsch and B. Elberling (2003) 'Jus Cogens v. State Immunity, Round Two: The Decision of the European Court of Human Rights in the Kalogeropoulou et al. v. Greece and Germany Decision', 4(5) *German Law Journal*, p. 14. The concept is subject to strong criticism, see e.g. S. D. Krasner (2002) 'Sovereignty: Organized Hypocrisy', in G. Kreijen et al. (eds.) *State, Sovereignty and International Governance*, Oxford: Oxford University Press. It is often pointed out that the notion of state sovereignty ought to be altered, initially due to the evolving character of human rights (see e.g. W. M. Reisman (1990) 'Sovereignty and Human Rights in Contemporary International Law', 84(4) *The US Journal of International Law*, pp. 866ff.), and more recently, with regard to the transboundary and unique characteristic of cyberspace, see R. H. Weber (2010) 'New Sovereignty Concepts in the Age of Internet', 14(8) *Journal of Internet Law*, pp. 12ff. and J. H. Jackson (2003) 'Sovereignty-Modern: A New Approach To An Outdated Concept', 97 *US Journal of International Law*, pp. 782ff.

7 On the modern meaning of sovereignty see e.g. F. H. Hinsley (1986) *Sovereignty*, 2nd edn., New York: Cambridge University Press, pp.126ff.

8 See e.g. Kelsen, op. cit., pp. 191ff. and Aust, op. cit., pp. 43ff.

9 For territory meaning land (including under ground), sea (including territorial waters, such as rivers or lakes) and air, see e.g. Oppenheim, op. cit., pp. 305ff and Shaw, op. cit., pp. 409ff.). The same powers as those over state territory are also vested with respect to the boarding of sea vessels and aircrafts as well as space vehicles registered in the state (the act of registration specifies such spatial link between the vehicle and the state by a right to hoist a flag of the state of registration).

of the state in a given space is the grounds for exercising state competence.[10] The scope of exercised power within a particular territory formed by the state authorities is complete and exclusive.[11] The completeness of competence is covered by the material aspect (that is, the authority to organize all domains of social life by regulating the course of events and status of things; *lex loci rei sitae; quidquid est in territori, est etiam de territorio*) as well as the personal aspect (that is, the authority to regulate behaviors of natural and juridical persons present in its territory, including citizens as well as those without citizenship of the state; *qui in teritorio meo est, etiam meus subditus est*). The exclusivity of the competence means its legitimate execution solely (exclusively) by state authorities, i.e. legislative, executive and judicial bodies. Therefore, as a rule this means an unlimited scope of powers, with the exception of limitations imposed by international law. State competence is, consequently, principally executed within the state territory. It is, however, also executed in spaces other than the 'own' territory of the state, such as politically organized spaces (i.e. territories of other states or areas of other political status – e.g. in the past such territories included the UN trust territories – and free (common) spaces not subjected to any state powers (e.g. the high sea).[12] The title to execute competence in those areas shall, in each and every case, flow from international law.[13]

When analyzing the jurisdictional activities of states, it should be noted that the object of a state's interests may be "physical" locations outside the territory of the state (for instance, trust territories), but also individual situations concerning persons, things and events located or staying outside the territory of the state. The most evident example of the above is the practice of translocation of natural and juridical persons onto territories of third countries and the unquestionable title of the state of nationality to not only render assistance to such persons, but also to

10 In the *Island of Palmas case* (*Netherlands* v. *USA*) (1928) the Permanent Court of Arbitration emphasised the development of international law, and in particular the principle of the exclusive competence of the sovereign state with regard to its own territory, as a key issue for regulating modern international relations. Available online at The Hague Justice Portal. <http://www.thehaguelegalcapital.nl/eCache/DEF/5/184.html> (accessed 5 February 2011).

11 The state power exercised within state territory is described as being "complete" and "exclusive", following the statement of Judge Huber in the above-mentioned decision, see also N. Q. Dinh, P. Daillier and A. Pellet (1999) *Droit International Public*, 6th edn., Paris: Librairie Generale de Droit et de Jurisprudence, pp. 470ff.

12 Cf. chapter 4 part 3.

13 The treaty between Great Britain and France on the exercise of state competences in the Channel Tunnel may serve as an example, as it allows for each state to exercise jurisdiction in the space of the Tunnel (The Channel Tunnel Act 1987). The Protocol between the Government of the United Kingdom of Great Britain and Northern Ireland and the Government of the French Republic Concerning Frontier Controls and Policing, Cooperation in Criminal Justice, Public Safety and Mutual Assistance Relating to the Channel Fixed Link, Sangatte, 25 November 1991, 1747 UNTS p. 109, <http://www.cps.gov.uk/legal/section2/chapter_f.html> (accessed 4 March 2011). It allowed French and British officers, acting on behalf of border authorities, to perform their duties in particular parts of the territory of the other state (the so-called "Control Zones"). Article 38(2)(a) of the protocol states that within "the Fixed Link each State shall have jurisdiction and apply its own law (i) when it cannot be ascertained with certainty where an offence has been committed or (ii) when an offence committed in the territory of one State is related to an offence committed on the territory of the other State, or

undertake jurisdictional activities against them.[14] The legitimacy of a state exercising laws with respect to events occurring abroad yet seriously affecting its territory is in no doubt. One of the first instances of acknowledging the (very limited at that time) jurisdictional powers of a state over events outside its territory is the resolution of the International Law Institute (ILI) dated 1879, which stipulated the right of states to sanction acts committed outside their respective territories and instances of breach of their criminal regulations by foreigners, insofar as such acts pose a threat to the existence of a state and are not penalized under the laws of the state in which they were committed.[15] Execution of jurisdiction outside the territory of the state indicates two things – first, a territorial context of sovereign activities of a state supplemented by their aterritorial, personal, aspect. Second, the entitlement of a state to execute jurisdictional competence over persons, things and events outside its territory raises questions fundamental to international law. Each and every attempt to exercise jurisdictional competence provokes a conflict of jurisdictions between that of the local authorities and that of the state attempting to exercise jurisdiction on grounds other than territorial. In such cases it is necessary to identify the rules for eliminating such conflict. States who are the parties to such a dispute may develop their own rules allowing conflict resolution. This was expressed by the Permanent Court of International Justice (PCIJ) in the *Lotus case* (1927) when the court, addressing the issue of state jurisdictional activities, stated:

> Now the first and foremost restriction imposed by international law upon a State is that (. . .) it may not exercise its power in any form in the territory of another State. In this sense jurisdiction is certainly territorial; it cannot be executed by a State outside its territory except by virtue of a permissible rule derived from international custom or from a convention.

The PCIJ stressed that international law does not prohibit a state from exercising sovereign powers outside its own territory, provided that such competence may be based on a relevant permissible rule of international law. International law provides for a wide measure of discretion in determining common rules for executing extra-territorial jurisdiction with only few limitations. The PCIJ emphasizes the variety of jurisdictional principles within the disposition of states, to be adopted by states in the absence of objection or complaint from other parties.[16]

(iii) when an offence has begun in or has been continued into its own territory". This solution supplements the traditional concept of the jurisdiction of states over their territory including under water, up to the state's border. Nevertheless, the protocol also stipulates that the state which was the first to receive the suspect into its territory has the priority in exercising jurisdiction. See also Shaw, op. cit., p. 582.

14 Cf. S. Rosenne, op. cit., p. 265.

15 See W. E. Hall (1904) *A Treatise on International Law*, Oxford: Oxford University Press, p. 213. The author also provides numerous examples of European states' regulations (between the nineteenth and twentieth centuries) beyond the limits specified by the ILI resolution. The author notices that the existence of such a right might be deemed a consequence of the state's right to self-preservation.

16 *France* v. *Turkey (the Lotus case)* (1927) PCIJ (Ser. A) No. 10 (PCIJ). <http://www.worldcourts.com/pcij/eng/decisions/1927.09.07_lotus/> (accessed 2 February 2011).

Without questioning the right of a state to perform jurisdictional activities against persons, things and events outside its territory, the PCIJ indicates that international law allows a certain liberty to states with respect to jurisdictional order.[17] According to the court, this state jurisdiction is determined by general principles regulating the manner of exercising jurisdiction that has been "adopted without objections or complaints"[18] from other parties or from conventions which allow states to exercise a particular, adopted jurisdictional regime.[19] Following the PCIJ reasoning, one should first and foremost point to the general principles of establishing jurisdictional regimes. They should be at the same time individualized and applied respectively to state capacity to establish certain rules (jurisdiction to prescribe), as well to state capacity to enforce them (jurisdiction to enforce). The US Law Institute's *Restatement of the Law* may prove helpful in ascertaining rules "accepted without objections or complaints" mentioned in the decision of the PCIJ.[20] Regarding the state capacity to establish rules, one may follow the approach presented in the *Restatement* that state jurisdiction to prescribe, apart from regulating the status of persons, things and events within the state territory, covers also events outside the state territory should they have or be intended to have substantial effect within the state territory.[21] It also includes activities, interests, status or relations of its nationals both outside and within its territory.[22] The prescriptive jurisdiction covers also conduct outside state territory by persons not being state nationals that is directed against the security of the state or against a particular category of other state interests.[23] The occurrence of all of the above generally described events and conduct requires, according to the *Restatement*, recognition by the law-maker and fulfillment of further prerequisites of reasonableness provided for in national legislation.[24]

17 See A. Bos (1993) 'The Extraterritorial Jurisdiction of States: Preliminary Report', 65(1) *Yearbook of the Institute of International Law*, p. 39, who names the spirit of discretional assessment the essence of the idea of jurisdiction, since it penetrates the awareness of international community and is liable for the relevance of the *Lotus case* decision; see also L. Reydams (2003) *Universal Jurisdiction: International and Municipal Legal Perspectives*, Oxford: Oxford University Press, p. 14.

18 *France* v. *Turkey (the Lotus case)*, op. cit.

19 Cf. S. Rosenne, op. cit., p. 265.

20 L. Henkin (ed.) (1987) *The Foreign Relations Law of the United States: Restatement of the Law*, New York: American Law Institute, hereinafter referred to as the *Restatement.*

21 The most obvious examples of such events are examples of shooting across the border and inflicting damage within a frontier zone or distributing libelous publications in a neighboring country, trading damage-inflicting products or telephone fraud (as in the case *Lamar* v. *US* (1916) 240 US 60 in which the court recognized that telephone fraud may be prosecuted as per the territorial jurisdiction of the state to which the call was made). <http://laws.findlaw.com/us/240/60.html> (accessed 5 February 2011).

22 The most typical examples are tax regulations imposing an obligation on nationals to pay tax on income generated abroad in the state of nationality.

23 The *Restatement*, § 402(f).

24 In accordance with the *Restatement*, § 403(2), whether exercise of jurisdiction over a person or activity is reasonable, is determined by evaluating all relevant factors, including, where appropriate: (a) the link of the activity to the territory of the regulating state, including the extent to which the activity takes place within the territory, or has a substantial, direct, and foreseeable effect upon or in the territory; (b)

The abovementioned, territorial, personal and effective aspects of exercising jurisdiction show the set of fundamental principles specifying the title to exercise jurisdiction, which manifests itself in national regulations. These principles are:

- the territoriality principle (the principle of territorial jurisdiction);
- the effects principle (the principle of effective jurisdiction);
- the personality principle (the principle of personal jurisdiction); and
- the protective principle (the principle of protective jurisdiction).

The territoriality principle (the principle of territorial jurisdiction) underlies any activity of the state to prescribe laws within its territory.[25] This principle is the primary fundamental rule of any normative activity. It reads that if any person, thing or event is present or occurs within the state territory, then such state has the authority to regulate the status of said persons, things or events. Limitations to this rule, if any, shall be stipulated by international law.

The effects principle (the principle of effective jurisdiction), being in close relation to the territoriality principle (and therefore also called the objective territoriality principle),[26] concerns "activities outside the state, but having or intended to have substantial effect within the state territory".[27] This principle justifies the classification of certain external events as within the jurisdiction of the state. Among contemporary instances of its exercise, provided in the resolution of the International Law Commission as early as in nineteenth century, we find execution of criminal jurisdiction over perpetrators of cross-border offences; that is acts committed abroad but having their "substantial effects" within the state territory.[28] More concerning examples of contemporary jurisdictional practice are statutes aimed at counteracting unfair competition in market relations covering the territories of third countries which concerns behaviors classified as illegal by the regulating statute where they are observed.[29]

the connections, such as nationality, residence, or economic activity, between the regulating state and the person principally responsible for the activity to be regulated, or between that state and those whom the regulation is designed to protect; (c) the character of the activity to be regulated, the importance of regulation to the regulating state, the extent to which other states regulate such activities, and the degree to which the desirability of such regulation is generally accepted; (d) the existence of justified expectations that might be protected or hurt by the regulation; (e) the importance of the regulation to the international political, legal, or economic system; (f) the extent to which the regulation is consistent with the traditions of the international system; (g) the extent to which another state may have an interest in regulating the activity; and (h) the likelihood of conflict with regulation by another state.

25 *The Restatement*, § 402(c).

26 "Jurisdiction with respect to activities outside the state, but having or intended to have substantial effect within the state's territory, is an aspect of jurisdiction based on territoriality, although it is sometimes viewed as a distinct category". See the *Restatement*, § 402(d).

27 Ibid.

28 It is worth indicating that the PCIJ in the *Lotus case* emphasized the obviousness of practices to penalize behaviors initiated abroad but which had effects in the territory of the state. Cf. M. Hirst (2003) *Jurisdiction and the Ambit of the Criminal Law*, Oxford: Oxford University Press, pp. 45–47.

29 The US law on counteracting unfair competition was supposed to regulate practices of business entities acting outside the United States, so that there are no adverse effects of such actions on US internal

The next principle is the personality principle (the principle of personal jurisdiction). Its fundamental form covers the exercise of a state's jurisdiction over those of its own nationals who are staying abroad, whether as persons residing there or those staying there temporarily. It is also referred to as the active personal jurisdiction, and at a basic level includes, apart from acts of diplomatic care, exercising laws (statutes) over persons, including those residing outside its territory. This first and foremost includes exercising jurisdiction over persons in breach of criminal laws thereof who leave the country in order to avoid any criminal liability.[30] The effectiveness of exercising this form of jurisdiction is substantially contingent upon extradition treaties. Another example might be the statutory practice of imposing an obligation to pay taxes in the state of nationality on state nationals performing commercial activites abroad. International double taxation agreements provide for the harmonious execution of this aspect of jurisdictional powers.[31] The scope of jurisdictional activities may be dictated not only by the interests of the state of nationality (such as administration of justice or reasonable budgetary inflows), but also the common interest of the state and its nationals. As an example of a state's interest requiring the application of certain categories of sovereign acts outside the state territory, one may point to the Convention on Jurisdiction and the Enforcement of Judgments in Civil and Commercial Matters[32] or other conventions on legal and administrative aid.[33] The personality principle also underlies the process of regulating all forms of activities of public servants acting outside the state territory at the time of peace, including the acts of military personnel. Exercising such activities is supported by relevant agreements.[34]

trade (it is worth mentioning that such statutes are adopted at state level; at federal level applicable statutes include the Lanham Act, 1946, 15 USC § 1125, Subchapter III and the Code of Federal Regulations, Title 16 (concerning the Federal Trade Commission). The compliance of business entities' operations outside the territory with internal statutes is assessed by US courts; see D. Carreau (2004) *Droit International*, Paris: Pédone, p. 362. For the external influence of other US statutes concerned with employment relations and stock exchange transactions see D. Carreau, op. cit., p. 362 and the decision in the case *United States* v. *Aluminium Corporation of America* (1945) 148 F 2d 416, in which the Supreme Court of the United States said that: "Any state may impose liabilities, even upon persons not within its allegiance, for conduct outside its borders that has consequences within its borders which the state reprehends". <http://hubcap.clemson.edu/~sauerr/classes/425/cases/alcoa.pdf> (accessed 5 January 2011). Cf. M. Hirst, op. cit., pp. 47–48.

30 Some criminal statutes provide for the punishment of state nationals for acts committed outside the state territory; see Aust, op. cit., p. 45.

31 See e.g., B. J. Arnold and M. J. McIntyre (2002) *International Tax Primer*, The Hague: Kluwer Law International, p. 29.

32 Convention on Jurisdiction and the Enforcement of Judgments in Civil and Commercial Matters, Lugano, 16 September 1988 ('the Lugano Convention').

33 For instance the European Convention on the Legal Status of Migrant Workers (Council of Europe), Strasbourg, 24 November 1977, Europ. T. S. No. 93, or the Convention on Mutual Administrative Assistance in Tax Matters, Strasbourg, 25 January 1988.

34 The Agreement on the Status of the North Atlantic Treaty Organization, National Representatives and International Staff, Ottawa, 20 September 1951 and the Agreement between the Parties to the North Atlantic Treaty regarding the Status of their Forces, London, 9 June 1951, regulate the legal and administrative conditions of member state armed forces stationed in territories of other member states in relation to the performance of tasks agreed by the parties. See also the Convention on the Safety of United Nations and Associated Personnel, 9 December 1994, GA Res., UN Doc. A/RES/49/59.

To be applicable to criminal cases, the principle of personal jurisdiction[35] requires, in general, satisfaction of the double criminality principle, which is that the act punishable in the state exercising jurisdiction is also deemed punishable by the state within whose territory the defendant committed the act.[36]

The regulation, by the domestic (criminal) law, of events taking place outside the state territory, but which involve damage by a foreign entity to the domestic state national is an accepted variant of the personality principle. The jurisdictional principle is then referred to as the passive personality principle. Its application in the past was rather rare for two reasons: diplomatic and moral. It was considered undiplomatic to suggest, by exercising this jurisdictional principle, that the legal regulations of a foreign sovereign did not provide sufficient protection to nationals of other states staying in its territories. Furthermore, determining the venue for the trial as per the nationality of the victim raised moral doubts, since it violated the *actor sequitur forum rei* principle, in that it was not the victim who stood trial. The state should rather focus its efforts on capturing the perpetrator to be able to apply its legal procedures towards them. Increasing exercise of the passive personality principle is being observed nowadays. This principle, by reason of an increasing number of terrorist attacks against nationals (including diplomats) staying outside the state territory, has been substantiated by, e.g., the US jurisdictional practice.[37] Anti-terrorist legislation of the United States authorises the prosecution of the perpetrators of terrorist attacks resulting in bodily injury or death, which are committed in any part of the world under the authority of a state which is a sponsor of terrorism, if the victim of such an act is a national of the United States or if a United States national files for prosecution thereof.[38]

35 For the exceptions and controversies see: D. McGoldrick, P. J. Rowe and E. Donnelly (2004), *The Permanent International Criminal Court: Legal and Policy Issues*, Oxford: Hart Publishing, pp. 79–80.

36 See e.g. R. Cryer, H. Friman and D. Robinson (2010) *An Introduction to International Criminal Law and Procedure*, Cambridge: Cambridge University Press, p. 89, in which the authors refer to the principle of 'double criminality' (or 'dual criminality') as "requiring that the underlying act (or omission) is criminal in both the requesting and the requested State."

37 A leading case for invoking this principle by the US courts was the *US* v. *Yunis* case (1991) 924 F. 2d 1086). <http://www.tkb.org/documents/Cases/87-CR-0377-Indictment.pdf> (accessed 12 February 2011). In *US* v. *Yunis* the issue concerned the apprehension of a Lebanese citizen by US agents in international waters and his prosectution in the US for alleged involvement in the hijacking of a Jordanian airliner. The only connection between the hijacking and the US was the fact that several US nationals were on that flight. The Court accepted that both the universality principle and the passive personality principle provided an appropriate basis for jurisdiction in the case. It was stated that although the latter principle was the most controversial of the jurisdictional principles in international law, "the international community recognizes its legitimacy". It was pointed out that although the US had historically opposed the principle of effective jurisdiction, it had been accepted by the US and the international community in recent years in the sphere of terrorist and other internationally condemned crimes.

38 A legal basis for the prosecution is provided for within the Antiterrorism and Effective Death Penalty Act (AEDPA), 28 USC § 2254 (1996) amendment to the Alien Torts Act <http://usinfo.state.gov/usa/infousa/laws/majorlaw/s735.htm> (accessed 4 March 2011). For more on the relevant US legislation and its application see R. Higgins (1994) *Problems & Process: International Law and How We Use It*, Oxford: Oxford University Press, pp. 66–68.

The last of the principles mentioned in the *Restatement* is the protective principle (the principle of protective jurisdiction).[39] The principle, as already mentioned, concerns actions initiated abroad directed against the security or vital interests of the state.[40] This principle, commonly accepted and exercised,[41] according to the *Restatement*, concerns only a limited class of offences directed against the security of the state or other offences threatening the integrity of its governmental functions, e.g., espionage, counterfeiting of the state's seal or currency, falsification of official documents, as well as perjury and conspiracy to violate the immigration or customs laws.[42] Current anti-terrorist acts also call upon this principle for their justification. The protective principle expresses the state's need to punish acts committed outside its territory but in which the state feels threatened. Executing criminal jurisdiction based on the protective principle does not require the double penalty prerequisite to be met.

The list of principles is completed by the universal jurisdiction principle, under which the state is vested with the title to adopt laws providing for the penalization of certain categories of acts that are considered by the international community as prosecuted in its interest. Each and every perpetrator is prosecuted regardless of the place where the act was committed. As examples of acts prosecuted in the international interest, the *Restatement* points to acts of maritime piracy, slave trading, attacks on sea and air vessels and their hijacking, acts of genocide and crimes against humanity as well as certain acts of terrorism.[43] Despite dubieties as to whether the list of abovementioned categories is an exhaustive and homogeneous set, and whether all of them are commonly subject to jurisdiction of all states,[44] the universal principle has certainly been stimulating treaty efforts directed at penalization and prosecution of offences qualified thereunder. For this reason the principle has pretensions to being referred to as quasi-universal,[45] which is the norm for acts provided for in treaties (as

39 "The protective principle may be seen as a special application of the effects principle, (. . .) but it has been treated as an independent basis of jurisdiction": the *Restatement*, § 402(f).

40 The *Restatement*, § 402.

41 Brownlie (1966) *Principles of Public International Law*, Oxford: Oxford University Press, p. 304; As I. Brownlie notes, almost all states exercise jurisdiction over foreigners for actions initiated abroad, if such actions affect the security of the state.

42 See the *Restatement*, § 402(f).

43 The *Restatement*, § 404.

44 The Draft Code Against the Peace and Security of Mankind, 1991, UN Doc. A/46/10 may provoke such considerations. Article 6 of the Draft reads that a state where the suspect of crimes against the peace and security of mankind stays shall initiate proceedings before court or effect extradition with respect to such a person. Crimes against the peace and security of mankind subject include aggression (Article 15), genocide (Article 19), apartheid (Article 20), particularly serious war crimes (Article 22), recruitment, use, financing and training of mercenaries (Article 23), international terrorism (Article 24) drug trafficking (Article 25), and causing intentional serious damage to the natural environment (Article 26).

45 For instance M. C. Bassiouni (1996) 'Accountability for International Crimes and Serious Violations of Fundamental Human Rights, International Crimes: Jus Cogens and Obligatio Erga Omnes, 59(4) *Law and Contemporary Problems*, pp. 63–74. Cf. T. H. Lee (2004) 'The US Supreme Court as Quasi-International Tribunal: Reclaiming the Court's Original and Exclusive Jurisdiction over Treaty-Based Suits by Foreign States against States', 104(7) *Columbia Law Review*. <http://ssrn.com/abstract=575583> (accessed 4 March 2011).

they are limited to those acts included by contractual consensus in the treaty). This can be contrasted with those acts which are *delicta iuris gentium* (classified as subject to the universal jurisdiction), such as genocide and war crimes. The statute of the International Criminal Court provides for a detailed and extensive description of their hallmarks (as well as of crimes against humanity).[46]

It should be assumed that the principles concerning jurisdiction which are listed in the *Restatement* reflect their already-established and still developing hierarchy; certainly the hierarchy may be considered established with respect to the territoriality principle (the principle of territorial, "effective" jurisdiction) and the subsidiary personality principle (the principle of personal jurisdiction) and still developing with respect to the protective principle (the principle of protective jurisdiction) and the universal principle.[47]

When discussing the capacity to enforce rules established by the state, one should first and foremost consider the capacity to enforce law by way of court proceedings hereinafter referred to as "the jurisdiction to adjudicate". We do not question instances of states exercising such jurisdiction, including with respect to those consequences of the actions of persons, status of things that are related to events outside the territory of the state.[48] The *Restatement* provides also for principles of exercising the jurisdiction to adjudicate which, similarly to the jurisdiction to prescribe, requires certain conditions to be met for the judicial enforcement measure to be deemed reasonable.[49]

The jurisdictional measures of the state are supplemented and exhausted, apart from exercising the jurisdiction to adjudicate, by the capacity of courts, enforcement and administrative authorities and police to apply measures forcing compliance with law, i.e. the jurisdiction to enforce. When touching upon the issue of jurisdiction to enforce, one should take account of the fact that state authorities, in order to enforce

46 Articles 5–8 of the Rome Statute of the International Criminal Court, 17 July 1988, 2187 UNTS 90; see also M. P. Scharf (2001) 'The ICC's Jurisdiction over the Nationals of Non-Party States: A Critique of the US Position', 64(1) *Law and Contemporary Problems*, p. 68. <http://www.law.duke.edu/journals/64LCPScharf> (accessed 7 April 2011); K. Roth (2001) 'The Case For Universal Jurisdiction', *Foreign Affairs*, October 2001. <http://www-stage.foreignaffairs.org/20010901faresponse5577/kenneth-roth/the-case-for-universal-jurisdiction.html> (accessed 7 April 2011).

47 For instance N. Q. Dinh, op. cit., p. 501; see also the Admissability Decision of the European Court of Human Rights, application no. 52207/99 in the case of *Banković* on the interpretation of Article 1 of the European Convention of Human Rights as to the meaning of the term "subject to jurisdiction" where the Court indicates limitations for invoking grounds for jurisdiction other than territorial grounds, as a result of the sovereign rights of other states.

48 The purpose of exercising judicial jurisdiction may, yet does not have to, enforce actions compliant with the law. See the *Restatement*, § 431: "Jurisdiction to adjudicate addresses links that justify a state in exercising jurisdiction to adjudicate in respect of person or thing, whether for purposes of enforcement or for other purposes".

49 A state jurisdiction to adjudicate is reasonable if a) the person or thing is present in the territory of the state, other than transitorily; (b) the person, if a natural person is resident in the state; (c) the person, if a natural person, is a national of the state; (d) the person, if a corporation or comparable juridical person, is organised pursuant to the law of the state; (e) a ship, aircraft or other vehicle to which the adjudication relates if registered under the laws of the state; (f) the person, whether natural or juridical, has consented to the exercise of jurisdiction; (g) the person, whether natural or juridical, regularly

compliance with rules they establish, may apply judicial[50] and nonjudicial measures.[51] The jurisdiction to enforce, to be fully effective, shall bear the hallmark of reasonableness, as is the case with the jurisdiction to prescribe and adjudicate.[52] Enforcement of rules may, therefore, concern the laws respecting the principles of territorial, effective, personal and protective jurisdiction, provided that legal norms meet the prerequisite of reasonableness.[53] Enforcement measures shall be in reasonable relation to acts and regulations they refer to; punishment for failure to comply shall be preceded with a proper specification of breach and be proportionate.

Finally, sovereignty of the state may be exercised over a person (natural or juridical) outside the territory of the state if the person is given such notice of the claims or charges against them that is reasonable in the circumstances and is given an opportunity to be heard, ordinarily prior to the application of enforcement measures, whether in person or by counsel or other representative. What is more, the enforcement ought to be done through the courts.[54] Various types of jurisdictional activities of the state invite a question about their mutual relation.[55] As regards the relation between the jurisdiction to prescribe, adjudicate and enforce, the *Restatement* considers that, in the light of international law, only a state that has jurisdiction to prescribe may enforce its laws, which it does through its courts insofar as its courts may enforce their jurisdictional powers.[56] The identification of types of jurisdictional activities and the principles regulating their enforcement (both already established and those still developing in the international arena), does not eliminate jurisdictional conflicts, in particular, when a state aspires to exercise its powers over entities and events outside the state territory. Assessments of reasonableness of actions taken by local authorities and third country agents competing in exercising jurisdiction within a given territory may overlap and lead (at least

carries on business in the state; (h) the person, whether natural or juridical, had carried on activity in the state, but only in respect of such activity; (i) the person, whether natural or juridical, had carried on outside the state an activity having a substantial, direct and foreseeable effect within the state, but only in respect of such activity; (j) the thing that is the subject of adjudication is owned, possessed or used in the state, but only in respect of a claim reasonably connected with that thing"; see also the *Restatement*, § 421(2).

50 The *Restatement*, § 431: "judicial enforcement measures include the imposition of criminal sanctions, such as fines and imprisonment, as well as other measures that may be ordered by a court in connection with judicial proceedings, whether civil, criminal or administrative, such as an order to produce a document or a sanction for failure to comply with such a order." Some measures taken by executive agencies subject to judicial confirmation or annulment, such as seizure of goods by the customs service, freezing of assets by fiscal authorities or execution of a warrant for arrest, have aspects of both judicial and nonjudicial enforcement.

51 The *Restatement* § 431: "nonjudicial enforcement measures comprise the following: denial of the right to engage in export or import transactions; removal from the list of persons eligible to bid on government contracts; suspension, revocation or denial of a permit to engage in particular business activity; prohibition of the transfer of assets".

52 The *Restatement* § 431.

53 The *Restatement* § 431(1).

54 Ibid.

55 See U. Kohl (2007) *Jurisdiction and the Internet: A Study of Regulatory Competence over Online Activity*, Cambridge: Cambridge University Press, p. 17.

56 The *Restatement* § 432.

hypothetically) to unanimous recognition of a right to act by one of competing entities;[57] however, assessments may also be mutually exclusive and provoke international disputes.[58] Nevertheless, one may presume that they constitute the starting point for the development of all jurisdictional configurations, their construal and assessment from the perspective of international law. Naturally, assuming such a role does not exclude individual solutions, where states competing for jurisdiction in respect of persons, things and events, may, thorough agreement, specify another detailed right to exercise jurisdiction with respect to the part thereof falling outside the state territory. In considering the possibility of individual solutions, one must also bear in mind the clear message of the decision in the *Lotus case*, that jurisdictional regimes[59] may be also established by way of a convention entered into by the states concerned, for examplethe typical treaties authorizing states to perform certain jurisdictional activities (for instance, extradition treaties), or treaties standardizing jurisdictional activities performed under national laws, i.e. on the basis of laws establishing the so-called private international law.[60] The essence here is the set of norms that serve to indicate the jurisdictional regime (the state's own or the foreign state's) that is appropriate to undertake a legal assessment of a given set of circumstances. The said circumstances may be, *inter alia* of a civil, family or guardianship nature, with the so-called alien element (relating to entities not formally found within the legal order of the territory which undertakes the assessment).[61] Regardless, such norms (referred to as "conflict of law rules" or "competence norms") serve as the basis for deciding whether a court of a state applies its own or foreign laws or delegates the case to another court for hearing. Situations with the so-called alien element increased in number, and growing need to decide upon the limits of competing jurisdictions caused states to develop strategies to meet that need. The scale of the phenomenon led to the establishment of the Hague Conference on Private International Law in 1893, the

57 Pursuant to the *Restatement* § 403(3), with respect to the exercise of jurisdiction to prescribe and an underlying obligation to meet the prerequisites of reasonableness (paras. 1–2 § 403), if prescriptions by the two states are in conflict, each state has an obligation to evaluate its own as well as the other state's interest in exercising jurisdiction and defer if the interest of the other state is clearly greater.

58 An example of radically different assessments of the right to exercise jurisdiction is the US practice (referrable to the principle of personal jurisdiction) of introducing, under the statute, economic restrictions of various nature (embargoes). Exercise of the said competence consists in adopting a broad definition of "persons subject to the US jurisdiction" covered by the regulation. The definition includes branches of US companies operating in third countries and it is this criterion that determines the effectiveness of law towards them. Such solutions provoke conflicts between the United States and states where the branches operate. The conflict is provoked not only by violation of the principle of territoriality being the fundamental principle determining the priority of jurisdiction, but the fact that branches of US companies, from a legal perspective, are subjects of the state they operate in; the said relations derive from the statutorily-specified registered office of the company or the place of registration. For more about jurisdictional conflicts of a similar nature between the US and European states, see D. Carreau, op. cit., pp. 363–365.

59 That is, a mutual, agreed order for exercising rights by competing states.

60 Cf. N. Q. Dinh, op. cit., p. 498.

61 For detailed analysis of the private international law treaties on state jurisdiction see F. F. Wang (2010) *Internet Jurisdiction and Choice of Law: Legal Practices in the EU, US and China*, Cambridge: Cambridge University Press; U. Kohl, op. cit.; J. Hornle (2009) *Cross-Border Internet Dispute Resolution*, Cambridge: Cambridge University Press.

purpose of which was to pursue harmonization of national norms as regards the manner of resolving legal issues with an alien element. Since 1954 more than 37 multilateral treaties have been concluded under the auspices of the organization.

Therefore, PCIJ decision seems to alert us to the possibility that there are two possible grounds for regulating jurisdictional issues. As A. Aust rightly notices, borders between international law and conflict of law rules are blurred, for many legal issues may be resolved using both international law instruments and conflict of law rules.[62] Naturally, public international law norms and private international law norms are different and originate from different legal orders. Nevertheless, the analysis of and the designing of solutions relating to jurisdictional powers of sovereigns in cyberspace may not disregard the acquis of international law (including also jurisdictional principles), nor the solutions already established or yet to be established, with respect to individual cases, by state regulations on conflict of law rules harmonized under relevant treaties.

The applicability to Internet of the aforementioned conclusions – that the issue of state jurisdiction is, above all, related to territorial aspect, and, furthermore, due to the sequence of commonly accepted principles; that it may concern entities and events outside the state territory; and the fact that the jurisdictional competence may, in such cases, be determined by the treaty agreed on by the parties concerned – can now be considered. Such confrontation between the principles of state jurisiction and the limitlessness and universal nature of the Internet raises a number of questions, the most significant of which are mentioned below.

In traditional, physical space the state exercises its exclusive competence within its territory, provided that no restraints have been imposed upon it under international law. This conclusion seems inescapable. At the same time, similar grounds for setting limits of state competence in cyberspace are not only ignored but impossible to apply. For it is not the physical location outside the cyberspace, but classification in DNS and TCP/IP that organize the presence of entities in cyberspace. Thus "presence" in cyberspace is identified by top level domain names and Internet protocol. Both the foregoing criteria of verification of entities presence in cyberspace – their creation or modification – fall beyond the competence of states. Consequently, presence and activity in cyberspace remains, to a large extent, beyond the traditional concept of jurisdictional competence of sovereigns. That competence has been vested in the private law entity of the State of California – Internet Corporation for Assigned Names and Numbers (ICANN).[63] ICANN delegates, for instance, rights to administer DNS code sequences (gTLDs and ccTLDs) to entities it selects. Also as regards ccTLDs, which could be recognized as reflections of online statehood, ICANN is not obliged to take account of the opinion of national authorities.[64] At the same time, it is clear

62 Aust, op. cit., p. 2; see also I. Brownlie, op. cit., p. 262.

63 ICANN; cf. chapter 4.

64 "The desires of the government of a country with regard to delegation of a ccTLD are taken very seriously. The IANA will make them a major consideration in any TLD delegation/transfer discussions. Significantly interested parties in the domain should agree that the proposed TLD manager is the appropriate party": ICANN (1999) *Internet Co-ordination Policy: Internet Domain Name System Structure and Delegation (ccTLD Administration and Delegation)*, (a). There is, however, a tendency to increase the role of governments within the ICANN structure, see chapter 4.

that assessing the competence limits of a state based on traditional, territorial definitions is impossible online. Therefore, it is necessary to establish the sequence of principles that would provide the grounds for a specific legal order in cyberspace. Such an order will need to be based on already existing principles adopted by the international community and extended by additional elements which reflect the the specific character of the multistakeholder community that cyberspace comprises. The analysis of basic, existing principles of mutual interaction of international arena actors, along with appropriate adjustment thereof to reflect the specific nature of cyberspace should be, therefore, the starting point. Such an analysis is presented below.

The application of territorial jurisdiction over cyberspace must be done with much caution, since territoriality directly contradicts the nature of transnational online interactions. It is clear that a state (through its authorities and bodies) may exercise its jurisdiction over its territory and persons physically located within its borders (subjective territorial jurisdiction). Therefore, it is, for example, authorized to prosecute all cybercrimes initiated from within its territory by its residents.[65] However, territorial jurisdiction in both criminal and civil matters is understood more broadly. It includes the competence to regulate not only the actions initiated within state borders, but also those whose effects appeared or were designated to appear therein[66] (the so-called objective territorial or effective jurisdiction).[67] Such application of territoriality would in fact result in global jurisdiction over all Internet activities,[68] since consequences of actions taken using the electronic network affect simultanously any place in which the Internet may be accessed. Effective jurisdiction was willingly exercised in early Internet-related cases[69] as any behaviour performed in cyberspace directly affected the territories of each sovereign aspiring to exercise jurisdiction over it. Its automatic application, however, for reasons mentioned above, raises serious doubts as it entails numerous dangers. A sovereign, when applying this principle, assumes that any information available in the state territory is subject to its jurisdiction and that the state shall regulate its content and underlying criteria. As a rule, such an assumption is contradictory to the social and civilizing goal of electronic contacts. The very fact of rendering certain content available within a certain geographic location cannot widen sovereignty to enable domestic powers to impose their legal regulations on authors of electronic content actually residing in various other states.[70] Such practice could lead to utter legal

65 See, e.g. Council of Europe Convention on Cybercrime, Article 22 para. 1.

66 As confirmed in e.g. the Council of Europe Convention on Cybercrime, Article 22, and para. 233 of the Explanatory Report. <http://conventions.coe.int/Treaty/EN/Reports/Html/185.htm>.

67 See e.g. C. C. Joyner (2005) *International Law in the 21st Century: Rules for Global Governance*, Oxford: Rowman & Littlefield, p. 150.

68 Even the prerequisite of double penalty might be insufficient, since states might call upon the supplementary protective principle of jurisdiction which does not require the prosecuted actions (or omissions) to be illegal within the state where they were initiated; see below.

69 See chapter 3 on US court practice.

70 In this context, the (controversial) blocking of electronic content deemed harmful by the sovereign, under statutes or discretionary agreements between service providers proves a practical solution (cf. chapter 3, filter policies).

uncertainty – nobody would dare to put any information or comments online for they would immediately become obliged to comply with rules of law of all states where the Internet is reachable. Furthermore, participants in Internet exchanges would be forced to take account of the potential legal consequences of their actions in the most distant parts of the globe, pursuant to the rules and regulations of which they are not even aware. The prospect of participation in court proceedings for breach of such foreign regulations could entail high costs. International companies would have to resign from operating online, as a result of fear of legal consequences they cannot even reliably assess. Thus it is certain that, even though the effective principle might prove helpful at regulating cyberspace relations,[71] it shall not serve as a fundamental principle, and shall be applied with much caution.[72] Existing attempts to limit the exercise of effective territoriality over cyberspace[73] certainly seem a step in the right direction, while application of the territoriality principle as the primary rule for cyberspace is destined for failure.[74]

Any assessment of the applicability of the personality principle in regulating relations in cyberspace should be commenced with the traditional notion of the personality principle, that of the active personality under which the state is competent to exercise jurisdiction with respect to all its nationals. The competence results, above all, from the attribute of statehood, an important element of which, apart from the fact of having actual state territory, is the requirement of a particular population being assigned to the terriory and functionally related to the state authority; a population which accepts the authority and abides by its regulations. It is the link between the two necessary elements of statehood – the territory and its citizens – that is the essence of nationality. It seems that, of all abovementioned principles, the personality principle is the most likely to set the limits for regulating online activities.

The personality principle enables the state to lay down, in a relatively certain manner, the rights and obligations of each national participating in online activities whilst at the same time subjecting them to a regime familiar both in terms of culture and geography. It also facilitates risk assessments related, for instance, to commencing business operations via the Internet. Naturally, application of the personality principle solely is insufficient and gives rise to further questions concerning the instances of conflicts of laws within, for example, transactions effected online. The passive personal jurisdiction

71 E.g. limited by the effects test or content targeting, cf. chapter 3 on US case law.

72 The *Granite Gate* and *CompuServe* cases may serve as an example of such negative consequences (cf. chapter 3).

73 See chapter 3 for the US effects test or European content targeting analysis.

74 The proposed concept of delimiting cyberspace through ccTLDs (see R. Uerpman-Wittzack (2010) 'Principles of International Internet Law', 11(1) *German Law Journal*, pp. 1256–1258) reflects a misunderstanding of the role of ccTLDs registrars, who are largely independent from state authority and operate based on an agreement with ICANN. It is rarely required that a ccTLD registrant must provide evidence of a factual link with the state or its territory, presented through the ccTLD's abbreviation in the ISO3166 list. The same argument goes for delimiting cyberspace with websites: not only may they be hosted on numerous mirroring servers (and therefore be physically located in multiple locations at once, see chapter 4), but also determining their targeted destinations might be impossible (especially with English language websites offering comprehensive services or content, see chapter 3 on the EU).

principle, by which a victim's nationality confers the title to exercise jurisdiction, constitutes an alternative to the foregoing principle. The principle is frequently invoked in cases relating to the Internet, in which claimants and courts refer to the principle along with the principle of effective jurisdiction. When assessing the usefulness of passive personality principle, one should invoke the very same doubt-raising arguments concerning the application of the effects principle to the Internet; the unserved consent to apply the principle produces the same, too far-reaching and unforeseeable consequences for all Internet users, in that it subjects them to countless number and categories of legal regulations.

Apart from the carefully applied effects principle, the personal jurisdiction principle could also be completed by the principle of protective jurisdiction. However in the days of controversies over the legal categorization of cyberterrorism,[75] the principle should be applied with much caution. Pursuant to this principle, states to which actions in cyberspace pose direct risk would be authorized to perform sovereign activities. The criteria applied to the assessment of whether it is reasonable of a particular entity to exercise jurisdiction are the same as those applied to cases not related to electronic activities. Some of them allow the application of analogy to already established legal institutions, whereas others require that law-makers, but also international law, apply a brand new approach especially towards the non-exhaustive catalogue of cybercrime.[76]

When applying the universal principle to the Internet, one should commence consideration by stating that its application is limited to the most serious international crimes and should, as a rule, result from international treaty.[77] Content that is "direct and public incitement to commit genocide"[78] and thus which can be prosecuted under universal jurisdiction is easy to find online; however, the legal categorization of so-called cyberterrorism as a crime subject to universal prosecution[79] may raise serious doubts.[80]

75 See e.g. F. D. Kramer, S. H. Starr and L. Wentz (2009) *Cyberpower and National Security*, Dulles: Potomac Books, Inc., p. 642; M. N. Schmitt (1999) 'The Principle of Discrimination in 21st Century Warfare', 2 *Yale Human Rights and Development Law Journal*, pp. 143ff.; see generally W. G. Sharp (1999) *CyberSpace and the Use of Force*, Falls Church: Aegis Research Corporation.

75 See e.g. N. Harvey (2010), 'Cyber Warfare: Addressing the Challenge', Chatham House session transcript 9 November 2010. <www.chathamhouse.org.uk/files/17800_091110harvey.pdf> (accessed 25 December 2010); J. Kulesza (2009) 'State Responsibility for Cyberattacks on International Peace and Security', 29 *Polish Yearbook of International Law*, pp. 139–152.

76 The catalogue is well defined in the CoE Convention on Cybercrime, although with the swift evolution of new technologies it may not stand the test of time.

77 Deriving universal jurisdiction from customary practice raises controversies: cf., M. Robinson (2006) 'The Princeton Principles', in S. Macedo (ed.) *Universal Jurisdiction: National Courts and the Prosecution of Serious Crimes under International Law*, Philadelphia: University of Pennsylvania Press, p. 27.

78 Convention on the Prevention and Punishment of the Crime of Genocide, Paris, 1948, Article III.

79 See e.g. Shackelford, S. J. (2009) 'From Nuclear War to Net War: Analogizing Cyber Attacks in International Law', 25(3) *Berkeley Journal of International Law*, pp. 191–250. <http://works.bepress.com/context/scott_shackelford/article/1004/type/native/viewcontent> (accessed 20 December 2010).

80 Most national legislation on crime anticipates that universal jurisdiction based on the existing international treaty regimes can be exercised to prosecute terrorist attacks. Examples of such treaties are the Convention on Offenses and Certain Other Acts Committed on Board Aircraft, Tokyo, 14 September 1963 ('the Tokyo Convention'), 704 UNTS 220; the Convention for the Suppression of Unlawful Seizure of Aircraft (Hijacking), The Hague, 16 December 1970 ('the Hague Convention'), 22 UST

The abovementioned jurisdictional principles may be applied at three different levels: public international law, private international law and international criminal law.

Public international law invokes the principles in the content and practice of applying treaties, or as the grounds for establishing and effecting commonly-applicable law, in the form and context presented above.

Private international law consists of the internal regulations of particular states, based on international treaties, and aiming at unification of civil law practices.[81] The purpose of such statutes and set of norms is to aid determination of which legal regime (a state's own or a foreign state's) is the appropriate one to undertake a legal assessment of a particular set of circumstances. The said circumstances may be the consequences of legal relations dealing with the aforementined alien element, be it an action causing results abroad, a foreign indivdual or an out-of-state physical object. Establishing the court venue may encounter numerous problems by reason of the aterritorial nature of the Internet, despite the application of common, analogous multilateral conventions,[82] conflict of law rules and traditional rules of private international law.

The views and practice of legal academics and commentators have, within a short period, established fundamental principles of transnational interactions in civil cases,[83] even though the consequences of their efforts have been met with criticism.[84]

The issue of criminal jurisdiction still poses a considerable challenge to international Internet regulations. Criminal law, being the reflection of ethical values characteristic of a local community, is closely related to the problem with criminal jurisdiction, since criminal law reflects regional/national/local values. Finding global solutions for effective criminal law enforcement is not possible due to these cultural differences – and we need global solutions to effectively regulate the global cyberspace. However, in the spirit of progressing globalization, the term "transnational criminal law" is becoming more and more popular.[85] A good embodiment thereof, with respect to the Internet, is the Council of Europe Convention on Cybercrime (CoE). The Convention unifies terminology and definitions of offences committed using computers and global network. Undoubtedly, the CoE constitutes a diplomatic, political, as well

1641; the Convention for the Suppression of Unlawful Acts Against the Safety of Civil Aviation (Sabotage), Montreal, 23 September 1971 ('the Montreal Convention'), 24 UST 564; and the International Maritime Organization Convention for the Suppression of Unlawful Acts against the Safety of Maritime Navigation, Rome, 10 March 1988 ('the Maritime Terrorism Convention'), 1678 UNTS 201. For examples of such national legislation see e.g. para. 6 of the German Penal Code (Strafgesetzbuch), or the Spanish Ley Organica del Poder Judicial at Article 23.4. Therefore, recognizing acts committed through electronic networks as acts of terrorism might result in universal jurisdiction over those who have participated in them.

81 See N. Q. Dinh, op. cit., p. 498; I. Brownlie, op. cit., p. 262.

82 E.g. the Convention on Jurisdiction and the Enforcement of Judgments in Civil and Commercial Matters, Brussels, 27 September 1968 or the United Nations Convention on Contracts for the International Sale of Goods, Vienna, 11 April 1980.

83 See generally F. F. Wang (2010) op. cit.; see also Chapter 3 for a brief description of national regulatory and judicial practice.

84 Cf. e.g. E. Gelbstein and J. Kurbalija (2005) *Internet Governance: Issues, Actors and Divides*, Msida: Diplo Foundation, p. 76.

85 See e.g. N. Boister (2003) 'Transnational Criminal Law?' 14(5) *EJIL*, pp. 953–976.

as legislative achievement – it is the first document of the international Internet law. However, the jurisdictional solution provided for therein, significant from the perspective of these considerations, discloses serious drawbacks.

The Convention stipulates no self-executing norms, which significantly limits its effectiveness.[86] Jurisdiction is discussed in Article 22 and gives priority to the territoriality principle, enabling states to exercise jurisdiction over crimes committed in their respective territories. Although Article 22 in para. 1 Provides for the possibility of exercising territorial jurisdiction on board a ship or an aircraft under a particular state's jurisdiction, as well as personal jurisdiction over state nationals, in the very next paragraph, para. 2, it enables each party to impose reservations upon the application of those other principles. It also enables states to exercise their jurisdiction according to their national laws (para. 3). Article 22 para. 5 exposes the weaknesses of the jurisdictional regimes laid down by the Convention. It states that, in the case of a dispute over jurisdictional competence, the parties shall negotiate "with a view to determining the most appropriate jurisdiction for prosecution" if they deem such procedure reasonable. The Convention does not introduce any arbitration mechanism or institutional supervision over the exercise of obligations by states, neither does it incorporate the *aut dedere aut judicare* principle common to anti-terrorist treaties.[87] It does not even provide an obligation upon the states to cooperate. Under Article 27 para. 4 a requested party may refuse assistance if the request for assistance concerns an offence which the requested party considers "a political offence or an offence connected with a political offence, or it considers that execution of the request is likely to prejudice its sovereignty, security, ordre public or other essential interests". Under this general clause both the jurisdictional provisions and performance guarantee mechanism stipulated in the Convention can be deemed ineffective.

Legal academics and commentators have presented an alternative to the Council of Europe concept. In 2000 a draft International Convention to Enhance Protection from Cyber Crime and Terrorism was formulated.[88] The proposal contains a sequence of exercising jurisdictional powers by states towards cyberoffence perpetrators. Pursuant to Article 5 para. 4 the state in which the alleged offender was physically present when the alleged offence was committed shall have the priority of jurisdiction (the subjective territoriality principle). If the state decides not to exercise its powers, the following priority of jurisdiction shall apply: (a) the state in whose territory substantial harm was suffered as a result of the alleged offence (the effects principle); (b) the state of the alleged offender's dominant nationality (the personality principle); (c) any state where the alleged offender may be found; and (d) any other state with a reasonable basis for jurisdiction. Moreover, the draft provides for self-executing norms obliging the state parties to take such measures as may be necessary for the authorized state

86 See e.g. CoE Convention on Cybercrime Articles 2 through to 14, beginning with the words: "Each Party shall adopt such legislative and other measures as may be necessary to establish as criminal offences under its national law, when committed intentionally . . .".

87 See e.g. L. Reydams, op. cit., p. 68.

88 Stanford Draft Convention on Protection from Cyber Crimes and Terrorism (2000) IWAR. <http://www.iwar.org.uk/law/resources/cybercrime/stanford/cisac-draft.htm> (accessed 13 January 2011).

to exercise jurisdiction.[89] Pursuant to Article 7, states shall comply with the *aut dedere aut judicare* principle. An agency for Information Infrastructure Protection (AIIP) was proposed to safeguard the treaty.[90] Whilst it is an interesting yet dogmatic proposal to distribute the jurisdictional competence of a state in criminal cases with respect to cyberspace, its analysis should, however, be carried out exclusively in the context of the Council of Europe Convention, which constitutes compromise to the fullest extent that the international community is prepared to tolerate.

State jurisdiction in international spaces

As mentioned above, the competence of a state is exercised also in spaces other than its (own) state territory; apart from "politically organized" spaces, competence may also be exercised in free (common) areas not subject to any sovereignty. It has also been proven that entitlement to exercise competence in those areas in each and every case must be based on the principles of international law. Therefore, the regulations concerning the said spaces (i.e. the high sea, Antarctic and outer space) have created a regime established so clearly that its rules may be compared with principles regulating the jurisdictional practices in state territories, for this reason it is often referred to as the "law of international spaces".[91] The analysis of its underlying assumptions, as manifested by several regulations, may prove useful for developing regulations concerning another international space: cyberspace.[92] We will therefore review the procedure for formulating the international spaces law and look at their solutions for the distribution of the jurisdictional competence of states. The history of international spaces commences with the law of the sea.

The modern law of the high sea originates, in substantial part, from Grotius in the seventeenth century.[93] The Law of the Sea has set the direction of discussion regarding international spaces as oceans have for a long time been a significant part thereof. The Antarctic was not properly discovered until 1820 and did not gain strategic – and what follows – political recognition until the 1950s.[94] Similarly outer space, even though known since time immemorial, has not been on the agenda of international law debates and remained unrecognized by 1957, when the world's first artificial

89 Article 5.

90 Article 12.

91 The encompassing, comprehensive term "law of international spaces" was introduced by J. F. Kish in his book (1973) *The Law of International Spaces*, Leiden: Sijthoff and invoked by D. C. Menthe (1998) 'Jurisdiction in Cyberspace: A Theory of International Spaces', 4 *Michigan Telecommunications and Technology Law Review*, pp. 69–103. <http://www.mttlr. org/volfour/menthe.pdf> (accessed 9 February 2011), and by T. Hillier (1998) *Sourcebook on Public International Law*, London: Routledge, pp. 261–262.

92 Cf. chapter 4.

93 H. Grotius (1609/2000) *Mare Liberum*, Ontario: Kitchener Batoche Books.

94 Interest in this area increased during the International Geophysical Year (1957–58), see R. MacDonald (2005) 'Challenges and Accomplishments: A Celebration of the Arctic Institute of North America', 58(4) *Infonorth* (Arctic Institute of North America). <http://pubs.aina.ucalgary.ca/arctic/Arctic58-4-440.pdf> (accessed 16 February 2011).

satellite "Sputnik" visited the near-Earth orbit for the first time.[95] In each international space the prospect of international conflict was the principal reason for formulating common regimes or regulating agreements.[96] Disputes over the Antarctic "pie" during the Cold War led to the development of a treaty regime, which, consequently, has frozen the shores of ice continent.[97]

The law of international spaces reads that state authority shall not extend over some spaces, i.e. high sea, sea bed and the deep sea, Antarctica, outer space and celestial bodies. Nowadays, the legal status of these areas, as areas impossible to appropriate, is quite well established (with the exception of Antarctica, the legal status of which, contrary to other territories, is based on freezing the existing territorial claims and prohibiting new ones). A feature common to all these areas is the obligation of peaceful use, freedom of research and use thereof under the same rights by all states, international organizations or other international law entities.[98]

Two concepts supported the establishment of the law of international spaces: *res nullius* and *res communis*. As international spaces are *res nullius*, that is, without an owner, as per the theory based on the Roman law and Locke's concept of natural law, each state may take over the territory if requirements traditionally imposed on state independence have been met. The debate over international waters space, Antarctica, the Moon and celestial bodies also concerned the possibility of exercising such powers by sovereigns. The principle of *res communis* [freely in the public domain] originates from Rome and has been confirmed on numerous occasions, by e.g., general principles of equality and independence incorporated in the Covenant of the League of Nations or the United Nations Charter.[99] A considerable part of modern international community (especially former colonies, which identified the concept of *res nullus* with imperial dominance of colonial powers) held that the said spaces were not *res nullius* but *res communis*. This view prevailed and is now reflected in such documents as the Convention on the Law of the Sea[100] or the Treaty on

95 N. Jasentuliyana (1999) *International Space Law and the United Nations*, The Hague: Martinus Nijhoff Publishers, p. 2.

96 This growing need for a coherent legal regime may also be the case for cyberspace.

97 For more about the use of international spaces, see e.g. D. C. Turack (2002) 'Concept of the Common Heritage of Mankind in International Law', *The Journal of Third World Studies*. <http://www.findarticles.com/p/articles/ mi_qa3821/is_200210/ai_n9115940> (accessed 13 February 2011).

98 The status may be rapidly and radically changed as a result of the discovery of new crude oil deposits under the surface of the continent, which was substantially affected by global warming. For more information see C. Di Leva and S. Morita (2009) 'Maritime Rights of Coastal States and Climate Change: Should States Adapt to Submerged Boundaries?' 5 *Law and Development Working Paper Series*, New York: The World Bank. <http://siteresources.worldbank.org/INTLAWJUSTICE/Resources/L&D_number5.pdf> (accessed 3 February 2011); or D. R. Rothwell (2008) 'The Arctic in International Law: Time for a New Regime?' 8(37) *Australian National University College of Law Research Papers*. <http://papers.ssrn.com/sol3/Delivery.cfm/SSRN_ID1317503_code734493.pdf?abstractid=1314546&mirid=5> (accessed 3 February 2011).

99 The Preamble of the Charter of the United Nations, San Francisco, 1945, states that the United Nations are determined to "reaffirm faith in fundamental human rights, in the dignity and worth of the human person, in the equal rights of men and women and of nations large and small". Similarly, the Covenant of the League of Nations, Paris, 1924, guarantees, under Article 3, that all Member States are equal.

100 The Convention on the Law of the Sea, Montego Bay, 10 December 1982, 1833 UNTS 397.

Principles Governing the Activities of States in the Exploration and Use of Outer Space, including the Moon and Other Celestial Bodies.[101] The former classifies the sea or ocean bed and its resources as the common heritage of mankind,[102] whereas the latter declares the impossibility of appropriation of outer space.[103] It is worth analysing the ways in which international spaces such as Antarctica, outer space, the high sea and the bottom of sea and ocean have been treated, as this enables us to consider the possibility of reapplying solutions utilised in such areas to cyberspace (those concerning not only jurisdictional principles, but also organizational schemes and a prospective future legal regime for cyberspace that is effective *erga omnes*).

Antarctica

The political borders of Antarctica are set out in Article 6 of the Antarctic Treaty;[104] pursuant to which Antarctica is an area south of 60° South Latitude including all ice shelves. Since its effective date, 1961, the Antarctic Treaty has evolved and developed into a multilateral regional regime often referred to as the Antarctic Treaty System (ATS). The Antarctic Treaty System consists of the Antarctic Treaty and the Convention for the Conservation of Antarctic Seals (CCAS) of 1972, the Convention for The Conservation of Antarctic Marine Living Resources (CCAMLR) of 1980 and the Protocol on Environmental Protection to the Antarctic Treaty (the Madrid Protocol) of 1991. The Treaty System has long been applied without any permanent body and only recently has the Antarctic Treaty Secretariat been established. The substitute for a decision-making authority has been the effective construction of consultative meetings held periodically between the "Consultative Parties", that is, the twelve original parties to the Treaty and seventeen states which have been assigned such status (Article IX.2) by "demonstrating their interest in Antarctica by conducting substantial scientific research activity there, such as the establishment of a scientific station or the dispatch of scientific expedition".[105]

The main purpose of the Treaty is provided for in Article I thereof, pursuant to which Antarctica shall be used for peaceful purposes only and no measures of military nature shall be allowed. The Treaty also ensures the freedom of scientific investigations (Article II), defines rules of exchanging information, scientific observations and

101 The Treaty on Principles Governing the Activities of States in the Exploration and Use of Outer Space, including the Moon and Other Celestial Bodies, New York, 27 January 1967, 610 UNTS 205, Article 1.

102 Article 136.

103 Article 1 qualifies bodies of the Solar system as the province of all mankind.

104 The Antarctic Treaty, Washington, 1959, 402 UNTS 71.

105 Article IX indicates two groups of participants of the Antarctic Treaty. These include 29 contracting parties with consultative status and other 16 observing states. The consultative states provide recommendations to their governments necessary to attain the objectives of the Treaty. Measures adopted by all consultative states are binding upon them. Detailed types of measures adopted by the consultative states were specified in 1995, see G. S. Schatz (1996) 'Antarctic Treaty Consultative Parties: Measures Relating to the Furtherance of the Principles and Objectives of the Antarctic Treaty', 35 *ILM* p. 1165.

personnel, as well as broadly understood co-operative working (Article III), prohibits nuclear explosions in Antarctica and the disposal there of radioactive waste material (Article V), and sets the territorial borders within which the Treaty shall apply, without defining and violating the principles pertaining to the high sea (Article VI). Article VII establishes the right of consultative states to conduct inspections with respect to all Antarctic areas and actions taking place therein.

The Antarctic Treaty itself does not establish any jurisdictional regime. Questions relating to the exercise of jurisdiction in Antarctica have been attached to the list of issues to be dealt with by consultative states at their regular meetings.[106] No regulations directly concerning the jurisdiction have been adopted so far. Nevertheless, the Treaty provides for partial regulation of the jurisdictional issue. Article VIII provides that observers designated under the Treaty and scientific personnel as well as members of the their staffs may conduct inspection and research. Pursuant to the provisions of the Treaty, the abovementioned persons are subject only to the jurisdiction of the states of which they are nationals. As regards other situations (e.g. jurisdictional competence concerning tourists), Article VIII stipulates that "Parties concerned in any case of dispute with regard to the exercise of the jurisdiction in Antarctica shall immediately consult together with a view to reaching a mutually acceptable solution".[107] The Article makes no reference to territorial jurisdiction or jurisdiction over floating islands (e.g. assumptions that the jurisdiction over all persons in the area of the facility shall be exercised by the state that organizes the facility).[108]

Subsequent treaties formulated the issue of exercising jurisdiction more directly. The Convention for the Conservation of Antarctic Seals reads: "Each Contracting Party shall adopt for its nationals and for vessels under its flag such laws, regulations and other measures, including a permit system as appropriate, as may be necessary to implement this Convention".[109] Such provision also expresses a more reserved attitude with respect to the territorial approach.

One of the reasons for avoidance of discussion about the territorial jurisdiction in Antarctica is the fact that seven states (Argentina, Chile, Great Britain, France, Norway, Australia and New Zealand) have raised concurrent claims with respect to different parts of ice tracts in Antarctica. All claims were suspended for the effective term of the Convention.[110]

It is worth perceiving Antarctica not only as territory governed by numerous treaty regulations, but as having one system or regime. The fact of such a regime being established is confirmed by the abovementioned treaties; it is also assumed in the Convention on the Regulation of Antarctic Mineral Resource Activities which states

106 Article IX § 1(e) of the Antarctic Treaty provides for the possibility of adopting measures "relating to the exercise of jurisdiction in Antarctica".

107 Antarctic Treaty, Article IX para. 2.

108 Antarctic Treaty, Article VIII.

109 Article 2.

110 Originally the Treaty was supposed to apply for 30 years, from 1961 to 1991 (the Antarctic Treaty footnote 64, Article XII § 2a). It cooled the Antarctic ambitions of the national powers who agreed to freeze the current status quo. The success of the regime was confirmed by the extension of the Treaty in 1991, after the end of the Cold War.

that "This Convention is an integral part of the Antarctic Treaty System, comprising the Antarctic Treaty, the measures in effect under that Treaty, and its associated separate legal instruments.[111] Thus, the intention of those who are parties to numerous conventions concerning Antarctica is to deem such conventions an integral part of a greater entirety – the Antarctic Treaty System, the core of which is the Antarctic Treaty.[112]

The current number of state parties to the Convention is 45 – all of them are, at least indirectly, interested in exploiting the resources of Antarctica. For this reason, whether the regime applies to third countries not being state parties to the Treaty is the subject of academic debates. However, legal commentators argue about whether the Antarctic Treaty System constitutes an objective, opposable legal regime. Although the Treaty itself does not stipulate *erga omnes* [owed to all] application thereof,[113] the general public may tacitly approve of this new order. Article 38 of the Vienna Convention on the Law of Treaties[114] (which clearly states that a single treaty shall not oblige third countries without their express consent)[115] reads that none of its provisions precludes a rule set forth in a treaty from becoming binding upon a third state as a customary rule of international law. It would be reasonable to presume that the Antarctic Treaty regime (being *res communis*, beyond the territorial designs of contenders) has developed, like the Law of the Sea, into a rightful customary international law.[116]

Outer space (celestial bodies)

As with Antarctica, outer space did not require, in international opinion, any legal regulations until it suddenly gained strategic and military meaning with the launching of a satellite by the USSR on 4 October 1957. None of the states raised any protest against violation of their territorial space, and therefore a precedent of a universal custom status was established. The fundamental principle governing behavior

111 Convention on the Regulation of Antarctic Mineral Resource Activities, Wellington, 2 June 1988, Article 2.1; see A. Watts (1993) *International Law and the Antarctic Treaty System*, Cambridge: Cambridge University Press, p. 292. The Convention has not entered into force and was replaced by the Protocol on Environmental Protection to the Antarctic Treaty, Madrid, 1991 ('the Madrid Protocol'). <http://www.antarctica.ac.uk/About_Antarctica/Treaty/protocol.html> (accessed 14 February 2011).

112 A. Watts, ibid.

113 The Antarctic Treaty does not directly provide that it applies to third countries not being its signatories. A strict positivist view would be that the Treaty does apply to such countries. However, the opposing view, which is more consistent with the general principles of international law, is that the regime of the Antarctic Treaty is a complex international system established on the basis of the Treaty system binding on the greatest powers, which slowly develops into customary international law (the view taken by most publications on the subject). For this reason, if a third country violates the rules of the Treaty, as for instance the prohibition on using armed forces or the Protocol on Environmental Protection to the Antarctic Treaty 1991, it shall be subject to condemnation by the united international community. Cf. A. Watts, op. cit., pp. 295–298.

114 1155 UNTS 331, 8 ILM 679.

115 Article 34.

116 B. Simma calls this an "objective regime", see B. Simma (1986) 'The Antarctic Treaty as a Treaty Providing for an "Objective Regime"', 19 *Cornell International Law Journal*, pp. 189–198.

in outer space is its availability to all members of international community and its non-appropriation.[117]

The legal regime of outer space (i.e. space between celestial bodies and the celestial bodies themselves in the universe) was established (unless one counts the Treaty Banning Nuclear Weapon Tests in the Atmosphere, in Outer Space and Under Water),[118] by the 1967 Treaty on Principles Governing the Activities of States in the Exploration and Use of Outer Space, Including the Moon and Other Celestial Bodies (the "Outer Space Treaty").[119] The Treaty consists of 17 Articles, many of which are taken directly from the Antarctic Treaty. Those fundamental rules set forth in the Outer Space Treaty and derived from the rules of the Antarctic Treaty comprise: the opening of the outer space for inspection and exploration by all States without discrimination of any kind (Article I); non-appropriation by claim of sovereignty, by means of use or occupation (Article II); the submitting of all activities in outer space to international law (Article III); the prohibition against placing in orbit around the earth any nuclear weapons or any other kinds of weapons of mass destruction, installing such weapons on celestial bodies, or stationing such weapons in outer space in any other manner (Article VI); and use of the Moon and other celestial bodies exclusively for peaceful purposes (Article IV).[120] As already mentioned, in each international space the prospect of international conflict (jurisdictional conflict) was the main reason for formulating customary regimes or regulatory agreements. Considerable interest in those areas, from the very first international initiatives and increasing as international activities in outer space intensify, has provoked inevitable conflicts.[121] This was expressed by the aforementioned Treaty itself; Article VI thereof reads that activities in outer space "shall require authorization and continuing supervision by the appropriate State Party to the Treaty", and the provisions of Article VII, in turn, oblige the states to bear liability for damage to outer space inflicted by any object launched by the state or from its territory.

117 See e.g. H. A. Wassenbergh (1991) *Principles of Outer Space Law in Hindsight*, The Hague: Martinus Nijhoff Publishers, p. 81; and R. P. Kroener (1997) 'International Agreements and Contracts', in G. Lafferranderie and D. Crowther (eds.) *Outlook on Space Law Over the Next 30 Years: Essays Published for the 30th Anniversary of the Outer Space Treaty*, The Hague: Martinus Nijhoff Publishers, p. 40.

118 Treaty Banning Nuclear Weapon Tests in the Atmosphere, in Outer Space and Under Water, Moscow, 5 August 1963, 480 UNTS 43. <http://www.state.gov/t/ac/trt/4797.htm> (accessed 16 January 2011).

119 610 UNTS 205.

120 Cf. R. P. Kroener, ibid.

121 Current activity in outer space includes the presence of approximately 4,000 satellites, mostly owned by the US and Russia, as well as China, Brazil and European states, spacecrafts, long-term human space flights, the so-called "spacewalks", exploration of the Moon and anticipated exploration of planets, and the launching of probes into extrasolar space. Apart from research activities, states perform actions of a military and civil nature: space controls, searching for natural resources, radio and television transmission as well as telephone transmission (GPS – Global Positioning System), meteorological observations, and the construction of conventional military systems in the space around the Earth (as the elements of the so-called "star wars" program). See A. M. Din (1983) 'Stopping the Arms Race in Outer Space', 20(3) *Journal of Peace Research*, pp. 221–225. <http://jpr.sagepub.com/content/20/3/221.full.pdf+html> (accessed 9 February 2011). An interesting challenge to the legal regime regulating outer space is its exploration by private entities, such as actions initiated by the Google Lunar X Prize Foundation, <http://www.xprize.org/>.

Article VII of the Outer Space Treaty, not only by imposesliability for damage caused by objects launched by or from a state, but also imposes liability to keep an appropriate register of objects both owned by the state and those from the "territory or facility" from which the object was launched.[122] The Treaty specifies that the "State Party to the Treaty on whose registry an object launched into outer space is carried shall retain jurisdiction and control over such object, and over any personnel thereof, while in outer space . . .".[123] The fact of registration is confirmed by marking the object and thereby indicating the jurisdictional competence of the state in whose register the object is entered.[124] The practice shows that states exercise jurisdiction over their "own" objects, appropriately marked, entered in registers or launched into space from their territories.

High sea

High (open) sea covers maritime areas outside the borders of territorial sea.[125] The main principle underlying international legal regulation of this space is the freedom of seas 'principle'. The principle, manifested in Article 2 of the Convention on the High Seas of 1958[126] (reiterated in Article 88 of the Convention on the Law of the Sea dated 10 December 1982)[127] is that the high sea is beyond any claims of sovereignty. The list of freedoms comprises: freedom of navigation, freedom of fishing, freedom to lay submarine cables and pipelines, freedom to fly over the high seas, freedom to construct artificial islands and other installations permitted under international law and freedom of scientific research. Some of the abovementioned freedoms may be limited if a coastal state establishes a contiguous zone, a continental shelf, an exclusive fishing zone or an exclusive economic zone. These zones alter the freedoms of high sea by defining what states may do within their area.[128] Limitations may be also imposed by international agreements, including the Convention on the Law of the Sea itself.[129]

Freedom of the high seas applies to all statesincluding those which are land-locked. (Land-locked states may have their own fleet, but access to ports and transit to those ports has to be agreed upon between the land-locked and the coastal state.)

The law specifies the issue of exercising jurisdiction over the high sea in an exhaustive manner. States exercise jurisdiction over ships flying their flag, the presence of which on the high seas, regardless of function, is a sign of the state's activity on the sea and evidence of its exercising freedoms of the high seas (freedom of navigation). Ships on

122 Cf. B. Cheng (1997) 'Space Objects and Their Various Connecting Factors', in G. Lafferranderie and. D. Crowther (eds.) op. cit., p. 206.
123 Article VIII of the Outer Space Treaty.
124 This is confirmed by the United Nations Convention on International Liability for Damage Caused by Space Objects, London, Moscow and Washington, 29 March 1972 (the "Liability Convention"), 961 UNTS 187, Article V.
125 Shaw, op. cit., p. 505.
126 450 UNTS 11 (No 6465).
127 The United Nations Convention on the Law of the Sea, op. cit.
128 Shaw, op. cit., p. 506.
129 Convention on the Law of the Sea, op. cit., parts VI and XIII.

the high sea are subject to international laws and the laws of the state under the flag of which they sail. This clear regime, of the submission of persons, things and events on board ship, to regulation by the state under the flag of which the ship is sailing, is decisive for the materialization of freedoms of the high sea. Pursuant to Article 91 para. 1 of the Convention on the Law of the Sea, each state fixes its own conditions for the grant of its nationality to ships in its territory. The only requirement imposed by the Convention is the obligation to prove that there exists a genuine link between the state and the ship. Ships on the sea are thus subject to the exclusive jurisdiction of the state under the flag of which they sail (Article 92 of the Convention on the Law of the Sea; "exclusive jurisdiction"). The scope of liability for its effective exercise is specified in Article 94 of the Convention which sets forth obligations of the State towards ships flying its flag and its crew with respect to administrative, technical and social matters.[130]

The jurisdiction of the flag state over the ship, similarly as over its territory is, as a rule, exclusive, yet it may be limited by international laws. Limitations stipulated by the law concern cases of a traditional nature: i.e. the right to visit, search and seizure, if there is a reasonable ground for suspecting that the ship is engaged in piracy or the slave trade, or if, despite flying a foreign flag, the ship is actually of the same nationality as the visiting warship. Pursuant to the Convention on the Law of the Sea,[131] the powers include the right to board ships "engaged in unauthorized broadcasting" or without nationality, as well as to exercise the right of hot pursuit, to act in circumstances of necessity (e.g. damage to a ship caused by a crash posing a serious threat to the natural environment)[132] or to deal with collisions at sea.[133]

Jurisdictional regime in international spaces

When searching for a principle which draws together the ways in which jurisdiction is exercised in international spaces, the conclusion seems inescapable that it con-

130 In particular, each State shall maintain a register of ships, assume jurisdiction under its internal law over each ship flying its flag and take such measures for ships flying its flag as are necessary to ensure safety at sea with regard to the construction, equipment and seaworthiness of ships, manning of ships, labor conditions and the training of crews, the use of signals, the maintenance of communications and the prevention of collisions. Each state is also required to conform to generally accepted international regulations, procedures and practices and to take any steps which may be necessary to secure their observance.

131 Article 110.

132 A coastal state may seize or destroy a ship to prevent ecological disaster, as in the 1971 Torrey Canyon case where an oil tanker under the Liberian flag, after having crushed the reef in Canal La Manche, was bombed by the British. For a detailed description of the case in the BBC News, see 'Bombs Rain Down on Torrey Canyon' from the BBC website <http://news.bbc.co.uk/onthisday/hi/dates/stories/march/29/newsid_2819000/2819369.stm> (accessed: 5 February 2011). Conduct in such cases is sanctioned by the Convention Relating to Intervention on the High Seas in Cases of Oil Pollution Casualties, Brussels, 29 November 1969, in force 6 May 1975, 9 *ILM*.

133 Article 97.1 of the Convention on the Law of the Seastates that "In the event of a collision or of any other incident of navigation concerning a ship on the high seas, involving the penal or disciplinary responsibility of the master or of any other person in the service of the ship, no penal or disciplinary proceedings may be instituted against such persons except before the judicial or administrative authorities either of the flag State or of the State of which such person is a national."

cerns, most of all, precisely specified spaces. In the case of the high seas, account is taken of the physical space of ships, platforms, artificial islands and other types of installations; in the case of outer space, for the time being, facilities launched into the space and (apart from facilities placed on geostationary orbit) passing through the space. Such spatial specification provided grounds for considering the exercise of jurisdictional competence with reference to the principle of territorial jurisdiction. The above-cited provision of the Convention on the Law of the Sea on the "exclusive jurisdiction" over the ship of flag state may, in this respect, be analogous to the practice with regard to the exercise of state jurisdiction over other areas: the authors of the *Restatement* take the view that applying laws to activities aboard a vessel, aircraft or spacecraft may be based on the principle of territoriality exercised within clearly defined spaces.[134]

A certain characteristic element that has to be invoked while considering the issue of exercising jurisdiction over international spaces is the provision of the Convention on the Law of the Sea requiring that the fact of a ship flying the flag of the state confirms the existence of a genuine link between the state and the ship.[135] The category of the "genuine link" is obviously taken from international law constructions concerning nationality.[136] Therefore, a question arises as to whether granting nationality to vessels, aircrafts or spacecrafts (and the act of registration is qualified as such[137]) provides grounds for invoking any special variant of personal jurisdiction, something which is yet to be further elaborated.

The said personal and territorial references should however, give way to a view that exercising jurisdiction over international spaces concerns not only its exercise aboard aircrafts, spacecrafts or Antarctica research facilities, but also, in the future most probably also in stations placed on the Moon and other celestial bodies.[138] The exercise of jurisdiction over such areas has to be justified otherwise than through attempts to link it to territory. The modern law of international spaces is based on the fundamental presumption that the nationality (broadly understood as the nationality of persons and vessels or facilities) constitutes the grounds for jurisdiction applied to outer space, Antarctica or the high seas.[139] In Antarctica the criterion is the nationality of the facility.[140] On the high seas the criterion is the nationality of the flag state ("flag law"). In extraterrestrial areas the state of registration (flag) of the spacecraft, whose

134 The *Restatement*, § 402(h).

135 Article 91 states that "Ships have the nationality of the State whose flag they are entitled to fly. There must exist a genuine link between the State and the ship."

136 See e.g., *Lichtenstein* v. *Guatemala* (the 'Nottebohm' case) (1955), available on the International Court of Justice website <http://www.icj-cij.org/icjwww/idecisions/isummaries/ilgsummary550406.htm> (accessed 2 February 2011).

137 N. Q. Dinh, op. cit., pp. 493–494.

138 Also drilling units on high seas.

139 E.g. Article 8 of the Antarctic Treaty or Article 6 of the Treaty on Principles Governing the Activities of States in the Exploration of Use of Outer Space, including the Moon and Other Celestial Bodies, op. cit.

140 Article 8 § 1 D of the Antarctic Treaty provides for a clause that scientific personnel and observers shall be subject only to the jurisdiction of their state.

register includes the launched object, retains jurisdiction and control over such object and its personnel.[141]

The modern law of international spaces is based on the assumption that the specific principle of state jurisdiction combining elements of the territorial and personal jurisdiction constitutes the grounds for exercising jurisdiction over high seas, Antarctica and outer space. The *Restatement*, without providing any special name, recognizes only an auxiliary role of the territorial jurisdiction in exercising the jurisdiction aboard vessels, aircrafts or spacecrafts.[142] The principle of so construed state jurisdiction seems to confirm this as correct.

Summary of jurisdiction-governing principles

The overview presented above, as to the fundamental principles on which states base their competence of sovereignty, enables us to determine the limits of state sovereignty in the existing geopolitical system. Analysis of the overview suggests that the main criterion on which state jurisdiction is based is territory. It is within a state's territorial bounds that the legal order established by state authorities applies – residents are obliged to respect it within a determined, physical area. The principle of territorial jurisdiction is a reflection of the equality of states and manifests itself in mutual respect of territorial integrity.[143] However, a sovereignty defined in terms of territory only is insufficient with respect to some of the complex circumstances that international law has to face. For this reason accompanying principles have been developed which specify special extensions of the principle of territorial jurisdiction and situations in which the principle may be restricted. One example of this is the principle of personal jurisdiction whereby a state exercises jurisdictional competence to regulate the behaviors of its nationals and other situations in respect of its nationals which take place outside the state territory (the active and passive personality principle).[144]

Apart from the construct that provides detailed description of circumstances where the interference in the territorial competence of another state is permitted, sovereigns have also developed principles concerning those areas of the globe, which in their opinion, should be common. The sovereigns deemed unacceptable the excessive increase in influence of any of the states in such areas, being *res communis* of all nations. Thus a concept of international territories has been developed which included circumpolar areas, sea areas except territorial waters, and outer space. Within these territories sovereigns decided to recognize a unique state jurisdiction regime. Nevertheless, the

141 The Convention on Registration of Objects Launched into Outer Space, New York, 12 Novermber 1974, in force since 1976 ('the Registration Convention'), 1023 UNTS 15 (No 15020). This national status functions as the concept of temporary presence dealt with in cases such as *The Schooner Exchange* v. *McFaddon* (1812) 11 US 116. <http://caselaw.lp.findlaw.com/scripts/getcase.pl?navby=case&court=us&vol=11&invol=116 (accessed 2 January 2011) and Brown v. Duchesne (1857) 60 US 183. <http://laws.findlaw.com/us/60/ 183.html> (accessed 2 February 2011).

142 The *Restatement*, p. 241.

143 With reservations regarding the necessity of modifying the existing scope of the concept of sovereignty.

144 Considering the abovementioned principle of double criminality.

abovementioned principles do not provide grounds for modern international relations and jurisdictional activities. The practice of states, and what follows (the views of legal academics and commentators), reveal further additional rules clarifying the exercise of powers by the states.

One of them is the effects principle (the principle of effective jurisdiction), which is becoming more and more popular by reason of forever closer and more complex economic and political relations between modern states. In the face of a considerable increase in the pace and scale of international interactions, it seemed reasonable for the states to go beyond their territorial jurisdiction to regulate conduct which entails potential risk to their economic and political situation. The popularity of the principle has been growing in modern international relations, when global threats of acts of terrorism and organized crime are becoming more tangible and serious than ever. The principle has been frequently applied, not only in circumstances where criminal law provisions were violated or which posed a risk to the existence of states, but also in the case of a conflict of laws, for the purpose of exercising rights by civil courts in situations where there was a legal dispute between nationals of two different sovereigns.[145] The effects principle has been invoked as the grounds for exercising competence by the judicial authorities of states in an increasing number of cases in the second half of the twentieth century, when the growth and popularization of trade and service exchange has been supported by an increase in the number of communication channels, mass media, telephones, faxes and, ultimately, the Internet. International consumers protection, which in the first half of the twentieth century was rather a question of academic considerations, has now, a hundred years later, become the subject of practitioners' debates and the grounds for numerous court cases. Media have emerged which do not adhere to traditional principles on which legal orders of states were built. Television broadcasting became a challenge to national legal regulations aiming at adjusting the provisions of law to new technical possibilities. However, no other media affected the modern law and regulations of international relations to such a considerable extent as did the global network of the Internet, for the traditional criterion of territoriality does not apply to relations established between nationals of different states within the area of cyberspace. It has become apparent that this new space of interpersonal relations needs to be regulated by the law and that the regulations applied so far are not sufficient to confront the electronic domain. The Internet has made it necessary to reinterpret such notions as sovereignty, jurisdiction or the immunity of states. An aterritorial and decentralized Internet, establishing a new supranational space of interactions between persons located in various territories, requires the introduction of new legal solutions and a thorough reconsideration of those already existing. The following part of the study details the new challenges posed by the electronic media to the law-makers, along with some proposed solutions.

145 In the context of exercising judicial jurisdiction, a particular example is the (US) Alien Tort Claims Act, 1982, 28 USC § 1350. On the basis of its provisions the Congress of the first term established that district courts shall have original jurisdiction with respect to any civil action by an alien for a tort only "committed in violation of the law of nations or a treaty of the United States". § 1350 stipulates the original jurisdiction of district courts over any civil action by an alien for a tort only, committed in violation of the law of nations or a treaty of the United States.

2 International Internet Law

Scope and sources

The need for International Internet Law (IIL)

The first part of this study was devoted to considerations of the fundamental principles governing the exercise of sovereign powers by states. In the second part the author compares these principles with the practice of state authorities exercising jurisdictional competence over entities acting via the Internet, within the area referred to as cyberspace.[1] As mentioned above, the purpose of this analysis is to compare principles developed so far, governing the distribution of jurisdictional powers among actors of international arena, with new circumstances, namely the effect of actions performed via the Internet. The difficulty in applying old principles to new circumstances results directly from the specific nature of global network, the limitlessness of which cannot be easily adapted to the present, mainly territorial models of distributing state competence: the Internet, in virtue of its limitless nature, may not be described using principles mainly based on the criterion of territorial sovereignty.

The Internet is often mistakenly identified with its most common application – the World Wide Web. The Web is then defined as a set of electronic documents placed on the hard drives of computers (servers) designed for this purpose in .html format, available when using the global computer network. As the World Wide Web Consortium describes it,[2] the "World Wide Web (WWW) is the universe of network-accessible information, an embodiment of human knowledge".[3]

1 The concept of cyberspace is used to specify common ground for exchanging information by all global network users. The characteristic feature of the cyberspace is its aterritoriality – it has no physical referent contrary to those spaces that international law has addressed so far. See e.g. D. R. Johnson and D. G. Post (1996) 'Law and Borders – The Rise of Law in Cyberspace', 48 *Stanford Law Review* <http://www.cli.org/X0025_LBFIN.html> (accessed 16 February 2011) or R. Bendrath and J. Hofmann (2005) 'The Return of the State in Cyberspace, Regulation and Legitimacy on the Internet: The Domain Name System and Privacy', paper delivered at the Lucerna conference on *The Internet and the Changing Face of International Relations and Security*, p. 3. <www.crn.ethz.ch/_docs/BendrathHoffmann_The-Return-of-the-State-in-Cyberspace-final.pdf> (accessed 16 February 2011).

2 For more about the World Wide Web Consortium (W3C) see chapter 4.

3 World Wide Web Consortium. <http://www.w3.org/MarkUp/html-test/cern/TheProject.html> (accessed: 2 February 2011); cf. the Internet Governance Project: "Thus, we define Internet as the global data communication system formed by the interconnection of public and private telecommunication networks using Internet Protocol (IP), TCP (Transmission Control Protocol TCP) and the

A moment's reflection shows that the Internet is far more than only the HTTP protocol constituting the foundations of the global electronic network, as it covers also many other devices and media using the network. The Internet is sometimes identified as the community of its users[4] or set of network-accessible resources. Possibly the most comprehensive definition of the Internet, for the purpose of our further considerations, is as a global data exchange system operating based on the interconnections of local networks distributed in a number of physical locations allowing simultaneous, multidimensional worldwide interaction of users. All areas of electronic interactions become the object of an independent regulation of sovereign states claiming the right to decide upon all content available in their territories. Functions of the Internet, apart from exchanging information or sending e-mails, also include online shopping (thus, commercial law is still being developed and amended)[5] or downloading and rendering accessible film and music files (the object of copyright and intellectual property rights regulations provoking a heated discussion among lawmakers, legal academics and commentators as well as users and authors themselves).[6] New possibilities gave rise to a series of new questions and challenges to national and international law makers. It followed that traditional principles of exercising jurisdiction had to be applied to a brand new arena of mutual interactions, common for various entities subject to different sovereigns. What is more, consequences of those actions are directly noticeable in the territory of each independent law maker; thus it comes as no surprise that each law maker claims the right to sanction harmful behavior and to remedy inflicted damage. This means that legal regulation of cyberspace is, by its nature, international. In order to show the scale of the phenomenon, it is useful to provide basic figures illustrating the dynamics of Internet development within recent years. It is assumed that the number of Internet users reaches almost two billion people all over the world.[7] The increase in the number of users within

protocols required to implement IP internetworking on a global scale, such as DNS and packet routing protocols". In the opinion of its founders, this definition takes account of the existence of numerous applications based on IPs, from which only a few constitute the grounds for the Internet functioning: Mathiason, J., Mueller, M., Klein, H. and Holitscher, M. (2004) 'Internet Governance: the State of Play', 04(001) *Internet Governance Project Papers*. <http://www.internetgovernance.org/pdf/ig–sop–final.pdf> (accessed 2 January 2011), p. 6.

4 Cf. e.g. J. James (2003) *Cyberpsychology: Principles of Creating Virtual Presence,* unpublished but available at the website of the University of Hawaii <http://www.soc.hawaii.edu/LEONJ/leonj/leonpsy/cyber.html#forming> (accessed 16 February 2011).

5 For example: Directive 1999/93/EC of the European Parliament and of the Council of 13 December 1999 on a Community Framework for Electronic Signatures (2000) OJ L 013, pp. 12–20 and a number of initiatives of the United Nations Commission on International Trade Law (UNCITRAL), such as the Model Law on Electronic Commerce adopted by the United Nations Commission on International Trade Law (1996) A/RES/51/162, which concerned legal issues related to Electronic Data Interchange (EDI) and related means of communication, or the draft of the Electronic Signatures Act.

6 For more about rights protecting intellectual property online, see chapter 2, sections 2 ('The Internet and Copyright') and 3 ('Domain Names – Internet and Trademark Law'), below.

7 For the cited statistical data see World Internet Users and Population Statistics at the Internet World Stats site <http://www.internetworldstats.com/stats.htm> (accessed 10 February 2011).

the last decade amounts to 450%, where the greatest growth was recorded in Africa (2,400%), even though the Internet penetration there is the lowest in the world (with only slightly over 10% of African residents having Internet access). The highest percentage of cybernauts resides in Asian countries (42%; that is over 825 million people), whilst in Europe the number of network users is smaller by almost a half (24% or 475 million people). Languages prevailing in the Internet data exchange are still English (27% of users)[8] and Chinese (slightly over 22% of users).

The data show clearly that the Internet is an international medium, and what goes with it – intercultural, yet everyday and judicial facts from all over the world – unambiguously shows that this sphere of life may not be disregarded by international legal regulation. The law, as a strict cultural creation, which varies depending on the longitude and latitude, requires compromise solutions to be applied globally. By reason of the increase in the Internet's popularity, sovereigns respecting their distinctness were confronted with a new challenge; while respecting established rules of international law and diplomatic courtesy, and without interference in the exclusive domain of other international law entities, they are obliged to effectively protect their interests and values.[9] This issue stems from proper interpretation and implementation of state jurisdiction practice within the limits set by international law. This necessity poses risk to, above all, the first of the fundamental assumptions of the synergic existence of an international community – that of the sovereignty of states based on the power to exercise jurisdiction. At the same time, this new situation threatens the fundamental principle of the state under the rule of law – legal certainty. If an Internet user may not be certain whether a geographically and culturally distant court is competent to assess his or her actions, measures aiming at convincing such a cyber traveler that his or her own state is democratic and governed under the rule of law can prove ineffective.

States took increasingly greater action to exercise their powers over online activities. They did this through enacting and executing national legislation. These numerous concurring national regulations simultaneously affected Internet users when they performed online activities that had international consequences, such as rendering online services to out-of-state consumers. US companies had to deal with European privacy protection. European online companies had to determine whether to pay taxes in Europe, or in the destination to which they had shipped their digitized goods. The legal consequences of their actions, often resulting from foreign national acts of law, took many users by surprise. Numerous examples presented below reveal the absence of a uniform practice and incidental decisions of authorities regarding key issues which require resolution in order to provide certainty to electronic interactions. One of the relevant questions is the issue of regulating cyberspace, and more

8 In 2004 the number was 35.4%.

9 Even though as A. Aust (op. cit., p. 43) notices, perhaps it is high time to note the occurrence of a new, superior principle governing the exercise of jurisdiction by states, provided that there exists sufficiently close relation between the state and regulated action and the state shall effectively overcome the interests of other states.

precisely, the ambit of competence of entities authorized to implement such regulation. At the same time, as more and more states decide to introduce such provisions, the scope of their powers goes far beyond their own territories.[10] Therefore, the only reasonable solution is to regulate the electronic interactions at international level, and the considerable experience of international law may enable us to apply already existing mechanisms (appropriately adapted) to the challenges of cyberspace. The catalogue of areas where the need for international regulations is explicit, is set out below. The areas show us the merits of the international Internet law.

The Internet and protection of copyright: fair use online

The international legal copyright protection regime is one of the best-regulated areas of international activity. Its pillar is the 1886 Berne Convention.[11] The purpose thereof is "*to protect, in as effective and uniform a manner as possible, the rights of authors in their literary and artistic works*".[12] Nevertheless, neither this document nor any accompanying agreements[13] establish any tool of international protection of copyright, which would automatically protect the rights of each author in every part of the world. Authors are entitled to national protection, the basic shape of which results from the Convention; the detailed scope of protection is clarified and implemented exclusively by the states. The Berne Convention is based on two fundamental principles:

- the minimum protection principle – signatories shall provide at least such protection under national law as the Convention provides for; and
- the assimilation principle – an author from another state shall be treated equally with nationals of a given member state.

As per the "minimum protection" principle, a member to the Convention shall protect foreign works if several easily verifiable conditions set out in Article 2 are met.[14] "National treatment" is described in Article 4 of the Convention, which provides for equal protection of the rights of authors in their country of origin and in countries other than their country of origin (even though the Convention stipulates a number of exceptions to these general rules). These Articles may be deemed the foundations of the international protection of copyright since they were accepted by 164 state parties.

10 For more, see D. R. Johnson and D. G. Post (1997) 'The Rise of Law on the Global Network', in B. Kahin and C. R. Nesson (eds.) *Borders in Cyberspace: Information Policy and the Global Information Infrastructure*, Cambridge, Mass.: MIT Press, p. 14.

11 Convention for the Protection of Literary and Artistic Works, Berne, 9 September 1886 ('the Berne Convention'), Rome version (1928).

12 Berne Convention, Preamble.

13 The Convention has been supplemented on numerous occasions, at Paris on 4 May 1896, revised at Berlin on 13 November 1908, completed at Berne on 20 March 1914, revised at Rome on 2 June 1928, at Brussels on 26 June 1948, at Stockholm on 14 July 1967 and at Paris on 24 July 1971 and subsequently amended again on 28 September 1979.

14 The expression "literary and artistic works" shall include any production in the literary, scientific and artistic domain whatever the mode or form of their expression.

The developed international copyright system, apart from the Berne Convention, consists of a number of other instruments, for instance the 1952 Universal Copyright Convention[15] (UCC), the 1961 International Convention for the Protection of Performers, Producers of Phonograms and Broadcasting Organizations (the Rome Convention) or the World Intellectual Property Organization whose 1996 "Internet Treaties" (WIPO Copyright Treaty (WCT)[16] and WIPO Performances and Phonograms Treaty (WPPT)[17]) adapted to the challenges of a modern world.

The purpose of the two latter documents was to reinforce the protection of copyright and related rights in times of electronic exchange, especially by taking account of digitization processes. The WCT constitutes a supplement to the Berne Convention and submits the object thereof to further protection. For instance, the provisions of Article 8 vest the authors with the right of authorizing any communication to the public of their works, by wire or wireless means, including on-demand display. The rights of communication referred to therein include distribution where the users may access these works from a place and at a time individually chosen by them.

Pursuant to Article 10 of the Treaty, states may, at their discretion, provide for regulations within the scope of fair private use; however, limitations of the copyright shall not unreasonably prejudice the normal use of the work or the legitimate interests of the author.

The WPPT duplicates the solutions of the WCT. It stipulates that artists, performers and producers of phonograms have the exclusive right to decide about introducing protected works within computer networks where they are available on demand. Despite formulating reliable unification and clarification mechanisms to regulate international copyright issues, it is this area that provokes most controversies. Domestic practice based on uniform international standards is substantially varied. Differences in domestic legislation, especially when exercised in court practice, result from different interpretation of the same provisions and jurisdictional competence by national courts. Two copyright elements raise most controversies: (a) contributory infringement and (b) fair use, as it is known in the US (fair dealing, as it is known in the UK). The disputes are exacerbated by the extensive reading of jurisdictional principles by national courts (the American construct of 'purposeful availment').[18] Both of them were invoked by reason of a particular computer data exchange system: the peer-to-peer (p2p) networks.

The first majorly popular p2p service – Napster – was closed down after a court judgment found, based on the controversial US Digital Millennium Copyright Act

15 As of February 2011, the 1952 United Nations Universal Copyright Convention in the 1971 Paris version gathered 100 state signatories, whereas the principles of the World Trade Organization Agreement on Trade-Related Aspects of Intellectual Property Rights concluded in 1994 in Marrakesh was approved by 153 WTO members.

16 Available at <http://www.wipo.int/treaties/en/ip/wct/trtdocs_wo033.html> (accessed 11 February 2011).

17 Available at <http://www.wipo.int/treaties/en/ip/wppt/trtdocs_wo034.html> (accessed 11 February 2011).

18 Cf. chapter 3 on US court practice.

(DMCA),[19] that it was subject to *contributory* copyright *infringement* done by its users.[20] According to the court decision, Napster contributed to copyright infringement by hosting illegal content.

The owners of Kazaa – the second majorly popular p2p site – were quick to learn from Napster's mistakes and provided their services using a different technology. Instead of hosting content itself, Kazaa just enabled links to content hosted by its users. Neither this substantial difference in the way of providing its service nor incorporating the company under the laws of Vanuatu freed Sharman Networks from a contributory infringement claim in the US. In presenting grounds for assessing the purposeful availment of Sharman Ltd to state jurisdiction, the Ninth Circuit District Court Judge Wilson argued:

> Here, there is little question that Sharman has knowingly and purposefully availed itself of the privilege of doing business in California. First, Sharman essentially does not dispute that a significant number of its users – perhaps as many as two million – are California residents. Indeed, given that Sharman's KMD software has been downloaded more than 143 million times, it would be mere cavil to deny that Sharman engages in a significant amount of contact with California residents.[21]

The same line of reasoning was given as grounds for liability damages ordered from other p2p service providers, such as Grokster or Streamcast[22] and repeated by the Australian judicature in its own case against Sharman.[23]

The Kazaa case is, however, of most interest from a jurisdictional perspective, as the very same factual circumstances presented before European courts lead to completely divergent decisions. The fact of not storing any illegal material and operating from a distant physical location made both the Dutch[24] and the Italian[25] court find

19 Digital Millennium Copyright Act (DMCA), 1998, 17 USC § 1201 (United States). <www.copyright.gov/legislation/dmca.pdf> (accessed 11 February 2011).

20 Napster: *A & M Records* v. *Napster* (2001), US Court of Appeals for the Ninth Circuit. <http://caselaw.findlaw.com/us-9th-circuit/1047162.html> (accessed 11 February 2011).

21 *MGM Studios, Inc. v. Grokster, Ltd.* (2005) 545 US 913. <http://laws.findlaw.com/us/000/04-480.html> (accessed 11 February 2011).

22 For further reference, see S. Smith (2003) 'From Napster to Kazaa: The Battle over Peer-to-Peer Filesharing goes International', 8 *Duke L. & Tech. Rev.* pp. 1–8. <http://www.law.duke.edu/journals/dltr/articles/PDF/2003DLTR0008.pdf> (accessed 11 February 2011).

23 *Universal Music Australia Pty Ltd* v. *Sharman License Holdings Ltd* [2005] FCA 1242, Federal Court of Australia <http://www.austlii.edu.au/au/cases/cth/federal_ct/2004/934.html> (accessed 11 February 2011).

24 See the decision of the Supreme Court of the Netherlands in *Vereniging Buma and Stichting Stemra* v. *Kazaa B.V.* (2006) Hoge Raad der Nederlanden, Eerste Kamer C02/186HR JMH/AT, Mudd Law Offices (trans.). <http://www.muddlawoffices.com/RIAA/cases/Netherlands.pdf> (accessed 11 February 2011).

25 *Italy* v. *Rizzi and Faretti* (2007) East Lombardi Appellate Court (Corte Di Cassazione). Sez. III Penale 149. <http://www.diritto–in–rete.com/sentenza.asp?id=331> (accessed 11 February 2011). See also the article 'Italy's High Court Rules that File Downloading not a Crime if not for Profit', *International Herald Tribune*, 22 January 2007. <http://www.post-gazette.com/pg/07026/756542-96.stm> (accessed 11 February 2011).

Shareman Networks Ltd outside their jurisdiction, regardless of the number of users located within the state borders of each of those countries. This case presents the clearest example of how a uniform legal framework can lead to contradictory decisions of national courts. The latest European court decision in The Pirate Bay (TPB) case goes to show that neither previous European jurisprudence nor the existing detailed copyright regulations warrant any legal certainty for those on trial. A Swedish court found the four owners of The Pirate Bay website, which enabled its users to exchange copyrighted content through torrent files (TPB hosted the addresses of the torrent files), liable for contributory infringement to copyright,[26] although this legal construction has never been applied in Europe to p2p networks.

The second element of existing copyright regulations that raises much controversy is fair use, mentioned in Article 10 of the Berne Convention. The idea behind it is to enable copyright protected works to be used without the permission of the copyright holder in particular cases, such as personal use or the statutory activities of libraries or media.

The public interest was the ground for the introduction of the fair use exception. Free access to the *acquis* of science and art was rightfully considered essential for further civilization development.[27] The concept of fair use, especially of personal fair use, proved to be a particularly problematic issue given the common availability and great popularity of digitized works. The territorial scope of the use of work constitutes one of the criteria separating fields of use and entitlement to use the work in the territory of a state in which the user has its registered office. This criterion was confronted with the limitless nature of the global network. Specification of recipients who can access the work within the personal fair use exception may prove the practical obstacle as many legal systems allow communication of works to variously defined "personal acquaintances", who, next to blood-relatives and in-laws, fall into the scope of permitted personal use eligible subjects. Similarly, doubts may arise with respect to the permitted "public" scope of fair use, especially in the context of problems of press regulation,[28] where law-makers provide special rights, in the context of fair use, to media.[29] The definition of the Internet or online publications as elements of so defined media proves problematic.

The interpretation of "fair use" has become the object of many doctrinal disputes, and most of all, divergent decisions of national courts made given similar facts. The liberal approach of European courts towards Kazaa presented above was reflected also in legislative proposals concerning fair use. The amendment to the Copyright Law of 2005

26 On 26 November 2010, a Swedish appeals court upheld the verdict, decreasing prison terms but increasing the fine. On 17 May 2010, following an injunction against the ISP, the site was taken offline.

27 The relevant provisions are stipulated in e.g. § 53 para. 1 of the German Copyright Law (Gesetz über Urheberrecht und verwandte Schutzrechte – Urheberrechtsgesetz) dated 9 September 1965 (BGBl I S 1273) as amended (uniform text: BGBl I S 2349).

28 J. Kulesza (2009) 'Which Legal Standards Should Apply to Web-Logs? The Present Legal Position of Internet Journals in the European *Iuris Prudence* in the Light of the European Parliament Committee's [sic] on Culture and Education report and Polish Supreme Court decision', 13(3) *Lex Electronica*. <http://www.lex-electronica.org/docs/articles_221.pdf> (accessed 5 February 2011).

29 See e.g. 17 USC § 107 allowing fair use for news reporting.

proposed by the French parliament[30] was to enable Internet users to download copyright protected files via peer-to-peer networks based on an extended concept of private fair use.[31] Such activity was to be permitted for own, private purposes only; however, the parliament proposed dispensing with the requirement of maintaining "close" and "permanent social relations" with the recipient, which had hitherto constituted an inherent element of the construct of the private fair use.[32] Such change would lead to peer-to-peer exchange being perfectly legal for over eight million French cybernauts, despite the fact that shortly beforehand the court issued a decision in favor of an organization dealing with copyright, holding that a file downloaded from the Internet may not be a private copy.[33] The phonographic industry immediately expressed their serious concerns about the proposed amendments and effectively prevented them; as a result the amended French Copyright Act has become one of the most restrictive laws of contemporary Europe.[34] This was the consequence of a heated discussion over the content of proposed amendments, by reason of which the amendment was forwarded to the French Constitutional Council (*Conseil Constitutionel*). The Council, by a decision of 27 July 2006, declared solutions proposed in the amendment inconsistent with the French Constitution and EU laws (in particular Directive 2001/29),[35] practically excluding the private use with respect to digitized works and emphasizing the liability of software producers for violation of copyright using their computer software. Another step was the introduction of a new type of sanction imposed on users violating the copyright – denial of Internet access (also known as the "three strikes law").[36] This controversial French proposal has not been assimilated by other EU legal systems (with the exception of Sweden), perhaps due to the fact that the French Constitutional Council deemed it a breach of fundamental civil rights, such as the right to access information and free communication.[37]

30 Loi No. 2006–961 du 1er Août 2006 Relative au Droit D'Auteur et aux Droits Voisins dans la Société de L'information (DADVSI), NOR: MCCX0300082L. http://www.legifrance.gouv.fr/WAspad/UnTexteDeJorf?numjo=MCCX0300082L (accessed 5 February 2011).

31 France Assemblée Nationale (2003) *Projet de Loi Relatif au Droit d'Auteur et aux Droits Voisins dans la Société de l'Information*, No. 1206. <http://www.assemblee–nationale.fr/12/projets/pl1206.asp> (accessed 5 February 2011). For the content of the amendment, see the website of the Assemblée Nationale: <http://www.assemblee-nationale.fr/12/projets/pl1206.asp> (accessed 5 February 2011).

32 The proposed amendment read: "authors shall not prohibit distributing their works in any form for private use, however, the purpose of obtaining such work shall in no event constitute direct or indirect commercial practice". Ibid.

33 *Anthony G.* v. *Société Civile des Producteurs Phonographiques* (2005). Decision of 8 December 2005, No. 12 Tribunal de Grande Instance de Paris, 31ème chambre/2, No. d'Affaire: 0504090091. <http://www.audionautes.net/pages/PDF/audionautestgiparis.pdf>. Also see the decision of 2 February 2005, Tribunal de Grande Instance Pontoise, 6ème chambre/3, in the case *SACEM, SDRM, SPPF and SCPP* v. *Alexis B Juris.com*. <http://www.juriscom.net/jpt/visu.php?ID=639> (accessed 5 February 2011).

34 See K. Fisher (2005) 'Schizophrenic on Intellectual Property Laws?' *Ars Technica*. <http://arstechnica.com/news.ars/post/20051222-5827.html> (accessed 5 February 2011).

35 Décision No. 2006–540 DC de Juillet 2006, Conseil Constitutionnel <http://www.conseil-constitutionnel.fr/decision/2006/2006540/index.htm>.

36 Loi No. 2011–669 du 12 Juin 2009 Favorisant la Diffusion et la Protection de la Création sur Internet ('La Loi Hadopi'), ORF No. 0135 du 13 Juin 2009 page 9666, Texte No. 2, NOR: MCCX0811238L.

37 Décision No. 2011–580 DC du 10 Juin 2009: Loi Favorisant la Diffusion et la Protection de la Création sur Internet. The decision became the grounds for formulating a thesis on the establishment of a new human right – the right to Internet access.

The jurisprudence of the ECJ based on Directive 2001/29 certainly supports the restrictive interpretation of fair use in Europe,[38] and constitutes the grounds for many EU member states to establish more stringent regulations on the responsibility for violating copyright leading to a practical collapse of the concept of fair use online.

It is not only the foregoing examples that prove that the unification of copyright protection practices is still a problematic issue. As an example of system ineffectiveness one may refer to the case of (no longer operational) Russian service www.allofmp3.com, which operated in compliance with the national provisions on copyright[39] yet failed to guarantee the protection of authors' rights, despite the fact that Russia is a party to the Berne Convention and did not violate its provisions. The discrepancy between international regulations and the provisions of Russian law arose in Article 39 of the Russian Copyright Law,[40] which represented the consequences of reservations made to the content of the Berne Convention.[41] Under an agreement with the Russian Organization for Multimedia & Digital Systems (ROMS), a 'collective society', the website owner offered, via the Internet, multimedia files in exchange for t a small payment. However, the owner did not guarantee the right to the authors of offered works to decide about the scope and manner of their distribution, and the remuneration was transferred to ROMS alone. The controversial ROMS was

38 Decisions of the ECJ to impose sanctions for failure to adapt the national laws to the requirements of Directive 2001/29 have been issued with respect to: Spain (*Commission of the European Communities* v. *Kingdom of Spain* (Case C-31/04), OJ (C 171) (9 July 2005), p. 3), Finland (*Commission of the European Communities* v. *Republic of Finland* (Case C-56/04), OJ (C 31) (5 February 2005), pp. 3–4), France (*Commission of the European Communities* v. *French Republic* (Case C-59/04), OJ (C 082) (2 April 2005), p. 5), the United Kingdom (*Commission of the European Communities* v. *United Kingdom of Great Britain and Northern Ireland* (Case C-88/04), OJ (C 045) (19 February 2005), p. 11), Sweden (*Commission of the European Communities* v. *Kingdom of Sweden* (Case C-91/04), OJ (C 019) (22 January 2005), p. 8) and Belgium (*Commission of the European Communities* v. *Kingdom of Belgium* (Case C-143/04) OJ (C 006) (8 January 2005), p. 20).

39 In 2007 Moscow's Cheremushkin District Court found Denis Kvasov, the owner of AllofMP3.com, not guilty of violating intellectual property laws; see T. Adelaja (2007) 'AllofMP3 Survives First Test In Court', *Moscow Times*, 16 August 2007. <http://www.themoscowtimes.com/news/article/allofmp3-survives-first-test-in-court/194998.html>

40 Article 39 of the Russian Federation Law on Copyright and Neighboring Rights, 1993, закон РФ N5351–1 (available in English translation at <http://www.literati.rus/npa_v.php?id=21>) allows public performance, distribution and broadcasting of the soundtrack or recording *without prior permission from the producer/performer of the recording (not authors)* against payment of due royalties. Article 45 para. 2 of the said Act provides for a collecting society to grant licenses for users of works which then allow the use of all works or objects of neighboring rights "on behalf of" all copyright and neighboring rights holders *including those who have not authorized the organization to manage their rights* (holders may, however, claim the exclusion of works from the domain managed by the organization).

41 Russia acceded to the Berne Convention on 13 March 1995 and under Article 18a reserved that the "effects of the above mentioned Convention shall not extend to the works which, at the date of entry into force of the said Convention in respect of the Russian Federation, are already in the public domain in its territory" (WIPO, Berne Notification 162). An analogous reservation was made by the United States when accessing the Convention in 1989. The possibility of making a reservation under Article 18a of the Convention raised certain doubts in the minds of legal academics and commentators as being inadmissible under Article 30(1) of the Convention, see L. I. Podshybykin and K. B. Leontiew (2002) 'Implementation of the Berne Convention in [the] Russian Federation'. <http://www.copyright.ru/publ-412.html> (accessed 11 January 2011) or P. B. Meggs and P. A. Sergiejew (2000) *Intellectual Property*, Budapest: Jurist, pp. 400ff.

legal in Russia at that time, even though it operated outside the International Confederation of Authors and Composers Societies (CISAC) seated in Paris. The amendment to the Russian Copyright Law,[42] introduced under political pressure from the US and threats of initiating proceedings by the RIAA (Recording Industry Association of America) along with the demand for compensation from Russian authorities in the amount of USD1.65 trillion has effectively solved the allofmp3 issue. Nevertheless, it did not prevent the creation of new websites operating on the same terms (a ROMS granted license), such as, Ukrainian MP3Count or Russian zaycev.net that offered free access to copyright protected content directly invoking the construct of private fair use.[43]

In circumstances where copyright protection is based on an incoherent system of international agreements, their inconsistent implementation and the endeavors of the some national legislures to entirely exclude the concept of fair use with respect to the Internet, must cause concerns. The limitation of users' rights introduced by state authorities under the pressure of a copyright collective society and international multimedia industry[44] results in an unreasonable imbalance. At the same time the fundamental copyright protection mechanism based on obligatory, individual license agreements between the author and each user does not fit the purpose and spirit of electronic exchange – immediate, simultaneous and multilateral.

The issue has become particularly noticeable as a result of adopting copyright protection for computer programs, especially towards the judicial practice of, *inter alia*, the United States, which permits the inclusion of software-based applications into the content of technical solutions protected with patents.[45] This troubling situation gave rise to specific legal solutions based on copyright, but, at least to the same extent, referable to the ethics of users themselves.

The concept of free software, introduced by R. Stallman in 1983, was the backlash against submitting computer software to the copyright regime.[46] The Free Software Movement initiated by Stallman at that time proposed a revolutionary solution, even though based on copyright. General Public License (GPL)[47] offered a new form of license agreement attached to each copy of the software rendered available thereunder.[48] Under the agreement the software author conveys to each user[49] a wide range of

42 On 1 January 2008 Russia introduced an amendment to the Copyright Law, superseding the said Act with a new part 4 of the Russian Civil Code. Pursuant to the amendment, only collective societies authorized by the state shall have the right to issue licenses (still) without the consent of copyright holders (one per each type of rights); Article 1244(3) part 4 of Russian Civil Code).

43 Cf. the user agreement at <http://www.zaycev.net> (accessed 2 August 2011).

44 See e.g. L. Lessig (2004) *Free Culture: How Big Media Uses Technology and the Law to Lock Down Culture and Control Creativity*, New York: Penguin, pp. 52 and 197.

45 For information about excessive freedom in granting rights under patents in the United States and its consequences, see G. Middleton (1999) 'Internet Patents', 10 *Journal of Law and Information Science*, p. 153.

46 S. Williams (2002) *Free as in Freedom: Richard Stallman's Crusade for Free Software*, Sebastopol, CA: O'Reilly Media, Inc., p. 105. A more extensive version of his thoughts, under the name GNU-Manifesto, was published in September 1985. Ibid.

47 GNU (2007) General Public License Version 3. <http://www.gnu.org/licenses/gpl.html> (accessed 18 December 2010).

48 GNU General Public License Version 3, section 4.

49 GNU General Public License Version 3, section 10, para. 1.

freedoms to use the software.[50] The only condition to be met by the user is to respect the copyleft principle,[51] that is the obligation to pass on the original version of the software or covered works on the same terms and conditions, under pain of termination of the license agreement.[52] As a consequence of the latter provision, the Open Source Software faction was established. USC Berkeley academics had proposed an alternative agreement to be attached to computer programs based on non-copyleft principle. The Berkeley Software Distribution License[53] leaves it to the licensee to decide whether to forward the received work or underlying covered work under a "free" or "open" license or to use it for commercial purposes under the copyright laws.

Free and open licenses may be deemed one of the first elements of the International Internet Law – their purpose is to offer a common legal solution for the entire global community. Despite the fact that the application of agreements encounters obstacles,[54] they effectively incorporate existing legal regulations and adapt them to new challenges posed by the Internet.[55] Thus, they have become inspiration for another type of agreement drafted for all categories of copyrighted works, the Creative Commons license. L. Lessig, the founder of Creative Commons, does not approve of law-makers' apparent disregard for reality. He questions the legitimacy of raising a whole generation as criminals.[56] In order to avoid establishing a law against the wishes of the community and rendering the powers over works to authors, he proposes instead a number of licenses that attain these goals. By December 2008, fifty versions of national license agreements had been developed, all based on the same principles. Their motto was the phrase coined by Lessig, "some rights reserved" as opposed to "all rights reserved" which underlies copyright. The range of possibilities CC licenses offer enables authors to modify the ambit of rights provided with respect to their works.[57] Although not free

50 GNU General Public License Version 3, section 10, para. 2 enumerates the right to run, modify and propagate the licensed work.

51 GNU General Public License Version 3, section 10, para. 3.

52 GNU General Public License Version 3, section 8, para. 1.

53 University of California at Berkeley (1998). For the license content, see <http://www.opensource.org/licenses/bsd-license.php> (accessed 18 December 2010).

54 For instance the consumer protection in the EU. Some rights, even though guaranteed under the agreement, go beyond the framework of obligatory protection granted to consumers in the EU. See B. Still (2007) *Handbook of Research on Open Source Software: Technological, Economic, and Social Perspectives*, Hershey, PA: Idea Group, Inc., p. 389.

55 See, for example, CeCILL (2005) Free Software License Agreement Version 2.0. <http://www.cecill.info/li- cences/Licence_CeCILL_V2-en.html> (accessed 13 January 2011).

56 L. Lessig writes about the "generation of criminals", which is raised bearing the mark of a breach of law without a sense of guilt for the alleged evil the generation commits. The author emphasizes that the natural availability of unlimited electronic resources shaped the awareness of the youngest generation of Internet users and naming them "criminals" does not fall within the goals the law is to achieve in a modern state. He asks about the influence of a generation of thieves on the community. In his opinion the condemnation of an entire generation is too high a price for attaining such goal. (L. Lessig (2008) *Remix: Making Art and Culture Thrive in the Hybrid Economy*, London: Bloomsbury Academic, p. XVII).

57 Excluding, for example, commercial use (non-commercial licenses) or works modifications (no-derivatives). CC license drafts also reflect the dispute referred to above concerning whether free/open software should include the "share alike" condition, analogous to the copyleft principle applied to GPL license. For more details, see <http://creativecommons.org/licenses/>.

from criticism[58] and problems related to practical implementation,[59] CC licenses have already proved effective in European court rooms.[60]

Domain names – Internet and Trademark Law

In the times of the so-called dotcom boom, that is in the second half of the 1990's,[61] domain names gained popularity to such an extent that they were proclaimed the trademarks of the twenty-first century. Such a simplification skillfully captures the essence of the issue related to the legal protection of domain names. The international protection of domain names using the industrial property protection system is even more challenging than the protection of digitized copyrighted works for at least two reasons. First of all, as is the case with copyright, entities eligible on a territorial basis shall enjoy industrial property rights comprising also the trademark protection right – the object thereof shall be effectively protected only within the borders of the state whose officers vested such rights. In principle, obtaining international protection requires such legal title to be received in each state where the entity with the right to trademark

58 The criticism of CC license focuses on two arguments. The first argument concerns the allegation of restricting the author's freedom by imposing limitations on users under licenses. The second argument concerns the inclusion of the CC movement as a globalist trend. See M. Pasquinelli (2010) 'The Ideology of Free Culture and the Grammar of Sabotage', in D. Araya (ed.) *Knowledge and Learning in the Age of Innovation*, Frankfurt: Peter Lang, p. 292. See also P. B. Tóth (2005) 'Creative Humbug', 2(24) *Indicare Monitor* pp. 8–12 <http://www.indicare.org/tiki-read_article.php?articleId=118> (accessed 18 December 2010) in which the author claims that CC movement has nothing to offer which has not been offered by traditional copyright law, and J. Dvorak (2005) 'Creative Commons Humbug', *PC Magazine*, 18 July 2005. <http://www.pcmag.com/article2/0,2817,1838244,00.asp> (accessed 18 December 2010) in which the author alleges that the solution proposed by the CC license authors is temporary and superficial.

59 These problems are most of all related to a different perception of what constitutes the public domain in national legal systems and the impossibility of waiving an author's moral rights under the continental copyright system, as opposed to the Anglo-Saxon copyright system; see L. Pallas Loren (2007) 'Building a Reliable Semicommons of Creative Works: Enforcement of Creative Commons Licenses and Limited Abandonment of Copyright', 14(2) *George Mason Law Review*, pp. 271ff., N. Elkin-Koren (2005) 'What Contracts Can't Do: The Limits of Private Ordering in Facilitating a Creative Commons', 74(2) *Fordham Law Review*, pp. 375ff. The lack of any possibility of verifying the licensee's rights, lack of identification of the parties to the civil agreement and actual problems with termination thereof or amendment thereto (by reason of an unspecified, open circle of licensees) also raise considerable doubts. Practical issues relating to applying CC agreements often result from free interpretation of jurisdictional principles by national courts in the context of protecting images in the content of licensed work. See, for example C. Pletcher (2009) 'Are Publicity Rights Gone in a Flash?: Flickr, Creative Commons, and the Commercial Use of Personal Photographs', 8 *Florida State Business Review*, p. 153.

60 The decision of the court in *Sociedad General de Autores y Editores (SGAE)* v. *Fernández* (2005) Procedimiento Ordinario 761/2005, File No. 15/2.006 (Court of First Instance No. 6, Badajoz, Spain). <www.extremaduracreativa.org/sentencia1.pdf> (accessed 18 December 2011); *Curry* v. *Audax* (2009) File No. 334492/KG 06–176 SR (Regional Court in Amsterdam). (for an English translation, see <http://mirrors.creativecommons.org/judgements/Curry–Audax–English.pdf> (accessed 18 December 2011)).

61 See e.g. F. B. Cross and R. A. Prentice (2007) *Law and Corporate Finance*, Cheltenham, UK: Edward Elgar Publishing, p. 81 on the dotcom boom history.

wishes to obtain protection (existing international trademark related agreements, contrary to patents, are not widely assimilated).[62] These circumstances produce another hardship as regards international protection of domain names using trademark-relevant legal instruments. As opposed to copyright vested in authors at the moment of materializing the work (even unfinished), industrial property rights are vested by way of a decision of national authorities, and the issue procedure entails high costs to be incurred by the potential eligible entity. However the problem of international protection of domain names is even more complex. All differences between traditional trademarks and domain names determine the deficiencies in and high costs of legal protection of trademarks. A moment's reflection shows that the territorial protection of domain names is clearly impossible. Insofar as the WIPO plays a supportive role with respect to international protection of industrial property rights (decisions to vest such rights fall within the competence of state authorities, even though based on international treaties and harmonized national laws), the shape of the domain names catalogue is determined by the ICANN exclusively.[63] It authorizes one body (a "registrar") to administer each TLD within which domain names may be registered. The specificity of the DNS has led to the creation of a unique set of arbitration rules: the 1999 Uniform Domain Name Dispute Resolution Policy (UDRP), applied by adhering organizations[64] (whose registrars have acceded to the policy) to disputes over domain names. The noble attempt to introduce a uniform set of rules has been a partial success,[65] nevertheless the policy has been adopted for domain names in the .com, .net, and .org gTLDs and certain ccTLDs.[66] The subject matter of the UDRP is limited to domain names identical or confusingly similar to a trademark or service mark previously registered.[67] Moreover, for the procedure to be performed, the alleged infringer must be demonstrated not to have any rights or legitimate interests in respect of the domain name and to be acting in bad faith.[68] If the domain name dispute is submitted to the UDRP regime, the decision shall not be final – each party

62 This is also the case with the International Convention for the Protection of Industrial Property, Paris, 1883, the trademark provisions of which have been subject to numerous reservations. See E. Clark et al. (2010) *Cyber Law in Australia*, The Hague: Kluwer Law International, p. 143. The WIPO is fostering work on two important documents: the Protocol Relating to the Madrid Agreement Concerning the International Registration of Marks, and the Draft Revised Trademark Law Treaty.

63 However, national governments are requesting more influence over the ccTLD string, see e.g., M. L. Mueller (2004) *Ruling the Root: Internet Governance and the Taming of Cyberspace*, Cambridge, Mass.: MIT Press, p. 244.

64 Those organizations include the Asian Domain Name Dispute Resolution Centre (ADNDRC), CPR Institute for Dispute Resolution (CPR), eResolution (eRes), The National Arbitration Forum (NAF) and WIPO. Also national ccTLDs registrars may adhere to the UDRP rules or propose regulations based on the original ICANN policy.

65 2011 saw the rise of a proposed UDRP reform, see ICANN (2011) GNSO Council Resolution, 3 February 2011. <http://gnso.icann.org/mailing-lists/archives/council/msg10635.html> (accessed 25 June 2011).

66 For a full list of ccTLDs using UDRP see http://www.wipo.int/amc/en/domains/cctld/index.html.

67 Paragraph 4(a) UDRP.

68 These most controversial criteria are described in more detail in Paragraph 4(b) UDRP.

has the right to initiate court proceedings[69] under provisions protecting trademarks or personal rights.[70] Parties quite often decide to submit the dispute to court.[71] Referring the dispute to court, however, entails yet another conclusion. Making the protection of domain names contingent upon previous protection by way of trademark of the claimant or complainant in the UDRP regime considerably and unreasonably limits the protection of a domain name holder. A breach of rights to a domain name may just as well entail the breach of trademark as the breach of personal rights of each natural (or juridical)[72] person under the law. The existing model of domain names protection, based on the UDRP, deprives the domain name right holder of personal rights protection. Naturally, accounting for this category of rights in rules on protection of domain names is a challenging task, if not impossible. The catalogue of personal rights is non-exhaustive and is supplemented over time by national courts within the national legal systems, for personal rights, above all, constitute the manifestation of cultural specifics. They reflect the international catalogue of human rights in the national law – virtues, which should be protected as inherent to human dignity (such as image protection, privacy or personal freedom).

Initiating court proceedings aiming at obtaining protection of rights to domain name produces one more difficulty being of fundamental importance from the perspective of these considerations. As mentioned above, the UDRP regime calls for arbitration and allows the party (Complainant) to select the forum – the organization which under the UDRP shall resolve the dispute. A decision not to solve the dispute amicably presents a difficulty in identifying a court competent to resolve the dispute. Domain name disputes, in themselves, are disputes comprising an "alien element" and require invoking already existing, intricate solutions of private international law.[73] From the very beginning of the discussion on the limits of jurisdictional competence in global network, domain names and protection of rights thereto constituted a paradigm of mismatch between the law and contemporary challenges.[74] It

69 Paragraph 4(k) of the UDRP Policy provides that the mandatory administrative proceedings requirement shall not prevent either the domain name registrant (Respondent) or the third party (Complainant) from submitting the dispute to a court of competent jurisdiction for independent resolution, see <http://www.wipo.int/amc/en/domains/guide/#a6>.

70 See Z. Efroni (2003) 'The Anticybersquatting Consumer Protection Act and the Uniform Dispute Resolution Policy: New Opportunities for International Forum Shopping?' 26 *Columbia Journal of Law & the Arts*, p. 335.

71 Cf. *Jay D. Sallen* v. *Corinthians Licenciamentos, Ltd. and Desportos Licenciamentos, Ltd.* (2001) 273 F. 3d 14 (United States Court of Appeals for the First Circuit), see also T. Hoeren (2006) *Internetrecht*, unpublished script p. 66, available on the Universität Münster website <http://www.uni-muenster.de/Jura.itm/hoeren/> (accessed 16 February 2011).

72 The existence of personal rights of juridical persons is subject to criticism by US legal academics and commentators (see i.e. the recent Supreme Court case *Citizens United* v. *Federal Election Commission* (2010) 558 US 08–205. European legal academics and commentators, however, still widely accept this view, even though the list of rights is shorter than of those vested in natural persons, cf. e.g. C. von Bar (2000) *The Common European Law of Torts: Damage and Damages, Liability for and without Personal Misconduct, Causality, and Defenses*, Oxford: Oxford University Press, pp. 131–132.

73 Cf. chapter 1 and U. Kohl, op. cit., pp. 33–35.

74 For more discussion on the subject see U. Kohl, ibid.

is obvious that effective jurisdiction shall not constitute the exclusive grounds for exercising jurisdictional powers by states – the mere electronic presence through a website is not sufficient for exercising jurisdiction over its owners or administrators, since such an assumption would surrender each website administrator to all jurisdictions in the world. This being the case, few states regard the mere accessibility of a webpage as insufficient for exercising their jurisdiction.[75]

Existing legal mechanisms provide sufficient protection neither for domain name holders, nor for those whose rights have been prejudiced through cybersquatters or gripe sites.[76] For the former, a *sui generis* domain name right, based on a uniform legal and ethical background, might be a feasible solution.[77] For the latter, nothing less than a uniform, global set of minimum standards for personal rights protection will suffice. In order to meet this challenging goal a critical look at the existing scope of human rights, in particular minimum restrictions of the freedom of speech and their possible practical application online is necessary.

Human rights and free speech

The shape of the human rights protection system is one of the most controversial issues in contemporary public international law.[78] The roots of this controversy lie in cultural diversity among nations resulting from their social, historical and political backgrounds.[79] The debate on the actual catalogue of human rights is still as vigorous as it was at the initial stage of their elaboration and efforts to reach consensus on whether the well-being of a single person should supersede the interest of the nation as a whole are deemed futile.[80] The notion of human rights has been rapidly

75 See C. T. Struve and R. P. Wagner, 'Realspace Sovereigns in Cyberspace: Problems with the Anticybersquatting Consumer Protection Act', 17(3) *Berkeley Technology Law Journal* p. 989 for more on the US Anti-Cybersquatting Protection Act practice, asserting *in-rem* jurisdiction over all gTLDs registered with a registrar located within a state. A recent controversial decision using *in-rem* jurisdiction was the botnet Waledac temporary restraining order (based on the Computer Fraud and Abuse Act (18 USC § 1030), Can-Spam Act (15 USC § 7704), Electronic Communications Privacy Act (18 USC § 2701), and the Lanham Act (15 USC 5 1125)). See chapter 3 for more details. See also W. T. Fryer III (2008) 'Handling Internet Domain Name Arbitration', 41(1) *The Maryland Bar Journal*, pp. 28–33.

76 D. Rowland (2006) 'Griping, Bitching and Speaking Your Mind: Defamation and Free Expression on the Internet', 110 *Penn St. L. Rev.*, p. 519.

77 See generally K. Komaitis (2010) *The Current State of Domain Name Regulation: Domain Names as Second-Class Citizens in a Mark-Dominated World*, Oxford: Routledge, and his proposition of "Lex Domainia".

78 J. Donnelly (2003) *Universal Human Rights in Theory and Practice*, New York: Cornell University Press, pp. 129ff. on the global human rights regime, and A. Hurrell (1999) 'Power, Principles and Prudence: Protecting Human Rights in a Deeply Divided World', in T. Dunne (ed.) (1999) *Human Rights in Global Politics*, Cambridge: Cambridge University Press, pp. 177–303.

79 Cf. J. Donnelly, op. cit., pp. 89ff. on cultural relativism, T. W. Laqueur (2003)'The Moral Imagination and Human Rights', in M. Ignatieff, A. Gutmann and K. A. Appiah (eds.) *Human Rights as Politics and Idolatry*, Princeton, NJ: Princeton University Press, pp. 127–140, and M. Ignatieff, 'Human Rights as Idolatry', in the same volume, pp. 53–100.

80 See e.g. B. G. Ramcharan (ed.) (1979) *Human Rights: Thirty Years After the Universal Declaration: Commemorative Volume on the Occasion of the Thirtieth Anniversary of the Universal Declaration of Human Rights*, New York: United Nations Publishing, p. 198.

evolving over the past sixty years to serve different needs and stand for altering values. This evolution, however, has never been as quick as has been the case over the last decade. It is most certainly because of the global phenomenon of the Internet that such concepts as freedom of speech or protection of privacy have taken on a whole new dimension and created the urge for a new, international consensus on the cyber-arena. The development of an age of borderless cyberspace and the popularity of the Internet that now reaches over one-third of the world population prove that a global consensus among cultures and policies on the limits of human rights is indispensable. Methods used by states to enforce national laws on freedom of speech or protect state secrets, for example, are no longer there for their nation only, as they result "in cyberspace", that is in almost[81] all states simultaneously. This fact is reflected directly in the human rights debate and raises serious questions about the shape and scope of a global human rights catalogue fit for the twenty-first century.[82]

Freedom of speech online is one of the most pressing issues that need to be resolved at international level. Since there is no strict global standard for free speech,[83] initially states attempted to regulate electronic content available within their borders by enforcing their national laws with traditional judicial means. Basing their competence on the objective territoriality principle, national courts tried to prosecute those foreign residents who exceeded national limits of free speech with certain electronic content, solely based on the fact that the content was accessible from within the forum state territory. The legal gridlock in the Yahoo! Nazi memorabilia case,[84] which still has not reached its final solution, serves as the clearest example that state jurisdiction over free speech needs to be dealt with at international level and executed independently of the traditional territorial jurisdiction of states.

The current approach to regulating electronic content is filtering.[85] Since practically no state allows freedom of speech to be exercised without any limitations, state authorities attempt to exercise their legislative restrictions also over online forms of

81 North Korea is regarded as the country with the lowest Internet penetration rate. Internet is available there through a link to China only to the fortunate few; however, a strongly filtered national network named Kwangmyong is used by a wide public. Actual lack of public Internet access does not stop successful international cyberattacks launched from North Korean territory.

82 States and international organizations are doing their share of work when it comes to seeking an international compromise on Internet rights. During the 2010 Internet Governance Forum taking place in Vilnius, Lithuania, the effects of nationwide efforts, incorporated in a document entitled 'Principles for the Governance and Use of the Internet' were presented. Civil society organized in various groups such as the Internet Rights and Principles Dynamic Coalition (working within and around the IGF) or the Association for Progressive Communications (APC) also successfully participate in ground-breaking initiatives aimed at proper application of human rights standards in the online environment.

83 See J. Kortteinen, K. Myntti and L. Hannikainen (1999) 'Traditions in Freedom of Expression', in G. Alfredsson and A. Eide (eds.) *The Universal Declaration of Human Rights: A Common Standard of Achievement*, The Hague: Martinus Nijhoff Publishers, pp. 399–401.

84 *Yahoo! Inc.* v. *LICRA and UEJF* (2006) 433 F.3d 1199 (United States Court of Appeals for the Ninth Circuit).

85 For a detailed analysis of states' practices of Internet filtering see chapter 3.

expression. Therefore, most of them[86] perform some sort of censorship ("Internet filtering") for different social, political or security reasons,[87] which results in limiting access to certain Internet content. The list of "filtering" countries is growing day-by-day and the record of countries violating the right to free speech through filtering presented by OpenNetInitiative includes over 40 entries (September 2010).[88] However, next to the filtering policies that clearly violate the present human rights standards of free speech by excessively[89] restricting access to certain content, there are those forms of filtering that leave much more room for controversy. The scope of Internet censorship is growing not only in countries recognized as autocratic, but also in model democracies. One could mention filtering done in libraries or schools for the protection of morality or child rights.[90] The common national practice in Europe allowing local ISPs to block sites with child-pornography,[91] for example, might be recognized as one of such actions.[92]

When discussing freedom of Internet access, human rights organizations oppose to any on-line censorship. At the same time state authorities present the clearly opposite opinion, attempting to protect their communities with all means available, both on and offline. However, blocking of electronic content is rarely initiated directly by law makers or executive authorities, even though, as an exception, it may also be effected by a judicial decision.[93] In democratic states blocking content is a

86 Internet filtering is performed even by states granting the right to internet access explicitly in their legal systems; e.g. Finland allows voluntary ISP filtering of child pornography, see the Act on Blocking Child Pornography ('Laki Lapsipornografian Levittämisen Estotoimista'), 2006, 1.12.2006/1068.

87 For global overview of Internet filtering see R. Deibert et al. (eds.) (2008) *Access Denied: The Practice and Policy of Global Internet Filtering*, Cambridge, Mass.: MIT Press.

88 www.opennet.net. The list presently consists of 40 countries, including, among others, Afghanistan, Algeria, Belarus, China, Cuba, Egypt, India, Iran, Iraq, Israel, Moldova, Morocco, North Korea, Pakistan, Saudi Arabia, Singapore, South Korea, Ukraine, United Arab Emirates, Uzbekistan and Vietnam.

89 Where "excessively" means outside the scope agreed upon in international contracts, see e.g. Article 10 para. 2 of the European Convention for the Protection of Human Rights and Fundamental Freedoms. The limits of such interference have also been proposed by the Council of Europe in May 2003 in a non-binding Declaration on Freedom of Communication on the Internet: <http://www.coe.int/t/informationsociety/documents/Freedom%20of%20communication%20on%20the%20Internet_en.pdf> (accessed 13 February 2011). Pursuant to the Declaration, measures may be taken by states to enforce the removal of clearly identifiable Internet content or, alternatively, the blockage of access to them, if the competent national authorities have taken a final decision on their illegality, provided that the safeguards of Article 10, para. 2, of the European Convention for the Protection of Human Rights and Fundamental Freedoms concerning the freedom of speech are respected.

90 E.g. the Children's Internet Protection Act (CIPA) (United States).

91 E.g. the latest German developments, see the EDRI report from 8 April 2009, 'ISPs Asked to Block Child Porn Sites on the Internet'. <http://www.edri.org/edri-gram/number7.7/pornography-blocked-isp> (accessed 29 October 2011).

92 Although even judicial interpretation of the US First Amendment recognizes blocking child pornography as legitimate: R.J. Deibert et al. (eds.) (2010) *Access Controlled: The Shaping of Power, Rights, and Rule in Cyberspace*, Cambridge, Mass.: MIT Press, p. 373.

93 For instance, the decision of the Italian court on blocking the PirateBay website for its users might have breached the copyright, e.g., Anonymous 'Italy cracks down on Pirate Bay', *New York Times* 14 August 2008. <http://www.nytimes.com/2008/08/14/technology/14iht-webpirate.15301147.html> (accessed 2 February 2011).

voluntary activity by the Internet service providers (ISPs).[94] Even in China, which is famous for its restrictive policy on the freedom of speech online, the burden of responsibilities, and what follows, the selection of methods and manner of restricting the access to specific content, rests with Internet service providers, though the legal obligation to control content is stipulated by both statutes and extra-legal "codes of conduct".[95]

When determining the international and legal nature of restricting the access to electronic content it is worth invoking the concept of state immunity. Today, the said construct assumes that actions of state authorities are twofold. They may either exercise exclusive powers vested therein under the international law (*acta de iure imperii*),[96] or act in the international arena as do private law entities, exercising competence not reserved for states (*acta de iure gestionis*).[97] The statutory limitation of the freedom of speech for internal safety reasons or protection of morality perceived from the perspective of the state falls within the first category – it constitutes an example of exercising state powers. The possibility of limiting the access to specific content by the ISP may be assessed by authorities of another sovereign state to that which has provided the statutory limitation, as per the *acts of state* doctrine deriving from the US case law and then assimilated by international law. The right to limit the access to electronic content exercised within the state territory and under a statutory permit by entities in the territorial jurisdiction of the sovereign arouses no doubts. Any suggestions concerning a possible obligation upon states amounting to the guarantee of access to electronic content are formulated only with respect to the freedom of international exchange guarantee (not within borders of a state) and fall within the ambit of demands of legal academics and commentators.[98] Any assessment of how the limiting of access to the Internet complies with international standards of human rights protection (possible breach of the freedom of speech and access to information of residents of a state whose authorities filter the content) is yet another issue. The 1966 International Covenant on Civil and Political Rights[99] provides for a (not prosecutable) obligation

94 Cf. J. Zittrain and J. Palfrey (2010) 'Internet Filtering: The Politics and Mechanisms of Control', in R. Deibert et al. (eds.) *Access Denied*, op. cit., pp. 32ff.

95 This solution is an exception on a global scale, for usually Internet service providers bear no direct responsibility for delivered content, unless they know that the content is illegal.

96 Such as, above all, exercising legislative, judicial and executive powers or the capacity to enter into contracts or exercising *ius legationis*.

97 See S. Sucharitkul (1976/7) 149 *Académie de Droit International de La Hague Recueil Des Cours* (*Collected Courses)*, The Hague: Martinus Nijhoff Publishers, p. 152.

98 The problem addressed here is when blocking a free transmission of electronic content in one state considerably and limits the access thereto in neighboring countries using the infrastructure of the filtering state. An example here may be the situation in 2008 during the Georgia and Russia conflict when the electronic infrastructure of Georgia was blocked, which resulted in the loss of Internet connection by Armenia (which uses the Trans Asian and European line passing through the territory of Georgia). Council of Europe (2009) *Internet Governance and Critical Internet Resources*, Strasbourg: Media and Information Society Division, Council of Europe, p. 22.

99 999 UNTS 171, entered into force on 23 March 1976.

to respect the right to freedom of expression.[100] Interpretation of the Article may be based on the content of the Resolution adopted by the Human Rights Council 12/16 related to the freedom of opinion and expression,[101] which requires the state parties to refrain from imposing restrictions on access to or use of information and communication technologies.[102] Existing international procedures for human rights protection sanction state practices which violate the said obligation. All UN procedures (both the international complaint procedure and special procedures) established for the protection of human rights may be initiated by the Human Rights Council, which is currently dominated by African and Muslim countries themselves imposing stringent restrictions on the freedom of speech.[103] In this context obtaining international consent to perform actions sanctioning extensive national censorship practices stands little chance of success. Without such consent, any actions[104] aiming at restricting the freedom of activities of filtering state are inconsistent with the international law. Even the controversial concept of "humanitarian intervention," which allows the use of force by one or several states in defense of some human rights without the consent of the United Nations Security Council, does not apply here since the rights to freedom of speech or communication are not of peremptory nature.[105] Although, as some have argued, the next generation of international humanitarian law might include protection of access to communications,[106] in the present shape of international law it is difficult to demonstrate that blocking the access to specific electronic content may constitute a violation of international law subject to sanctions, and thus the grounds for any intervention in the internal affairs of the blocking state.

Such observations produce two conclusions. The principle of subjective territorial jurisdiction may be exercised in cyberspace with respect to the freedom of speech only by applying the filter – blocking the access of residents of the regulating state territory to specific content, authorized under the internal laws. Another conclusion that seems inescapable relates to the growing role of ISP, for the issue of freedom of speech pertains not only to the question about the scope of content permitted online, but also about entities which should protect the compliance with the principles and

100 Article 19 of International Covenant on Civil and Political Rights (ICCPR).

101 Resolution of the 12th session of the Human Rights Council on 2 October 2009, 'Freedom of Opinion and Expression', A/HRC/RES/12/16.

102 Section (p)(iii).

103 Cf. R. Evans 'UN Chief Tells Rights Body Drop Rhetoric, Blocs', *Reuters*, 12 December 2008. <http://www.reuters.com/article/2008/12/12/us-un-rights-idUSTRE4BB67820081212> (accessed 12 February 2011).

104 Also those supporting or tolerating actions of private entities operating from the territory of the state with a view to preventing the effects of national policy, cf. The Clinton Doctrine.

105 Cf. J. Pattison (2010) *Humanitarian Intervention and the Responsibility to Protect: Who Should Intervene?* Oxford: Oxford University Press, p. 50, in which the author claims that the *opinio iuris* constituting humanitarian intervention as a customary law mechanism was acknowledged in only a few situations so far; none of them concerned the protection of free speech as the sole ground for intervention (p. 75).

106 OpenNet Initiative (2004) *A Starting Point: Legal Implications Of Internet Filtering.* <http://opennet.net/research/reports> p. 13.

bear responsibility for their breach.[107] It is their will which determines the scope of information available online.[108]

The key issue to be considered while looking for an answer to the limits of freedom of speech online is the question of morality and moral standards. The bottom line is that even right now a certain, basic common ground for some of the most widely condemned practices can be found: the prosecution of child pornography or human trafficking seems to be present in most national criminal codes. Values represented through such legislation seem to be a safe starting point for the discussion on limits of free speech online.[109] On the other hand, hate speech (spreading Nazi propaganda,[110] Holocaust denial[111]) or promoting genocide are among the most difficult issues in present international politics. An irresolvable problem in this area will naturally be the politically motivated censorship that occurs, according to the authorities exercising it, in order to protect the integrity and stability of the nation itself. This set of issues must be left as the last to be discussed and compromised. However, the era of Internet forces the initiation of a serious debate on the limits of national power over Internet content, and no consensus has been reached on this. The key to such difficult issues might be the clear "delimitation" of cyberspace[112] by a set of guidelines based on the sequence of applying international jurisdictional principles.

Systems convergence – Internet and media

The complexity of setting limits to free speech online is increased by one more specific element of electronic communications: the Internet may be described as

107 This issue was also raised by the French association 'J'Accuse' in its activities for eradicating racism from the Internet, when in June 2001 the association brought an action against thirteen French companies operating as Internet service providers, for they facilitated the access to US websites with racist and Nazi content: *J'Accuse* v. *Gen. Communications, et al.* (2001) T.G.I. Paris, No. RG 01/57676. <http://www.juritel.com/Ldj_html-445.html> (accessed 25 June 2011).

108 That the issue is not an easy one is proved, for instance, by the famous dispute between Google and the Chinese authorities from the end of 2009. See M. Beutz Land (2010) 'Google, China, and Search', 14(25) *ASIL Insights*. < http://www.asil.org/insights100805.cfm>; P. Moloney Figliola et al. (2010), *US Initiatives to Promote Global Internet Freedom: Issues, Policy, and Technology*, Darby, PA: Diane Publishing Co., p. 10. For information on the liability for contents, see below.

109 The practical example of successful negotiations on such basic standards could be the Council of Europe Convention on Cybercrime, regarding the definitions of crimes rather than the jurisdictional mechanism presented therein. On the subject of free speech, its Additional Protocol, although ratified by only six states, might be a particularly good starting point for further debate: Additional Protocol to the Convention on Cybercrime, Concerning the Criminalization of Acts of a Racist and Xenophobic Nature Committed through Computer Systems, Strasbourg, 28 January 2003. <http://conventions.coe.int/Treaty/en/Treaties/Html/189.htm> (accessed 11 January 2011).

110 §§ 86, 86a German Penal Code (Strafgesetzbuch) op. cit.

111 Penalized under §§ 130(3) and 220a(1) German Penal Code. A similar regulation prohibiting the denial of crimes against humanity has been adopted by the Republic of Poland (Article 55 of the Institute of National Remembrance Act, 1998, 155(1016) Dz. U. [*Journal of Laws*] and, *inter alia*, France, Canada and the USA.

112 With respect to such a concept of delimited cyberspace the terms: "Splinternet" or "Cyberbalkanization" are often used, although they refer to self-imposed limits set in cyberspace by communities

all media known to man combined into one, and then reinvented. Traditionally, national laws have paid much attention to specifying the particular (usually, more rigid) rules for journalistic freedom of speech. With the Internet incorporating television, radio and press in a new, interactive way, all those national standards have come to be tested. It is challenging to ascertain how national laws or international standards ought to be applied to mass-communications effected via the Internet. Below we take a brief look at the crucial problems and the solutions that have been presented.

Free speech is the cornerstone of free media. Free media are the cornerstone of democracy. All national and international press law regulations aim at guaranteeing the freedom of all mass media on the one hand (by affording journalists exclusive rights and permissions)[113] and providing for its professionalism on the other hand (by imposing particularly high moral and ethical obligations on journalists – of due diligence and high professional standards).[114] Those are, however, the only two generalizations to be made in the area discussed. Not only do states which regard themselves as democratic vary considerably in introducing those standards through national legal regulations, but many modern day sovereign countries have different understandings of the role media play in their national systems.[115]

What follows is a relatively simple question that appears in political and legal discussion, but to which no simple answer can be found: should the Internet be regarded as media, and if so – which (radio, press, television)? Is it solely a telecommunications network, just as the telephone, or is it more of mass medium, like television or printed press?

Originally an analogy between the Internet and television was based on the physical resemblance between computer monitors and TV sets. Nowadays a more subtle parallel is based on the fact that both media are used for broadcasting even though

themselves rather than national legislations. See M. van Alstyne and B. Brynjolfsson (1996) 'Electronic Communities: Global Villages or Cyberbalkanization?' 5 *ICIS Proceedings Papers* <http://aisel.aisnet.org/icis1996/5>; A. F. Wood and M. J. Smith (2005) *Online Communication: Linking Technology, Identity, and Culture*, Oxford: Routledge, pp. 138–140. For more on the role of cyber-communities in forming an international legal regime for cyberspace see chapter 4.

113 See the jurisprudence of the ECHR regarding the interpretation of Article 10 e.g. *Castells* v. *Spain* (1992), Application no. 11798/85, para. 43 where the courts refer to the crucial role of free speech exercised in public interest or *Obeschlick* v. *Austria (No 2)* (1997) Application no. 20834/95, para. 57 regarding defamation of a politician by journalists in media. Generally on the individual confines of free speech in media see e.g. United Kingdom House of Commons' Culture, Media and Sport Committee on *Press Standards, Privacy and Libel: Second Report of Session 2010–2011, Volume 2: Oral and Written Evidence,* London: The Stationery Office, pp. 424–444.

114 In the ECHR jurisprudence see e.g. *Vereniging Weekblad 'Bluf!'* v. *The Netherlands* (1995) 20 EHRR 189, paras. 44ff., *Goodwin* v. *United Kingdom* (1996) 22 EHRR 123, paras. 42–45 and D. Ehlers and U. Becker (2007) *European Fundamental Rights and Freedoms*, Berlin: Walter de Gruyter, p. 115.

115 See P. Norris and R. Inglehart (2010) 'Limits on Press Freedom and Regime Support', in P. Norris (ed.) *Public Sentinel: News Media & Governance Reform*, Washington, DC: World Bank Publications, pp. 193–221; and see generally M. Fandy (2007) *(Un)civil War of Words: Media and Politics in the Arab World*, Westport: Greenwood Publishing Group, pp. 19–39 on the impact of governments on the media content of e.g. influential al-Jazeera and Al-Arabiya.

they differ considerably.[116] Another possible parallel would be to compare traditional telephony to the early days of the Internet (when the global network was connected only via a telephone modem) or the growing popularity of the Internet telephony (VoIP based services). There is also some sort of a functional analogy between them: communication via instant messaging and emailing is similar to telephone; however, such comparison disregards websites and interactive services. In the context of the freedom of speech, early decisions of the US Supreme Court drew a distinct line between the Internet and other media. Analogies between the Internet and television were invoked by those who endeavored to censor electronic content by claiming that, as the Internet exerts influence on society comparable to mass media, it should meet the set decency standards of other media. The General Public Prosecutor of the United States made an attempt to invoke the analogy in the *Reno* v. *ACLU* case.[117] The Supreme Court of the United States did not admit the analogy between the Internet and television and provided the electronic network with the highest protection possible within the scope of the freedom of speech, declaring the Communications Decency Act ineffective.[118] Nevertheless, nowadays, state authorities more and more often refer to the analogy and extend it considerably, including the Internet into the catalogue of mass media, next to press, radio and television, and submitting it to restrictions of the press and television laws.[119] Consequently each person who renders content[120] available via the Internet should meet the higher standards of due diligence applied towards professional journalists. On the other hand, this means that Internet content providers may enjoy special rights vested in journalists, for instance journalistic

116 Television is based on broadcasting information from one broadcaster to numerous recipients, while the Internet includes a multitude of various communication types (one-to-one, one-to-many, many-to-many).

117 *Reno* v. *American Civil Liberties Union* (ACLU) (1997) 521 US 844 (United States Supreme Court). The case pertained to the entering into force of the Communications Decency Act (CDA) 47 USC 151 adopted by the US Congress on 1 February 1996 as an amendment to the Communications Act, 1934. <http://www.epic.org/free_speech/CDA/cda.html> (accessed 7 February 2011). Developed by Congress as Title V of the Telecommunications Act 1996, the CDA provided for strict control over content available online to prevent exposing minors to pornographic and obscene content (and stipulated the responsibility of electronic services providers for statements of persons using their services, thereby regulating their legal situation otherwise than for publishers of non-electronic content).

118 In the opinion of the Court, CDA provisions constituted a gross breach of the First Amendment to the US Constitution guaranteeing freedom of speech, as they did not allow parents to freely decide about content available to their children.

119 E.g. in July 2009 all Kazakh online communications and content were given the same legal status as the news media and thereby their authors, editors and publishers were exposed to the possibility of criminal prosecution (see Reporters without Borders, 'Call for Revision of Repressive Internet Law as it Goes into Effect', 15 July 2009 <http://en.rsf.org/kazakhstan-call-for-revision-of-repressive-15-07-2009,33808>). A similar regulation introduced in Hungary on 1 January 2011 aroused much national and international controversy (see 'EU-Hungary Row over Media Law Cools Down', BBC News, 2 February 2011 <http://www.bbc.co.uk/news/world-europe-12343319>). A 2007 Polish Supreme Court decision, confirmed in December 2010, required the registration of all "electronic press" with regional courts (see Kulesza, J. op. cit.)

120 Although note that the Polish press law referred to above defines press as "periodically published general information", not all publicly available content.

professional secrecy, protecting informers or anonymous publishing. Such analogy entails many threats, as from among the immensity of electronic content only a part constitutes or even aspires to be referred to as media transmission. The so-called weblogs – publicly accessible electronic diaries – constitute a special category here. Along with the growing interest in the Internet, many found weblogs their chance to pursue a lifelong dream of becoming a journalist. As the Internet became the most influential network of the twenty-first century, the significance of the opinions presented therein considerably grew. The web was filled with self-proclaimed journalists who demanded "real-life" protection for their activities exercised online. Their demands were set against those who presented controversial or libelous opinions on public issues and claimed to take no liability for their words on the grounds that online publishing was not the same as publishing in print. The question of the legal status of online information and whether it deserved the same protection as printed articles came in full force in the *Apple* v. *Does* ('the Apple News Sites case'),[121] where Apple accused the operators of blogs about their technological advancements of revealing Apple's trade secrets. The Santa Clara County Court awarded the administrators of those pages secrecy privileges similar to those of journalists.[122]

The question of the legal status of electronic publications seems irresolvable in the present state of international debate on the freedom of speech. Freedom of speech standards, and what follows from them (freedom of press standards) are based on the peculiarity of national laws. Only reaching a global consensus with respect to some minimum standards of restricting the freedom of speech and harmonization of the procedures for enforcing online laws by particular sovereigns could produce a solution to the problem. For that matter, the only practical solution at the very moment is to resort to ethics. On the one hand those who, while rendering electronic publications available, expect to be awarded the status of journalists should clearly declare such an intention on their websites and voluntarily meet higher standards of due diligence that only journalists are required to observe. At the same time, state authorities should refrain from generalizing the status of all transmissions of electronic content and make awarding the status of a journalist (for content providers) or press (for websites) contingent upon the will of authors themselves. The media law should thus be applied only to those authors of electronic content who declare such will online[123] or, should such an obligation be created by national laws, report to relevant state bodies. Others should bear responsibility for their own words under general principles of law such as non-journalists expressing their opinions in public (e.g. in town squares).

121 The decision is available online at <http://w2.eff.org/Censorship/Apple_v_Does/memo_of_points.pdf> (accessed 13 August 2011). See *O'Grady* v. *Superior Court* (2006) 139 Cal.App.4th 1423 (United States Cal.App.).

122 Anonymous 'Apple pays $700,000 for bloggers' legal fees', *MACNN*, 29 January 2007. <http://www.macnn.com/articles/07/01/29/apple.pays.legal.fees/&startNumber=10> (accessed 13 August 2011).

123 See the controversial proposal of the European Union Parliament Culture Committee 'Report on Concentration and Pluralism in the Media in the European Union" (2007/2253(INI)) recommending that member states "encourage their [web-logs'] voluntary labeling according to the professional and financial responsibilities and interests of their authors and publishers", p. 9.

The popular term "convergence", which covers both technical convergence and services convergence is associated with the process of showing similarities between the Internet and traditional media. The term "technical convergence" means the integration of telecommunication and electronic infrastructure with technical equipment and services. The "services convergence" comprises, *inter alia*, radio transmission via the Internet or Voice over Internet Protocol (VoIP).[124] Consequently, "convergence" means a combination of various services and their content. There is a high probability that in the near future the Internet will enable to offer various types of services, and particular market sectors will be combined. Intensification of services convergence has led to popularization of the term "Internet of Things" (IoT), meaning "an emerging global, Internet-based information service architecture facilitating the exchange of goods in global supply chain networks [. . .] developing on the technical basis of the present Domain Name System; drivers are private actors".[125] What we deal with here is a number of personalized services. Based on information registered by e.g. Radio Frequency IDentifiers (RFIDs) and transmitted via, *inter alia*, the Internet (but also the traditional cellular telephone network) to established centers designed to process data so downloaded,[126] service providers are in a position to personalize their offerings.[127]

IoT is a problem concerning telecommunication regulations, in particular the scope of responsibility of providers of telecommunication services via which some data are transmitted or their possible obligations related to data retention.[128] Technical convergence delegates the authority to decide with whom and on what terms the access rights will be vested to the providers of access to data transmitting network (the so-called "cerberus" scheme).[129]

The European Union emphasized the significance of the telecommunications revolution in a 1997 Green Paper.[130] It is owing to this document that convergence has become a synonym for the merging of various media market sectors as

124 The popularity of the service has considerably affected the market position of traditional telecommunication companies.

125 R. H. Weber (2009) 'Internet of Things – Need for a New Legal Environment?' 25(6) *Computer Law & Security Review*, p. 522.

126 The centers are often "virtual" centers operating in electronic "cloud". Consequently, they use the processing capacity of many computers in physically distant locations cooperating via electronic connections.

127 Knowing the behavior of customers in supermarkets – the time spent in particular sections, based on data from RFID installed in discount loyalty cards – owners of the stores are able to offer goods to their customers which will be of interest to them.

128 The controversial EU data retention Directive 2006/24 requires telecommunications companies to store data about all of their customers' communications.

129 C. Palzer and C. Hilger (2001) 'Media Supervision on the Threshold of the 21st Century – Structure and Powers of Regulatory Authorities in the Era of Convergence', 8 *IRIS Legal Observations of the European Audiovisual Laboratory*, p. 8.

130 The European Commission (1997) *Convergence of the Telecommunications, Media and Information Technology Sector, and the Implications for Regulations – Towards an Information Society Approach*, Commission Green Paper, COM (97) 623 <http://aei.pitt.edu/1160/01/telecom_convergence_gp_COM_97_623.pdf> (accessed 5 February 2011).

a result of new technological possibilities. With reference to the Green Paper, the European Commission carried out extensive consultations to produce, after two years, the so-called "Communications Review" in 1999.[131] The outcomes included in the review served as the Commission's grounds for developing proposals for five directives[132] and a number of regulations which aimed at superseding and simplifying the existing telecommunications sector regulation system. The Commission, noticing the role of IoT, devoted its recommendations of 2009 to the role of RFIDs.[133]

However, the most noticeable aspect of media convergence, by reason of IoT, is the right to privacy protection. If, when using inexpensive, easy to operate and capacious information carriers, almost all data about users may be gathered and processed, the significance of any legal guarantee whereby the scope of such data is determined by the user himself grows dramatically. Therefore, the following section of the study is devoted to the protection of privacy online.

Privacy

The need for effective international protection of privacy arises out of numerous applications of the Internet, such as social networks,[134] new media[135] or the "Internet of Things" ("IoT").[136] They all pose a unique threat to users' privacy as they allow gathering,

131 The European Union Commission (1999) *Towards a New Framework for Electronic Communications Infrastructure and Associated Services*, COM (99) 539. <http://europa.eu/scadplus/leg/en/lvb/l24216.htm> (accessed 5 February 2011).

132 The Commission proposed: (a) Directive 2002/21/EC of the European Parliament and of the Council of 7 March 2002 on a Common Regulatory Framework for Electronic Communications Networks and Services ('the Framework Directive') OJ (L 108) pp. 33–50; (b) Directive 2002/19/EC of the European Parliament and of the Council of 7 March 2002 on Access to, and Interconnection of, Electronic Communications Networks and Associated Facilities ('the Access Directive') OJ (L 108) pp. 21–32; (c) Directive 2002/20/EC of the European Parliament and of the Council of 7 March 2002 on the Authorization of Electronic Communications Networks and Services ('the Authorization Directive') OJ (L 108) pp. 21–31; (d) Directive 2002/22/EC of the European Parliament and of the Council of 7 March 2002 on Universal Service and Users' Rights Relating to Electronic Communications Networks and Services ('the Universal Service Directive') OJ (L 108) pp. 51–77; and (e) Directive 2002/58/EC of the European Parliament and of the Council of 12 July 2002 Concerning the Processing of Personal Data and the Protection of Privacy in the Electronic Communications Sector ('the Directive on Privacy and Electronic Communications' OJ (L 201/37) pp. 37–47.

133 Commission Recommendation of 12 May 2009 on the Implementation of Privacy and Data Protection Principles in Applications supported by Radio-Frequency Identification, SEC (2009), pp. 585–586.

134 See generally S. Gutwirth, Y. Poullet and P. De Hert (eds.) (2010) *Data Protection in a Profiled World*, New York: Springer Science.

135 Including media convergence and applying legal regulations applicable to conventional media (television, press) to the Internet. See e.g., Council of Europe Committee of Experts on New Media (MC-NM) *Report of the Meeting of 25–26 March 2010*, Strasbourg. <http://www.coe.int/t/dghl/standardsetting/media/MC-NM/MC-NM%282010%29006_en%20FIN%20Report%202nd%20meeting.asp#TopOfPage> (accessed 20 December 2010).

136 See R. H. Weber and R. Weber (2010) *Internet of Things: Legal Perspectives*, New York: Springer, pp. 41ff.

storing and analyzing data in a scope and manner never possible before.[137] The problem with privacy protection online is twofold. First, it is the lack of a universal accord on the status of personal data protection.[138] Since the scope of the right to privacy is primarily shaped by the acknowledged scope of protected personal data, their diverse status in various jurisdictions leads to the actual ineffectiveness of any national or international personal data protection online, since it may not be effectively exercised.[139] The second problem with protecting privacy online is the very definition of "privacy". Even the EU states, proud of their human right protection regime, find it difficult to define the scope of privacy protection when faced with such new challenges as the legal status of data presented by Google Street View and the possible legal responsibility in Europe for the infringement of users privacy by the Mountain View, California based Google Inc.[140] Below, an attempt to define the right to privacy has been made and two proposals for solving the global protection problem have been described.

In national continental legal systems privacy is defined with reference to three sets of norms: personal data protection, personal rights protection and the constitutional right to privacy construed in categories of human rights.[141] This privacy protection construct was reflected in European Community law, entered in national laws and was derived by legal academics and commentators from constitutional norms.[142] In the European international treaties system the right to privacy is guaranteed under Article 8 of the European Convention for the Protection of Human Rights and Fundamental Freedoms, as part of the protection of a right to respect for private and family life this right may only be restricted in special cases provided for in the Convention. Below, detailed reference to these three groups of regulations is made.

The first legally binding international instrument providing for protection of

137 See generally The United Kingdom House of Lords Select Committee (2009) *Surveillance, Citizens and the State*, London: The Stationery Office, p. 130.

138 There are various international accords on the data protection issue, however, the universal status of personal data is not uniform; see Organization for Economic Co-operation and Development (2003) *Privacy Online: OECD Guidance on Policy and Practice*, Paris: OECD Publishing, p. 390; C. J. Bennett (1992) *Regulating Privacy: Data Protection and Public Policy in Europe and the United States*, New York: Cornell University Press; and D. L. Baumer, J. B. Earp and J. C. Poindexter (2004) 'Internet Privacy Law: a Comparison between the United States and the European Union', 5(23) *Computers & Security*, pp. 400–412 (discussing the EU data protection regime and the California Online Privacy Protection Act ("OPPA") of 2003).

139 See generally M. Bezzi et al (eds.) (2010) *Privacy and Identity Management for Life*, New York: Springer; M. Petković and W. Jonker (eds.) (2007) *Security, Privacy and Trust in Modern Data Management*, New York: Springer.

140 The Polish data protection ombudsman (the *Generalny Inspektor Ochrony Danych Osobowych or* "General Personal Data Protection Inspector", found Facebook outside Polish jurisdiction, see '*Facebook poza polską jurysdykcją: nie można go ani pozwać, ani skontrolować*' ('Facebook Outside Polish Jurisdiction: Cannot be Sued or Controlled'), *PAP/Gazeta Prawna*, 19 November 2010. <http://prawo.gazetaprawna.pl/artykuly/466155,facebook_poza_polska_jurysdykcja_nie_mozna_go_ani_pozwac_ani_skontrolowac.html> (accessed 25 December 2010).

141 See e.g. F. Moos and J. Kirchner (2009) 'Data Protection and Monitoring', in J. Kirchner, P. R. Kremp and M. Magotsch (eds.) *Key Aspects of German Employment and Labour Law*, New York: Springer, p. 109, referring to the protection of privacy in Germany with respect to employees.

142 See e.g. A. J. Marcella and C. Stucki (2003) *Privacy Handbook: Guidelines, Exposures, Policy Implementation and International Issues*, New York: John Wiley and Sons, p. 118, referring to the legal construction introduced in Slovenia.

data was the Council of Europe Convention for the Protection of Individuals with Regard to Automatic Processing of Personal Data,[143] which opened for signature on 28 January 1981.[144] Nowadays, the European legal academics and commentators define personal data also on the basis of the Directive 95/46/EC on the Protection of Individuals with Regard to the Processing of Personal Data and on the Free Movement of such Data.[145] Pursuant to Article 2 of the Directive "personal data" shall mean any information relating to an identified or identifiable natural person; an identifiable person is one who can be identified, directly or indirectly, in particular by reference to an identification number or to one or more factors specific to his or her physical, physiological, mental, economic, cultural or social identity. This general definition is clarified by subsequent, detailed provisions of the Directive, especially by the definition of "data processing", which provides for a set of actions permitted with respect to personal data and the rights and obligations of persons using such data. The Directive introduces higher standards for processing specific categories of sensitive data (Article 8) including data revealing racial or ethnic origin, political opinions, religious or philosophical beliefs or trade union membership, and data concerning a data subject's health or sex life. The provisions of the Directive have been reflected in national laws of member states, which specify provisions thereof, and the protection model provided for in the Directive has been assimilated by many non-European states. Present challenges related to the implementation of the Directive are addressed by the Working Party on the Protection of Individuals with regard to the Processing of Personal Data under Article 29 of the Directive.[146] The scope of privacy protection guaranteed under the provisions of Directive 95/46/EC may be substantially altered by Directive 2006/24/EC.[147] A practical result of introducing the said regulation is the requirement that electronic communication services providers in Europe retain data about their users ("data retention") – data generated automatically during the performance of network services ("traffic data"). The official purpose of the regulation is to facilitate the work of enforcement authorities and prevent crimes specified in the laws of each member state; however, the actual purpose is collecting, storing and providing enormous volumes of personal data without reference to statutory legitimacy (as mentioned above, the limitation of the right to privacy requires pointing to exceptional, reasonable need as stipulated, for instance, in Article 8, section 2 ECHR). The Directive was met with strenuous objection on the part of European organizations safeguarding human rights as well as negative

143 ETS, No. 108. <http://www.netdialogue.org/initiatives/coeautoprocess> (accessed 20 February 2011).

144 For more about European protection of personal data and privacy on the Internet, see C. Kuner (2003) *European Data Privacy Law and Online Business,* Oxford: Oxford University Press, pp. 1–49.

145 (1995) OJ (L 281), p. 31 amended by the Regulation (EC) No 1882/2003 of the European Parliament and of the Council of 29 September 2003 (2003) OJ (L 284) p. 1.

146 The Working Party homepage is at <http://ec.europa.eu/justice/policies/privacy/workinggroup/index_en.htm> (accessed 23 June 2011).

147 Directive 2006/24/EC of the European Parliament and of the Council of 15 March 2006 on the Retention of Data Generated or Processed in Connection with the Provision of Publicly Available Electronic Communications Services or of Public Communications Networks and Amending Directive 2002/58/EC, OJ (L 105) (13 April 2006), p. 54.

opinions by national constitutional tribunals that the Directive constitutes a gross violation of the right to privacy guaranteed under certain constitutions.[148]

Neither Community regulations, nor the rich case law of the European Court of Human Rights relating to the protection of Article 8 of ECHR and the right to respect for one's personal life, provide any definition of the right to privacy. The court functions on case study basis adapting the interpretation of the convention to a particular case, and the minimum standard of protection may be defined as "a right to establish and develop relationship with other human beings".[149] The leading guidelines for the admissibility of interference in the protected sphere of privacy is specified by Article 8 section 2, which provides for such interference only if the provisions of law allow and it "is necessary in a democratic society in the interests of national security, public safety or the economic well-being of the country, for the prevention of disorder or crime, for the protection of health or morals, or for the protection of the rights and freedoms of others." Those standards are reflected in the interpretation of corresponding constitutional provisions, guaranteeing the right to privacy under national laws of ECHR state parties.

Constitutional or treaty-based privacy protection standards concern protection against excessive interference by state authorities in the lives of persons under state jurisdiction. However, they do not provide protection for relations between the individuals themselves.[150] Such protection is guaranteed solely by the civil law protection of personal rights; in the EU this is often specified in reference to the German civil concept of the theory of spheres. Pursuant to this idea any information relating to a human being may be qualified as belonging to his or her public, private or intimate sphere. The public sphere covers information concerning activities or features of a person pertaining to the public function he or she holds, and as such shall not be subject to protection. The privacy sphere comprises information not related to the public function and subject to protection, unless the person concerned waives such protection (by disclosing information to the public), in which case such information is not protected as falling within the sphere of privacy. The highest degree of protection is provided with respect to the intimacy sphere, which roughly includes data considered "sensitive" under the Directive 95/46/EC. Disclosure of such information, even by the person concerned, shall neither exempt from the protection obligation nor

148 The decision of the German Constitutional Court (Bundesverfassungsgericht) of 2 March 2010, 1 BvR 256/08, 1 BvR 263/08, 1 BvR 586/08, found the obligation imposed by the Directive 2006/24/EC unconstitutional in light of Article 10 of the German Constitution (Grundgesetz). An earlier, similar, decision was issued by the Romanian Constitutional Court: Constitutional Court Decision No. 1258 of 8 October 2009. <http://www.ccr.ro/decisions/pdf/ro/2009/D1258_09.pdf> (for an unofficial English translation, see <http://www.legi-internet.ro/english/jurisprudenta-it-romania/decizii-it/romanian-constitutional-court-decision-regarding-data-retention.html>.

149 See the United Kingdom House of Lords Select Committee Report (2009) *Surveillance, Citizens and the State*, op. cit., p. 31.

150 Directive 95/46/EC in Article 3 para. 2. states "This Directive shall not apply to the processing of personal data . . . by a natural person in the course of a purely personal or household activity." The scope of "personal use" in the online environment is particularly difficult to assess. See e.g., M. Birnhack and N. Elkin-Koren (2011), 'Does Law Matter Online? Empirical Evidence on Privacy Law Compliance' 17 *Michigan Telecommunications & Technology Law Review*, pp. 380–382.

exclude such information from the protected sphere of privacy. The civil protection of personal rights, including the right to privacy, enables one to effectively demand that an infringement be brought to an end (e.g. by removal of information) and can require pecuniary compensation (damages).[151]

Even though in US case law the right to privacy was defined in 1890 as "the right to be left alone", subsequent definitions proposed by common-law parliamentary bodies fit into the rules of the abovementioned European guidelines. The British 1990 Calcutt Committee on Privacy and Related Matters defined it as: "The right of the individual to be protected against intrusion into his personal life or affairs or those of his family, by direct physical means or by publication of information".[152] In spite of the apparent concurrence of definitions, European and US privacy protection systems differ considerably. Inasmuch as in the continental system the right to privacy is viewed in terms of human rights, in the United States the concept is derived from economic and commercial grounds (where processing of personal data constitutes quite a considerable part of the entire market sector). The US government is unwilling to introduce a uniform, federal regulation by reason of the fact that, as commerce representatives claim, universal regulation pertaining to privacy would have an adverse effect on the development of e-commerce. First and foremost, however, the government raises the argument of complexity of state privacy regulations unification.[153] US legal academics and commentators assume that government interference in this regulatory field is unnecessary. The US model ensures only a few positive rights. The intention is that self-regulation and market forces jointly are to establish the protection of data and privacy. The European model, however, assumes that the government is responsible for privacy protection for nationals, and to this end it is the government that should demonstrate active involvement.[154] In order to enable personal data flows from Europe, where the data are protected under Directive 95/46, to the United States, the US Department of Trade has developed safe harbor principles. US entrepreneurs wanting to use European databases shall either accept these principles or join one of the self-regulating programs on the protection of personal data (TRUSTe or BBBOnLine) which are compliant with the principles.[155]

151 See G. Arzt (1970) *Der Strafrechtliche Schutz der Intimsphäre*, Tübingen: Mohr Siebeck, pp. 101ff even though the literature provides more detailed distinctions such as in U. Branahl (2009) *Medienrecht: Eine Einführung*, Wiesbaden: VS Verlag, p. 135, where a social sphere (Sozialsphaere) and secret sphere (Sekretsphaere) are also distinguished.

152 United Kingdom House of Commons (1990) *Report of the Committee on Privacy and Related Matters*, Chairman David Calcutt QC, Cmnd. 1102, London: The Stationery Office, p. 7.

153 The debate is similar to the discussion on intellectual property rights and the postulated necessity of their globalization. Conclusions drawn from the debate showed that copyright on the Internet is rigorously protected by, most of all, entrepreneurs and commercial organizations.

154 *KU* v. *Finland* (2008) Application No. 2872/02 (European Court of Human Rights).

155 See: H. Farrell (2002) 'Negotiating Privacy across Arenas: The EU-US "Safe Harbor"', in A. Heretier, (ed.) *Common Goods: Reinventing European and International Governance*, Colorado: Rowman & Littlefield. Also available at <www.henryfarrell.net/privacy1.pdf> (accessed: 18 December 2011). Full information about the safe harbor principles is available at <www.export.gov/safeharbor. asp>

Another element restricting the scope of common privacy protection is the so-called data havens,[156] i.e. computers or electronic networks including personal data protected in Europe or the United States which are located in a state having no personal data regulations or where such regulations are not consistently observed, and most often having no relevant extradition agreements in place.[157] There are various purposes to establishing data havens, from providing access to content uncensored by authorities to users from states where filtering policies are pursued, gathering content inciting social unrest, software violating existing national licenses, enabling breach of copyright, pornography restrictions or gambling prohibitions, to direct circumvention of data protection laws. Defenders of such places declare that the content is not used to support spam, terrorism or child pornography, yet many such locations do serve this purpose.[158]

These examples of ineffective international privacy protection highlight the need for intensifying international collaboration. We are in a time where of global electronic exchange continuously exposes new risks to privacy. To this end, efforts have been made by numerous international organizations, even though an international treaty regulating these issues is yet to be formulated. Those documents that have been developed are non-binding and call for the unification of ethical standards by addressees and signatories.

The 1980 OECD *Guidelines on the Protection of Privacy and Transborder Flow of Personal Data*[159] may serve as an early example. The purpose of the guidelines is to prevent breaches of fundamental human rights such as unlawful retention, retention of false personal data or data abuse and unauthorized disclosure. The guidelines have laid down frameworks for a number of national regulations in this field (including, *inter alia*, Great Britain, Australia, Canada and Hong Kong).[160] Under the OECD declaration pertaining to the transborder data flows,[161] the parties undertake to protect access

156 The term was first used (in the literary rather than legal context) by B. Sterling in his 1988 book *Islands in the Net* (Southport: Arbor House), where such havens protect "free" content against censorship; see also D. Loundy (1997) '"Data Havens" May Protect Online Enterprises', *Chicago Daily Law Bulletin*, 9 January 1997. <http://www.loundy.com/CDLB/Jurisdiction2.html> (accessed 14 January 2011), p. 6.

157 See e.g. C. D. Raab and C. J. Bennett (2003) 'The Governance of Global Issues: Protecting Privacy in Personal Information' paper presented at the European Consortium for Political Research Workshop on the Governance of Global Issues: Effectiveness, Accountability and Constitutionalization, Edinburgh. <http://www.essex.ac.uk/ECPR/events/jointsessions/paperarchive/edinburgh/ws11/RaabBennett.pdf> (accessed 24 January 2011), p. 6.

158 For more information see C. D. Raab and C. J. Bennett, op. cit., p. 19.

159 Organization for Economic Co-operation and Development (1980) *Guidelines on the Protection of Privacy and Transborder Flows of Personal Data*. Paris: OECD. <http://www.oecd.org/document/18/0,2340,en_2649_34255_1815186_1_1_1_1,00.html> (accessed 9 January 2011).

160 See: C. L. Mann (2000) *Transatlantic Issues in Electronic Commerce*, Washington, DC: Institute for International Economics. <http://www.iie.com/publications/wp/00-7.pdf> (accessed 29 January 2011), p. 18.

161 Organization for Economic Co-operation and Development (1985) *Declaration on Transborder Data Flows*, Paris: OECD Publishing. <http://www.oecd.org/document/60/0,2340,en_2649_34225_2373500_1_1_1_1,00.html> (accessed 9 January 2011).

to data and to avoid establishing unreasonable barriers for their circulation. States undertook to develop clear regulations on information exchange, communication and computer services affecting international data transmissions.[162] The following 1998 OECD *Ministerial Declaration on the Protection of Privacy on Global Networks* is of supplementary nature.[163] The states declare their support for transposing the applicable privacy policy to electronic media for the purpose of enabling users to familiarize themselves with it and guarantee effective implementation mechanisms. They undertake to raise users' awareness of the need to protect their data in electronic environment and bring to their attention available means of protection. The document, however, serves to provide documentation for disputable areas rather than to make an attempt at reaching an actual international compromise.

Such solutions show the current approach to regulating key areas of electronic operations. Given the fact that developing treaties is time consuming and difficult (it requires extensive compromise), the existing proposals for solving the privacy problem are soft law: self regulation based on common ethical standards, described in non-binding declarations or guiding principles. Unlike in the case of traditional public international law, those documents are not always created by intergovernmental organizations, but more often directly by the governed. Initiatives such as the Google Global Network Initiative[164] resort to industry self-regulation, calling upon other industry representatives (social platforms operators, Internet service providers) to adhere to a set of rules and principles aimed at granting international privacy protection to their users.[165] Such initiatives and the scope of the existing privacy protection challenge reach for the wealthy soft-law background available in public international law.

Self-regulation does seem to be the current tendency in regulating privacy online; however, one more interesting, although less practical, proposal ought to be mentioned. The crucial arguments for cyberspace autonomy presented by J. P. Barlow in 'A Declaration of the Independence of Cyberspace'[166] in 1996 echo an earlier proposal by D. Barnes of Austin Cyberpunks. Barlow claimed that national authorities "have no sovereignty" in cyberspace, whose "citizens" will form their "own Social Contract, according to the specifics of their world". Barnes proposed a complete anonymization of electronic interactions.[167] Such a solution would not only guarantee

162 For more about the European protection of personal data and privacy on the Internet, see C. Kuner, op. cit. pp. 1–49.

163 Organization for Economic Co-operation and Development (1998) *Ministerial Declaration on the Protection of Privacy on Global Networks.* <http://www.oecd.org/dataoecd/39/13/1840065.pdf> (accessed 9 January 2011). The document is not subject to international sanctions for breach.

164 <http://www.globalnetworkinitiative.org/>

165 On the results of such efforts, see Global Network Initiative (2010) *Inaugural Report: Our Work, Our V ision, Our Progress.* <http://www.globalnetworkinitiative.org/cms/uploads/1/GNI_annual_report_2010.pdf> (accessed 25 December 2010).

166 J. P. Barlow (1996) 'A Declaration of the Independence of Cyberspace', paper published online <https://projects.eff.org/~barlow/Declaration-Final.html>

167 D. Barnes (1994) 'Coming Jurisdictional Swamp of Global Internetworking', unpublished, Austin, TX: Austin Cyberpunks <http://www.io.com/~cman/swamp.html> (accessed 29 November 2004). See also I. A. Goldberg (2000) *A Pseudonymous Communications Infrastructure for the Internet,* unpublished PhD thesis, University Of California At Berkeley. <http://www.cypherpunks.ca/~iang/

a complete equality of all users but would also provide full privacy protection. Each user would receive an "electronic passport" and as part of a transaction would allow e.g. companies intending to provide controversial materials to verify the nationality of the end recipient. Companies willing to enhance credibility could resign from being anonymous and render identification certificates available to the general public, even though, as a rule, companies would have to give up their real-world reputation, based on already established trade names or trademarks, in return benefitting from services of anonymous agents distributing their products online. Along with the companies' development of an electronic reputation associated with an electronic pseudonym, the loyalty of consumers would increase. Those users who wished to ensure the certainty and safety of electronic exchange could request their state authorities or generally recognized organization supporting trade (e.g. ICC or WTO) for arbitration and thus obtain information about the true identity of the business partner. If the partner proves untrustworthy and the transaction fails, the user could address an organization or certificate issuing authority in order to obtain assistance. Such a solution would allow us to resolve disputes resulting from online operations using agreed set of universal principles or arbitration procedures. Should the idea be consistently effected and users actually refrain from providing their true identity, general anonymity should resolve the question of jurisdiction or personal liability and would guarantee privacy.

The simplicity of the proposal of a complete anonymization of electronic exchange is tempting. Indeed, it would be easier to follow the behavior of few "de-anonymized" than to leave the issue of business partners' identification to e.g. auction website operators. Today, it is common knowledge that the issue of online reputation is not to be underestimated. There is a high probability that the concept will grow in popularity along with the intensifying attempts of state authorities to wholly invigilate users. Although these arguments would undoubtedly appeal to private users and are already effective, for instance in the world of auction websites,[168] large companies would probably be unwilling to resign from the reputation and goodwill they have been earning for years in the real world. The proposal of anonymization may be considered a partial solution, specific to some cyber-communities. So far, however, in order to establish content liability, the traditional rules specified below apply.

thesis-final.pdf> accessed 20 January 2011); see also G. Hosein (2000) *A Brief Coverage Of Anonymity and Animosity: The Socio-Technical Network And The Role Of Freedom*, unpublished, London: The London School of Economics and Political Science <http://academic.research.microsoft.com/Publication/4647681/a–brief–coverage–of–anonymity–and–animosity–the–socio–technical–network–and–the–role–of–freedom> (accessed 20 January 2011); and I. Goldberg, D. Wagner and E. A. Brewer (1997) 'Privacy-Enhancing Technologies for the Internet' paper delivered at the 42nd IEEE Spring Computer Society International Conference, San Jose, California. <http://citeseer.ist.psu.edu/rd/35710544%2C54687%2C1%2C0.25%2CDownload/http://coblitz.codeen.org:3125/citeseer.ist.psu.edu/cache/papers/cs/788/http:zSzzSzwww.cs.berkeley.eduzSz%7EdawzSzprivacycom pcon97.pdf/goldberg97privacyenhancing.pdf> (accessed 20 January 2011).

168 Cf. chapter 4; for the role of reputation online see J. L. Zittrain (2008), *The Future of the Internet and How to Stop It*, New Haven: Yale University Press, pp. 216–221.

Content liability

The issues of liability for electronic content may concern civil liability or criminal responsibility. First, and most importantly, the subject matter of these deliberations is civil liability, with special consideration being given to the liability of Internet service providers.

Electronic content liability may be borne by three groups of entities: 1) Internet content providers (ICPs), 2) Internet service providers (ISPs), also referred to as Internet Access Providers (IAPs), and 3) end users. An Internet content provider is, most often, the author of information or data placed online. An Internet service provider is an entrepreneur who offers Internet connectivity (many ISPs are telecommunications companies).[169]

Inasmuch as the liability of authors of content placed online raises no doubt, the issue of any liability of Internet access providers for content to which they provide access is still a subject of heated discussion. They actually have the physical control over content availability (and may make the decision to disable access thereto); nevertheless, it is disputable whether and to what extent they should exercise such power, and on what grounds. Such questions are especially relevant in states deemed democratic where the scope of liability of the ISPs (if any) is restricted. In the United States relevant legal acts regulate only the exemption of liability of ISPs within the scope of their activities as publishers[170] and the breach of copyright.[171] Provisions regulating the nature of ISP liability in European Community law are provided for in Articles 12–15 of the Directive on Electronic Commerce.[172] Pursuant to the said Articles, ISPs shall not be liable for actions consisting in providing services of "mere conduit" (Article 12),[173] catching (Article 13)[174] and hosting

169 For details on the division of ISPs, see W. Lehr (1998) *Understanding Vertical Integration in the Internet*, Cambridge, Mass.: MIT Internet and Telecoms Convergence Consortium. <http://itc.mit.edu/itel/pubs/Lehr. pdf> (accessed 4 February 2011), p. 2.

170 47 USC section 230 has been criticized for being too beneficial to the ISPs. For example, see *Kenneth M. Zeran* v. *America Online Inc.* (1997) US Cert. Pet. 97–1488. <http://laws.findlaw.com/4th/971523p.html> (accessed 2 February 2011) and *Blumenthal* v. *Drudge* (1998) 992 F. Supp. 44 <http://legal.web.aol.com/decisions/dldefam/blumenop.html> (accessed 2 February 2011). In these cases America-OnLine has been exempted from liability for providing access to defamatory content, when it refused to remove the content.

171 17 USC, section 512, introduced as part of Digital Millennium Copyright Act of 1998.

172 Directive 2000/31/EC of the European Parliament and of the Council of 8 June 2000 on Certain Legal Aspects of Information Society Services, in Particular Electronic Commerce, in the Internal Market ('the Directive on Electronic Commerce').

173 Where a service is provided that consists in the transmission in a communication network of information provided by a recipient of the service (e.g. email), or the provision of access to a communication network, the service provider is not liable for the information transmitted, on condition that the provider does not initiate the transmission, does not select the receiver of the transmission, and does not select or modify the information contained in the transmission.

174 Where a service is provided that consists in the transmission in a communication network of information provided by a recipient of the service, the service provider is not liable for the automatic, intermediate and temporary storage of that information, performed for the sole purpose of making more efficient the information's onward transmission to other recipients of the service upon their request, on condition that the provider does not modify the information, the provider complies with

(Article 14).[175] Provisions of the Directive, however, leave member states much room for discretion to demand from a service provider, by way of a decision of court or competent administrative authority, the termination or prevention of an infringement, observing at the same time the laws of the state. Article 15 exempts service providers from the obligation to monitor delivered content,[176] even though internal provisions of the Member State may impose the obligation on ISPs to inform the competent public authorities of alleged illegal activities undertaken, or information provided, by recipients of their service or the obligation to communicate to the competent authorities, at their request, information enabling the identification of recipients of their service with whom they have storage agreements (Article 15.2).[177]

Consequently in Europe and America it is a common practice to exempt service providers from content liability. The case is totally different, however, in most Asian countries where service providers are legally bound to filter content they provide and bear liability for materials they are not able to block.[178] Such a solution entails high risk. The obligation resting with service providers to filter content makes them *actually* censors. If an ISP is to be liable for materials which it puts into circulation, a logical consequence is limiting the risk by blocking the access to those which could potentially

conditions on access to the information, the provider complies with rules regarding the updating of the information, the provider does not interfere with the lawful use of technology, widely recognized and used by industry, to obtain data on the use of the information, and the provider acts expeditiously to remove or to disable access to the information it has stored upon obtaining actual knowledge of the fact that the information at the initial source of the transmission has been removed from the network, or access to it has been disabled, or that a court or an administrative authority has ordered such removal or disablement.

175 Where a service is provided that consists in the storage of information, the service provider is not liable for the information stored, on condition that the provider does not have actual knowledge of illegal activity or information and, as regards claims for damages, is not aware of facts or circumstances from which the illegal activity or information is apparent, or the provider, upon obtaining such knowledge or awareness, acts expeditiously to remove or to disable access to the information.

176 Article 15.1 reads: "Member States shall not impose a general obligation on providers to monitor the information which they transmit or store, nor a general obligation actively to seek facts or circumstances indicating illegal activity".

177 The principle is also included in the Council of Europe Declaration on Freedom of Communication on the Internet. Principle 6 says that "Member States should not impose on service providers a general obligation to monitor content on the Internet to which they give access, that they transmit or store, nor that of actively seeking facts or circumstances indicating illegal activity. Member States should ensure that service providers are not held liable for content on the Internet when their function is limited, as defined by national law, to transmitting information or providing access to the Internet. In cases where the functions of service providers are wider and they store content emanating from other parties, Member States may hold them co-responsible if they do not act expeditiously to remove or disable access to information or services as soon as they become aware, as defined by national law, of their illegal nature or, in the event of a claim for damages, of facts or circumstances revealing the illegality of the activity or information. When defining under national law the obligations of service providers, due care must be taken to respect the freedom of expression of those who made the information available in the first place, as well as the corresponding right of users to the information. In all cases, the above-mentioned limitations of liability should not affect the possibility of issuing injunctions where service providers are required to terminate or prevent, to the extent possible, an infringement of the law."

178 For more information, see chapter 3.

expose the ISP to liability Representatives of digital liberalism and Western countries who believe that the scope of content available online ought to be determined solely by Internet users providing it strenuously object to the above-mentioned practice. Recent decisions of European national courts seem, however, to reject this approach, as can be seen in the decision to impose liability upon Google Video administrators for failure to remove content harmful, in the opinion of the Italian court, to a third party's right to privacy.[179]

As much as assigning content liability to ISPs raises controversy, it is clear that ICPs may be held liable for their actions. By the same token, they are the ones directly exposed to the jurisdictional principles jigsaw presented in the previous chapter. Administrators and owners of websites make attempts to secure their legal situation by diverse means, including terms of use stipulating the jurisdiction. Those clauses are used to protect the website operator against the liability in all locations where the site is available. Numerous sites introduce general terms and conditions of use which often provide for regulations on the legal system to which a given "place" in cyberspace is to be subject.[180] Operators and administrators of websites invoke the most favorable and convenient legal system to regulate mutual relations between them and the users. It is the intention of authors that such clauses be equivalent to traditional arbitration clauses. However, they might be considered "adhesive" agreements, which considerably limit the equal position of parties to a legal relationship. The main defect of such contractual provisions is that users most often do not read them, disregard them or are unaware of their existence. Therefore, the effectiveness of providing consent by website users to the provisions of law specified by the website operator seems doubtful. At the same time, it is the most popular solution for the administrator to avoid problems with foreign jurisdictions, as it is an unambiguous way to establish the legal system governing the parties and relations between the author, administrator and users. Nowadays, the solution frequently applied to avoid the foregoing allegation of poor "visibility" of terms and conditions in electronic transactions is that the user should click a screen "button" to agree to the terms and conditions as well as the regulations of the website (referred to as click-agreements or click-wrap agreements).[181] Such security puts the author in a position to argue that regulations relevant to the website content have been clearly indicated. Still, such documents are most often of

179 *Italy* v. *Drummond et al.* (2010) Tribunale Ordinario di Milano, Sezione 4 Penale, 2 February 2010, Sentenza No. 1972/2010. Available in Italian at <http://speciali.espresso.repubblica.it/pdf/Motivazioni_sentenza_Google.pdf>. See also A. Liptak, 'When US and European Ideas of Privacy Collide', *New York Times*, 27 February 2010.

180 Google's Terms of Service state: "Terms for use of this Website shall be subject to and comply with the laws of the State of California, without prejudice to the binding rules of private and public international law of your stay. If for any reason the court of competent jurisdiction deems any or all provisions of these Terms inapplicable, other provisions shall remain in force". <http://www.google.pl/intl/pl/terms_of_service.html> (accessed 17 January 2011).

181 For more on click-agreements see P. Richardson 'Internet Buyers Beware of "Click" Agreements'. <http://www.mbf-law.com/pubs/articles/166.cfm> (accessed 15 January 2011); for information about the low effectiveness of such agreements see H. Bidgoli (2006) *Handbook of Information Security: Threats, Vulnerabilities, Prevention, Detection and Management*, New York: John Wiley & Sons, p. 567.

extensive length and most users do not bother to read them. Moreover, it is difficult to identify the individual who actually provided the consent.[182] Arguments raised by opponents of so formulated and presented adhesive agreements also pertain to computer software licenses (shrink-wrap agreements), where a user is forced to consent to a long and complex license agreement (including jurisdictional regulations) before the installation of the software he or she wishes to use.[183]

So far, content has been subject to several practical solutions. The liability for websites should be borne undoubtedly by those who exert direct impact on their content. It seems unreasonable, however, to impose liability on Internet Service Providers, who on the one hand are not practically in a position to meet the obligation, and on the other hand are vested with powers far exceeding the competence resulting from functions they hold.

Cybercrime and network security

Given the fact that the issue of combating cybercrime falls directly within the ambit of national criminal regulations, the abovementioned low level of international co-operation in criminal cases applies here. The existing international crime-related agreements are limited to prosecution of the most serious crimes (crimes against humanity or terrorist crimes). The nature of cybercrime and the specificity of combating thereof require, however, a review of the traditional approach to criminal regulations. Inasmuch as a traditional concept of combating crime directly affected the level of security in the territory of the regulating sovereign, a cybercrime produces harmful effects in many physical locations simultaneously. If such damage is extensive and is related to key electronic state infrastructure, cybercrime should be deemed a type of terrorist crime and, as such, should be subject to common sanctions. Both issues are discussed in detail below.

The first international organization to successfully provide treaty-based regulations on cybercrime was the Council of Europe. The 2001 Convention on Cybercrime constitutes the first hard law document that can be deemed an international Internet law act. It pertains to offenses committed via the Internet and other computer networks, with special consideration to violation of copyright, computer fraud, child pornography and breach of network security. States joining the Convention assimilate definitions of cybercrime contained therein and established co-operation frameworks. The Convention provides also for delegations and procedures enabling searching of the computer network and interception of data. These actions are to be undertaken by

182 In trade contracts it is often the case that terms and conditions limit or deprive the purchaser of guarantee rights or stipulate an exemption of the seller from liability for possible loss or damage resulting from using the object of the transaction. Such regulations often submit the entire transaction to the jurisdiction of the seller's state, consequently the consenting purchaser loses the privilege to submit the case to a near and convenient court.

183 For examples of decisions pertaining to such agreements see R. L. Dickens, 'Finding Common Ground in the World of Electronic Contracts: The Consistency of Legal Reasoning in Clickwrap Cases', 11(2) *Marquette Intellectual Property Law Review*, pp. 381–411 at p. 392. For information about the very nature of such agreements see ibid., p. 382.

way of developing relevant national provisions and increasing international co-operation. An auxiliary document to the Convention is the Additional Protocol sanctioning racist and xenophobic material in cyberspace.

As already mentioned, the jurisdictional solution provided for in the Convention should be assessed critically. As discussed, Article 22 only reiterates the general principles of international law and accords a wide margin of discretion to state parties in their application. The Convention provides no answer to the question about which state is competent to prosecute a crime, and does not contain a definition of "place of commitment" on which the competence of state jurisdiction depends.[184] The Convention allows a state to unilaterally refuse its aid in combating cybercrime.[185] It must be emphasized that a more detailed or rigorous solution to the jurisdictional issue was not politically possible at the time of negotiating the CoE Cybercrime Convention. From a strictly academic point of view, the Stanford Draft, referred to in the previous chapter, must be mentioned. In its Article 5 it successfully tackles the problem of Internet jurisdiction by proposing a sequence (rather than a list) of jurisdictional principles to be used when regulating online actions.[186] Article 3 specifies the subject matter of the proposed Draft Convention, including interfering with the function of a cyber system, cyber trespass, tampering with authentication systems, interfering with data, trafficking in illegal cyber tools, using cyber systems to further offenses and targeting social infrastructures. The Draft disregards more controversial issues such as intellectual property rights protection and distribution of political or religious content. The Stanford Draft Convention is important for one more reason – it brings together the regulation of cybercrime and cyberterrorism in one regulatory framework. Following the practice of other existing treaties aimed at combating terrorism, it introduces in Article 7 the *aut dedere aut judicare* principle. It also recommends the establishment of an institution for the protection of Convention provisions: the Agency for Information Infrastructure Protection (AIIP).[187]

In light of recent events,[188] the question of network security is attracting forever more academic and political attention. There is no doubt that network security

184 Article 22 stipulates an alternative application of each known ground for exercising jurisdiction depending on the decision of state authorities.

185 Article 29 para. 5b) that allows a state requested to render legal aid in the case of cybercrime prevention or prosecution to refuse such aid if "the requested Party considers that execution of the request is likely to prejudice its sovereignty, security, *ordre public* or other essential interests".

186 Para. 4, in particular, specifies the sequence in detail: "Each State Party will exercise its rights and fulfill its obligations under this Convention to the extent practicable in accordance with the following priority of jurisdiction: first, the State Party in which the alleged offender was physically present when the alleged offense was committed; second, the State Party in which substantial harm was suffered as a result of the alleged offense; third, the State Party of the alleged offender's dominant nationality; fourth, any State Party where the alleged offender may be found; and fifth, any other State Party with a reasonable basis for jurisdiction."

187 Article 12.

188 Such as the 2007 cyberattacks on Estonia which originated from Russian territory, or the 2010 case of the Stuxnet worm attacks aimed at the Iranian nuclear power plant. For more information see e.g. J. Markoff (2010) 'A Silent Attack, But Not a Subtle One', *New York Times*, 26 September 2010.

and stability is a necessary condition for the further existence and development of the information society. The principle of network security – the common obligation to protect the Internet infrastructure – has been expressly defined in all WSIS documents[189] and acknowledged by the doctrine.[190]

The basic controversy surrounding the practical application of this principle relates directly to public international law: it is the question of the limits of state responsibility for cyberattacks initiated or conducted through infrastructure located within its territorial jurisdiction. There is a common accord that states ought to bear responsibility for these kinds of events; a strong controversy arises, however, over the suitable international law mechanism to be applied.[191] The majority position is the US doctrine[192] supported by numerous European politicians[193] and international law researchers,[194] which strongly holds that cyberspace is "the fifth battlefield" and a cyberattack is just another act of armed aggression, allowing for armed self defense,[195] including pre-emptive measures.[196]

<http://www.nytimes.com/2010/09/27/technology/27virus.html> (accessed 15 December 2010). For a detailed analysis of the Estonia case see S. J. Shackelford, op. cit. *See generally* D. Delibasis (2007) *The Right to National Self-Defense in Information Warfare Operations*, Bury St Edmunds, UK: Arena Books, and D. Delibasis (2006) 'State Use of Force in Cyberspace for Self-Defence: A New Challenge for a New Century', (8) *Peace Conflict and Development: An Interdisciplinary Journal*, pp. 13ff.

189 United Nations World Summit on the Information Society (2003) *Declaration of Principles*, section B5 paras. 35–37, p. 5; WSIS (2003) *Plan of Action*, section C5 para.12, p. 6; United Nations WSIS (2005) *Tunis Agenda* para. 42, p. 13 (emphasizing the importance of an appropriate commeasure of means used for protecting security and human rights); para. 45, p. 14; para. 57, p. 15; paras. 58 and 68, p. 16 and Annex 1, section C5, p. 26 (assigning ITU as the unit responsible for co-ordinating international measures on IT security).

190 See e.g: A. Pisanty (2010) 'Security: the Key to Trust and Growth of the Internet', in W. J. Drake (ed.) *Internet Governance: Creating Opportunities for All*, New York: United Nations Publishing, pp. 46–56; Internet Governance Forum (2010) *Legal aspects of Internet governance: International cooperation on cyber–security* (Transcript of session 123, Vilnius, Lithuania, 15 September 2010). <http://www.afilias.info/webfm_send/138> (accessed 15 December 2010).

191 See: J. Kulesza (2009) 'State Responsibility for Cyberattacks on International Peace and Security', 29 *Polish Yearbook of International Law*, pp. 139–152.

192 See e.g., F. D. Kramer, S. H. Starr and L. Wentz, op. cit., p. 642; M. N. Schmitt, op. cit., pp. 143ff., and see generally W.G. Sharp, op. cit.

193 See e.g., N. Harvey (2010) 'Cyber Warfare: Addressing the Challenge', Chatham House session transcript 9 November 2010. <www.chathamhouse.org.uk/files/17800_091110harvey.pdf> (accessed 25 December 2010), p. 6, where N. Harvey, UK Minister of State for the Armed Forces said: "The integration of cyber and physical attack would seem to be the most likely use of cyber in the military sphere. We must therefore win the battle in cyberspace, as well as the battle on the ground. So the first thing we should recognize is that actions in cyberspace form part of the future battlefield, rather than being separate from it. It adds a new and modern dimension to conflict, but what it seeks to achieve should be subject to the same strategic and tactical thought as a conventional military operation. We will encounter the same adversaries with the same motivations in cyberspace as we do in the real world – albeit in a new environment which has its own unique characteristics. As Clausewitz believed, war is an expression of politics by other means. This means we should also be able to prevent, deter, coerce or even intervene in cyberspace."

194 P. Cornish et al. (2010) *On Cyber Warfare: A Chatham House Report*, London: Chatham House.

195 See e.g. Schmitt, op. cit., pp. 143ff and by the same author (2001) 'Computer Network Attack: The Normative Software', 4 *Yearbook of International Humanitarian Law*, pp. 53–85.

196 See e.g. Sharp, op. cit., p. 95 and p. 129.

The opposite line of reasoning holds that states are obliged to undertake due diligence in preventing cyberattacks and they may only be held responsible for a cyberattack if it can be demonstrated that they have failed to meet the due diligence standard. This is the position presented by, for example, the Council of Europe Ad Hoc Advisory Group on Cross-Border Internet, which proposes[197] an international law mechanism for "prevention and management of and response to Internet disruptions and interferences", based on the "the principle of prevention in the International Law Commission's Draft Articles on Prevention of Transboundary Harm from Hazardous Activities".[198] It widely refers to the existing environmental law standards[199] and the Law of the Sea[200] and attempts to set the basic terms of reference for a due diligence standard in cyberspace.[201] However, it disregards the direct applicability of traditional state-responsibility mechanisms to cyberattack prevention,[202] obliging the international community to further develop an appropriate international law framework.[203]

The CoE draws from public international law in one more area – the legal qualification of Critical Internet Resources (CIRs). This term refers to the key network elements upon which its functioning relies, such as root-servers, the large interconnected networks that form the Internet (the "Internet backbone") or the DNS.[204] Most of those elements belong to private companies; they, however, serve the global network and the universal information society. Presently they do not have public law status, however it is forever more strongly raised they ought to. Since those elements

197 Interim Report of the Ad Hoc Advisory Group on Cross-Border Internet to the Steering Committee on the Media and New Communication Services, Incorporating Analysis of Proposals for International and Multi-Stakeholder Cooperation on Cross-Border Internet, Strasbourg, December 2010, p. 20.

198 The CoE Ad Hoc Advisory Group proposes that "States should, in cooperation with each other and with all relevant stakeholders, take all reasonable measures to prevent, manage and respond to significant transboundary disruption of and interference with the stability, robustness, resilience and openness of the Internet, or at any event minimize the risk and consequences thereof."

199 See pp. 26ff.

200 Para. A5, p. 26: "*Responsibility*. With the objective of ensuring accountability in respect of adverse consequences on the stability, robustness and resilience of the Internet, states should engage in dialogue and cooperate to the further development of international law relating to the responsibility and liability for the assessment of and compensation for damage as well as the settlement of related disputes." In para. 81 of the explanatory notes, the Group explains that "this principle is inspired by and modeled after the United Nations Convention on the Law of the Sea of 10 December 1982" and its Article 235.

201 See para. 72, p. 24: "The commitment of a state in respect of taking measures to prevent, manage and respond to transboundary disruptions or interferences would be one of due diligence. It is the conduct of the state in question that would determine whether it has complied with its duty of due diligence. This duty is the standard in international treaty law in respect of the protection of the environment (see paragraph 61 above). Acting with due care imposes on state a duty to do all it can, or in other words, to take all appropriate measures at its disposal to prevent and minimize foreseeable significant transboundary harm."

202 See p. 86.

203 See p. 87.

204 See Council of Europe (2009) *Internet Governance and Critical Internet Resources*, Strasbourg: Media and Information Society Division, Council of Europe, pp. 9ff.; M. L. Mueller (2010) *Networks and States: The Global Politics of Internet Governance*, Cambridge, Mass.: MIT Press, pp. 215ff. See generally S. D. Personick and C. A. Patterson (eds.) (2003) Critical Information Infrastructure Protection and the Law: An Overview of Key Issues, Washington, DC: The National Academies Press.

of network infrastructure are of key significance to Internet security,[205] they ought be considered Common Heritage of Mankind and governed under international law.[206] Such proposals remain in the *avant-garde* of IIL. However, with the growing importance of network security such a possible transposition of key CIRs status may not be ignored.

Cybersecurity presents one of the key challenges to IIL. It requires a skilful application of international law mechanisms. Principles derived from environmental law, the Law of the Sea[207] or human rights law[208] might be applicable to cyberspace.

Electronic commerce

While e-business may be broadly defined as any economic activity among Internet community members (both private or corporate) with the use of an electronic computer network, e-commerce means only the part of such activity that consists in the sale or purchase of goods and services.[209] However, these terms are often used interchangeably. The concept of e-business exceeds the scope of e-commerce, as it includes integration of telecommunications technologies with professional economic activity. E-commerce may take various forms: it may mean a relation between the entrepreneur and consumer (business-to-consumer, also known as B2C) most frequently encountered in trade (represented for example by all websites offering online sales of goods or services). The second dynamic area of electronic exchange is the one pertaining to mutual relations between entrepreneurs (business-to-business or B2B). Another type of e-commerce covers transactions between the business and governmental sectors (business-to-government or B2G), which plays a special role in the practice of granting e.g. state permits.[210] Last but not least, natural persons not

205 Root-server attacks have been attempted, so far with little success; see ICANN (2007) *DNS Attack Factsheet 1.1*, California: ICANN. <http://www.icann.org/en/announcements/announcement-08mar07.htm> (accessed 25 December 2010).

206 See *Internet Governance and Critical Internet Resources*, op. cit., pp. 24ff; A. Segura-Serrano (2006) 'Internet Regulation: A Hard-Law Proposal', 10 *The Jean Monnet Working Papers*, p. 48.

207 See *Internet Governance and Critical Internet Resources*, op. cit., p. 23; Segura-Serrano, op. cit., p. 48 and Council of Europe *Interim Report of the Ad-hoc Advisory Group on Cross-border Internet*, op. cit., pp. 20ff.

208 See e.g., A. Segura-Serrano (2006) 'Internet Regulation and the Role of International Law', in A. von Bogdandy and R. Wolfrum (eds.) 10 *Max Planck Yearbook of United National Law*, Leiden: Koninklijke Brill, pp. 264ff.

209 See e.g., S. L. Jarvenpaa and E. H. Tiller (1999) 'Integrating Market, Technology, and Policy Opportunities in E-Business Strategy', 8 *Journal of Strategic Information Systems* (<http://www.reedsresearch.com/SupplyMgt/Jarvenpaa.pdf> (accessed 29 January 2011)), p. 235 for a discussion of the broadly understood automation of transactions, and communication and interaction using computers and communications technologies for commercial purposes, using the terms "electronic business" or "e-business". For numerous definitions of e-commerce see e.g. Z. Qin (2009) *Introduction to E-Commerce*, New York: Springer, pp. 7ff. See also: S. M. Rahman and M. S. Raisinghani (2000) *Electronic Commerce: Opportunity and Challenges*, Hershey, PA: Idea Group, Inc., p. 103.

210 For instance, a party offering B2G services could do so by offering access to one place online, where tax statements and official forms could be submitted. Co-operation may naturally be closely related to the possibility of performing e-work in offices or the lease of applications or databases to governmental institutions.

conducting economic activity may effect transactions online (consumer-to-consumer or C2C), where the most popular formula includes the so-called auction websites. An appropriate definition of e-commerce carries numerous practical and legal implications. Special principles are applied, for example, related to tax or customs duties depending on the classification of a given transaction as an electronic transaction. Differences arise at the very comparison of national and international definitions of e-commerce. For instance for the US government the key element differentiating traditional commerce from e-commerce is an "electronic obligation to sell goods or services".[211] This means that each commercial contract concluded in an electronic form should be deemed an electronic transaction even if the performance thereof consists in the provision of services outside cyberspace.[212]

E-commerce has, above all, triggered the necessity to redefine some traditional trade-related issues. For example, one can consider the question about classifying musical works, a problem that still remains unanswered: do musical works change their nature from goods to services depending on whether they are delivered on CD (a physical medium) or via the Internet (a digital medium)? A positive answer to such question may lead to the situation where the same musical work may have a varied commercial nature and thus be subject to different regulations, depending on the media via which it is transmitted. The issue of classification has far reaching consequences as various regulatory mechanisms are applied to goods and services. No clear answer has been provided to the abovementioned question; nevertheless, it seems that the nature of goods should not change depending on the transaction medium.[213]

Pursuant to the WTO definition, "electronic commerce" is understood to mean "the production, distribution, marketing, sale or delivery of goods and services by electronic means."[214] The limitlessness inherent in the Internet is best reflected by the sudden increase in the number and value of international transactions. Commercial relations based on electronic data exchange most often include a foreign element linking more than one state territory. Electronic commerce and the increase in consumer confidence in electronic transactions that is necessary for its development and the increase in the safety of electronic commerce itself – which goes hand it hand with it – are priorities for the further development of this medium. Detailed analysis of e-commerce in terms of its private and legal implications has become the subject matter of numerous deliberations. Therefore, within this study only those issues requiring international co-operation will be touched upon.

211 US Census Bureau (2006) *Quarterly Retail E-Commerce Sales 1st Quarter 2006*. <http://www.census.gov/mrts/www/data/html/06Q1.html> (accessed 15 January 2011).

212 According to the US government definition, the sale of books by book websites is an e-transaction, despite the fact that the goods are, most often, supplied by traditional mail.

213 For more information, see W. F. Fox and M. N. Murray (1997), 'The Sales Tax And Electronic Commerce: So What's New?' 50(3) *National Tax Journal*, pp. 573–592. The authors argue that the tax base should not depend on whether the payment is made for the transfer of data, access to services or their content, p. 585.

214 World Trade Organization (1998) *Work Programme on Electronic Commerce*, Geneva: WTO. <http://www.wto.org/english/tratop_e/ecom_e/wkprog_e.htm> (accessed 15 January 2011).

One of the most assimilated and significant international initiatives as regards e-commerce is the UNCITRAL Model Law on Electronic Commerce.[215] The key point of interest in the document is the mechanism designed for integration of e-commerce within the functioning of traditional transactions (e.g. recognizing the effectiveness of e-documents). The Model Law has laid foundations for e-commerce regulations in many states, but does not, however, directly deal with the place and time at which a contract is concluded,[216] leaving the problem to be regulated by traditional private international law mechanisms.

The EU adopted the Directive on Electronic Commerce and a number of directives pertaining to electronic signatures, protection of personal data and electronic financial transactions. As a result of these directives, e-commerce principles were harmonized within the EU (including also by relevant amendments to national legal regulations). However, due to the global nature of e-commerce, the ambit of these laws have been insufficient. In the Asia-Pacific region the main arena for co-operation is the Asia-Pacific Economic Co-operation (APEC) forum. APEC established the Electronic Commerce Steering Group, which deals with all e-commerce relevant issues such as consumer protection, personal data protection, spam and network security. An achievement of APEC is the development of the APEC's *Paperless Trading Individual Action Plan* (IAP),[217] aiming at reducing or eliminating the requirement for mandated paper-based documents in cross-border trade. The Plan has been initiated by the Electronic Commerce Steering Group (ECSG). Like all APEC Individual Action Plans, the *Paperless Trading Individual Action Plan* requires each APEC member to provide an annual report of actions taken in order to liberalize and facilitate trade and investment.

For e-commerce to function and develop properly, two types of actions are necessary: introduction of safe mechanisms for effecting transactions, and winning consumers' confidence. An effective legal tool for winning confidence is the introduction of consumer protection rules. Provisions on e-commerce should protect consumers within several areas: at transfer of information on payment cards, when faced with unfair advertisements or when supplied with damaged products. Needless to say, it is necessary to establish international regulations on consumer protection, especially

215 UNCITRAL Model Law on Electronic Commerce, New York, 1996. <http://www.jus.uio.no/lm/un.electronic.commerce.model.law.1996/> (accessed 14 January 2011). The Commission deemed the harmonization of law by way of model laws most effective. The Draft Convention can be found at <http://www.un.or.at/uncitral/english/sessions/wg_ec/wp-77.htm> (accessed 28 January 2011).

216 Article 15 of the Law specifies only the place and time of sending data and the place and time of their receipt. Only under the said provision is it possible, applying the internal regulations of the analyzing state, to determine the time and location of the conclusion of the contract. Pursuant to Article 15 of the Law, the dispatch of a data message occurs when it enters an information system outside the control of the originator. Therefore the concept recognizing the time of accepting the offer as the time when the addressee could have actually read the offer is rejected.

217 APEC (2004) *Paperless Trading Individual Action Plan* <http://www.apec.org/apec/documents_reports/electronic_commerce_steering_group/2004.MedialibDownload.v1.html?url=/etc/medialib/apec_media_library/downloads/taskforce/ecsg/mtg/2004/pdf.Par.0037.File.v1.1> (accessed 15 January 2011).

given the fact that the significance of this issue in traditional commerce was minor (demand for international consumer protection was rather low). As e-commerce grows, so does the number of transactions effected across state borders. To this end the OECD adopted two sets of recommendations, the 1999 Council *Recommendation concerning Guidelines for Consumer Protection in the Context of Electronic Commerce*[218] and the 2003 *Guidelines for Protecting Consumers from Fraudulent and Deceptive Commercial Practices Across Borders.*[219] These laid down fundamental principles currently adopted by several business associations, including the International Chamber of Commerce.[220] The 1999 *Recommendation* sets forth in great detail the most significant features of effective consumer protection in business-to-consumer online transactions. Part IV of the *Recommendation* emphasizes the meaning of international co-operation to combat fraudulent, misleading or unfair transborder commercial conduct. The work of the OECD committee consisted in the assessment of state authorities' activities and preparation of a report including general information regarding the enforcement of law at transborder level,[221] and a report for discussion.[222] The committee decided to formulate common frameworks of consumer protection against such practices. The OECD in the latter document (2003) recommends that authorities safeguarding consumer rights in member states cooperate in the enforcement of national laws against such practices and work to establish frameworks for closer, faster and more efficient co-operation among authorities. The committee also encouraged non-OECD members to take account of the *Recommendation* with appropriate implementation assistance from member states.[223]

What is significant for international e-commerce are doubts and questions concerning which state is competent to exercise control over it. Two views may be distinguished as regards the appropriate jurisdiction in electronic commerce. The first approach provides for privilege of the seller and is based on the jurisdiction of the

218 Organization for Economic Co-operation and Development (1999) *Recommendation Concerning Guidelines for Consumer Protection in the Context of Electronic Commerce.* <www.oecd.org/dataoecd/18/13/34023235.pdf> (accessed 9 January 2011).

219 Organization for Economic Co-operation and Development (2003) *Guidelines for Protecting Consumers from Fraudulent and Deceptive Commercial Practices Across Borders.* <http://www.oecd.org/dataoecd/15/51/34011414.pdf> (accessed 9 January 2011).

220 It should be noted that OECD Guidelines are voluntary and not subject to sanctions.

221 OECD (2003) *Guidelines*, op. cit.

222 Electronic Commerce Steering Group Meeting, Santiago, Chile, 26–27 February 2004.

223 The co-operation should include, *inter alia*: establishing a domestic system for combating cross-border fraudulent and deceptive commercial practices against consumers; enhancing notification; information sharing and investigative assistance; improving the ability to protect foreign consumers from domestic businesses engaged in fraudulent and deceptive commercial practices; improving the ability to protect domestic consumers from foreign businesses engaged in fraudulent and deceptive commercial practices; considering how to ensure effective redress for victimized consumers; and co-operating with relevant private sector entities. Pursuant to the document, the Secretary-General shall keep a record of the consumer protection enforcement or policy agency designated as a contact point, and instruct the Committee on Consumer Policy to exchange information on progress and experiences regarding the implementation of this Recommendation, review that information, and report to the Council on this subject.

place of origin of the goods or the jurisdiction indicated by the seller.[224] Supporters of this approach claim that companies dealing mainly with e-commerce may rely on a predictable and well-known legal environment (the basis for the so-called click agreements, for example). The second approach, which places the consumer in a privileged position, is based on the state law of the destination of the goods.[225] The main defect of this solution is that companies may simultaneously be subject to many jurisdictions. One remedy to this would be to intensify the harmonization of consumer protection principles, rendering the jurisdiction issue less significant.[226]

Determining the global value of e-commerce is hard, if not impossible, both because of the lack of a uniform definition of e-commerce, and because of tax issues. Almost all state authorities make attempts to implement online economic activity taxation. However, the task is difficult due to, for instance, varied tax bases.[227] Ever since the beginning of the Internet the United States has made attempts to propagate it as a tax-free zone,[228] whereas the OECD and EU firmly oppose this stance, claiming that the Internet should not enjoy special benefits as regards taxes. The 1998 Ottawa Principles[229] clearly stipulate that there is no difference between tax on traditional transactions and e-transactions.[230] Many US companies raise the same argument, expecting the government to tax online transactions.[231] This quasi-ideological

224 Cf. e.g. S. Ham and R. D. Atkinson (2001) *A Third Way Framework for Global E-Commerce*, Washington, DC: Progressive Policy Institute (<http://www.ndol.org/documents/global_ecommerce.pdf> (accessed 29 January 2011), pp. 11ff.), even though entrepreneurs targeting their conduct at foreign territories are excluded. For more information see International Chamber of Commerce (2001) *Jurisdiction and Applicable Law in Electronic Commerce Policy Statement.* <http://www.iccwbo.org/id478/index.html> (accessed 28 January 2011).

225 E.g. Article 5 of the 1968 Brussels Convention reads that as regards a dispute arising out of sales agreements the place of supply is the venue of dispute resolution; nevertheless, provisions do not mention e-contracts. The opponents of this approach argue that in the case of e-contracts, determination of the place of supply may be difficult. See e.g. N. Rosner (2002) *International Jurisdiction in European Union E-Commerce Contracts*, online only at the Law Library Resources Exchange <http://www.llrx.com/features/eu_ecom.htm> (accessed 29 January 2011). The issue is explicitly disregarded by the Directive on Electronic Commerce: Article 1 para. 4 thereof states that "This Directive does not establish additional rules on private international law nor does it deal with the jurisdiction of Courts".

226 This was the original intention of participants to the drafting of the Hague Convention; however, its scope has been limited to business to business contracts.

227 D. Pinto (2003) *E-Commerce and Source-Based Income Taxation*, Amsterdam: International Bureau of Fiscal Documentation (IBFD) Publications BV, pp. 69–126.

228 In 1998 the United States Congress adopted the Internet Tax Freedom Act, Title XI of PL 105–277 and the Omnibus Appropriations Act.

229 Organization for Economic Co-operation and Development (1998) *Electronic Commerce: Taxation Framework Conditions* ('the Ottawa Principles'). <http://www.oecd.org/dataoecd/46/3/1923256.pdf> (accessed 14 January 2011). For more information see J. Owens (2000) *Taxation in the Wired World*, Paris: OECD. <http://ncsi-net.ncsi.iisc.ernet.in/cyberspace/societal-issues/202/202.pdf> (accessed 14 January 2011).

230 Section II.4.: "The taxation principles which guide governments in relation to conventional commerce should also guide them in relation to electronic commerce".

231 For more information, see D. A. Thomas (2001) 'Current Issues in US State and Federal Taxation of Electronic Commerce', paper delivered at the 16th BILETA Annual Conference, University of Edinburgh. <http://www.bileta.ac.uk/01papers/thomas.html> (accessed 20 January 2011).

dispute is closely related to the question about the relevant place of taxation, and this is yet to be resolved by the United States and the EU. The Ottawa Principles indicate the place of destination, rather than the place of origin. It is in the interest of the US government to collect tax in the place of initiation of the transaction, as most companies dealing with e-commerce have their registered offices in the United States. *A contrario*, endeavors of the EU to levy tax in the place of destination result from a higher concentration of e-buyers than sellers in the old continent. The main initiative as regards the unification of e-transaction customs duties at national level is the 1998 WTO *Ministerial Declaration on Global Electronic Commerce*.[232] The Declaration was for the last time explicitly applied during the 2001 WTO meeting in Doha, and due to the failure of negotiations in Cancun, in 2003, the issue has not been subject to further official discussion, leaving the question of application of the *Ministerial Declaration on Global Electronic Commerce* to the discretion of states. It seems that today it is a common belief that there are no prerequisites for exempting e-transactions from tax.[233]

Another element related to e-commerce and the uncertain status of transaction confidentiality is the scope of state authorities' control over online actions taken by their nationals. The request by the Attorney General of the State of New York that Paypal and Citibank stop effecting transactions using e-money to make payments to Internet casinos, is an example of controversial practice.[234] Such a request directly links e-payments and enforcement of provisions of law by local authorities. At the same time, various forms of e-payments have so far been established in states withwell developed economies. E-payments require a stable, certain and effective legal background. Nevertheless, many developing states still function with economies operating mostly with cash. If non-cash transactions are at all possible in those states (e.g. by debit and credit cards), usually a hand-written signature has to be affixed.[235] This substantial discrepancy directly affects the possibility of further development of e-commerce and expands the gap between the "rich North" and the "poor South" still further. Contrary to the recommended means for reducing the gap, consisting in enabling poorer states to purchase electronic equipments and rendering e-payments available, remedying this issue requires gradual, evolutionary changes to the entire legal and commercial systems of the states, in a manner coherent with existing mechanisms and regulations of developed countries.

The key question as regards e-payment regulations and, above all, tax on e-transactions is which entities are competent to enforce them, i.e. concerning the limits of state fiscal jurisdiction. The tax jurisdiction depends on the physical location

232 World Trade Organization Ministerial Conference (Second Session, 18–20 May 1998) *Ministerial Declaration on Global Electronic Commerce*, Geneva: WTO. <http://www.wto.org/English/tratop_e/ecom_e/mindec1_e.htm> (accessed 29 January 2011).

233 The statistical data shows that 58% of respondents see no prerequisites for such privileged treatment of e-commerce; see S. Basu (2008) 'International Taxation of E-Commerce: Persistent Problems and Possible Developments', 1 *Journal of Information, Law & Technology*, p. 12.

234 For the subsequent agreement, dated 16 August 2002, see Attorney General of the State Of New York Internet Bureau, *Assurance of Discontinuance in the Matter of Paypal, Inc.* <http://www.oag.state.ny.us/bureaus/internet_bureau/pdfs/paypal.pdf> (accessed 28 February 2011).

235 See E. Gelbstein and J. Kurbalija, op. cit., p. 110.

and status of the taxable person since tax regulations are national and thus territorial. Consequently, it is also necessary to assign a specific geographical location to each transaction. Here, one needs to determine whether, as per the principle of tax chargeability at the place where the taxable amount arises, authorities should have powers at the place of registration/residence of the operating entity[236] or at the place where the transaction was effected. One should pay attention to two aspects of tax jurisdiction – legislation and enforcement. This differentiation poses a question about the powers of states, on the one hand to impose the tax obligation (direct taxation) and on the other hand to enforce the obligation through entities subject to their jurisdiction (indirect taxation).[237] Again it proves necessary for international governmental bodies to provide an answer to this issue as well as to those more detailed, practical issues resulting from it.[238]

International Internet Law challenges

The digital divide

The digital divide may be defined as the distance between those who for technical, political, social or economic reasons have access to and the possibility of using ICT, and those who do not.[239] Since the digital divide exists at various levels, opinions as to the extent and significance of the divide are varied: between states, as well as within a state, between urban and rural communities, rich and poor, young and old, women and men. The divides are caused by levels of education, health protection, place of residence, standard of living, employment, and access to clean water and food.[240] The development of information and telecommunication technologies reveals an

236 It should be mentioned that methods of effective and reliable geo-location of users are still being developed.

237 For more, see S. Basu, 'International Taxation of E-Commerce', op. cit., pp. 9ff. and S. Basu (2007) *Global Perspectives on E-Commerce Taxation Law*, Burlington, VT: Ashgate Publishing Ltd, pp. 29ff.

238 More about tax jurisdiction on the Internet, see W. Hellerstein (2003) 'Jurisdiction to Tax Income and Consumption in the New Economy: A Theoretical and Comparative Perspective', 38 *Georgia Law Review*, pp. 1–70; S. Basu, *Global Perspectives*, op. cit., p. 32; and, on BIT tax, J. Stehn (2002) *Leviathan in Cyberspace: How to Tax E-Commerce*, Kiel: Institut für Weltwirtschaft, p. 14.

239 According to the OECD definition, "digital divide" means: "the gap between ICT 'haves' and 'have-nots'": OECD Directorate for Science, Technology and Industry, Committee for Information, Computer and Communications Policy (2005) *Guide to Measuring the Information Society* Paris: OECD, p. 8. <http://www.olis.oecd.org/olis/2005doc.nsf/0/49b3a67e2dbbab51c12570b300392351/DocPDFEng/0.A6?OpenElement&FieldElemFormat=gif> (accessed 7 February 2011), p. 69. However, per H. Williams, the digital divide is "a structural divide between developed and developing countries, and within a country between urban and rural communities, rich and poor, young and old, able and disabled and women and men". See H. Williams (2005) 'Driving the Public Policy Debate: Internet Governance and Development', in W. J. Drake (ed.) *Reforming Internet Governance: Perspectives from the Working Group on Internet Governance (WGIG)*, New York: United Nations Publishing, p. 148.

240 Cf. Summary of the First Meeting of the G8 Digital Opportunity Taskforce (the Dot Force) 30 November 2000. <http://www.g7.utoronto.ca/dot_force/summary-nov-00.html> (accessed 28 February 2011).

enormous disparity between developing and developed states, a disparity which is growing faster than even before and affecting all areas of life.[241]

Opponents of the term digital divide claim that statistics are often misleading and the divide itself *actually* does not increase. In their opinion, traditional statistics based on the number of computers, websites and available data transmission bandwidth should be replaced with data that would allow concentration on the more extensive effects of modern technologies on developing states.[242] China or India are provided as examples of unreliable statistical data: statistics show that China or India are separated from, for instance, European states by the digital divide, but their actual significance and achievements in the IT area far exceed many developed states.[243]

Apart from the problem of the digital divide, another issue often raised in discussions on the division of communities by the criterion of IT use is the issue of so-called common access; that is the access to information and modern technologies for all community members.[244] In order to combat the effects of the digital divide, the WSIS established the Digital Solidarity Fund to support developing states in building telecommunications infrastructure.[245] However, actual worldwide operations aiming at counteracting the existing situation are only occasional. The UN initiated the Digital Diaspora Network to support the development of Africa, Latin America and Caribbean regions by mobilizing resources and assistance on technologies, business and vocational counseling.[246] UNESCO initiatives are of special importance to social issues relating to the digital divide, thanks to the Convention on Protection of Cultural Diversity and the initiation of several projects aimed at propagating linguistic and cultural diversity.[247]

241 This fact was confirmed in the United Nations (2005) *Development Programme Report: International Cooperation at a Crossroads: Aid, Trade and Security in an Unequal Word*, New York: United Nations Publishing. <http://hdr.undp.org/reports/global/2005/> (accessed 14 January 2011), p. 115 and the International Labor Organization's World Commission on the Social Dimension of Globalization (2004) *A Fair Globalization: Creating Opportunities for All.* <http://www.ilo.org/public/english/wcsdg/docs/report.pdf> (accessed 14 January 2011), p. 29. For more information, see S. Nanthikesan (2000) 'Trends in Digital Divide', Mass: Harvard Center for Population and Development Studies. <http://hdr.undp.org/en/reports/global/hdr2001/papers/nanthikesan-1.pdf> (accessed 14 February 2011).

242 See: E. Gelbstein and J. Kurbalija, op. cit., p. 115.

243 More detailed data are presented by S. Nanthikesan, op. cit., pp. 28ff.

244 Cf. chapter 4.

245 Article 28 of the United Nations Agency for Information and Communication Technologies (ITU) (2005) *World Summit on the Information Society Tunis Agenda for the Information Society*, Geneva: ITU. <http://www.itu.int/wsis/docs2/tunis/off/6rev1.html> (accessed 4 January 2011). For more about the document, see chapter 4.

246 The Digital Diaspora Network for Latin America and the Caribbean can be found at <http://www.ddn-latinamericacaribbean.org/index.htm> (accessed 7 February 2011) and Digital Diaspora Network for Africa at <http://www.ddn-africa.org/> (accessed 7 February 2011). More information about both initiatives can also be found on the UNESCO website at <http://portal.unesco.org/shs/en/ev.php-URL_ID=6126&URL_DO=DO_TOPIC&URL_SECTION=201.html> (accessed 1 May 2011).

247 These include numerous conferences, round table meetings, reports, publications and studies. A complete list is available on the UNESCO website at <http://portal.unesco.org/culture/> (accessed 2 January 2011).

Notwithstanding the genesis of the existing divergence between the standards of information technology and literacy within different communities, finding a proper way to reduce them requires sovereigns to accept a common approach towards the potential of the information era. The starting point for any international discussion on the division of competence in the electronic domain is to consider the abovementioned national and regional aspect of legal regulations applied to the Internet. Only when the discussion on a new way of network governance takes account of those so far disregarded issues will sovereigns be in position to reach an effective international compromise.

Teleworking

The Internet has also changed our way working. The global network has perfectly adapted to altering employment relations. The labor market is forced to react promptly to changing national and global economies, thus parties to an employment contract expect it to be, above all, flexible. For employers this means shorter notice periods and for employees the need for better social protection. Apart from the increasing pace of economic and social changes in the tenty-first century, the considerable impact of teleworking on shaping those changes has been observed. It is teleworking, particularly, that induces employers to willingly resign from entering into long-term contracts of employment with many-week notice periods. They are effectively replaced by flexible contracts traditionally falling under provisions of civil law.

Teleworking[248] has become more and more popular, especially given the general availability of broadband Internet via which teleworking may take place, maintaining proportionate outlays and resources. A traditional employment relationship, based on personal performance by an employee, is modified when an employee and an employer enter into a teleworking contract.

The literature defines the phenomenon as "computer-supported activity regularly or temporarily exercised partly outside the main premises of the employer".[249] At the same time it is emphasized that telework, being a relatively new notion, is yet to be assigned a clear set of references. It is said to include, *inter alia*, electronic homeworking,[250] tele-cottages and neighborhood centers,[251] mobile or nomadic

248 "E-working", "e-work", "telework", "telecommuting", "working from home" (WFH) all refer to work performed away from premises usually used for this purpose, such as offices or plants, by employees in their own homes, cars, airplanes or from abroad. Work may also be performed in an electronic form and be delivered to the employer. See C. L. Sia et al. (2004) 'Effects of Environmental Uncertainty on Organizational Intention to Adopt Distributed Work Arrangements', 51 *Engineering Management*, pp. 253–267. Telework can mean work rendered through other media, such as telephone or teletext.

249 W. Hromadka and F. Maschmann (2000) *Arbeitsrecht Band 1: Individualarbeitsrecht*, 3rd edn., New York: Springer, pp. 99–100.

250 Work is performed in the place where the employee resides, and the employee communicates with the employer via electronic means. See L. Mitrus (2001) *Telepraca jako nowa forma zatrudnienia*, 3 *Transformacje Prawa Prywatnego*, pp. 11–12.

251 This type of telework is based on common use by several tele-employees of devices available in a telecenter in the vicinity of their place of residence. However, the organization of such telecenters is not specified - should the devices be a joint investment of employees, employer (one or several, for whom the work is to be rendered) or of local authorities (public libraries or similar institutions)? Ibid.

networks,[252] group or team telework[253] and call-centers and remote offices,[254] although it would be challenging to indicate clear divisions between the existing forms of telework.[255] By reason of inconsistent views from legal academics and commentators,[256] the concept of telework has not been clearly defined in legal terms and currently combines many definitions and, in principle, is based on two distinctive formal criteria: the place of work (outside the registered office of the employer)[257] and the use of modern technologies to undertake the work.[258] It should be also noted that the notion of telework may not be used to refer to work consisting of the manufacturing of material goods; it is rather reserved for the provision of services or information.[259] Modifications introduced by telework to the concept of employment,[260] changed the quality of employment structure. Wider access to the Internet means that temporary and short-term work has been substantially popularized. Frequent renewal of short-term employment contracts for the performance of a specific task has become a common practice. The direct consequence of this employment structure modification is the reduction of employee social care standards – if the employee is to perform his or her

252 The term refers to work performed not only from the place of the employee's residence, but from any place where the employee decides to perform it. Ibid.

253 Work performed by a team of employees, whose cooperation is not based on personal contacts but on exchange of digitized information. Ibid.

254 This term refers to "auxiliary" offices established by companies, which have contact with the supervising company exclusively by an electronic network. Ibid.

255 The criterion of division is the place of work performance (if it is the place of residence of the employee, such work is referred to as "home based teleworking"; if the work is performed outside the place it is referred to as "nomadic teleworking"; and "ad hoc teleworking" is if the work is performed occasionally outside the registered office of the employer). Another division based on time spent on performing the work via an electronic network is proposed by P. James in (2004) *Is Teleworking Sustainable? – An Analysis of its Economic, Environmental and Social Impact*, Peterborough, UK: SusTel Project. <http://www.sustel.org/documents/Reports/final%20report%20-%20july%202004%20v2.pdf> (accessed 27 February 2011) p. 8.

256 The International Labor Organization presented an extensive study pertaining to teleworking, see V. Di Martino (2001) *The High Road To Teleworking*, Geneva: ILO. <www.ilo.org/public/english/protection/safework/telework/hrdptl.pdf> (accessed 27 February 2011).

257 It does not have to be the place of residence of the employee. The only condition to recognize a given type of performance as telework is that the work or a considerable part thereof is performed outside the office of the company.

258 Not only the Internet; telework also includes contacting the employer via a telephone.

259 W. Hromadka and F. Maschmann, op. cit., p. 100.

260 The key element that distinguishes telework is the lack of a fundamental feature of the contract of employment, i.e. the obligation to render work in place indicated by the employer. In the case of work performed by electronic networks, this obligation is groundless; what is significant in this context is the performance of a task delegated to an employee in an agreed manner and not the actual physical location of the computer the employee uses to perform the task. Telework is thus directly related to considerable changes in work organization. The office space and specific conditions the employer is usually obliged to ensure are unnecessary. The employee decides about the circumstances in which he or she renders work, at the same time the costs of organization and maintenance of workplaces are considerably reduced on the part of the employer, as it does not have to maintain premises. From economic perspective, this inherent feature of telework saves time for the employee, who may resign from everyday commuting to work. Modern telecommunication has blurred the traditional division of employees' time into work, free time and time for rest or sleep (traditionally separated into three, equal, 8-hour intervals). The beginning and end of work time are more and more difficult to determine.

functions without a (previously commonly applicable) contract of employment for an unspecified period, but within periods specified by the employer, the employee will not benefit from e.g. obligatory health benefits or insurance that are within the traditional scope of employment contracts. Consequently, the employee social care standard is considerably reduced, and in this case it is the employee that is liable for providing sufficient working conditions as well as health and social care. From the perspective of law, telework does not clearly fall into traditional legal categories, for it may refer to persons running their own business (the self-employed) and traditional employees as well as persons working under civil contracts. Therefore, each of the three groups, even though falling within the ambit of teleworking, is subject to different regulations. Labor law provisions, having direct effect within the area of tax and social insurance laws, do not apply to two out of the three abovementioned groups.[261]

There is no escaping the fact that the current formulation of labor law does not keep abreast of the requirements set by developing modern technologies. To this end it will be necessary to answer the fundamental question – should and may teleworking be regulated by labor law, or would it be more reasonable to exclude the concept from this branch of law? To reformulate the question, one may also suggest the possibility of extending the scope of labor law into other fields traditionally regulated by civil law. Beyond any doubt, traditional labor law provisions stipulating the fundamental principle that the work is to be rendered in person in the office of the employer, do not apply to teleworking.[262] Offshoring of IT services has also increased with the advent of call centers and information or data processing centers. The direct and first effect of such practice is the internationalization of employment relations, which should be followed by the internationalization of worker protection standards. It is also necessary to modify the labor law system as it pertains to permissible weekly or daily work performance periods (and the possibility of verifying whether such provisions are observed). Such amendments shall require new labor law principles regulating such issues as working hours, protection of employee rights and, equally important, remuneration. Nowadays, so-called virtual enterprises are established which give up traditionally understood employment plants in favor of teleworkers.[263] Equally important is the issue of privacy in the work place and legally set limits to employer interference in electronic data by or about their employees.[264] Apart from the traditional concept of electronic data confidentiality, meaning emails stored in the employer's server, will there be any new areas in which employer will be able to interfere? Should cookie files of teleworkers be verified? Or is it only results of their work that should be subject to review?[265]

261 The International Labor Organization recommends the application of the ILO Convention (No 177) and Recommendation (No 184) pertaining to work at home. Neither of the said documents directly refers to the issue of telework, and their application raises serious doubts or even objection: V. Di Martino, op. cit., p. 107.

262 For more about the debate concerning the nature of telework from the labor law perspective, see V. Di Martino, op. cit., pp. 104–105, which specifies the extra-legal features that form the notion of a telework relationship.

263 Cf. P. James, op. cit., p. 9.

264 For a detailed analysis see N. B. Fairweather (1999) 'Surveillance in Employment: The Case of Teleworking', 22(1) *Journal of Business Ethics*, pp. 39–49.

265 To date, the legal frameworks of France, Portugal and Great Britain indicate a trend to limit supervision over employees. An employer is generally obliged to warn an employee before any monitoring actions

Another crucial aspect that cannot be disregarded is the considerable influence of the Internet on the situation of disabled persons on the labor market. If there is no problem of commuting between home and workplace and adapting office premises to the needs of a disabled person, he or she becomes a full labor market participant with the same rights. The opportunities that the Internet offers for the employment of disabled persons is one of the aspects that must be considered in any discussions on telework regulation.[266]

Traditionally, labor law has been regulated by national provisions. Nevertheless, in the era of globalization, and especially the dominating influence of the Internet, it seems necessary to internationalize such regulations. Given the growing number of employees rendering work to foreign entities and cooperating with teams of a supranational nature, an urgent need to introduce relevant international regulations arises. It is necessary to lay down minimum standards of teleworker protection, not to mention the development of an appropriate legal scheme within which telework should be performed. In the light of the considerable globalization of the labor market it may prove necessary to modify existing international agreements on labor law so that they can be applied to workers rendering work via electronic means. It also seems necessary to specify whether such agreements shall be subject to labor law provisions (if so, the agreements have to be substantially modified to taking account of those issues mentioned above), or whether such agreements will be deemed civil law agreements (if so, they have to take account of previously mentioned international agreements on the unification of international trade and the clear limits of sovereign state competence). Another issue directly relating to state jurisdiction is the resolution of employee disputes when the registered office of the employer and the place of the employee's residence are not located within the area of one state's competence.

E-government

It is not only citizens of information communities, but also governments all over the world, who have learned to appreciate the advantages of electronic communication. Developed and developing states, central and local authorities, find their place

were taken. In Denmark, a court held that the dismissal of an employee for sending private emails and visiting chat rooms of pornographic content was incompliant with the law as the employer failed to draw up Internet use regulations stipulating a prohibition on using it for private purposes. Another reason given by the court was that the manner in which the employee used the Internet did not have negative impact on the employee's professional duties (see M. Møller Johansen (2003) *New Technology and Respect for Privacy/Private Life at the Workplace – the Case of Denmark*, Dublin: European Industrial Relations Observatory. <http://eurofound.europa.eu/eiro/2003/07/word/dk0304103s.doc> (accessed 29 January 2011), p. 6). A 1999 decision of the German *Labor Court Brunswick case* (Arbeitsgericht Braunschweig) that 60 graphic files containing child pornography, kept by the employee of a municipal kindergarten on a computer the employee used at work, justified dismissal without notice if there was a suspicion that he downloaded the files due to pedophile tendencies: Judgment 3 Ca 370/98 NZA-RR 1999, 192. <http://www.netlaw.de/urteile/agbr_01.htm> (accessed 15 January 2011). The European Trade Union Confederation presents a very precise solution to the issues concerned, suggesting that teleworkers should be entitled to switch off from the network, see V. Di Martino, op. cit., p. 108.

266 For more about the impact of telework on occupational status, see V. Di Martino, op. cit., pp. 82ff.

in the electronic network. E-government is the use of information and communication technology in public administrations, which combine with organizational change and new skills in order to improve public services and democratic processes and strengthen support for public policies.[267] As with e-commerce, which enables entrepreneurs to effect transactions more efficiently (B2B) and approach the customer (B2C), e-government aims at establishing closer relations between the government and citizen (G2C, government-to-citizen), government and businesses (G2B, government-to-business) and mutual relations between governmental bodies (G2G, government-to-government).[268] The idea of e-government can only be found among national practices.[269] Research on the practice and mission of e-government comprises three areas:[270] e-government,[271] e-service[272] and e-learning.[273]

267 European Commission (2004) *Staff Working Paper. e-Europe 2005 Mid-Term Review*, Background Papers, COM (2004) 108. <http//ec.europa.eu/information_society/eeurope/2005/doc/highlights/whats_new/mtr_wp_isc_version1.41.doc> (accessed 1 June 2011), p. 5. The World Bank defines e-government as the use of IT technologies by governmental bodies, enabling them to effect relations with nationals, businesses and other branches of power. The purpose of the activities is to ensure better quality of services provided by the government, improvement of relations with industry and entrepreneurs and reinforcement of society's influence on decisions. Benefits resulting from e-government also include eliminating corruption and increasing the transparency of the state apparatus.

268 For more information see K. Barzilai-Nahon and H. J. Scholl (2007) 'Similarities and Differences of E-Commerce and E-Government: Insights from a Pilot Study', paper given at the 40th Annual Hawaii International Conference on System Sciences (HICSS'07). <http://csdl.computer.org/comp/proceedings/hicss/2007/2755/00/27550092c.pdf> (accessed 4 February 2011). For a detailed study of e-democracy problems and perspectives, see OECD (2003) *Promise and Problems of E-Democracy*, Paris: OECD. <http://www.oecd.org/dataoecd/9/11/35176328.pdf> (accessed 4 February 2011).

269 The World Bank is responsible for gathering information on the progress of the evolution.

270 See Commonwealth Centre for Electronic Governance (2002) *International Tracking Survey Report No. 1 – E-Government, E-Governance and E-Democracy: A Background Discussion Paper*, London: Commonwealth Centre for Electronic Governance. <http://www.electronicgov.net/pubs/research_papers/tracking5/IntlTracking%20Report%20Number%201Jan02.doc> (accessed 4 February 2011). Cf. e.g. OECD *Promise and Problems*, op. cit., p. 151, which indicates the necessity of developing the 5-way information exchange necessary for effective e-democracy functioning: 1. Government to Citizen (G2C), 2. Citizen to Government (C2G), 3. Representative to Citizen (R2C), 4. Citizen to Representative (C2R), and 5. Citizen to Citizen (C2C).

271 E-government is the use of information and communication technology in public administrations combined with organizational change and new skills in order to improve public services and democratic processes and strengthen support to public policies: European Commission (2004) *Staff Working Paper. e-Europe 2005 Mid-Term Review*, op. cit., p. 5.

272 E-services consist in allowing the access to government services using electronic means. They concern those actions of state administrations which may be rendered online. This means, *inter alia*, the possibility of lodging a request for a license or for advice and consultations, and the provision of services directed at their addressees (e.g. request for residence permit, information about traffic or weather or free e-mail services). Many contacts between local authorities and citizens are maintained only when there is a one-off practical need – instances include passport services, marital status records and entries to official registers and databases, which may be effected via an electronic network. The indicator of e-government development in Europe is the availability of 20 basic public services (12 services for citizens; 8 for business). For the availability of services and the degree of their interactivity, see European Commission (2004) *Staff Working Paper: e-Europe 2005 Mid-Term Review*, p. 7.

273 E-learning means using communication technologies to gain knowledge. The *e-Europe Review* does not define the term, it only mentions that the telecommunications infrastructure is used to improve

The potential of e-democracy considerably exceeds previous public e-services achievements. Instances of the application of electronic solutions in public administration can be found in Europe,[274] as well as in the United States[275] and China.[276] It is reflected both by the availability of state offices' websites on the Internet, as well as providing citizens with the possibility of using the Internet to performing state administration actions (submitting tax returns, obtaining licenses etc.). The Internet also holds much potential for organizing democratic elections.[277] Today, IT technologies within the scope of public administration are still an experiment, rather than carefully organized joint undertakings; nevertheless, the underlying potential may not be disregarded. Procedures for introducing changes into political organizations and cultures require time, and most of all, outlays and infrastructure development. Problems of a technical nature, however, underlie these considerations. Fundamental international challenges to e-government and e-democracy include territorial, national and regional obstacles. Effective functioning of state institutions online requires unification of procedures falling outside the ambit of the Internet. Consequently, along with the planned establishment of, for example, medical records and entries to health fund records, which the insured would carry on him on herself, it would be necessary to unify the scope of data collected in particular states so that it could be used by the common system (such plans so far concern only the European Community, nevertheless, it seems that the universality of the Internet requires us to consider the possibility of a far reaching extension of the function). Should

qualifications and learning; European Commission (2004) *Staff Working Paper: e-Europe 2005 Mid-term Review*, p. 10.

274 The first parliamentary elections in the world which enabled one to vote via the Internet were held on 26–28 February 2007 in Estonia, and were mainly a media success (only 3 % of voters participated in the elections via the Internet). For more information, see 'Estonia Scores World Web First in National Polls', *Information Week*, 28 February 2007. <http://www.informationweek.com/management/showArticle.jhtml?articleID=197700272> (accessed 9 January 2011).

275 Attempts to use the Internet to exercise the democratic functions of the state were made in the United States during the presidential elections in 2004. However, the results of applying available technologies were far from expected. In New Orleans several ballot machines broke down on the day of elections and long queues were formed to cast a vote. In Ohio, one ballot machine unexpectedly counted four thousand votes in favour of George Bush and in North Carolina over 4,500 votes were lost as a result of the failure of the electronic data storage system. In the United States almost one third of all votes in the 2004 presidential elections were cast via an electronic network. Most machines operated using software which was neither publically disclosed nor subject to public verification (for safety and protection against interference reasons). Almost none of the suppliers provided voters with the possibility of verifying the fact that their votes were actually forwarded to final counting. It turned out that most machine operators were not properly qualified. At the same time, the technical support personnel for the ballot machines had unlimited access to the system during voting. This experiment proved that mechanisms underlying e-democracy are still not sufficiently developed to be safely applied to democratic procedures. The result of the numerous errors was a series of actions brought against the relevant electoral commissions, e.g. *Schade* v. *Maryland State Board of Elections* (2007) 401 Md.1; *Americans for Safe Access* v. *County of Alameda; Soubirous* v. *Riverside County (California Court of Appeals); Gusciora and others* v. *Codey and others (New Jersey)* and so on. For more information, see Electronic Frontier Foundation 'E-Voting'. <http://www.eff.org/Activism/E-voting/> (accessed 23 January 2011).

276 Ibid.

277 Taking account of remarks made above.

e-government, and *a fortiori* e-democracy, exceed the borders of particular states, it would be essential to unify those regulatory provisions to which e-government would apply (in particular privacy protection or data security). E-government is one of the priorities of the European Community, expressed in the eEurope 2005 Action Plan[278] and the i2010 plan.[279] In her address delivered at the end of 2005, Viviane Reding, the EU's Commissioner for Information Society and Media, summed up the implementation of the eEurope 2005 plan by the member states and pointed to further development of the sector. Benefits accruing from the implementation of electronic state services include reducing the administration costs and the time spent by the public in visiting state offices. If used reasonably, e-government will allow maintenance of an existing social policy model and contribute to increasing the effectiveness of government functioning.[280]

Jurisdiction

All of the foregoing issues concerning the regulation of actions taken using the Internet have one common denominator. Each problem boils down to the confusion over the limits of competence of particular regulating states. Various regulations relating to telework or the freedom of speech collide in the limitless space of the Internet. Therefore, jurisdiction is the aspect of the debate on Internet governance that requires immediate attention and solution. The number of Internet-related disputes is still growing. Lack of clarity regarding jurisdiction may produce two effects within a short time: the inability of a state to exercise its legislative and executive power and the inability of natural and juridical persons to enjoy the right to a fair and public hearing of their case. Other potential consequences include the lack of legal certainty on the Internet, slower development of e-commerce, and the informal division of the Internet into independent spheres of relative legal certainty. The relationship between jurisdiction and the Internet comprises an inherent element of uncertainty, for

278 European Union Communication from the Commission to the Council, the European Parliament, the European Economic and Social Committee and the Committee of the Regions (1999) *e-Europe 2005: An Information Society for All*, COM (1999) 687. <http://ec.europa.eu/information_society/eeurope/2002/news_library/documents/eeurope2005/eeurope2005_en.pdf> (accessed 14 January 2011).

279 In the first year of implementation of the initiative (2005–2006) it covered a wide spectrum of actions, including, *inter alia*, a detailed review of existing EU regulations pertaining to e-communication, comparing quantitative particulars as regards broadband access, updating the Television-Without-Frontiers Directive, initiating the Film Online project to promote electronic distribution of cinematographic works, analyzing and implementing radio frequency identification technologies, further implementing e-inclusion and e-government initiatives or intelligent cars; see European Commission, Information Society and Media DG (2006) *A Summary of the First Year's Results: The Single European Information Space Achievements May 2005/2006*, Information sheet 7.5. <http://ec.europa.eu/information_society/eeurope/i2010/docs/info_sheets/7-5-i2010-results-en.pdf> (accessed 4 February 2011).

280 The address of Commissioner Viviane Reding, at Stockholm on 9 December 2005 ('Open Government and Governance in the On-Line Society') can be located at <http://ec.europa.eu/information_society/activities/egovernment_research/doc/minconf2005/keynote_speech_%209.12.pdf> (accessed 11 January 2011).

jurisdiction is, above all, based on geographical divisions of the entire globe into state territories which may not be made in the electronic space. As mentioned above, there are three fundamental aspects of jurisdiction. It may be perceived as looking for an answer to the question about the competence of the court (judicial jurisdiction), the rights applicable to particular circumstances (substantive, legislative jurisdiction) or the manner of implementation of courts' or law-makers' decisions (executive jurisdiction). The following three types of relations, specified above, are used for indicating the grounds for the exercise of jurisdiction: territorial relations, personal relations and effects relations. Issues relating to Internet jurisdiction arise when disputes include extraterritorial elements (e.g. persons from various states or international transactions). Drawing analogies with, or applying provisions of traditional real world regulations to Internet-related issues produce major problems which restrict the scope of their application, such as the laws governing e-transactions between residents of two different states, controversial questions about the limits of freedom of speech and privacy on the Internet or, in the case of telework, a need to establish international standards for the legal protection of employees. International agreement proves even more essential with respect to all issues relating to criminal law, where, next to imperfect technology for identifying individuals online, it is necessary to establish effectively a functioning co-operation network within the scope of crime detection and investigation (the Council of Europe Convention on Cybercrime, in spite of the intention of its authors and the hopes attached to it, does not play this role). International provisions regulating international telecommunications services are equally significant, with special consideration needed regarding respecting the right to freedom of speech, local understanding of morality protection, provisions on the freedom of competition and a ban on unfair competition. On top of the wide range of legislative needs is a growing necessity to guarantee global network security consisting in, above all, international co-operation. Possible solutions to the problem of jurisdictional conflicts may be based on modernization of private international law, harmonization of national laws, use of international arbitration and/or the application of technical solutions that would enable one to determine the origin of data placed on the Internet more precisely than it is possible today. Nevertheless, state authorities are not in a position to resolve practical problems relating to jurisdictional conflicts on their own, and very few international legal acts make any attempt to address Internet-related jurisdictional issues, while international co-operation is essential if we are to resolve such problems. Jurisdictional issues constitute a key concern of participants to the international debate on Internet governance.

3 Examples of current national practice

Summary of differences

Preliminary comments

As mentioned before, in light of the existing international law theory and practice, the jurisdictional powers of a state are limited by the need to respect the interests and actions of foreign sovereigns. Each state is obliged to impose restraint and self-limitation in the exercise of jurisdiction in cases with a foreign element and should avoid unjustified interference in the competence of others.

Legislative competence is the grounds for exercise of all jurisdictional powers, and constitutes the first and fundamental element of all analyses. It is the form thereof that actually determines state competence.

The traditional form of state legislative jurisdiction is based, above all, on the criterion of territorial powers. This criterion is also applied with respect to Internet-related regulations: law makers establish national provisions to regulate the Internet content available in their territory, however, the effects of direct application of the territoriality principle in this context substantially exceed the physical borders of the regulating entity. States make attempts to maintain as extensive sovereignty as possible to control activities outside their territories, if such activities produce effects within their territories (even if such control tends to be ineffective). The outcome of this is the conflict of state competence within the scope of actions taken using the electronic network. Therefore, it is necessary to establish international co-operation frameworks specifying the area of competence of each sovereign as soon as possible.[1]

In the absence of legal regulations adapted to the specificity of the Internet, and attempts to regulate the medium by reference to existing practice in areas not related to this medium, various states developed individual approaches to the manner of resolving legal issues pertaining to electronic contacts. The complex issues of legal regulation of the Internet also include the fact that the key decision-maker as regards the technical aspects of the global network (including the issues related to assigning of domain addresses) is ICANN, which remains an entity of US national law.

A general reflection on the problem briefly outlined in the previous chapter suggests that it poses many challenges not only to international law: the problem of *national* regulation of the Internet still remains a legislative Gordian knot. Law-makers' existing

1 Cf. D. Johnson and D. Post (1996) 'Law and Borders – the Rise of Law in Cyberspace', op. cit.

endeavors mostly concern national spaces and are adaptations of the existing local laws (including private international law regulations) to actions performed on the Internet. They refer, above all, to economic activity and national defense assurance, disregarding such issues as the privacy protection and other human rights. Adopted regulations are fragmentary and of very limited territorial scope. Previous international consensus, arrived at primarily by way of developing case law, has determined only that the place of potential availability of a transmission placed on the Internet or the location of equipment enabling data storage and transmission (i.e. servers or routers) should not be the basis for determining state jurisdiction and relevant laws, even though there is no clear written agreement as to that content and some judicial decisions on the issue still vary. The agreement pertaining to the contract law is also drawn with a thin line: two ways of resolving civil disputes arising in connection with the Internet are postulated (however, still requiring sufficient legal awareness of trade participants and providing no fundamental principles should the parties fail to meet their obligations or not be content with the outcome). First and foremost, it is postulated that contractual relations be subject to the legal system specified by the parties themselves; so far the selection of governing law has been the most effective solution. The other possible solution is to submit Internet-related disputes to commercial arbitration[2] (as mentioned above, such services in disputes over Internet domains are rendered by ICANN, WIPO and local arbitration courts). The obvious conclusion, however, is that these ways are effective only when both parties consent to the specified resolution of the conflict. The best solution would be to develop mechanisms which identify bodies competent to resolve international disputes in the absence of any contractual settlement among or between the disputing parties. Whilst such a mechanism might be possible for civil law disputes, however, on the issue of exercising criminal jurisdiction, no uniform practice among states has been developed so far and considering the cultural differences reflected in national criminal legislations, is unlikely to follow.[3]

In this part of the study the author will present three approaches to the manner of regulating the Internet, each radically different and at the same time most significant for further development of the international practice. It is arguable that only two stances should be presented: European – based on the principles of the private international law, as applied to electronic exchange and its results; and North American (US and Canadian) – based on an analogy with earlier inter-state and international case law, issued under the "minimum contact" provisions and the purposeful

2 For more about the resolution of disputes in cyberspace by arbitration, see e.g., C. B. Springer (2001) 'Master of the Domain (Name): a History of Domain Name Litigation and the Emergence of the Anticybersquatting Consumer Protection Act and Uniform Dispute Resolution Policy', 17 *Computer & High Technology Law Journal*, pp. 316ff.; E. E. Katsh, M. E. Katsh and J. Rifkin (2001) *Online Dispute Resolution: Resolving Conflicts in Cyberspace*, New York: Jossey-Bass; M. E. Katsh (1996) 'Dispute Resolution In Cyberspace' 28 *Connecticut Law Review* p. 953. <http://www.umass.edu/legal/articles/uconn.html> (accessed 18 January 2011); and H. H. Perritt (2000) 'Dispute Resolution in Cyberspace: Demand for New Forms of ADR', 15(3) *Ohio State Journal on Dispute Resolution*. <http://works.bepress.com/henry_perritt/20/> (accessed 19 April 2006).

3 See generally B. Wojciechowski (2010) *Philosophical Approach to the Interculturality of Criminal Law*, Frankfurt: Peter Lang.

availment principle. The comparison of just these two examples of state practice (Europe and US/Canada), even though based on similar legal approach to regulating cyberspace, reveal irreconcilable discrepancies in approach. Nevertheless, in order to depict a more complete, global view of the trends in Internet policies and regulations, the author will also consider the regulatory approaches of China and Singapore, which are representative of effectively functioning Asian filtering policies, yet utterly different from the abovementioned Western ones. The author's consideration will focus on the limits of state competence, based on decisions made by state authorities and provided justifications. Numerous areas of legislation are to be compared, the common denominator of which will be the jurisdictional basis for the exercise of powers by state authorities. The expected conclusion of this analysis is to present a picture of various approaches to the problem of regulating actions arising through cyberspace.

North America

The position and practice of the United States towards regulating cyberspace are of particular significance: being the cradle of the Internet, the United States has the potential technical capability to influence the functioning of the Web worldwide, through US-based organizations administering key Internet resources (primarily ICANN, IANA and the majority of gTLDs registrars). As opposed to most situations regulated by the law, the condition precedent to effectively regulating cyberspace is having appropriate technology. Thus, the one who administers Internet root zone files and protocols actually holds crucial power over the entire network. The technical form of the key DNS protocol is actually determined by ICANN.[4] Also, US courts were the first to face the legal challenges posed by mass electronic contacts and are thus the originators of Internet case law. Lessons learned from the application of jurisdictional principles to inter-state cases were subsequently transferred to international disputes. Decisions issued in the United States and the established line of adjudication have become the basis of further resolutions in the entire American continent and have also been reflected in European legal documents.

The basis for exercising jurisdiction by district courts is 28 USC § 1331. It states that district courts shall have original jurisdiction over all civil actions arising under the Constitution, laws, or treaties of the United States. The application of this principle is complemented by the explanation in the *Restatement*: "a state may exercise jurisdiction through its courts to adjudicate with respect to persons or a thing if the relationship of the state to the persons or thing is such as to make the exercise of jurisdiction reasonable".[5] Therefore, the exercise thereof shall in each case be reasonable if the claim concerns a defendant physically located in the territory of the forum state (as per the international principle of exercising territorial jurisdiction). Additionally, US practice requires that several additional prerequisites be met with respect to an

4 Cf. chapter 4.

5 *Restatement* § 421 (1).

out-of-state defendant. First and foremost, the requirements of due process must be met, that is above all that the state may exercise its powers only if the defendant maintains "minimum contacts" with the forum. This requirement is imposed by the Fifth Amendment to the US Constitution, which stipulates that a state shall not "deprive any person of life, liberty, or property, without due process of law". Section one of the Fourteenth Amendment to the US Constitution refers this obligation onto state authorities, consequently state constitutions reflect the same constitutional principles. For this reason in inter-state cases the court has jurisdiction if it is possible in the light of two regulations: the relevant local long-arm statute and the constitutional due process clause.

Long-arm statutes are state statutes of varied form. Provisions thereof specify the principles of state jurisdiction over defendants outside the state in civil procedure. Most existing statutes of such type are based on the model statute, the Uniform Interstate and International Procedure Act (UIIPA) approved by the Commission on Uniform State Laws in 1962. In light of the provisions thereof, the district court may exercise personal jurisdiction over a natural person residing in the state, as well as a juridical person incorporated under the laws of the state or having the main place of operations in the state. UIIPA names the grounds for exercising personal jurisdiction as a jurisdiction based upon an enduring relationship (§ 1.02 UIIPA). Furthermore, the court may exercise personal jurisdiction with respect to a person who, acting directly or through an agent, conducts business in the state, enters into contracts with the state for the supply of services or goods, or by actions or omissions in the territory of the state inflicts damage therein. The court may also recognize its jurisdiction with respect to those defendants who inflict damage in the forum state territory by actions or omissions conducted outside the territory of the state, if they conduct regular business or participate in any continuous actions or generate income on trading in goods or rendering services in such state. Exercising state jurisdiction may also result from the fact that real property, with respect to which the defendant has a legal interest, is located in the state's territory. This set of principles is referred to as personal jurisdiction based on conduct (§ 1.03 UIIPA). The long-arm statute of Illinois of 1955 constituted the basis for developing the UIIPA.[6] As it slightly differs from the framework proposed by the Commission on Uniform State Laws, it has become the model for a particular group of such statutes. The bases for jurisdiction indicated therein include carrying out business in the territory of the state, committing a tort in the territory of the state and owning, holding or using real property in the territory of the state. They also include agreements on liability for exercising ownership rights in the territory of the state, including strict liability. More importantly, the long-arm statute of Illinois includes an additional clause stipulating the possibility of exercising jurisdiction "on any other basis now or hereafter permitted by the Illinois Constitution and the Constitution of the United States" (the so-called "catch all" clause). The clause allows for the maximum extension of jurisdictional competence of the state authorities without failing to meet the due process requirements.

6 Illinois 'long-arm' statute, 1955, 735 ILCS 5/2–209.

Whether or not the requirement of due process in inter-state cases is met is determined on the basis of the "minimum contacts" requirement. In accordance therewith, a defendant from outside the state has to have maintained certain minimum contacts with the forum, following which that defendant may reasonably expect to be summoned before a court of a given state in the event of a dispute arising. The constitutional obligation to guarantee due process to defendants was elaborated on by the Supreme Court of the United States in the case *International Shoe Co.* v. *Washington.*[7] The Court held that "due process requires only that, in order to subject a defendant to a judgment *in personam*, if he be not present within the territory of the forum, he have certain minimum contacts with it such that the maintenance of the suit does not offend 'traditional notions of fair play and substantial justice'".

In accordance with this judgment, the minimum contacts standard is not a mechanically carried out test but a case-by-case verification, the result of which depends "upon the quality and nature of the activity in relation to the fair and orderly administration of the laws". Consequently, if the nature and quality of actions are regular and systematic, the district court is entitled to exercise the jurisdiction.

Generally speaking, the existence of a jurisdictional right is proved based on continuous, regular and systematic contacts between the defendant and the forum. Special jurisdiction, however, exists when the claim results directly from contacts of the defendant with the forum state. Since the *International Shoe* decision, the Supreme Court and courts of appeal have established additional criteria to determine whether jurisdiction over a non-resident is justified. In order for these criteria to be met it has to be proved that the defendant purposefully availed himself or herself of the laws of the forum state, so that he or she may reasonably expect to receive a claim from such state[8] and that the forum state has a reasonable interest in resolving the dispute.[9]

These state jurisdictional principles were confronted at the end of 1990s with a hail of claims resulting from inter-state interactions performed via the Internet. The first decisions pertaining to inter-state relations based on electronic contacts were issued in the second half of the 1990s. They were characterized by extreme discrepancies in the interpretation of inter-state jurisdictional principles. Many judges decided to apply the simplest analogy, disregarding the special, global nature of the medium they had to face. They decided to exercise their jurisdictional powers only if the effects of actions taken outside the state were noticeable within its territory.[10] Most often the judges invoked the personal jurisdiction resulting from actions of the entity (§ 1.03 UIIPA),[11] which is that the defendant, when producing effects within the

7 (1945) 326 US 310.

8 The concept has been developed in the following cases: *Burger King Corp.* v. *Rudzewicz* (1985) 471 US 462, 475, *Schwarzenegger* v. *Fred Martin Motor Co.* (2004) 374 F.3d 797, 802 (9 Cir.), *United States* v. *Swiss American Bank, Ltd.* (2001) 274 F.3d 610, 623–24 (1 Cir.), and *Ballard* v. *Savage* (1995) 65 F.3d 1495, 1498 (9 Cir.).

9 E.g. *Coughenour* v. *State Auto Property and Casualty Insurance Company* (1995) 62 F.3d 1423 and *Panavision Int'l, L.P.* v. *Toeppen* (1998) 141 F.3d 1316 (9 Cir.).

10 See: the *Granite Gate* case, discussed further herein.

11 In continental terms this may be compared to invoking the effects principle.

forum territory, should have been aware of the responsibility he or she would bear within its area. The effects principle was also applied to criminal cases.

In the case *United States* v. *Thomas*, which concerned the operator of e-bulletin distributing, *inter alia*, to Tennessee, pornographic materials forbidden therein, the Sixth District Court held that "the effects of the Defendants' criminal conduct reached the Western District of Tennessee, and that district was suitable for accurate fact-finding."[12] Similarly, in the first international case concerning trademark infringement online, *Playboy Enterprises, Inc.* v. *Chuckleberry Publishing, Inc.*,[13] the New York court recognized its jurisdiction to hear the case based on the availability of services provided online in the US directly from Italy, yet it also consciously held that:

> The Internet is a world-wide phenomenon, accessible from every corner of the globe. [The defendant] cannot be prohibited from operating its Internet site merely because the site is accessible from within one country in which its product is banned. To hold otherwise 'would be tantamount to a declaration that this Court, and every other court throughout the world, may assert jurisdiction over all information providers on the global World Wide Web'.

The most significant decision based on the local effects of actions performed using the global network was the 1997 decision in the *Minnesota* v. *Granite Gate Resorts, Inc.*[14] case. Following the "Warning to all Internet Users and Providers"[15] – a Minnesota Attorney General memorandum, published shortly before the case was presented to the Minnesota court – the Minnesota Attorney General, H. H. Humphrey III, brought to justice operators of websites residing and operating from outside the state, based solely on the fact that the website they had operated made available information on gambling services which were prohibited within the state (the website contained an advertisement for an Internet casino which was about to commence operation). The website administrators were convicted of violation of state gambling laws even though they did not offer gambling services within the state. The court, acknowledging the arguments raised by Attorney General, concluded:

> computer hits on Defendants' Websites and the fact that the advertisements give consumers phone numbers to call, along with the fact that (. . .) mailing list include Minnesota residents, are more than sufficient evidence that Defendants

12 *United States* v. *Thomas* (1996) 74 F.3d 701 (6 Cir.). It is worth mentioning that the defendant, as part of its website operation, required that subscribers first register and provide their personal data and place of residence. Therefore he was aware of the geographical location of the recipients of its electronic dispatches.

13 (1996) 939 F. Supp. 1032 (SDNY).

14 (1997) 568 NW 2d 715 (Minn. Ct. App.).

15 This document warned that state jurisdiction would be exercised with respect to "persons who transmit information via the Internet knowing that information will be disseminated in Minnesota." Pursuant to the warning, "principles of Minnesota law apply equally to activities on the Internet. Individuals and organizations outside of Minnesota who disseminate information in Minnesota via the Internet and thereby cause a result to occur in Minnesota are subject to state criminal and civil laws."

> have made a direct marketing campaign to the State of Minnesota. Therefore, it is not unforeseen nor unreasonable to Defendants to be required to come to Minnesota to defend themselves (. . .) The Defendants attempt to hide behind the Internet and claim that they mailed nothing to Minnesota, sent nothing to Minnesota, and never advertised in Minnesota. This argument is not sound in the age of cyberspace.

Should such reasoning be applied to all websites, their operators would be facing world-wide liability.

Access to the website in the forum state was also a key argument of the district court in the case *Maritz, Inc.* v. *Cybergold, Inc.*[16] of 1996, where the court recognized its jurisdiction over the out-of-state defendant based on the number of hits onto their website:

> its intent is to reach all internet users, regardless of geographic location. (. . .) Through its website, [the defendant] has consciously decided to transmit advertising information to all internet users, knowing that such information will be transmitted globally.

Similar decisions were issued by civil courts in other states: in the case of 1996 *Inset Systems, Inc.* v. *Instruction Set, Inc.*[17] the district court in Connecticut based its jurisdiction on an advertisement by the defendant available on the Internet, and held that the defendant:

> continuously advertised over the Internet, which includes at least 10,000 access sites in Connecticut. Further, unlike hard-copy advertisements (. . .) Internet advertisements are in electronic printed form so that they can be accessed again and again by many more potential consumers.

In the court's view, the advertisement transmitted via the Internet was a commercial offer sufficiently repeatable to allow the application of the jurisdictional statute of Connecticut.

However, in the early days of Internet case law, more balanced decisions were also being made. The district court in the case *American Library Association* v. *Pataki*[18] rightly held that Internet users are not able to determine in advance the age of their potential recipients protected under the New York law and its territorial jurisdiction. In the case *Cybersell, Inc.* v. *Cybersell, Inc.*[19] the court arrived at a similar conclusion, recognizing that it would not "comport with traditional notions of fair play and substantial justice" for Arizona to exercise personal jurisdiction over an allegedly infringing Florida website advertiser who had no contacts with the forum other than maintaining a webpage accessible within the forum state.

16 947 F. Supp. 1328 (ED Mo.).
17 (1996) 937 F. Supp. 161 (D. Conn.).
18 (1997) 969 F. Supp. 160 (SDNY).
19 (1997) 130 F. 3d. 414 (9 Cir.).

Extensive application of personal jurisdiction was also negatively assessed by the New York court in the case *Hearst Corp.* v. *Goldberger.*[20]

> [A] finding of personal jurisdiction in New York based on an Internet website would mean that there would be nationwide (indeed, worldwide) personal jurisdiction over anyone and everyone who establishes an Internet website. (. . .) Even if Goldberger's Internet website could be considered an "offer for sale" where, as here, Goldberger has no produce or service yet available for sale, jurisdiction does not exist in New York based merely on his placing the offer on the Internet outside New York.

Other courts made attempts to supplement the insufficient effects test with new elements specific to the electronic medium. And so in the *Bensusan Restaurant Corp.* v. *King*[21] case the court invoked website targeting as a necessary, additional criterion. The court held that the:

> mere fact that a person can gain information on the allegedly infringing product is not the equivalent of a person advertising, promoting, selling or otherwise making an effort to target its product in New York. (. . .) mere foreseeability of an in-site consequence and a failure to avert that consequence is not sufficient to establish personal jurisdiction.

In the court's opinion, personal jurisdiction may be exercised only if the actions of the defendant were targeted directly at the forum state (considered purposeful availment).

The same reasoning was followed by the court in the *CompuServe, Inc.* v. *Patterson*[22] case, where the court held that

> the defendant knowingly made an effort and, in fact, purposefully contracted – to market a product in other states, with Ohio-based CompuServe operating, in effect, as his distribution center. Thus, it is reasonable to subject Patterson to suit in Ohio, the state which is home to the computer network service he chose to employ.

The interpretational efforts of courts from late 1990s were concluded by the Pennsylvania District Court in the leading *Zippo Manufacturing Co.* v. *Zippo Dot Com, Inc.*[23] case. In its decision, the court proposed the division of websites into three categories: active, passive and "middle ground". Based on previous inter-state case law, the court held that the likelihood that personal jurisdiction can be exercised is directly proportionate to the nature and quality of the commercial activity that an entity conducts over the

20 (1997) WL 97097 (SDNY).

21 (1996) 937 F. Supp. 295 (SDNY), affirmed 126 F. 3d. 25.

22 89 F.3d 1257 1996).

23 (1997) 952 F. Supp. 1119 (ED Penn.).

Internet. The Pennsylvania court held that at one end of the spectrum are situations where a defendant uses websites to conduct business with the forum state and at the opposite end are situations where defendant simply uses the website only as a tool for making information available to those who are interested in it. If the defendant enters into contacts with residents of a foreign jurisdiction that involve the transmission of computer files over the Internet, effective jurisdiction may be exercised (*CompuServe* v. *Patterson*). At the opposite end of the spectrum are situations where a defendant has simply posted information on an Internet website which is accessible to users all over the world. A passive website that does little more than make information available to those who are interested in it is not grounds for the exercise of personal jurisdiction (*Bensusan* v. *King*). The third "middle ground" category covers those websites where a user can exchange information with the host computer, however, that exchange is not the essence of the interaction being conducted. In these cases, the exercise of personal jurisdiction is determined by examining the level of interactivity and the commercial nature of the exchange of information that occurs on the website (*Maritz* v. *Cybergold*). The "*Zippo* continuum" scheme is presented in Figure 3.1.

The *Zippo* test is a milestone in US case law on adapting general jurisdictional principles to the specificity of the global network. The Pennsylvania court emphasized that exercising jurisdiction over all actions causing effects in the forum state would mean exercising universal jurisdiction over actors within the cyber-realm. Wishing to avoid such an undesirable situation, the court proposed to restrict the application of state jurisdiction to interactive websites; that is those used as the medium to provide traditional services. This leading case decision has, however, some drawbacks that limit the possibility of its practical application. The middle ground category of websites

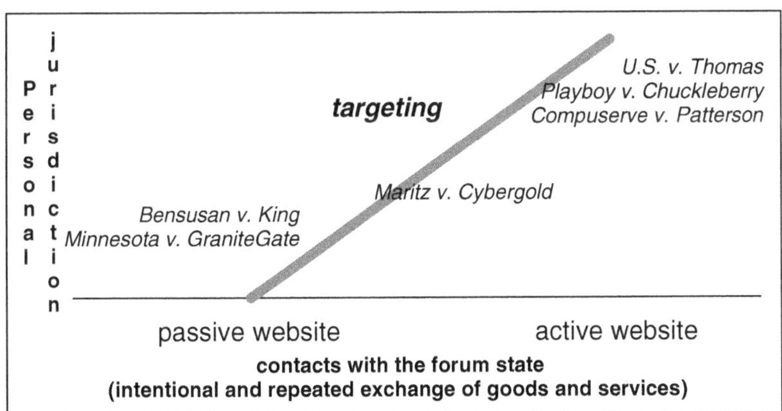

Figure 3.1 The *Zippo* Continuum.[24]

24 Derived from H. H. Perritt and M. G. Stewart (2000) 'ABA Internet Jurisdiction Project', a presentation at the Chicago-Kent College of Law, Illinois Institute of Technology <www.kentlaw.edu/cyberlaw/ottawa3.ppt> (accessed 10 April 2011) p. 5.

poses the most interpretational problems, since most websites belong there. They are not designed to provide a specific service, but among their numerous functionalities is the performance of some services. The proposal to exclude passive websites, those no different from traditional advertisements, from the state exercise of effective jurisdiction should be assessed positively, just as we should accept the suggestion that courts exercise their powers with respect to parties whose only intention is to provide online services targeted at the state. The difficulties with determining the principles of applying jurisdiction with respect to the third, middle-ground category has been further considered in later state court decisions.[25]

And so, in the 2001 *Mattel, Inc.* v. *Adventure Apparel*[26] case the New York District Court supplemented the *Zippo* scheme with an additional "effects test". Jurisdictional competence would thus result not only from the very interactive nature of the website but also from its actual use. In the *Mattel* case the court invoked the decision in *Calder* v. *Jones*[27] and held that the possibility of applying effective jurisdiction depended not only on the availability of services offered within the forum territory, but also the occurrence of a harmful effect therein. Consequently, state jurisdiction would be exercised only with respect to interactive, targeted websites, if a result of their operation would be that a harmful effect occurred in the forum state.

The targeting test was further supplemented in 2006 by the US Court of Appeals for the Ninth Circuit in the *Pebble Beach Company* v. *Caddy*[28] case. In order to provide grounds for exercising jurisdiction in the United States, one should prove that the defendant had "purposefully availed himself" of the privilege of conducting activities in the forum state or the United States as a whole, or "purposefully directed" his activities towards one of those two forums.

The above-described evolution of US case law on inter-state electronic contacts ought to be assessed highly favorably. It has moved from the inconsiderate application of effective jurisdiction (as in the *Granite Gate* case) which would expose all Internet users to worldwide liability, through the attempts to restrict liability made by the court, with varying degrees of success, in the *Zippo* case, to the multi-element test that considerably limits the scope of parties to be held accountable for their online actions. This valuable evolution seems to be contradicted, however, by recent US case law and legislative trends.

Controversial decisions affecting the situation of out-of-state parties have so far been issued in cases related to the registration of domain names based on the Anticybersquatting Consumer Protection Act (ACPA) of 1999. This Act permits a trademark

25 In more recent US decisions, these shortcomings of the *Zippo* continuum were depicted (e.g. *Millenium Enterprises, Inc.* v. *Millenium Music LP* (1999) 33 F. Supp. 2d 907 (D. Or.). <www.internetlibrary.com/pdf/Millennium-Enterprises-Millennium-Music.pdf> (accessed 2 February 2011) where the "court finds that the middle interactive category as described in *Zippo* needs further refinement to include the fundamental requirement of personal jurisdiction: 'deliberate action' within the forum state. Such action could include transactions between the defendant and forum residents through the defendant's Web site or conduct of the defendant purposefully directed at residents of the forum state through the Web site."

26 (2001) WL 28672 (SDNY).

27 (1984) 465 US 783.

28 (2006) 453 F. 3d 1151 (US Court of Appeals for the Ninth Circuit).

owner to file a civil action against an alleged trademark infringer with a court where the registrar of the infringing domain name is located[29] (*in rem* jurisdiction).[30] As three most popular top-level domains (.com, .net and .org) are administered in Virginia, any holder of a domain name of the said extension may be summoned by a Virginia court. Pursuant to the ACPA's provisions, it is permissible to file an *in rem* civil action as regards the domain name; as a consequence, the owners of such domains are deemed absent owners of tangible property located in Virginia. The first Virginia court decision based on these provisions concerned the claim of the British company Harrods in respect of 60 domain names including the word "Harrods" (*Harrods Ltd.* v. *Sixty Internet Domain Names: harrodsargentina.com, et al.*[31]) The Court of Appeals for the Fourth Circuit upheld the decision of the court of first instance and ordered that 54 domain names held by out-of-state residents be granted to the British entity. An action recently brought by Microsoft pertaining to the botnet Waledac follows this line of adjudication,[32] citing, however, a wider jurisdictional basis than just the ACPA.

Another controversial document is the USA PATRIOT Act,[33] passed by the US government in response to the tragic events of 11 September 2001 and extended for another 4 year term in 2011. The Act considerably expands the definition of "protected computers" by amending US criminal legislation intended for combating computer fraud and abuse.[34] Before the Act entered into force, only computers operating from the territory of the United States were subject to the regulation (considered "protected"). However, pursuant to the provisions of the USA PATRIOT Act, protected computers include: "a computer located outside the United States that is used in a manner that affects [the] interstate or foreign commerce or communication of

29 Section 3002 (d) (2) (a) ACPA.

30 See D. Campbell (2006) *The Internet: Laws and Regulatory Regimes*, Salzburg: Yorkhill Law Publishing, p. 455.

31 (2002) 302 F. 3d 214, (4 Cir.).

32 *Microsoft Corporation* v. *John Does 1–27, civil action no. 1_10CV156 (LMBIJFA)* where Microsoft lodged a complaint (filed under seal) with the United States District Court for the Eastern District of Virginia (Alexandria Division) against John Does 1–27 who operated a computer botnet allegedly causing damage to the company and its clients. The Doe defendants were presented with allegations that they operated 273 domain names ("Harmful Botnet Domains"). The violation consisted in damaging the reputation of the company built up over time and with considerable resources and efforts. Through the botnet, its operators used the Microsoft software inconsistently with its purpose and caused harm to its users. The plaintiffs invoked 28 USC para. 1331 as the grounds for court jurisdiction to hear the case, while allegations of common law breach were based on para. 1367 of the same section of USC which states that district courts have original jurisdiction over all civil actions with respect to which their jurisdiction is exclusive (on the basis of para. 1331). The issue is to establish a relationship so that the claims are a part of the same case or question on a point of law as per Article III of the U.S. Constitution. The plaintiffs invoked para. 1391(b) section 28 USC and justified the exercise of jurisdiction by stating that the domain name is deemed to have its *situs* in the judicial circuit in which the domain name registry that registered or assigned the domain name is located. As already mentioned, the registry of .com is administered by Verisign, seated in Virginia. This constituted the grounds for exercising personal jurisdiction by the district court (*Microsoft Corporation* v. *John Does 1–27*, p. 5).

33 Uniting and Strengthening America by Providing Appropriate Tools Required to Intercept and Obstruct Terrorism (USA PATRIOT) Act, 2001 (HR 3162).

34 Computer Fraud and Abuse Act, 18 USC § 1030.

the United States".[35] In these circumstances, even if the suspect, victim and the victim's computer are outside the territory of the United States, US law grants itself jurisdiction over their actions, if the said computer is used in any way which could "affect" communications in the United States. Taking account of the architecture of the Internet, the Act provides for a dangerously broad competence on the part of the US authorities. The controversial[36] Protecting Cyberspace as a National Asset Act[37] (presently a bill only) also follows this legislative tendency. On the other hand, however, the "International Strategy for Cyberspace" recently (May 2011) proposed by the Obama administration might be considered a symbolic outreach to the rest of the international community on the issue of cybersecurity and Internet governance.[38]

US court practice exerts a strong impact on the legislation of neighboring states. Canadian case law on Internet disputes serves as an example of the direct assimilation of US solutions. The influence is noticeable even in assimilating the division into passive and active websites, as proposed in the *Zippo* case. This may be illustrated by the decision over the application of Quebec local laws on the protection of French language in *Attorney General of Quebec* v. *Hyperinfo Canada, Inc.*[39] The Canadian court found that a disclaimer stating that "the Website is not intended for Quebec residents for it fails to meet the Charter of the French Language requirements" was not sufficient to deem the website not addressed to the province residents. Similarly, blocking IP addresses with a ".qc" extension proved insufficient and barely effective.

Following earlier US decisions, the Newfoundland Supreme Court, in a 1998 case, held it reasonable for Canadian courts to exercise jurisdiction in a tort case based solely on the availability of online information.[40] The defendant neither sold their stocks in Canada nor published a disputed statement in the Canadian press nor maintained direct contact with Canadian stockholders. It was Canadian stockholders, however, who brought an effective action against the business in Canada.

35 USA PATRIOT Act, section 814.

36 Initially the bill had stipulated that central government assumed liability for the safety of key electronic infrastructure and the rights of the US President to "shutdown" the Internet. According to Section 18 the President was to be able to declare a cybersecurity emergency and order the limitation or shutdown of Internet traffic to and from any compromised Federal Government or United States critical infrastructure information system or network. At the same time, pursuant to Section 14 (b), the bill was to ensure that the Trade Secretary had access to "all relevant data concerning such networks without regard to any provision of law, regulation, rule, or policy restricting such access", which raised serious privacy concerns. These controversial elements were eventually struck from the bill.

37 § 3480, which in Section 249 (a) (1) ("National Cyber Emergencies") allows the US President to issue a declaration of a cyber emergency to national critical infrastructure (as specified by the President). Following such a declaration, the owners and operators of the critical infrastructure are obliged to implement response plans provided by the US authorities.

38 The White House (2001) *International Strategy for Cyberspace*. <www.whitehouse.gov/sites/default/files/rss_viewer/international_strategy_for_cyberspace.pdf> (accessed 4 February 2011). For more on this document, see chapter 4.

39 (2001) No. 550–61–000887–014 (CQ). <http://aix1.uottawa.ca/~geist/hyperinfo.htm> (accessed 4 February 2011).

40 The case concerned publishing by the defendant of false and misleading information intended tor increase the stock value of the company (*Alteen* v. *Informix Corporation* (1998) 164 Nfld. and PEIR 301, 507 APR 301). <http://aix1.uottawa.ca/~geist/alteen.html> (accessed 4 February 2011).

A completely different decision of the Canadian court that reflected the evolution of the US case law following the *Zippo* case was issued in 1999, when the Court of Appeals heard the allegation of a libelous statement placed on the stock exchange website by a Canadian resident. The Canadian company Braintech brought an action in a Texan court against the person who placed libelous information and was awarded damages in the amount of USD 400,000. When the company made attempts to enforce the judgment in Canada, the Canadian court held that the Texan court had been wrong to recognize its jurisdiction since communications were placed on a passive website, and refused to enforce the judgment.[41] Yet another decision that confirms the assimilated case law was the decision in *3DO* case,[42] where the court found that a court may exercise state jurisdiction based on the interactivity of a website and the fact that it produced a specific effect in a given territory. A similar decision was issued in the case *Dostana Enterprises LLC* v. *Federal Express Corporation*,[43] where the court confirmed that the location of the server is not relevant to recognition of the jurisdictional competence of the United States.

Suffice it to say, US case law has definitely contributed to the legal regulation of cyberspace. Careful analyses of jurisdictional principles presented in the abovementioned decisions enable legal practitioners and theorists to construe and define the Internet itself, as well as the legal principles to be applied thereto. Early decisions undoubtedly had to bear the burden of their pioneer nature. Nevertheless, principles developed in such cases as *Maritz* or *Zippo* constitute invaluable help to those who attempt to apply traditional, territoriality principles to the aterritorial Internet. The stance they took in negating the exercise of powers with respect to the owners of passive websites considerably contributed to the guarantee of Internet users' freedom from the worldwide jurisdiction of other states. This principle should, with all confidence, be commonly assimilated. However, more recent changes, both in the approach of adjudicators and in US legislation, are disturbing. They are an incentive for Internet de-centralizing and particularizing tendencies. Submitting all computers in the network to US jurisdiction as per the PATRIOT Act directly decreases the certainty level of all electronic contacts. If the said approach was largely assimilated by national legal orders, this would be the most pessimistic possible scenario for the Internet – the Internet would become the object of universal, global jurisdiction where each user could be subject to the jurisdiction of all sovereigns who ascertain the user's actions to be potentially harmful to the interests of the state or its residents. Such situation naturally requires intervention and negotiations before the information society loses its most efficient communication medium.

41 *Braintech, Inc.* v. *John C. Kostiuk* (1999) BCCA. 0169 (Court of British Columbia). <http://www.courts.gov.bc.ca/jdb-txt/ca/99/01/c99-0169.txt> (accessed 2 February 2011).

42 *3DO Co.* v. *PopTop Software, Inc.* (1998) US Dist. LEXIS 21281 (ND Cal.) <http://www.perkinscoie.com/casedigest/icd_results.cfm?keyword1=trade%20secrets&topic=Trade%20Secrets> (accessed 2 February 2011).

43 *Dostana Enterprises LLC* v. *Federal Express Corporation* (2000) WL 1170134 (SDNY). See C. B. Springer, 'Master of the Domain (Name)', op. cit., p. 338.

Europe

The relationship between European law and its regulation of actions taken via the Internet results from the traditional approach of European private international law. When resolving jurisdictional issues, one should consider the general competence of courts and other state authorities to hear and resolve civil or criminal cases and perform other procedural actions.

In civil law suits concerning the activity in the global network, there is usually a clear element that determines the international nature of a given case, which is based on the so-called "foreign element".[44] Due to the aterritorial nature of the Internet, determination of the court of venue may encounter numerous problems. Even though the "place" or "location" of the Internet does not exist, linking the legal acts with a particular territory is assumed to be possible, and consequently so is the submission of such acts to a specific legal regime. Based on traditional principles, two models of resolving Internet disputes within the ambit of the European civil law can be considered

The first model consists in the assumption that it is possible to resolve Internet disputes based on few international substantive general regulations, for example the Vienna United Nations Convention on Contracts for the International Sale of Goods dated 11 April 1980 whose application is restricted to commercial enterprises. Under the second model, applied more often, the conflict of law rules of private international law apply to the resolution of Internet disputes, including, in particular, jurisdictional rules indicating the competence of court of a given state to resolve the dispute, along with narrowly defined conflict of law rules that point to the substantive regulations applying to a given case.[45] In spite of modifications and amendments to many regulations of state law, the simplest and the most effective way to avoid problems in determining the competent jurisdiction is for the parties themselves to explicitly choose the governing law and competent court. The very nature of electronic activities considerably increases the significance of indicating the competent court and governing law for a contractual relationship, since, as already mentioned, the place or location might prove difficult to determine in cyberspace.

The Brussels Convention on Jurisdiction and the Enforcement of Judgments in Civil and Commercial Matters of 27 September 1968 constitutes the origin of European procedural law and has a special place in jurisdictional regulation of civil cases.[46] Article 220 of the Treaty of Rome, which established the European Economic Community in 1957, stipulated the need to simplify formalities relating to recognition and

44 Cf. *inter alia*, M. N. Shaw (2003) *International Law*, op. cit., p. 573 and G. J. H. Smith (2007) *Internet Law and Regulation*, London: Sweet & Maxwell, p. 467.

45 These include, in particular, Council Regulation (EC) No 44/2001 of 22 December 2000 on Jurisdiction and the Recognition and Enforcement of Judgments in Civil and Commercial Matters OJ (L 012) (16 January 2001) (hereinafter referred to as 'Regulation (EC) No 44/2001'), which was modeled on the Brussels Convention and the Lugano Convention, referred to below, and the conflict of law rules contained in the Rome Convention on the Law Applicable to Contractual Obligations of 1980 (OJ (C 27) (26 January 1998), p. 34).

46 Convention on Jurisdiction and the Enforcement of Judgments in Civil and Commercial Matters, Brussels, 27 September 1968, OJ (C 27) (26 January 1978).

enforcement of court and arbitration decisions. The Parties to the Brussels Convention increased the number of states taking this view.[47] The convention regulates three groups of issues: it provides for norms on judicial jurisdiction; specifies prerequisites and procedures for conduct within the scope of recognizing and enforcing foreign decisions; as well as specifying the effects of *lis pendens* before a court of one of the state parties. The convention applies only in civil and commercial matters (Article 1 para. 1 of the convention).[48] Adopting the Brussels Convention enabled harmonization of procedures for recognizing and enforcing decisions within the European Community, by guaranteeing uniform interpretation of convention provisions notwithstanding the differing legal systems of the member states. Under the Protocol of 3 June 1971 member states' supreme courts may request interpretation by the European Court of Justice in Luxembourg. Positive experiences pertaining to the functioning of the convention encouraged non-member states who were members of the European Free Trade Association (EFTA) to adopt solutions based on the Brussels Convention. As the group of state parties to the Brussels Convention is, as a rule, limited to EU member states, another convention, the so-called Parallel Convention to the Brussels Convention, was developed; this restates the regulations of its predecessor, the Brussels Convention. On 16 September 1988 in Lugano a convention of the same title as the Brussels Convention was signed.[49] The Lugano Convention was signed by members of the European Community and six EFTA states.[50] The similarity of both conventions is manifested with identical wording of provisions and the same numbering of articles. The Lugano Convention is an open treaty[51] consisting of three protocols. The first protocol concerns jurisdictional issues, procedures and enforcement; the second, uniform interpretation of the convention; and the third, the relation to other conventions.[52] Unlike the Brussels Convention, the European Court of Justice is not competent to construe the Lugano Convention provisions since EFTA states did not consent to it. The second additional protocol to the convention stipulated an interpretational solution by reference to precedents – courts of each contracting state, applying the provisions of the convention, shall take account of the interpretations by courts of other states. To ensure the circulation of

47 On 9 October 1978 Denmark, Ireland and Great Britain (in the so-called Luxembourg Convention) acceded to the Convention, on 25 October 1982 Greece (in the so-called 2 Luxembourg Convention) did so, on 26 May 1989 Spain and Portugal (in the so-called Donostia-San Sebastian Convention) and finally on 19 February 1996 Finland, Austria and Sweden did so.

48 Explicit exclusions are provided for in para. 2 Article 1: "The Convention shall not apply to (. . .) to revenue, customs or administrative matters, marital status or legal capacity of natural persons, rights in property arising out of a matrimonial relationship, wills and succession, bankruptcy, proceedings relating to the winding-up of insolvent companies or other legal persons, judicial arrangements, compositions and analogous proceedings."

49 Convention on Jurisdiction and the Enforcement of Judgments in Civil and Commercial Matters, Lugano, 16 September 1988 ('the Lugano Convention'), OJ (L 319) (25 November 1988), pp. 9–48.

50 Austria, Finland, Iceland, Norway, Switzerland and Sweden.

51 This means that apart from EU and EFTA Member States the convention may be acceded to by states invited by Switzerland (as a depositary), at the request of one state party to the convention and upon the consent of all other state parties.

52 The Lugano Convention, Article 57.

information an obligation was formulated to forward decisions issued both under the Lugano and Brussels Conventions.[53] The Lugano Convention may be applied irrespective of the nationality of parties to the proceedings.[54] The subject matter of the Lugano Convention includes civil and commercial matters, even though the phrase "civil and commercial matters" is not defined therein.[55] Only the Lugano Convention may be applied when the defendant resides in a state that is party to the Convention but not an EU member state or when the provisions of the Lugano Convention grant jurisdiction to such state. The convention, in principle, supersedes other international agreements concluded by parties as regards the subject matter it regulates. The convention regulations also supersede the provisions of the internal laws of state parties to the convention which pertain to the same subject matter.[56] The solutions provided for in the Lugano Convention substantially facilitate international trade, however, they do not provide an answer to problems relating to global electronic activities – to facilitate them, a general extension of the scope thereof would be necessary.

The regulation of state jurisdiction set forth in the Lugano Convention is, above all, based on the *actor sequitur forum rei* principle. Therefore, when establishing the grounds for direct jurisdiction, the circumstances of the defendant are taken into consideration, for, among all possible criteria, the convention is based on the principle of the defendant's domicile.[57] Persons domiciled in the territory of state parties to the convention

53 Thanks to the establishment of this link between both abovementioned Conventions it is possible to apply the *acquis* of the case law under the Brussels Convention in order to construe the Lugano Convention.

54 The ECJ has held that, under the Brussels Convention, all persons to whom the convention applies have equal rights and obligations thereunder, irrespective of domicile or nationality. (*LTU Lufttransportunternehme GmbH & Co. KG* v. *Eurocontrol*, Case 29–76, [1976] ECR, p. 1541). The Lugano Convention is similar in structure and contents to the Brussels Convention and reflects its legal reasoning and jurisprudence, Therefore, the legal reasoning applied in respect of the Brussels Convention can also be applied to the Lugano Convention notwithstanding that the ECJ has no competence regarding the latter.

55 Decisions issued under the Brussels Convention assume that none of the laws of state that are party to the convention is relevant to interpretation of the term "civil and commercial matters", therefore the purpose, scope and definitions of the convention and the general principles resulting from the legal systems of state parties to the convention should be followed. The case law developed by the European Court of Justice suggests that criteria determining the civil and commercial nature of a case are as follows: type of pursued claims, type of actions taken or their legal grounds. The convention regulations also pertain to, e.g., cases heard in adhesive proceedings before criminal courts, or even cases heard in administrative proceedings. Exclusions from the Lugano convention (Article 1 para. 3) are the same as those indicated above with respect to the Brussels Convention. As regards the status and legal capacity of natural persons, the following are excluded: validity of marriage and changeability of marital status, separation, minors' status, rights of custody, legal capacity and capacity to perform acts in law, nationality, place of residence and stay, custody, guardianship and adoption; see F. F. Wang, op. cit., p. 219.

56 The convention allows invocation of national law only if the law is more favorable than the convention regulations.

57 Pursuant to Article 2 para. 1 of the Lugano Convention, persons domiciled in a state bound by this convention shall, whatever their nationality, be sued in the courts of that state. Establishing that the defendant is domiciled in a state bound by the convention constitutes not only grounds for the court to apply state jurisdiction, but is the only and sufficient reason for applying the convention jurisdictional norm instead of the internal jurisdictional norm.

may be summoned before courts of other state parties only pursuant to the convention regulations. Other norms stipulated by internal provisions specifying other jurisdictional criteria (e.g. place of residence) shall thus not apply.[58] If the defendant does not reside in the territory of one state, the judicial jurisdiction of a foreign state is determined in accordance with the provisions of such state.[59] However, the Lugano Convention does not define the domicile criterion. A person domiciled in the territory of state parties may be sued before the courts of another state pursuant to the Convention regulations pertaining to alternative jurisdiction (Article 5 and 6 of the convention).

Article 16 enumerates situations where exclusive jurisdiction shall apply. Another option is provided for in Article 17, pursuant to which parties may enter into an arbitration agreement under which disputes which have arisen or which may arise in connection with a particular legal relationship must be submitted to a court of a particular contracting state.[60] The principle of free selection of jurisdiction by the parties is a sign of freedom of contract and an exercise of free will by the parties to a contractual relationship. This element is especially significant compared with the concept of determining the judicial jurisdiction by the claimant (*actor sequitur forum rei*), which bears the risk of forum shopping.[61]

If parties to the agreement decided to choose the governing law, jurisdictional issues pose a minor problem in comparison with the one that may occur when parties fail to specify the governing law and thus the general principles of international law apply to disputes between them. The Lugano Convention, as mentioned above, applies to disputes between European states that are parties to the convention, that is EU and EFTA states. Regulation No 44/2001 which, in all EU member states except Denmark, superseded the 1968 Brussels Convention, is of fundamental meaning to EU member states on the issue of civil jurisdiction.[62] Both the Lugano Convention and Regulation 44/2001,[63] modeled on the Brussels Convention, refer to analogous solutions. Their subject matter covers civil and commercial matters.

To conclude: the territoriality principle is the principle under which general jurisdiction is determined in respect of a contractual relationship where the parties failed to indicate the governing law. Under this principle, persons domiciled in a member state or contracting state of either the Brussels or Lugano Conventions, regardless of their nationality, can be sued before the courts of such state; this is provided for in Article 16 of each of the conventions. The abovementioned provision

58 The provisions stipulating jurisdiction based on such grounds (referred to as exorbitant jurisdiction) are set forth in Article 3 of the Lugano Convention.

59 Apart from exclusive jurisdiction (Article 16 Lugano Convention).

60 The said provision regulates the form of the agreement in detail.

61 See U. Kohl, op. cit., p. 178; D. J. B. Svantesson (2007) *Private International Law and the Internet*, The Hague: Kluwer Law International, p. 298.

62 The situation of consumers (a particular category of individuals entering into a trans-national private law contract, a category defined by the Regulation) is regulated differently in the Regulation compared to the provisions of the Brussels Convention. The latter makes no particular difference to the situation of a consumer. The Regulation entered into force on 1 March 2002.

63 Council Regulation (EC) No 44/2001, op. cit., pp. 1–23.

incorporates the general principle of civil action: *actor sequitur forum rei*. The principle is neither modified nor clarified by the electronic character of the parties' interaction. The criterion assumed by both acts concerned is the domicile of the parties. Pursuant to Article 5 para. 4 of the Lugano Convention, the only and sufficient premise of applying the said norm instead of the provisions of the internal laws is the determination of the domicile in the territory of the state party. Nevertheless, both acts provide for no definition of "domicile".

Apart from formulating the general principle, both documents allow for the possibility of applying an alternative jurisdiction. If parties fail to indicate the law governing contractual relations, in the light of the Lugano Convention (Article 5) and Regulation 41/2001 (Article 5) a party may be sued in a state other than the state of its domicile or its registered office. The state of performance of the obligation in question may be considered the forum to hear the case. Such provisions may raise controversy when applied to online contracts.[64] Regulation 44/2001 clarifies the concept of the "the place of performance of the obligation" as "in the case of the sale of goods, the place where, under the contract, the goods were delivered or should have been delivered" (Article 5). In the case of the provision of services, it is the place where, under the contract, the services were provided or should have been provided.[65]

The increased feeling of freedom or even impunity of Internet users while online often makes the global network a tool for committing offences. Apart from traditional civil law torts,[66] new types of breach occur which are specific to the Internet: cyber squatting, spam, linking or framing.

Article 5 para. 3 of the Lugano Convention and of Regulation 44/2001 grant jurisdiction in tort cases to courts competent in the location where the harmful event occurred.[67] The place where the harmful event occurred may mean the physical

64 It would be incredibly difficult to determine the "place of contract performance" in the case of e-transactions, where the contract performance itself is limited to transfer of data from one computer to another (downloading). The key question that, if answered, will allow one to attempt to apply the cited provision pertains to the place of obligation of the performance: is it the seat of the seller (where it places its product online) or the buyer (to whose location the ordered content is transferred)? Wang suggests considering the place of dispatch or receipt, or the place to which the online activities are directed. (F.F. Wang, op. cit., p. 55). Such a solution might show insufficient consideration of the multiplicity of options and practical obstacles in determining the place of website targeting.

65 Special exception to the principle of Article 2 of the Lugano Convention is provided for in Article 5 para. 5 thereof. It states that a business may be sued in the place in which its branch, agency or other establishment is situated. This, however, is an exception, and as such, does not allow extensive interpretation – therefore, websites cannot be deemed branches.

66 E.g. breach of personal rights, fair competition and industrial property, intellectual property (e.g. misleading potential consumers as to the company name or torts committed by online services), violation of privacy and protection of personal data.

67 Similar criteria are assumed in the draft Hague Convention on Jurisdiction and Foreign Judgments (based on the Lugano and Brussels conventions and case law related thereto.) Article 10 para. 3 of the draft Hague Convention would be the most significant as regards Internet torts, as it establishes prerequisites for jurisdiction based on the place of harm, but does not apply where the defendant undertook appropriate measures to avoid the effects in a given state or to target the activities to the territory of a different given state. The provision would be of special importance to Internet economic activity (a question arises as to whether it is sufficient to use *disclaimers* on websites to meet this condition).

location where the acts (or omissions) that resulted in harm were performed (territorial jurisdiction) as well as the place where harm was caused (effective jurisdiction).[68] Should this be the case, the claimant may choose whether to lodge a claim with the court competent in the place where the perpetrator acted (or failed to act) or with a court competent in any place where the harm was suffered. Considering the nature of cyberspace, harm might be so widespread as to result in worldwide jurisdiction.

The place where the act was committed may be the place where the perpetrator uploads data to the computer network.[69] However, the place where the harm was caused via the Internet is more difficult to identify. The application of a concept of the place where the harm is caused, stipulated by the provisions, raises doubts in the context of the already mentioned multi-site effect of all actions taken via the Internet. It is necessary to presume that the potential availability of information in a given state does not provide grounds for establishing that harm may be caused therein. The minimum condition for a possible application of the construct of the place of the occurrence of harm is, undoubtedly, the analysis of the intention accompanying the author of the harmful content – it would be necessary to establish whether the perpetrator foresaw that his message would reach a given state and, if so, the perpetrator might bear liability. Courts adjudicating in cases pertaining to electronic contacts should draw on US case law, where too broad an interpretation of the facts of the case based on the effects principle proved unjustified. While searching for a relevant clause specifying jurisdictional competence towards electronic activities, one could restrict jurisdiction solely to the place where the harmful content was uploaded. The law of the state where the business is conducted, irrespective of the fact that services are actually offered on the Internet, will be the governing law in most cases. In the case of a natural person not conducting economic activity, the law governing contractual obligations is the law of the state where the person permanently resides. The provision of Article 4 para. 5 of the Rome Convention (now replaced by a similar regulation within the Rome I Regulation (Regulation (EC) 593/2008 Article 4 para. 4) also seems significant – the abovementioned presumption does not apply if characteristic performance cannot be determined, and the presumptions in paragraphs 2, 3 and 4 will be disregarded if it appears from the circumstances as a whole that the contract is more closely connected with another country. When analyzing these provisions vis-à-vis electronic transactions, such circumstances may comprise, for example, the registered office or place of residence, place of contract conclusion, possibly the website's language, the domain within which the website is registered, its currency or any disclaimers. Undoubtedly, courts, when interpreting these provisions, should not consider the place where the servers, onto which the website or its elements are uploaded, are actually located.

Generally, one may point to several common models of procedure followed by Western countries and aimed at the adjustment of applicable conflict of law rules to

68 A defendant may be sued in the place where the "harmful event occurred" which cover[s] both the place where the damage occurred and the place of the event giving rise to it (*Shevill* v. *Presse Alliance SA*, case 68/93, [1995] ECR 1–415 at para. 20; see also Kohl, op. cit., p. 124.

69 At the same time, the possibility of virtual space on the Internet or the location of technical devices allowing data upload to be deemed such a place, should be rejected.

factual circumstances pertaining to the Internet. Above all, the state of origin principle and the state of receipt principle are indicated. The former principle aims at submitting the case to the law of the state in the place where electronic content was uploaded.[70] The latter principle is based on the criterion of a place of receipt of information (place of harm) relating to the person receiving specific information – his or her domicile or place of residence. Each of the proposed solutions is more favorable to different entities – depending on the source of the obligation, the solution may be in favor of either the injured party rather than the perpetrator or the business rather than the consumers from various states. All applicable treaties that regulate the cross-border jurisdiction referred to hereinabove (the Brussels Convention, the Lugano Convention, Regulation 44/2001 and the Rome Convention) apart from the traditional principle of the state of origin, provide also for the principle of jurisdiction by the state of receipt. An exception in favor of the state of origin, by application of a specific internal market clause, is implemented under Article 3 of the Directive on Electronic Commerce.

Pursuant to Article 3 of the Directive on Electronic Commerce, information society services must be assessed under the laws of the state where the business is seated (an example of the state of origin principle). Information society services include, in particular, providing access to, transmitting and searching for commercial information or data storage.[71] Article 3 paras. 1 and 2 of the Directive sets forth two prerequisites for applying this principle. First of all, authorities of the state where the service provider is established must verify that its actions comply with that nation's domestic provisions. Secondly, a state must not discriminate against foreign services. The authentic interpretation of Article 3 para. 2 (that is, the interpretation of the authors of the Directive, the European Council) suggests that any restriction of the freedom to provide information society services, except those referred to in the Annex, are prohibited. The reason for this is the principle that commercial enterprises who submit to the laws of the state where they are seated, being the community state, should not be forced to be subject to additional limitations in the state where their services are received. In this form, the state of origin principle underlies e-commerce under the 2000 Directive on Electronic Commerce. One should not disregard the fact that the state of origin principle was also applied to provisions of European Community *acquis*, e.g. Articles 2 and 3 of the Television without Frontiers Directive.[72]

70 Ibid. "Source of the transmission" means the business seat, or the place in which the activity, commitment of an act or omission giving rise to liability in tort takes place.

71 Directive 2000/31/EC, op. cit. See G. J. H. Smith, op. cit., p. 792.

72 Directive 1989/552/EEC of the European Parliament and of the Council of 3 October 1989 on the Coordination of Certain Provisions laid down by Law, Regulation or Administrative Action in Member States concerning the Pursuit of Television Broadcasting Activities, OJ (L 298) (17 October 1989), pp. 23–30. Its provisions are based on the principle of applying the laws of the broadcaster's country, which is to ensure the freedom of service provision. Member States must, by appropriate means, ensure, within the framework of their legislation, that television broadcasters under their jurisdiction comply with the broadcasting provisions of their state. Other Member States must not impose additional provisions on the broadcaster, but must guarantee free access and no restrictions to broadcast television programs. These principles were also envisaged in the amendments to Directive 2007/65/EC.

Following the state of broadcast principle does considerably affect the level of substantive law harmonization. It seems sensible that conflict of law rules should be applied in favour of the state of broadcast, since only the regulations of the broadcaster's state are valid. It is worth emphasizing that mutual recognition of the state of origin principle by state of receipt courts is permissible only if the state of origin provides for an effective guarantee that services rendered by service providers in its territory, which are then received by other states, are compliant. Therefore, the state of origin principle, in order to be effective, requires that all national regulations observe it: in order to provide a coherent assessment of IT services, a collective analysis of all legal regulations of a Member State is necessary. This approach by the Directive on Electronic Commerce is a novelty in European regulations and presents the principle of freedom to provide IT services in a completely new light. Nevertheless, pursuant to the Directive on Electronic Commerce, the scope of application of the principle is restricted to information society services. *Lex specialis* with respect to the state of origin principle is set forth in section 57 of the preamble to the Electronic Commerce Directive, which permits a member state to retains the right to take measures against a service provider that is established in another member state but directs all or most of his activity to the territory of the first member state. *Ratio legis* of the exception shall be the intention to prevent attempts to circumvent the state law by establishing the business outside the state at which the services are actually targeted.

One must consider whether the provisions of the above Directives derogate from the conflict of law rules of traditional private international law. Are these rules *lex specialis* against the traditional private international law treaties? How is one to construe provisions of Article 3 of the Directive in the light of international practice?

The explanation provided in the explanatory notes to the directive, state that Article 3 was not aimed at the exclusion of the provisions of Regulation 44/2001. The lack of such intention is also confirmed by the provision of Article 1 para. 4 of the directive, which states that it neither establishes additional rules on private international law nor deals with the jurisdiction of courts. The state of origin principle does not violate the rules on private international law, even though as the Article says, national law cannot limit freedom of service provision. Such a formulation leads to numerous doubts, which may need to be considered in practice or upon amendment of the rules.

The latest step towards a harmonized regulation of non-contractual obligations in Community law is the so-called Rome II Regulation.[73] Pursuant to Article 3 thereof, the Regulation is to be of universal nature, that is, it shall be applied irrespective of whether the law of a member state or a third country has been selected as the governing law. Within this, it further specifies the criteria for selection of a competent court in tort-related matters. As a general rule, presented in Article 4, the law applicable to a non-contractual obligations arising out of a tort shall be the law of the country in which the damage occurs, regardless of the country or countries in which the indirect consequences of the event may be observed. Although such a formulation further

73 Regulation (EC) No 864/2007 of the European Parliament and of the Council of 11 July 2007 on the Law Applicable to Non-Contractual Obligations (Rome II).

narrows the scope of potential fora, it does not clarify the interpretation of the "place where the harm occurred" expressed hereinabove, thus still providing for the possibility of forum shopping by the plaintiffs.

It is impossible to establish one conflict of law rule applying to all tortious obligations arising via the global network. The place of commission of the tort, often being the fundamental criterion, seems insufficient in the context of a wide range of new possible tortious obligations. As a result of amendments initiated by law makers, the focus of regulation has moved from the harmful act to the damage and ways to remedy it. When summing up the abovementioned brief review of European jurisdictional regulations, one should highlight the fact that, as a rule, assuming a specific range of jurisdictional criteria depends mainly on the national law-maker, acting in the context of international obligations taken on by the state. The said criteria may be more or less flexible. The most commonly applied criterion is the place of conclusion of the contract (*lex loci contractus*). The criterion of the place of performance of the obligation (*lex loci solutionis*) and the criterion of the place of service supply/provision (*lex loci originalis*) are also often invoked. Furthermore, the theory of characteristic performance is applied, which means that the contractual relationship is subject to the laws of the state where the person rendering the performance characteristic of a given legal relationship, e.g. supply of goods, is domiciled or has its registered office. The principle that, due to its greater flexibility, seems the most practical in Internet obligations is the theory of applying the law most closely and naturally related related to a given contract. The application of this principle requires, however, that the judge examining the facts of the case have sufficient experience to provide a reasonable and well-grounded assessment.

The simplest way to avoid jurisdictional problems in Internet disputes is to specify the law governing a given legal relationship within a contract. Should, however, the parties disregard such an option, current European legislation allows for much freedom in claiming jurisdiction by national courts and leaves much confusion to the defendants in potential Internet cases. What is more, the wide and ambiguous catalogue of jurisdictional guidelines allows states to apply their national laws on civil and criminal jurisdiction. What follows is considerable legal uncertainty over the possible legal effects of actions performed online and much possibility for forum shopping for potential plaintiffs.

Before the final conclusion of consideration of European legislation on jurisdiction in matters pertaining to electronic contacts, European case law in Internet-related cases is worth mentioning. Envisaging the early US case law, discussed above, based on the extensive exercise of effective jurisdiction, two early 1990s decisions of European courts should be mentioned – the German *CompuServe* case and the French *Yahoo!* case.

In the 1999 *CompuServe* case[74] the German regional court (Landesgericht) in Munich held the CEO of CompuServe GmbH (a German branch of the US based CompuServe Inc.) responsible for having made available content of violence and child

74 Amtsgericht München, 8340 Ds. 465 Js 173158/59 and judgment of 17 November 1999, Landgericht München and 20 Ns 465 Js 173158/95 (AG München I). <http://www.netlaw.de/urteile/lgm_12.htm> (accessed 2 February 2011).

pornography within the territory of Germany, which constituted a breach of Article 184 para. 3 of the German Criminal Code. The court found that CompuServe Inc. had the technical expertise to block access to discussion groups from German territory, including the said content at any time, and decided not to do so. In the court's opinion the CompuServe Inc. Board acted intentionally, breaching German law in order to obtain profits. The defendant was held accessory to the crime, for CompuServe GmbH ensured access to CompuServe Inc. services to German subscribers of the latter, which constituted its core economic activity, and shared the profit with CompuServe Inc. The decision was subject to much criticism, as it eventually subjected to the German court decision actions conducted by an out-of-state enterprise (CompuServe Inc.) and was the initial point for discussion on intermediary liability (the intermediary in this case being CompuServe GmbH).

A relatively similar French case that provoked a public discussion on the freedom of speech and the limits of jurisdictional competence of national courts as regards the assessment of actions performed via the Internet is the French case against Yahoo![75] (*LICRA (The League Against Racism and Antisemitism) and the Union of Jewish Students of France* v. *Yahoo!, Inc.*). The US based company Yahoo! enabled within its auction service the sale of Nazi memorabilia by a US resident. French Internet users could, without any obstacles, visit both the US and French version of the website and freely participate in the auction. Pursuant to the French law which prohibits incitement to racial hatred, the Paris court judge, J. J. Gomez, imposed a fine on Yahoo! for "insulting collective memories" of the French. Defendants' arguments based on the freedom of speech guaranteed by the First Amendment to the US Constitution have been decisively rejected in all court instances. The French court ordered the website administrators to block the access to the controversial US website; however before executing the judgment and instead of initiating a cassation hearing in France, Yahoo! brought an action in the US expecting the District Court for the Northern District of California in San Jose to confirm the impossibility of enforcement of the French sentence in US territory. When the court did issue a decision in favor of Yahoo!, it seemed that the situation was indeed locked in a stalemate, however in a decision of January 2006, the US Court of Appeals for the Ninth Circuit recognized US jurisdiction to hear the case, but provided no final resolution and prohibition to enforce the French decision in the US.[76] Finally, in 2006, the Supreme Court denied certiorari thus ending the case undecided. The *Yahoo!* case is the prime example of how the

75 Decision of the regional court in Paris of 20 November 2000, N° RG 00/05308, <http://www.eff.org/legal/Jurisdiction_and_sovereignty/LICRA_v_Yahoo/20001120_fr_int_ruling.en.pdf> (accessed 16 January 2011).

76 *Yahoo! v. La Ligue Contre Le Racisme et l'Antisémitisme*, 2006 WL 60670 (9 Cir. 2006). <http://www.ca9.uscourts.gov/ca9/newopinions.nsf/3DF703F416DC0608882570F40006DDCF/$file/0117424.pdf?openelement> (accessed 16 June 2006). The US Court of Appeals for the Ninth Circuit reversed the decision of the regional court and delegated the case for another hearing with the recommendation to dismiss the claim holding that "Yahoo! argues that it has a First Amendment right to violate French criminal law and to facilitate the violation of the French criminal law by others. (. . .) The] extent or the very existence of such an extraterritorial right under the First Amendment is uncertain" (p. 6).

existing confusion in applying jurisdictional principles to online contacts may lead to gross legal uncertainty for both the users and the service providers. Insofar as the legal and jurisdictional consequences are of the essence of the case concerned, the Internet aspect stresses the complexity of interdependence between the online world and traditional borders. In dissenting opinions, US judges presented their completely divergent views on the judgment, holding that the French court decision could in no way be enforced outside French borders.[77]

In early European cases, in spite of clear provisions of international law on the infringement of intellectual, industrial property or personal rights, European national courts would recognize their jurisdiction even towards passive websites. In the *Mecklermedia Corp.* v. *D.C. Congress GmbH*[78] case the British court recognized its jurisdiction in a case brought by a US company and its British branch against a German-based enterprise. In order to recognize jurisdictional competence over the act of unfair competition it was sufficient to show that the German defendant was liable in tort by maintaining websites which resulted in harm effected in Great Britain (as that was where the damage to goodwill and reputation of the claimants occurred).[79] This 1997 decision reflects the expansive execution of effective jurisdiction, characteristic also of mid-1990s US adjudicature. However, the following evolution, specific of US jurisprudence aimed at limiting the scope of plaintiffs in Internet-related cases, was not reflected in European courtrooms,[80] probably due to the fact that positive law, as described above, is not flexible enough to meet the challenges posed by cyberspace.

The current stage of development of case law seems to indicate that, where the provisions of the state of origin do not apply (as per the E-Commerce Directive) and where the governing law was not indicated by the parties, one should apply the state of broadcast principle modified in accordance with the foregoing suggestions. Courts, before hearing cases relating to the issues concerned, should, as per the categorization proposed in the *Zippo* case, make a general division into passive and active websites and assess the level of interactivity and nature of information only of the active ones. Supplementary conditions, such as website targeting, would make the distinction clearer. Such a practice might facilitate the approximation of the European stance to the United States' "minimum contacts" rule.

It is also worth mentioning that there is an area where states have always been unwilling to assume too broad or too detailed international obligations: the criminal jurisdiction. Existing conventions applied towards so-called international criminal law[81] combine elements of war law and pertain to the gravest crimes against human-

77 Cf. M. Geist (2006) 'The Law, Borders, and the Internet', *BBC News,* 24 January 2006. <http://news.bbc.co.uk/2/hi/technology/4641244.stm> (accessed 16 June 2011).

78 *Mecklermedia Corp.* v. *D.C. Congress GmbH* [1997] TLR (Ch.).

79 *Mecklermedia Corp.*, ibid. See J. Beltran, op. cit.

80 See F. F. Wang, op. cit., p. 89, which differentiates US-specific jurisdiction, base on the *Zippo* "effects" and "targeting" criteria and European special jurisdiction, as an exception to the general jurisdictional principles.

81 See e.g. C. C. Joyner (2005), *International Law in the 21 Century: Rules for Global Governance*, Oxford: Rowman & Littlefield, pp. 133–160.

ity,[82] whereas the only international agreement on criminal activities conducted through cyberspace – the CoE's Convention on Cybercrime referred to above, contains the aforementioned, significant procedural defects. The lack of consensus as regards the principles of criminal liability for actions taken via cyberspace carries considerable implications for the status of Internet service providers. While in the abovementioned legal regimes the generally accepted principle is that of ISPs' non-liability for provided content should they not be aware of its criminal or infringing character, and the responsibility for illegal content lies instead with the content providers, a thoroughly different approach is taken by most Asian states. Those that attempt to look at cyberspace as just another emanation of their territorial authority build electronic and legal safeguards to protect that territory. Often at the forefront of protection for the national community from the risks of the cyber-realm stand the ISPs, obliged to censor unwanted or potentially dangerous content. Those policies rely on effective content filtering.

Asia and the problem of electronic content filtering

China

Given the tremendous role that Asia plays in online relations (China holds the first place worldwide in the number of Internet users, with over 360 million),[83] the approach adopted by Asian countries towards regulating cyberspace is of crucial importance. The Asian country that has devoted most time and resources to effectively filtering electronic content available from within its territory is China.[84] According to Berkman Center for Internet & Society[85] research, in early 2000 China was already blocking the access to several thousand websites, using various filtering techniques,[86] including strict requirements imposed on search engine providers. In accordance with the OpenNetInitiative (ONI) report, the censorship system in China consists of several levels of legal regulations and technical control.[87] Filtering is effected not only at Internet Exchange Points (IXPs) but also as a result of actions taken by individual service providers bound by the provisions of national law and community ethical standards. China, by means of legal and technical instruments, blocks access to potentially dangerous political and social content (including those referring to events in Tiananmen square, liberation movements in Tibet, the spiritual community Falun Gong, discussions

82 See e.g. M. C. Bassiouni (1980) *International Criminal Law: A Draft International Criminal Code*, The Hague: Brill Archive, pp. 11–37.

83 See <http://www.internetworldstats.com/top20.htm> (accessed 22 January 2010)

84 See R. Deibert et al. (eds.) (2010) *Access Controlled*, op. cit., p. 4.

85 See J. Zittrain and B. Edelman (2003) *Empirical Analysis of Internet Filtering in China*, Mass.: Harvard University, Berkman Center for Internet and Society. <http://cyber.law.harvard.edu/filtering/china/> (accessed 21 January 2011).

86 Some websites are blocked by IP numbers, others by the domain name, still others through DNS kidnapping (the user while trying to reach a given Internet address is forwarded to another website or to a website with information about an error).

87 OpenNetInitiative (2005) *Internet Filtering in China in 2004–2005*. <http://cryptome.org/cn/cn-filter.pdf> (hereinafter referred to as 'ONI *Internet Filtering*'), (accessed 14 January 2011), p. 9.

on lack of social justice or independent media, and calls for democratization or the opening of borders).[88] The state also filters "inappropriate" materials, i.e. sexual, pornographic or others considered obscene. Handbooks on methods of evading the censorship blockage are also removed.[89] National provisions name numerous state entities supervising Internet content, subject either to the State Council Information Office (SCIO) or the Propaganda Department of the China Communist Party.[90] Control over electronic content includes provisions on criminal and civil liability, the obligation to license and register online activities as well as self-monitoring by both ISPs and ICPs.[91] At the same time, the Ministry of Industry and Information Technology (MIIT) controls the use of infrastructure. With its consent direct access to the network is provided to the Chinese by nine licensed Internet Access Providers (IAPs). Each IAP has at least one connection to the global backbone network via one of the abovementioned IXPs. Internet service providers (ISPs) connect to the Internet using services offered by IAPs.

MIIT (then known as the Ministry of Information Industry or MII) initially did not allow foreign companies to participate in the national telecommunications market; the situation has changed since China acceded to the World Trade Organization in 2001.[92] The first statute that specified the manner of using the Internet by Chinese residents was the State Council Order no. 147, under which the Minister of Public Security in December 1997 issued the "Computer Information Network and Internet Security, Protection and Management Regulations".[93] These regulations set out fundamental purposes for which the Internet may *not* be used.[94] The provisions of Article 20 stipu-

88 Human Rights Watch (2005) *World Report: China*. <http://hrw.org/english/docs/2005/01/13/china9809.htm> (accessed 19 January 2011).

89 Ibid.

90 See R. Deibert et al. (eds.), op. cit., pp. 456–457.

91 Ibid., p. 458.

92 C. D. Marsan (2004) 'China: ISPs Report Major Growth in 2004', *Network World Fusion*, 20 December 2004. <http://www.nwfusion.com/newsletters/isp/2004/1220isp1.html> (accessed 19 January 2011).

93 China Computer Information Network and Internet Security, Protection and Management Regulations Article 1, English translation. <http://www.asianlii.org/cn/legis/cen/laws/cinaispamr904> (accessed 13 January 2011).

94 Article 4 states that no individual may use the Internet to harm national security, disclose state secrets, harm the interests of the state, of society or of a group, the legal rights of citizens, or to take part in criminal activities. Article 5 states that no individual may use the Internet to create, replicate, retrieve, or transmit information inciting resistance or breach of the Constitution or laws or the implementation of administrative regulations, incite the overthrow of the government or the socialist system, incite the division of the country, harm national unification, incite hatred or discrimination among nationalities or harm the unity of the nationalities, make falsehoods or distort the truth, spread rumors, destroy the order of society, or promote feudal superstitions. Materials containing sexually suggestive content, gambling, violence or murder are also forbidden, as is information promoting terrorism or inciting others to criminal activity, openly insulting other people or distorting the truth to slander people, injuring the reputation of state bodies, or any other activities against the Constitution, laws or administrative regulations of the state. Pursuant to Article 6, no unit or individual could engage in the following activities which could harm the security of computer information networks. No one could use computer networks or network resources without getting proper prior approval, no one could without prior

lated penalties for violation of the said prohibitions: warning, confiscation of the illegal content, fine not to exceed RMB 5000 (approx. EUR 600) and, for more serious offenses, computer and network access to be closed down for up to six months. The State Council supplemented the foregoing document with the "Telecommunications Regulations" (State Council Order No 291 of 11 October 2000),[95] which prohibited natural persons from using the telecommunications network to produce, reproduce, disseminate or transmit specific categories of information.[96] The situation of Internet content providers has also been regulated restrictively. The State Council Order No. 292 (Measures for Managing Internet Information Systems), established the first formal content restrictions binding on ICPs.[97] Those among them, who found illegal data on their administered websites were obliged to submit a complete report to relevant authorities. Two years later, on 27 June 2002 the General Administration of Press and Publication (GAPP) along with the MIIT developed the "Interim Administrative Provisions on Internet Publishing".[98] The new provisions were to harmonize the principles governing traditional and electronic publications and submit them to supervision by all governmental bodies exercising control over the traditional, printed press. China has also developed principles for Internet audio-visual broadcasting. In January 2003 the State Council issued rules on Administration of the Broadcasting of the Audio-Visual Programs on the Internet and other Information Networks pursuant to which information providers shall obtain licenses from the State Council Information Office before commencing activities. At the same time, the Ministry of Culture, on 10 May 2003, issued its own Interim Provisions on the Administration of Internet Culture, which reiterated previous regulations. The Ministry again imposed the obligation on all ICPs to register with their regional or central office. The principles extended previously implemented restrictions on freedom of speech and press including information sent to mobile phones and other wireless devices, as well as other forms of electronic transmission such as video games.[99]

permission change network functions or add or delete information, no one could without prior permission add, delete, or alter materials stored, processed or transmitted through the network, and no one could deliberately create or transmit viruses, or perform other activities, which harm the network.

95 An English translation can be found at <http://tradeinservices.mofcom.gov.cn/en/b/2000-09-25/18619.shtml> (accessed 6 January 2011).

96 Information with content that: 1. opposes the fundamental principles determined in the Constitution; 2. compromises state security, discloses state secrets, subverts state power or damages national unity; 3. harms the dignity or interests of the state; 4. incites ethnic hatred or racial discrimination or damages inter-ethnic unity; 5. sabotages state religious policy or propagates heretical teachings or feudal superstitions; 6. disseminates rumors, disturbs social order or disrupts social stability; 7. propagates obscenity, pornography, gambling, violence, murder or fear or incites the commission of crimes; 8. insults or slanders a third party or infringes upon the lawful rights and interests of a third party; 9. includes other content prohibited by laws or administrative regulations.

97 Article 12 requires content providers to ensure the lawfulness of information distributed using their services and shall record and keep a copy of their records for 60 days. Article 15 provides for nine categories of information whose production, reproduction, release, or dissemination is prohibited.

98 Interim Provisions on the Administration of Internet Publication (hereinafter referred to as 'the Interim Provisions'). An English translation is available at <http://www.cecc.gov/pages/virtualAcad/index.phpd?showsingle=1563> (accessed 19 January 2010).

99 See ONI, *Internet Filtering*, op. cit. p. 17; see also: R. Deibert et al. (eds.), op. cit., p. 456.

According to ONI, at least twelve entities decide about the scope of electronic content available in the state territory.[100] Principles determined thereby are often incompatible. Meeting the imposed requirements is even more difficult since their statutory definitions are vague and general. The interest of state authorities in regulating the Internet has increased after the year 2000, and as a consequence the number of regulations pertaining thereto and the number of authorized implementing bodies have also grown. The circumstances may imply competitive actions taken among Chinese authorities in the fight for the casting vote as regards the Chinese Internet.

Those bodies originally authorized to regulate electronic content were the bodies responsible for printed and telecommunications media. The General Administration of Press and Publications (GAPP) grants licenses for the press, including journals, periodicals and websites. GAPP activities are supported by the General Customs Administration, which confiscates materials deemed "harmful to the government". At the same time the Chinese State Administration of Radio, Film, and Television supervises radio and television (including the satellite and Internet broadcasting) in collaboration with MIIT. The latter is responsible for controlling the software industry and licensing the ICPs. The Ministry of Public Security is liable for general regulation of Internet access. The State Secrets Bureau keeps a register of all categories of state secrets which shall be kept by all the Chinese.[101] Finally, the guarantee that Chinese publishers publish only materials falling within the communistic party ideology is the responsibility of the Central Propaganda Department.[102] Apart from the detailed central regulation of the scope of available electronic content, China also exercises control over the actions of service providers, content providers, service subscribers and Internet café users. To regulate all aspects of electronic activities, the State Council, on 25 September 2000, issued Order No. 292 Administrative Measures for Managing Internet Information Systems. The document introduced a special category of websites, both profit-making and non-profit, that "relate to information, the publishing business, education, medical and health care, pharmaceuticals, and medical apparatus etc."[103]

Pursuant to this order, Internet service providers operating within Chinese territory, before commencing their activities, must apply for a license issued by MIIT. Obtaining the license obliges them to record and keep records of the email addresses of the client, along with his or her telephone number and IP number. Also in accordance with this Order, and contrary to Western states' regulations, Chinese service

100 ONI names the Central Propaganda Department, Department of Commerce, Department of Telecommunications, General Administration of Press and Publications, Ministry of Culture, Ministry of Information Industry, Ministry of Public Security, Public Security Bureau, State Administration of Radio, Film, and Television, State Council, State Council Information Agency, State Secrets Bureau; see ONI, *Internet Filtering*, op. cit., p. 54.

101 State Security Law of 22 February 1993. An English translation can be found at <http://www.cecc.gov/pages/virtualAcad/exp/explaws.php> (accessed 19 January 2011).

102 See: ONI, *Internet Filtering*, op. cit., p. 10.

103 State Council Order no. 292 of 25 September 2000 (Administrative Measures on Internet Information Services). <http://www.chinaitlaw.org/?p1=print&p2=050306173518> (accessed 13 January 2011) ('the Measures').

providers bear legal responsibility for the content they provide. Failure to meet their obligations will result in license cancelation and personnel detention.[104] ICPs shall adapt to national provisions not only the information they provide themselves but also entries on discussion forums available on their websites. Furthermore, they shall keep records of all content rendered available. Order No. 292 imposes an obligation on commercial ICPs to apply for a commercial license to the Ministry of Information Industry,[105] but also providers conducting non-commercial operations must keep official records of services provided.[106] They also have to apply for the license if they wish to distribute electronic "bulletins" or administer distribution letters.

Provisions on the Administration of Internet Electronic Messaging Services[107] issued by the Congressional-Executive Commission on 27 October 2000 extended the requirements of Order no. 292. Any Internet content provider who intends to render services allowing the electronic exchange of views must not only apply for the consent of the Minister of Information Industry,[108] but also develop a comprehensive set of regulations, compliant with applicable laws, which shall be binding on the users of the website.[109] Such regulations (being a distant counterpart of the non-binding provisions of netiquette used in Western culture) must be placed on the website in a noticeable place.[110] Under the provisions of the same act, ISPs shall keep records of activities of their users and keep copies of such records for 60 days and possibly provide them to the relevant state authorities on their demand.[111] ISPs and ICPs were obliged to monitor any information rendered available on their websites and to promptly remove and report any "inappropriate" and "unlawful" information.[112] Wishing to meet the above-mentioned requirements, ISPs often apply their own measures of monitoring and censorship, thus further limiting the users' access to information. Restrictions on the freedom and monitoring of electronic information also concern foreign service providers for whom the Ministry of Information Industry issued, in 2000, the Public Pledge on Self-Discipline for the China Internet Industry. Acceding to the document is a de facto condition precedent, even though extralegal, to conduct business in China.

Chinese law-makers also directly address web users. The State Council Decree of 1996 requires all subscribers to register with their local police bureau within the first

104 International Centre for Human Rights and Democratic Development (2001), *Review of China's Internet Regulations and Domestic Legislation*. <http://www.ichrdd.ca/english/commdoc/publications/globalization/legislationInternetChinaEng.pdf> (accessed 16 January 2011); see also: R. Deibert et al. (eds.), op. cit., p. 459.

105 The Measures, Article 7.

106 The Measures, Article 8.

107 China Congressional-Executive Commission decision on Provisions on the Administration of Internet Electronic Messaging Services of 27 October 2000. For an English translation see <http://www.cecc.gov/pages/virtualAcad/index.phpd?showsingle=1568> (accessed 13 January 2011) (hereinafter referred to as 'the Provisions').

108 The Provisions, Article 5.

109 The Provisions, Article 6.

110 The Provisions, Article 10.

111 The Provisions, Article 14.

112 The Provisions, Article 13.

30 days of signing up with an ISP. The same Decree sets up police computer investigation organizations to investigate alleged violations.[113] Those who wish to avoid this type of filtering are offered cybercafés (wangba), which are very popular in China. The number of such cafés has grown in recent years, even though only some of them are licensed. China periodically increases its supervision over Internet cafés.[114] Formally, the owners of such cafés are required to install software that blocks websites purportedly containing pornographic or "subversive" content. Cafés must keep detailed logs including users' identities (by asking them to produce their identification cards), linking users to the pages they visited and recording access to any blocked pages. Cafés must keep these records for at least 60 days and submit them to the Public Security Bureau. The goals of the regulations are to "provide good service to users and to promote socialism".[115] Cafés must follow all applicable regulations established by several state administrative bodies. Culture Departments of the government at the county level or above are entitled to observe and promote new facilities of such type and control the already existing ones. The Public Security Bureau is responsible for "information safety" including within cybercafés. The Commerce Department registers cafés, issues permits and inspects the premises, checking whether the owners hold relevant licenses.[116]

Another element of the "Great Firewall of China" is the Law on State Secrets, which defines a "state secret" as secret information within the scope of social, technological and internal relations development, national and economy security.[117] In accordance with the Law, state secrets include, for example, "secrets in the building of national defense", "secrets concerning major policy decisions on state affairs", "secrets in national economic and social development", "secrets concerning science and technology" and secrets concerning criminal proceedings as well as the secrets of political parties.[118] These provisions effectively limit the amount of critical views on state policy available to Chinese Internet users.[119] The State Secrets Bureau enjoys extensive discretionary powers when defining new categories of "state secrets".[120] The authorities have assigned this status to numerous types of information with a

113 See ONI, *Internet Filtering*, p. 12.

114 In 2001, the State Council conducted a three month investigation into public Internet service providers, closing over 8,000 Internet cafés. The police installed filtering software to block pornography and other "harmful" information.

115 See ONI, *Internet Filtering*, p. 12.

116 Cafés must obtain permits before commencing service. Companies that offer this type of service must have adequate capital, fire prevention systems, methods for controlling access to information, and appropriate technical and security personnel. Cafés cannot be located within 200 meters of an elementary school, middle school, or residential building. See ONI, *Internet Filtering*, p. 12.

117 Law of the People's Republic of China on Protection of State Secrets. An English translation is available at <http://www.cecc.gov/pages/newLaws/protectSecretsENG.php> (accessed 8 January 2011).

118 Law on Protection of State Secrets, Article 8.

119 Cf. Amnesty International (1996) *State Secrets – a Pretext for Repression*, AI INDEX: ASA 17/42/96, section 1.

120 Cf. Human Rights in China (2004) *Who's Who in Labor & State Secrets*. <http://www.hrichina.org/public/contents/article?revision%5fid=18104&item%5fid=18103> (accessed 20 January 2006).

retrospective effect. China's Constitution requires all citizens to "safeguard" state secrets.[121] Violations of the State Secrets Law must be reported to authorities. Penalties for failure to comply with state secrets regulations are severe: the Supreme People's Court ruled that serious cases of state secrets violations can be punished with up to 10 years of imprisonment, and violators may face the death penalty for cases of severe harm.[122] An additional obligation rests with the electronic content providers who "shall conscientiously perform secrecy protection duties and establish sound administration systems to strengthen supervision and monitoring".[123] Current information may be published online only by licensed publishers,[124] whereas obtaining a license for electronic press requires following the same procedure as the that applied to printed press. As a consequence of this legal scheme, Chinese authorities are satisfied that any information available to citizens comes from sources controlled by the state. These legal means have, more recently, been complemented by the introduction of new technical tools aimed at increasing state surveillance over its residents. The "Green Dam" and the "Golden Shield" are codenames given to recent government programs aimed at, respectively, introducing filtering to all computers sold in China and organizing a digital nationwide surveillance network covering public security units.[125]

Electronic content control in China is also exercised through non-regulatory measures. The Internet Society of China (not being a chapter of The Internet Society) exerts strong pressure on content and service providers to agree to a "Public Pledge of Self-Regulation and Professional Ethics" developed by the Ministry of Information.[126] Acceptance of this document by Western commercial enterprises has been severally criticized by media and social organizations of democratic states.

In order to develop a common international Internet policy it is necessary to take account of the positions of states conducting filtering policies, such as the People's Republic of China. To achieve a consensus, one should undoubtedly start with areas common to all states: protection of nationals against international terrorism, sexual crime and weapons of mass destruction etc. This "initial position" may form a basis to further discussions. The key to determining a relevant model of cooperation may be to determine the principles of exercising jurisdiction by reference to human rights protection. There are views that breach of such rights, including on the Internet, could become the grounds for general repression.[127]

121 See ONI, *Internet Filtering*, p. 17.

122 'Supreme People's Court on Stealing State Secrets', *Xinhua News Agency*, 21 January 2001.

123 Provisions on the Administration of the Protection of Secrets on Internationally Networked Computer Information Systems, Articles 8 and 10. An English translation is available at <http://www.cecc.gov/pages/virtualAcad/exp/expsecurity.php> (accessed 16 January 2011).

124 The Provisions Article 19.

125 See R. Deibert et al. (eds.), op. cit., p. 463.

126 Public Pledge of Self-Regulation and Professional Ethics for China Internet Industry. For an English translation, see <http://www.isc.org.cn/20020417/ca102762.htm> (accessed 16 January 2011).

127 So considers J. Nolan (2008) 'The China Dilemma: Internet Censorship and Corporate Responsibility', 57 *University of New South Wales Faculty of Law Research Series*, pp. 11ff.

To picture an interesting compromise between the control of electronic content and values common to international community it is worth taking a closer look at the development and practice of another Asian country that interferes in the content available within its territory to a completely different extent.

Singapore

Singapore has one of the most advanced and comprehensive modern technology development strategies in the world, supported by significant infrastructure investment administered by the government. The authors of Singapore's information policy have aimed at transforming the small Asian country into the ICT hub for the entire Asian sub-continent, investing in the exchange of thoughts rather than commodities exchange.[128] Since 1995, Singapore has been a member of the World Trade Organization; as a result, in 2000, it introduced full liberalization of its ICT market. The implementation of national laws pertaining to information technologies is supervised by the Media Development Authority, formerly the Singapore Broadcasting Authority.[129]

The authorities have used a wealth of experience in managing the national network.[130] Earlier experiences of Singapore relating to press or television law served as the model for its Internet regulations. Many renowned publishers adapted to standards set by the authorities of the island when they established their own regional offices in Singapore. A combination of available infrastructure, production and distribution factors, proceeds from advertisements and other pro-commercial circumstances must have prevailed over the stringent policy drawbacks. A similar tendency has been observed with respect to electronic media.

The idea of establishing a regional broadcasting center in Singapore for the Asian and Pacific regions proved successful. Singapore serves as the centre for recognized international television stations to conduct their activities within the territory of Asia. Interestingly enough, although private satellite receivers are forbidden in Singapore,[131] programs for the rest of Asia are broadcast from the island. The practice of international companies to date has been based to a large extent on extralegal ethical rules, thereby proving that there is no need for the authorities to directly interfere in the content broadcast by such companies. Generally speaking, cable television providers offer politically indifferent material such as music or sport, addressed to a wide family audience, thereby demonstrating the conservative values supported by the government. The filtering software applied in Singapore is designed to block general access

128 See G. Rodan (1996) 'Information Technology and Political Control in Singapore', 26 *Japan Policy Research Institute Working Papers*. <http://www.jpri.org/publications/workingpapers/wp26.html> (accessed 18 January 2011).

129 Ibid.

130 In 1992, the National Computer Board put forward a new strategic statement, *IT 2000: A Vision of an Intelligent Island*. Under *IT 2000* (see G. Rodan, op. cit.), it is now envisioned that all 750,000 households on the island will have been connected to a comprehensive computer network with broadband coaxial.

131 See G. Rodan, op. cit.

to specific content.[132] Singapore authorities decided to demonstrate the comprehensive nature of their technologies as early as in 1994, when scan of public Internet accounts made it possible for the government to search over 80,000 private files, of which five were considered to be pornographic.[133] The government stressed that it did not intend to search any further: such a display of power at the beginning of the Internet in Singapore was designed to make citizens aware that the government did not wish to amend or formulate a more lenient policy directed at protecting the morality of nationals for the mere fact of emergence of a new medium.[134]

The fundamental legal instrument establishing such control is the Singapore Broadcasting Act.[135] Pursuant to the Act, the Media Development Authority enjoys the right to require the blocking of specific external sites or domains and to mandate the removal or moderation of "objectionable" content hosted by service providers. An Internet Code of Practice[136] has been developed by the Authority and defines forbidden content ISPs must block.[137] Singapore's official position is that the state filters Internet content to promote social values and maintain national unity,[138] with the goal of denying access to objectionable material, especially pornography and content inciting ethnic or religious strife. Each of Singapore's three primary Internet service providers offers optional, filtered Internet access services that block additional sites for a minimum monthly fee (other than from the "black list").[139] The scope of filtering effected by the Singapore authorities is, *de facto*, minimum.[140] Similar content is readily available on other sites on the Internet.

132 Such software as e.g. Surf Watch, Cyber Patrol or Cyber Sentry. Some of them search for key terms on a website and display pages containing such terms. This software may, however, result in the blocking of websites which include not only prohibited material.

133 See G. Rodan, op. cit.

134 Ibid.

135 Singapore Broadcasting Act 1994.

136 Media Development Authority *Internet Code of Practice*. <http://www.mda.gov.sg/wms.file/mobj/mobj.497.internet_code.pdf> (accessed 16 January 2011). Similar Internet Codes of Practice are non-binding in other countries: in Great Britain it is a document of a voluntary nature, and in New Zealand the document is proposed by the modern technology industry as a form of self-regulation.

137 In considering what "prohibited material" is, the following factors should be taken into account: whether the material depicts nudity or genitalia in a manner calculated to titillate, whether the material promotes sexual violence, whether the material depicts a person or persons clearly engaged in explicit sexual activity, whether the material advocates homosexuality, whether the material depicts a person who is, or appears to be, under 16 years of age in sexual activity, whether the material advocates homosexuality or lesbianism, or depicts or promotes incest, zoophilia, pedophilia, and necrophilia, whether the material depicts detailed or relished acts of extreme violence or cruelty or whether the material glorifies, incites or endorses ethnic, racial or religious hatred, strife or intolerance. Internet Code of Practice, section 4.

138 OpenNet Initiative (2005) *Internet Filtering in Singapore in 2004–2005*. <www.opennetinitiative.net/singapore/> (accessed 16 January 2011), hereinafter referred to as ONI *Singapore*, p. 3. Cf. R. Deibert et al., *Access Denied*, op. cit.

139 Ibid.

140 According to ONI research, only eight sites of 1,632 tested websites were blocked (0.49%). The blocked sites focused on pornographic content, one site on illegal drugs and another one on fanatical religion; ibid.

Internet content regulation is based on entirely different grounds than is the case with China – not on modern, comprehensive technological solutions, but mainly on controlling access (through the license requirement for websites with political content) and legal pressure (claims for defamation and deprivation of liberty). These effectively prevent the placing of objectionable content online.

In comparison with other countries applying obligatory filtering, the technical filtering applied in Singapore is one of the most limited. The Singapore Telecommunications Act requires all Internet service providers as well as political parties, Internet content providers,[141] and owners of sites providing materials about political or religious topics to register with the Media Development Authority (MDA) as representatives of a specific category of providers.

The Media Development Authority (MDA), established on 1 January 2003 (formerly the Singapore Broadcasting Authority), is a governmental body authorized to regulate media. The powers of the MDA are directly provided in the Media Development Authority of Singapore Act[142] under which it was established. Pursuant to its provisions, both service and content providers shall operate in accordance with the Internet Code of Practice. All Internet service providers shall be subject to a relevant Class License.[143] In this way Singapore enforced regulations constituting a barrier to unlimited creation of Internet content, thus rendering regulations on content itself more stringent. It is worth stressing that some websites of political content, especially those expressing critical views on the government, are placed on foreign servers to circumvent national regulations. So far, the government has undertaken no special steps to counteract this practice, concentrating on national actions. The Internet Code of Practice provides neither for penalties nor restrictions with respect to users; nevertheless, the violation of other rights, such as the ban on possessing pornography, may result in criminal sanctions. Moreover, the Media Development Authority may impose penalties on content providers for violating the rules, including fines or license suspension or cancellation for failure to comply with Code of Practice.[144]

More far-reaching regulations are provided for in the Computer Misuse Act and legislation pertaining to electronic commerce adopted in 1998,[145] which vested broad

141 The Media Development Authority defines Internet service providers as "Internet Access Service Providers (IASPs) who function as main "gateways" to the Internet, and Internet Service Resellers (ISRs) who obtain Internet access from the IASPs and resell such access to the public. Internet Content Providers are defined as "information providers on the World Wide Web... [who] include web authors and editors, web publishers and web server administrators." See the MDA's *Internet Industry Guide*. <http://www.mda.gov.sg/wms.file/mobj/mobj.496.internet_industry_guide.pdf> (accessed 16 January 2011).

142 Media Development Authority of Singapore Act. <www.parliament.gov.sg/Legislation/Htdocs/Bills/020037.pdf> (accessed 7 January 2011).

143 For more information, see Singapore Media Development Authority *Internet Service Providers*. <http://www.mda.gov.sg/Documents/PDF/licences/mobj.487.ClassLicence.pdf> (accessed 21 May 2011).

144 Ibid., p. 1.

145 Computer Misuse Act, 1993, Chapter 50A as amended. <http://statutes.agc.gov.sg/non_version/cgi-bin/cgi_retrieve.pl?actno=REVED-50A&doctitle=COMPUTER%20MISUSE%20ACT%0A&date=latest&method=part> (accessed 7 June 2011).

competence in the police to seize and search computers without first obtaining a warrant, and to decode electronic messages.[146] Furthermore, other service providers (e.g. universities) also apply the practice of blocking websites. Similarly to the Authority, they neither disclose addresses of websites nor provide the reasons for blocking them.[147] The findings of a report on censorship prepared by a committee established by the government determined that access to "content that undermines public order and the nation's security, denigrates race and religion or erodes moral values" should be limited.[148] The committee found certain content "clearly immoral and demeaning", that is "pornography, deviant sexual practices, sexual violence, child pornography, bestiality".[149] The report pointed to the discrepancy in definitions of "violence, nudity and homosexuality", especially recommending a less clear-cut definition of homosexual content.[150]

An important, if not the most important, measure of controlling the media in Singapore is to raise claims based on provisions prohibiting defamation, libel and slander.[151] "Defamation suits in Singapore are a common tactic for controlling speech, especially that related to Singapore's government and politics. Defendants who lose such suits often face hundreds of thousands of dollars in liability. Self-censorship by the media is common"[152] since the burden of proof rests with the defendant; he or she has to prove the truth of the statements. "The Defamation Act presumes that defamatory words are false and the plaintiff need do no more than prove that the defamatory words have been published by the defendant."[153]

Internet censorship in Singapore is quite rigorous; however, the approach taken differs utterly from the Chinese approach. The government uses non-technical and extralegal measures to prevent the placing of specific content online and to hinder access thereto, in particular that content referring to political groups other than the ruling party and religious or ethnic issues. The threat of extremely high fines or even criminal prosecution as a result of defamation lawsuits, imprisonment without court decision under the Internal Security Act, and police monitoring of computer use may deter users in Singapore from creating or obtaining access to potentially objectionable materials.[154] Singapore's filtering regime, despite being rather low-tech, is still extremely effective.

146 Ibid., section 14 on investigations by police and law enforcement officers.

147 ONI *Singapore*, p. 10.

148 Singapore Ministry of Information, Communication and the Arts (2003) *Censorship Review Committee: 2003 Report*. <www.mda.gov.sg/wms.file/mobj/mobj.316.Censorship_Review_ 2003.pdf> (accessed 7 January 2011), p. 15.

149 Ibid., p. 6.

150 Ibid., p. 32. This may be related to the fact that Singapore is becoming the center of homosexual culture in its region (see: ONI, *Singapore*, p. 4).

151 Singapore Defamation Act. <http://statutes.agc.gov.sg/non_version/cgi-bin/cgi_retrieve.pl?&actno=Reved-5&date=latest&method=part> (accessed 13 January 2011).

152 See: ONI *Singapore*, p. 6.

153 See ONI *Singapore*, p. 7. The practice was disapproved, *inter alia*, by the US Department of State in (2005) *Singapore: Country Reports on Human Rights Practices*. <http://www.state.gov/g/drl/rls/hrrpt/2004/41659.htm> (accessed 9 January 2011).

154 Ibid.

Between effective jurisdiction and filtering – a summary of state practice

In traditional terms, the fundamental basis for restrictive laws is "maintaining social values", protection of "morality" or the safeguarding of "social standards". Efforts to uphold morality sometimes leverage legal concepts of "indecency" and "obscenity", whose definitions vary widely from country to country. For instance, South Korea has banned content dealing with euthanasia and hacking.[155] Legislation in India blocks sites that "appeal to the prurient interest", and Australian law prohibits sites that include "information about crime or drug use".[156] Egypt bans Internet content on "taboo issues" such as criticism of its president, and Uzbekistan prohibits accessing materials critical of the country's president or based on religious extremism.[157]

The second fundamental rationale for Internet filtering is "national security". A number of states used the 911 terrorist attacks, as well as argument about the potential threat of terrorist attacks, to justify tighter restrictions on Internet content.[158] Anti-terrorist legislation often allows governments considerable latitude in monitoring and censoring Internet content viewed by their citizens. Other countries filter Internet content more extensively, stating that such censorship is necessary to preserve national security. As mentioned above, protecting national security in China includes banning materials that could threaten "national unity"; Burma, Egypt, and Malaysia, on the other hand, forbid any content that criticizes the ruling party. Liberia has blocked websites that contain "anti-Liberian materials", while Zimbabwe disables foreign sites that publish anything "likely to cause alarm or despondency".[159] In 2001, India adopted the Communications Convergence Bill governing "the content and transmission of all communications in India, regardless of the medium".[160]

Internet filtering often raises doubts about the protection of the rights to freedom of expression, the press, privacy or religion. Here it should be emphasized that the nature and extent of these civil liberties vary substantially from country to country. The extent to which filtering does not violate fundamental freedoms is a vital issue arising on the introduction of a filtering regime by a state. Blocking may be overbroad (blocking of websites with dangerous content interferes in citizens' freedoms guaranteed by a state)[161] or under-inclusive – failing to meet its purpose.

155 See ONI (2004) *A Starting Point: Legal Implications of Internet Filtering*, p. 6.

156 Ibid., p. 6.

157 Ibid.

158 See e.g. Great Britain, Regulation of Investigatory Powers Act, 2000.

159 *Privacy International and the GreenNet Educational Trust (PIGNET)* 'Silenced: An International Report on Censorship and Control of the Internet.' <http://www.privacyinternational.org/survey/censorship/silenced.pdf> (accessed 15 January 2011), p. 20, hereinafter referred to as 'PIGNET *Silenced*'.

160 Bill No 89 of 2001. <http://www.dot.gov.in/Acts/CCBill_of_pages_41.doc> (accessed 5 January 2011). Quote from ONI *A Starting Point*, p. 7.

161 "The United States Supreme Court, for instance, upheld a requirement for Internet filtering of materials 'harmful for minors' in schools and public libraries as a condition of receiving federal financial support": ONI *A Starting Point*, p.8. See also B. Edelman (2003) *Sites Blocked by Internet Filtering Programs*, Harvard University Berkman Center for Internet and Society. <http://cyber. law.harvard.edu/people/edelman/mul-v-us/> (accessed 5 January 2011).

Naturally, the issue must be classified in terms of a state's violation of its competence as vested under the international law. For, "when a state filters packets flowing through physical elements of the global network located within its geographic boundaries, that state affects the communications of citizens not only in its own territory, but potentially worldwide."[162] One state's powers exercised over email sent from its territory directly affect the ability of other states' residents to impart and receive information. Filtering might only block access within a country's borders to certain websites, but it might also alter network traffic within its borders and impede access even by users from abroad. If one state's filtering inflicts damage on a resident of another state (for instance, as a result of non-delivery of an electronic package or simply an email), the injured party typically has limited legal recourse.

> She must choose between pursuing action in that state's courts, which will likely be unsuccessful (either because filtering is legally authorized there or because government actions are protected by the doctrine of sovereign immunity), or bringing suit in her home jurisdiction, which may lack authority to hear the dispute or the power to enforce a judgment.[163]

The Internet's global content distribution and the intermediary role played by multimedia companies make clashes between state jurisdictions inevitable. Disputes may be resolved by international dispute settlement bodies, such as the WTO or by relevant agreements between countries, the latter solution being more permanent. Existing private international law allows for much discretional power on the part of the states applying them. Discrepancies in application of private international law regulations are particularly likely with disputes regarding Internet content filtering, "as it involves two issues at the core of a state's sovereignty: the government's authority to regulate its telecommunications infrastructure, and local cultural standards on acceptable content. States most often view these interests as determinative in making judicial decisions".[164] Thus, while filtering raises serious jurisdictional concerns, states tend to assert the primacy of their laws in disputes on the limits of freedom of speech or communication online.

However, one should not express any outward disapproval of filtering and Internet censorship as such. Instances of government Internet monitoring may be encountered in Europe[165] as well as the US.[166]

> The ability to enforce a court decision imposes a practical limit on a sovereign's jurisdiction. While an unenforceable judgment may still have value (for example,

162 ONI *A Starting Point*, p. 8.

163 ONI *A Starting Point*, op. cit., p. 10.

164 ONI *A Starting Point*, op. cit., p. 10.

165 One should mention the controversial Data Retention Directive (European Union Directive 2006/24/EC of the European Parliament and of the Council of 15 March 2006 on the Retention of Data Generated or Processed in Connection with the Provision of Publicly Available Electronic Communications Services or of Public Communications Networks and Amending Directive 2002/58/EC, OJ (L 105) (13 April 2006), pp. 54–63.).

166 E.g. the aforementioned USA PATRIOT Act.

> to signal a state's position on a contested issue or to affirm a litigant's abstract rights) – it does not generally alter a defendant's behavior or compel obedience . . . Traditionally, enforcement of a judgment requires a state to have either direct power over the defendant orher property or a binding agreement with another state requiring enforcement of the first state's judgments . . . Absent one of these two arrangements, states were generally powerless to enforce decisions beyond their borders. Filtering, however, makes enforcement relatively easier for sovereigns. A state's control over Internet infrastructure, service providers, content providers, or users can be sufficient to enforce its decisions through filtering.[167]

A state's power to resolve a dispute has always been practically limited by the state's geographical boundaries. With Internet filtering the state can control a defendant's or respondent's conduct, by, for example, preventing that state's residents from accessing the content or services that the defendant enables.

The issue of Internet governance is closely related to the jurisdiction question.

> Filtering sharpens the problem of governance by effectively devolving control from international organizations and standards-setting bodies to individual states and ISPs. The focus is shifting from the original disputes over domain names allocation and the structure of the Internet Corporation for Assigned Names and Numbers to broader issues like filtering, spam, network security and other tricky, distributed problems.[168]

International law provides for several potential tools to analyze Internet filtering (through provisions pertaining to human rights or the protection of intellectual property), yet it does not regulate a country's ability to filter the Internet access of its citizens. There are no international treaties directly safeguarding free and open Internet. It seems that market forces themselves may ensure a minimum level of Internet access as it guarantees production growth and gains for the economy. Further steps, however, need to be taken by the international community as a whole.[169]

The United States has taken steps to commence such a debate. The initial step was the 2005 draft Global Internet Freedom Act[170] that would ensure worldwide protection of human rights online through, among others, the efforts of the Office of Global Internet Freedom. Although the bill never became law, the idea behind it is being reintroduced in recent US declarations, such as the "Clinton Doctrine".[171] On 21 January 2010, Hillary Clinton, the US Secretary of State, announced the commencement

167 ONI *A Starting Point*, op. cit., p. 11.

168 ONI *A Starting Point*, op. cit., p. 12.

169 See chapter 4.

170 Global Internet Freedom Act, H.r. 2216. <http://www.govtrack.us/congress/billtext.xpd?bill=h109-2216> (accessed 5 January2011).

171 S. Gorman 'Web Access Is New Clinton Doctrine', *Wall Street Journal*, 21 January 2010. http://online.wsj.com/article/SB10001424052748703405704575015461404882830.html?mod=WSJ_hpp_MIDDLETopStories<http://online.wsj.com/article/SB10001424052748703405704575015461404882830.html> (accessed 21 January 2011).

of implementation of "Internet Freedom",[172] a new program against the censorship of electronic content propagated by state governments. The Secretary has condemned China, North Korea, Egypt, Vietnam, Tunisia, Uzbekistan and Saudi Arabia as countries restricting the free flow of information, violating the privacy of citizens discussing politics and using the Internet as a tool to spy and reduce people of various beliefs to silence.[173] She had declared that the US would use its resources to aid those who suffer from extensive limitations of access to information and communication freedom. Criticism of the initiative was based on cultural differences on the limits of the freedom of speech – US standards differ substantially from the standards of other states, while each state enjoys equal powers, under the principle of sovereignty, to decide about the limits applicable to its community.

The next step towards an international debate on human rights standards online was the May 2011 "International Strategy for Cyberspace", proposed by Barack Obama. It invited the worldwide community to work together on elaborating international standards for human rights online, with the Universal Declaration of Human Rights[174] and its Covenants[175] as the starting point for deliberations. This seems the only possible direction for seeking consensus on regulating the World Wide Web, since "any type of legal or diplomatic solution risks interfering with a state's traditional sovereignty. The definition of 'indecent' materials in the United States would let pass materials that would be deemed off-limits in much of Europe, and certainly in countries like Saudi Arabia or other parts of the Middle East. A quick survey of national views on 'indecency' reveals the enormous complexity of formulating an international standard".[176]

It is necessary to seek an international consensus on the principles and limits of state power in cyberspace. Such a process would have to:

> confront the clash of local standards and norms with an international medium whose design resists barriers and blocks [both technical and legal]. There is no simple way to establish and enforce a single legal standard for Internet content across every state. Countries with divergent perspectives on governance, civil liberties and culture are unlikely to achieve consensus on a filtering regime.[177]

172 D. Gross 'Aide: Clinton will Address China in Internet Freedom Speech', *CNN*, 21 January 2010. <http://www.allbusiness.com/legal/constitutional-law-freedom-speech/13752059-1.html> (accessed 21 January 2011).

173 Ibid.

174 Universal Declaration of Human Rights, G.A. res. 217A (III), UN Doc A/810 at 71 (1948).

175 International Covenant on Civil and Political Rights, 1966, UN Doc. A/6316 and the International Covenant on Economic, Social and Cultural Rights , 1966, UN Doc. A/6316, which together form the "International Bill of Rights".

176 ONI *A Starting Point*, p. 15. Note 48 on p. 16 states that in Algeria, indecency is defined as "material that undermines public order and morale" and includes the "denigration of the president through insults or defamation." Kazakhstan has a similar prohibition against "harming the honor and dignity" of the President. Bahrain blocks sites that are "platforms for spreading biased news, rumors and lies". See also PIGNET *Silenced*, op. cit., pp. 20–21.

177 ONI *A Starting Point*, p. 16.

Nevertheless, the reform of filtering seems "both desirable and possible . . . [the] filtering regime should embrace three cardinal principles: transparency, accountability, and inclusiveness".[178]

The reform seems an attainable objective. International organizations and states themselves are unable to execute the changes they consider appropriate in borderless cyberspace. However, through their local practice, standards, declarations and negotiations a common consensus may be developed.

The current courtroom practice provides valuable lessons from which the sought-after consensus ought to be derived. They clearly show that applying territorial jurisdiction in Internet-related cases must be limited.

The subjective territorial jurisdiction would only be welcomed in cases of cybercrime, especially the ones leading to cyberattacks, where the country from whose territory the harmful actions are initiated is the first to seek and punish the culprits. Should it fail to act, the victim states ought to be entitled to exercise their jurisdiction (the *aut dedere aut judicare* principle for cybersecurity threats ought to be introduced within an international framework treaty[179]). Should there be more than one state entitled to act (as would probably usually be the case), traditional extradition regimes could be applied.

In civil law cases the application of effective jurisdiction should only be limited to those instances where the US *Zippo* and effects test criteria are met, that is when a particular service or website content is targeted at the forum state (through language, content or currency), there is actual interaction with the state and actual harm had been caused. The mere availability of certain content within a state territory ought not be the ground for exercising jurisdiction.

Such a limitation of their power would be unsatisfactory to most states, forever more eagerly wanting to execute their national laws in cyberspace. For those states, the way of protecting local community from potential harm caused by electronic content would be Internet filtering – blocking access to certain categories of electronic content recognized by the local community as inappropriate or harmful. Standards for introducing Internet filtering ought to be carefully elaborated on the international level, based on human rights standards, and be accountable and transparent.

Certainly, at the current stage of development, establishing a negative standard would be possible – a standard prohibiting dissemination of materials such as child pornography or producing weapons of mass destruction. A possible way of further elaborating those standards and a mechanism for seeking such consensus is presented in the following chapter. J. P. Barlow was right to say that "one cannot separate the air that chokes from the air upon which wings beat";[180] nonetheless, the international community has no other option but to make such attempt.

178 ONI, ibid.
179 The principle may be enacted only within a treaty regime.
180 J. P. Barlow, op. cit.

4 From international governance to International Internet Law

Internet governance – new actors in international law

So far, the success of numerous international organizations and national governments in regulating the World Wide Web through law has been moderate. The reasons for their failure are twofold and they both originate from the nature of the network, designed as a decentralized one, resilient to a direct attack.[1] First, it is the very architecture of the network, composed of three interrelated but dissimilar layers, that makes it impossible to efficiently render it subject to any unilateral regulation. The second reason is a consequence of the first one – since the network is decentralized, all of its actors hold an equally strong position in defining its character.[2] The key to regulating the Internet lies in a comprehensive, coherent co-operation of all stakeholders,[3] achievable solely through international multi-stakeholder collaboration.

Following Benkler's "layers of communications"[4] scheme, successful rule over the

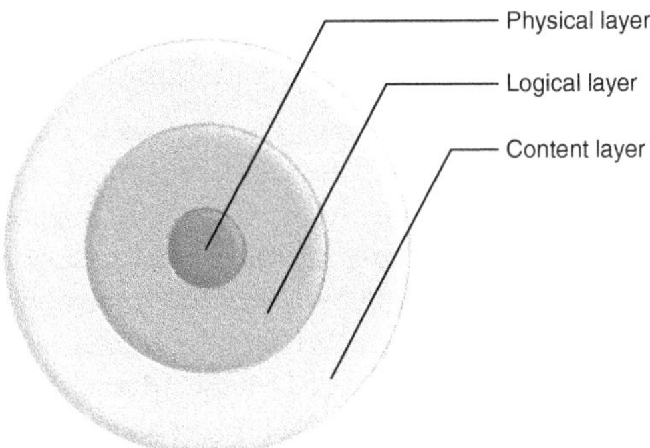

Figure 4.1 Schematic Representation of Internet layers.[5]

1 See generally: B. van Schewick (2010) *Internet Architecture and Innovation*, Cambridge, Mass.: MIT Press.

2 See generally: Lessig (2006) *Code: Version 2.0*, New York: Basic Books, pp. 1–30.

3 In accordance with the principle of multi-stakeholderism, discussed in detail below.

4 See e.g. Y. Benkler (2006) *The Wealth of Networks: How Social Production Transforms Markets and Freedom*, New Haven: Yale University Press, pp. 392ff., L. Lessig, op. cit., p. 144, but see also p. 368, where a fourth layer – the "application layer" – is mentioned.

5 Own study after Y. Benkler, *The Wealth of Networks*, op. cit., p. 393.

Internet would require harmonizing the regulation of all three layers simultaneously. This means a legal and practical coordination of:

- the physical layer: the technical layer allowing various elements of the Internet to interact;
- the logical layer: software-based coordination of key protocols enabling Internet functioning; and
- the content layer: conducting social policy through co-operation by state authorities and entities involved in electronic exchange.

Primarily, non-governmental organizations (such as IETF)[6] currently deal with the first two issues. They act upon open procedures developed by a wide spectrum of members, representing academia, business and the civil community. The third, most outer layer incorporates a traditional, exclusive competence of state authorities acting through their legislative bodies. In order for the global network to function efficiently, all parties participating in the debate on regulating the Internet ought to consider the specifics of all three layers and differences between them. This facilitates the clarification of what is otherwise vague and guarantees that key entities involved in electronic activities, including governments, accurately define their views on each of the elements separately, thereby setting clear-cut co-operation frameworks. The middle, logical layer is of key significance to such considerations, as the purpose of its functioning is to determine who governs the network and how entities involved in political or economic life may participate in such governance. The connection thereof with the content layer is especially important. At the confluence of the two layers – between the technical coordination of the code and its application to safeguard national laws – emerge issues comprising international Internet law.

The logical layer operation is based on already developed procedures (developed by IETF and ISPs worldwide) while any co-operation intended for international content layer governance is at its initiation stage. Lessons learned from the logical layer governance mechanisms could allow for the development of new, improved institutions for the content layer and underlying international legal regulation. Therefore, a brief description of the logical layer governance mechanism is depicted below.

In the 1980s technical supervision over what was to become the Internet was exercised by a number of agreements and "requests for comments" submitted by US government bodies, including *inter alia*, the US Defense Advanced Research Project Agency, DARPA. After the Internet Society (ISOC) was established in 1992, it took over the financing of such activities. This form of organization has, over time, transformed into a task force of mutually related institutions and committees working on technical standards, the most important being the Internet Architecture Board (IAB) and the Internet Engineering Task Force. By 1998, many functions of the Internet Assigned Numbers Authority (IANA) which had operated under agreement with ARPA, was subsumed by the Internet Corporation for Assigned Names And Numbers (ICANN) which was

6 The Internet Engineering Task Force. The ITU-T also plays a major role in all telecommunications regulations.

established for the purpose of assuming the abovementioned obligations (other than IP addressing) as well as new duties. The corporation was financed by businesses and operated under an agreement with the US Department of Commerce.[7] Despite the fact that the organizations were primarily joined with the US government, their structure was presumed to be autonomous and independent. The operation standards and structures of the said bodies were developed by the individuals involved (mainly volunteers) in a process based on compromise, discussion on technical issues and thorough analyses of circumstances. At this point it seems reasonable to present a short review of organizations which played or are still playing a significant role in the technical administration of the greatest global network.

The Internet Engineering Task Force[8] is a large open international community of network designers, operators, vendors, and researchers concerned with the evolution of Internet architecture and the interoperability of the network. It is the main body engaged in elaborating new Internet standards. The IETF Secretariat is largely financed with fees for participating in IETF meetings and hosted by a non-profit organization (the Corporation for National Research Initiatives). The organization operates an open consultation process via standardization proposals published online and presents the Internet Engineering Steering Group (IESG) with Requests for Comments as regards technical issues. IETF facilitates compromise on technical solutions based on the engagement of ICT experts from all over the world and issues recommendations to the IESG on matters relating to setting protocol standards. IETF membership and participation are open to any interested individual. To become a member of IETF, an individual has to register with the working group falling within the ambit of his or her interest, with respect to which he or she may offer a significant contribution.

IESG[9] is responsible for the technical management of IETF activities and Internet standards development. It administers the processes according to rules and procedures that have been adopted by the ISOC. IESG initiates working groups of IETF and, depending on needs, approves their participation or calls upon them to participate in further works. The IESG consists of the Area Directors who are selected by the Nominations Committee and are appointed for two years (the Nominations Committee is randomly selected from among the IETF volunteers).

The Internet Society[10] was established in 1992 in the United States to safeguard financial and legal aid for IETF operations. The organization has evolved into an international non-profit organization which promotes Internet development, including *inter alia*, by availing its legal and financial resources to IETF, IESG and IAB. ISOC supports the activities of numerous entities (including its national and regional chapters), co-ordinates public communications and the external relations of the abovementioned organizations and encourages businesses to engage in creating Internet infrastructure.

7 ICANN (1998) *Memorandum of Understanding Between the US Department of Commerce and Internet Corporation for Assigned Names and Numbers*. <http://www.ntia.doc.gov/ntiahome/domainname/icann-memorandum.htm> (accessed 16 January 2009).

8 Homepage: <www.ietf.org>.

9 Homepage: <www.iesg.org>.

10 Homepage: <www.isoc.org>.

The Internet Architecture Board (IAB)[11] is a committee organizing and supervising the IETF. IAB is responsible for strategic oversight of ISOC and IETF operations. It is informed about relevant long term challenges connected with the Internet functioning and pays special attention to new, advanced initiatives. Moreover, IAB sponsors and organizes operations of the Internet Research Task Force and conducts innovative workshops to collectively analyze specific Internet architecture issues. IAB members are selected by the Nominating Committee in an open procedure – anyone may apply, and decisions are, as a rule, made unanimously. The IAB provides oversight of aspects of the architecture for the protocols and procedures used on the Internet and processes used to create Internet standards. The IAB serves as an appeal board for complaints of improper execution of the standards setting procedures by IESG. The IAB acts as a representative of the interests of the IETF against other standards developing organizations (e.g. ICANN). it also acts as a source of advice and guidance to the Board of Trustees and Officers of the Internet Society concerning technical, architectural, procedural, and (where appropriate) internal policy matters pertaining to the Internet and its advanced technologies. However, the governance of the logical layer includes other entities operating outside the abovementioned scheme.

The International Telecommunication Union Standardization Sector (ITU-T) is one of three International Telecommunication Union sectors and from the very beginning of work on Internet regulation it has played a significant role (*inter alia*, as WSIS coordinator). It develops non-binding technical recommendations serving as standards within all telecommunication fields. The Telecommunications Standardization Bureau (TSB) is the secretariat of ITU-T. Every four years the ITU convenes a conference to determine main policy objectives, adopt a five-year strategic and financial scheme and select senior management. ITU-T offers three types of membership: state membership, sector membership and associated membership.[12]

The World Wide Web Consortium (W3C) deals with developing interactive technologies (specifications, guidelines, software and tools) to support evolution and improve interoperability of the World Wide Web. Future works of W3C are likely to include ensuring access to the entire network using various devices and extending access. Consortium groups are composed of member organizations' representatives, the Consortium representatives and invited experts. It is working groups that develop most of W3C's technical reports, open source software and electronic service concepts. W3C welcomes technical products and services sellers, Internet content providers, laboratories, standard-setting organizations and governments. Consortium decisions are consensus based.

Beyond any doubt, the most significant entity that governs the code layer is ICANN. The Internet Corporation for Assigned Names and Numbers is an entity incorporated under the laws of California as a non-profit organization acting for charitable or public purposes, under the California Nonprofit Public Benefit Corporation Law.[13] The Corporation is managed by a Board of Directors comprising twenty-one

11 Homepage: <www.iab.org>.

12 Associates include ICT providers, equipment manufacturers and companies. An associate may join only one working group, thus small national companies often participate as associates.

13 California Corporations Code, § 5000.

members.[14] Three Supporting Organizations play a key role in ICANN structure. The first of these is the Generic Names Supporting Organization (GNSO) which deals with policies on generic top-level domain (gTLDs) governance. The Country Code Names Supporting Organization (ccNSO) operates within the field of country code top-level domains (ccTLDs), whereas the Address Supporting Organization (ASO) is to develop recommendations on Internet Protocol (IP) address policies. Each of the abovementioned organizations is composed of representatives of entities directly administering the said resources.

ICANN structure also comprises advisory committees, whose role is limited to issuing non-binding recommendations to the Board of Directors. These include the Governmental Advisory Committee (GAC),[15] the At-Large Advisory Committee (ALAC),[16] the Root Server System Advisory Committee (RSSAC) which provides advice on DNS operation; the Security and Stability Advisory Committee (SSAC) composed of Internet experts reviewing the network and the Technical Liaison Group (TLG) comprising representatives of other international technical organizations dealing with the Internet. ICANN operates using regular meetings organized in various parts of the world (to engage individuals from various local communities in the dialogue). Resolutions of the ICANN Board of Directors, reports and memoranda are published on the ICANN website.

Duties of ICANN include administration, co-ordination and allocation of IP numbers and domain names; administration and co-ordination of root name server system; overseeing mutual relations of entities such as regional or national domain name registrars; promoting fair competition at TLD level and any and all issues related to the exercise of the abovementioned functions, such as domain dispute resolution.[17] The role of ICANN is relevant in the context of international law if one takes account of its competence with respect to ccTLDs. The manner in which the ccTLDs are regulated slightly differs from gTLDs governing by reason of assumptions made at an early stage of Internet development in RFC 1591.[18] This document was instigated

14 The ICANN Board of Directors comprises the ICANN President, six representatives of Supporting Organizations (i.e. ICANN sections dealing with particular areas of the organization's activity); eight independent representatives of the public interest selected by the Nominating Committee consisting of ICANN representatives. The last from among the voting directors is selected by the At-Large Advisory Committee representing web users. Two representatives (non-voting liaisons) are nominated by Advisory Committees and two by the Technical Liaison Group and Internet Engineering Task Force. Since 2009, one director has been appointed by the Governmental Advisory Committee.

15 The GAC is composed of representatives of state authorities and is the only body where government representatives may attempt to influence ICANN policy. The basic area of GAC operations includes issues related to ccTLDs governance.

16 Since 2002, as a result of a reform, there no longer is a direct election of the At-Large representative, as the procedure did not focus as much information society members' attention as expected (now the two-stage voting is done by elected representatives). Details can be found in the report of 19 August 2002 *Assistance Group on Proposed Implementation of an At-Large Advisory Committee Report to the Evolution and Reform Committee*. <http://www.icann.org/en/committees/evol-reform/alacag-report-19aug02.htm>.

17 *Memorandum of Understanding*, op. cit., part B.

18 IETF (1994) *IETF Standard RFC 1591 Domain Name System Structure and Delegation*. <http://www.isi.edu/in-notes/rfc1591.txt> (accessed 1 January 2009), p. 4. RFC are not legally binding IETF technical standards ("*de facto* standards"); they constitute commonly followed technical procedures and protocols

by the founder of DNS, J. Postel, who noticed the need to develop guidelines for creating and allocating ccTLDs, which would enable avoidance of the arbitrariness and uncertainty of both ccTLDs creation and governance. RFC 1591 refers to ISO 3166-1 to avoid, when assigning country domain names, situations where a private entity allocating such names freely decides about recognizing or refusing the recognition of sovereignty of an entity applying for rights to a specific World Wide Web address. In RFC 1591 two letter codes of geographical regions are provided, currently applied by ICANN to TLDs designated for states and territories (over 240 categories). Most ccTLDs in use today are taken from the ISO 3166-1 list or from the list of exceptionally reserved code elements defined by the ISO 3166 Maintenance Agency,[19] however, there are a few ccTLDs not included in the ISO 3166-1 that the ICANN decided to introduce (e.g. the .eu for European Union). Controversially, ICANN also grants TLDs (although generic) to geographical areas without independent statehood.[20]

ICANN, as the entity administering root-servers, also decides which domain is administered by which server. It may also decide about altering the administration method with respect to a given domain or about changing the domain registrar. A formal power of ICANN is to delegate rights to administer domain name to another entity, if such action, in the opinion of ICANN, is taken to ensure proper DNS functioning, and if there are no direct objections to such solutions.[21] Such conduct does

agreed on by entities involved in the Internet's operation. They aim at ensuring "equitable, just, honest and competent" exercise of administrative functions. Currently RFC 1591 has been supplemented by ICANN's *Internet Co-ordination Policy: Internet Domain Name System Structure and Delegation* (*ccTLD Administration and Delegation*) of May 1999. <www.icann.org/icp/icp-1.htm> (accessed 1 January 2009) and IANA's document *ccTLD Redelegation Step-by-Step Overview*. <www.iana.org/cctld/redelegation-overview-19jun02.htm> (accessed 1 January 2009). Other documents on ccTLDs governance include ICANN (2000) *Yokohama Meeting Topic: ccTLD Delegation and Administration Policies* (<www.icann.org/yokohama/cctld-topic.htm> (accessed 1 January 2009)), (2000) *Letter from GAC Chairman Paul Twomey Transmitting GAC Views on ccTLD Delegation and Administration Principles* (<www.icann.org/committees/gac/twomey-letter-23feb00.htm> (accessed 1 January 2009)) and ICANN (2000) *March 2000 ICANN Meeting in Cairo: ccTLD Delegation and Administration Policies*. <www.icann.org/cairo2000/cctld-topic.htm> (accessed 1 January 2009). For a selection of documents, see M. Watkins (2005)'Government Regulation of the Dot-ca. Domain Name Space', 2(1) *University of Ottawa Law & Technology Journal*. <http://www.uoltj.ca/articles/vol2.1/2005.2.1.uoltj.Watkins.145-172.pdf> (accessed 29 January 2009), p. 152.

19 According to the ICANN (2007) *Issues Paper: Selection of IDN ccTLDs Associated with the ISO 3166-1 Two Letter Codes*, there are two sources used by ISO to develop the 3166 list, the United Nations Terminology Bulletin Country Names or the Country and Region Codes for Statistical Use of the UN Statistics Division.

20 Although granted with the consent of the Spanish government, the 2005 decision on the .cat domain for representing Catalonian culture still remains the leading case. See P. Gerrand (2006) 'A Short History of the Catalan Campaign to Win the .cat Internet Domain, with Implications for Other Minority Languages', 8 *Digithum*. <http://www.uoc.edu/digithum/8/dt/eng/gerrand.pdf> (accessed 17 December 2010). The plans for GAC to be vested rights allowing each member to veto new gTLD proposals seem forever more controversial. Cf. M. Mueller (2010) 'Handing Control of the Internet to Governments: Bad Idea', *CBS TechNews*, 3 February 2010.<http://www.cbsnews.com/8301-501465_162-20030583-501465.html>.

21 ICANN (1996) *Internet Domain Name System Structure and Delegation*, op. cit. para. (a) "The IANA may choose to make partial delegations of a TLD when circumstances, such as those in a developing country, so dictate. . . . (f) In cases where there is misconduct, or violation of the policies set forth in this document and RFC 1591, or persistent, recurring problems with the proper operation of a domain,

not have to require consulting the government of the state the domain concerns; however, ICANN makes the position of state authorities its "major consideration".[22]

Based on RFC 1591, in February 2000, the GAC issued *Principles for Delegation and Administration of ccTLDs.*[23] The content thereof reiterates rules formulated by J. Postel that the ccTLD administrator "is the trustee of the top-level domain for both the nation, in the case of a country code, and the global Internet community".[24] Nevertheless, unlike in the case of the RFC 1591, the GAC rules strengthen the position of governments, stipulating that the country domain administrator "should recognize that ultimate public policy authority over the relevant ccTLD rests with the relevant government or public authority".[25] One should note that the GAC Principles has no binding force and reception thereof is not similar to that of RFCs.[26]

ICANN is thus an important international scene actor and a significant element in modern international relationships where the Internet is gaining more and more significance. Consequently, the situation by which the US authorities had special competence over this entity was subject to strong criticism until the end of September 2009 when the Joint Project Agreement between the US Department of Commerce (DoC) and ICANN (under which the US government (through the DoC), as the only authority in the world, could exercise indirect influence over the Internet backbone) expired. (The *Memorandum of Understanding* had terminated in 1998 and was extended in 2003 through the Joint Project Agreement or JPA). Critical views were expressed by civil society organizations, state governments and international organizations.[27]

ICANN reserves the right to revoke and to redelegate a Top Level Domain to another manager". See also M. Stuart Lynn (2004) *President's Report: ICANN – The Case for Reform.* <www.icann.org/general/lynn-reform-proposal-24feb02.html> (accessed 1 January 2009) and the controversial ccTLDs .ht registry decision. <http://www.iana.org/reports/2004/ht-report-13jan04.html>.

22 *ICANN Internet Domain Name System Structure and Delegation*, (a) "The desires of the government of a country with regard to delegation of a ccTLD are taken very seriously. The ICANN will make them a major consideration in any TLD delegation/transfer discussions. Significantly interested parties in the domain should agree that the proposed TLD manager is the appropriate party".

23 ICANN GAC (2000) *Principles for Delegation and Administration of ccTLDs.* <http://www.isi.edu/in-notes/rfc1591.txt> (accessed 1 January 2009).

24 RFC 1591, op. cit., p. 4.

25 GAC, *Principles*, op. cit. para. 4.4.

26 GAC also suggests the formalization of a trilateral relationship between ICANN, the country domain administrator and the government in the form of relevant contracts. Ibid, para. 3.5. The suggestion has been approved by ICANN, which intends to contractually regulate their relations with national administrator.

To this end it formulated two framework agreements: the first one concerns the situation where the ccTLD registrar is being authorized without the direct involvement of governmental authorities, and the second concerns the trilateral relationship, where ccTLD is delegated to an entity formally approved by the government, who is also party to the delegation agreement. So far such trilateral agreements have been concluded by only a few states, including Japan (Japan Registry Service Co. Ltd.), Australia (.au Domain Administration Limited) and Taiwan (Taiwan Network Information Center). See M. Watkins, op. cit., p. 155).

27 The climax of this criticism was the address of European Commissioner for the Information Society and Media, Viviane Reding, in *Commissioner Reding's Weekly Videomessage*, 4 May 2009, 'The Future of Internet Governance: Towards an Accountable ICANN'. <http://ec.europa.eu/commission_barroso/reding/video/text/message_20090504.pdf>.

The system under the *Memorandum of Understanding* stipulated ICANN's obligation to submit annual reports on its operations to the US DoC. It was this US authority that had the unique influence on ICANN's activities,[28] whereas state governments or international organizations had no actual impact on its board's decisions. The GAC is their only representation, and the GAC's powers, as at the end of September 2009, had been insignificant. It is composed of 100 government representatives from all over the world (from among which only 40 are actively taking part in GAC proceedings), a European Commission representative and several organizations with observer status (such as UNESCO and OECD).[29] By 2009 the role of GAC consisted in providing non-binding advice on public policy issues, i.e. when "there may be an interaction between ICANN's policies and national laws or international agreements".[30]

This meant that the participation in developing ICANN policies by authorities other than US DoC was insignificant.[31] However, the Barack Obama administration kept their word, given during the election campaign, and allowed for a revolution in global DNS management, at the same time exposing itself to the criticism of its own legislative arm.[32]

The parties to the *Affirmation of Commitments* (AoC) signed on 1 October 2009, as well as to preceding agreements, are ICANN and the US Department of Commerce; however, the mechanism behind it is a new one. The official purpose of the document is "to institutionalize . . . the technical coordination of the Internet's domain name and addressing system (DNS), globally by a private sector led organization".[33] These commitments of the parties concern four areas of activity: (1) ensuring that decisions related to the global technical co-ordination of the DNS are made in the public interest and are accountable and transparent; (2) preserving the security, stability and resiliency of the DNS; (3) promoting competition, consumer trust, and consumer choice in the DNS

28 The ".xxx" gTLD case serves as an example of excessive, although indirect and informal, US influence on ICANN decisions; the domain was to denote erotic websites, however, ICANN rejected the registration proposal (in May 2006) mainly under pressure exerted by American society on the US Department of Commerce. It took 5 years, time-consuming court proceedings and (last but not least) a new US President for the ".xxx" gTLD to be finally approved by the ICANN Board in 2011.

29 Pursuant to Article XI, section 2 of ICANN and information included on ICANN's homepage, "It is open to participation by representatives of national governments each of which may appoint a representative and an adviser to the Committee. Membership is also open to distinct economies as recognized in international fora, and multinational governmental organizations and treaty organizations on the invitation of the GAC Chair." For more information about the GAC, see <http://gac.icann.org/about-gac/>.

30 Ibid.

31 The Committee had no such causative power, as the Generic Names Supporting Organisation (GNSO), whose decisions are made by supermajority vote, is binding on the ICANN board if the board does not reject the decision by 2/3 of votes.

32 E.g. 'ICANN Be Independent', *The Economist*, 24 September 2009. <http://www.economist.com/businessfinance/PrinterFriendly.cfm?story_id=14517430>; see also J. Fildes, 'US Relaxes Grip on the Internet', *BBC News*, 30 September 2009. <http://news.bbc.co.uk/2/hi/technology/8283310.stm>.

33 ICANN (2009) *Affirmation of Commitments by the United States Department of Commerce and the Internet Corporation for Assigned Names and Numbers*, 30 September 2009. <http://www.icann.org/en/affirmation.htm> (accessed 25 December 2010), Preamble.

marketplace; and (4) facilitating international participation in DNS technical coordination.[34] The document affirms Bill Clinton's policy of decentralized, private DNS system governance. The fourth commitment affirms the parties' commitment to a model in which all social groups will be engaged (multi-stakeholder policy). This is emphasized by paragraph 8, which states that: "ICANN is a private organization and nothing in this *Affirmation* should be construed as control by any one entity".[35] ICANN commits to adhere to transparent and accountable budgeting processes and pursue policies based on facts and the outcomes of discussions between particular social groups. A significant change is the commitment of ICANN to publish each year an annual report that sets out ICANN's progress against ICANN's bylaws, as well as its future plans. Moreover, ICANN commits to provide a thorough and appropriate explanation of decisions taken, the rationale thereof and the sources of data and information on which it relied.

Para. 6 of the document is of key importance here, under which the parties also affirm the US DoC's commitment to participation in ICANN's Governmental Advisory Committee and recognize the important role of the GAC with respect to ICANN decision-making and execution of tasks. They emphasize the importance of GAC input on the public policy aspects and technical procedures of the Internet DNS developed by ICANN.

The AoC established new international DNS coordination system – it introduced the community legitimization, sough so long, to Internet backbone management.[36] ICANN review is to be performed no longer by the DoC alone, but by a volunteer community members review team, including the GAC Chair, the ICANN Board Chair, the DoC Assistant Secretary for Communications and Information (reviewing, however, only the first of the four key areas of ICANN's commitments), representatives of ICANN Advisory Committees and Supporting Organizations and independent experts. Composition of the review team will be agreed jointly by the GAC Chair (in consultation with GAC members) and the Chair of the ICANN Board.[37] The AoC therefore constitutes the synergic co-operation of all international electronic arena actors – both representatives of information society and government representatives (via GAC).[38] Another element of the new system is the commitment of the parties to preserve the security, stability and resiliency of Internet resources; this is the object of the agreement and is subject to a similar review proceedings.[39] To show the transparency of ICANN procedures, the results will be published for public comment. Each review team shall take account of public comments in their review when it deems it appropriate. The AoC entered into force on 1 October 2009. Pursuant to the provision of para. 11, the agreement is intended to be long-standing, but may be amended at any time by the mutual consent of the parties.

34 *Affirmation of Commitments*, para. 3.

35 *Affirmation of Commitments*, para. 8.

36 *Affirmation of Commitments*, para. 9.

37 Recommendations resulting from the reviews will be provided to the Board and posted for public comment. The Board will take actions within six months of receipt of the recommendations, and the performance thereof shall be the object of another review: *Affirmation of Commitments*, para. 9.1.

38 Ibid., para. 9.1.

39 Ibid., para. 9.2.

The document ought to be assessed positively. It meets the expectations of the international community, clearly formulated since 2005, as confirmed by comments from companies' executives and state leaders,[40] including Commissioner Reding.[41] The document incorporates the idea of international, decentralized DNS co-ordination and might be considered a blueprint for the global Internet governance model, as it allows for participation of all stakeholders on a representative basis.

The specific character of this new unique media that is the Internet, became clear to the United Nations no earlier than 2003.[42] Only then did the United Nations Secretary General call upon the World Summit on the Information Society (WSIS) to look into the issue of international Internet governance (IG) and present its opinions and guidelines.[43] The initial 2003 WSIS Geneva meeting resulted in the *Declaration of Principles*[44] where the participants agreed that "International Internet Governance issues should be addressed in a coordinated manner".[45] They called for "the Secretary-General of the United Nations to set up a working group on Internet governance"[46] (WGIG), which presented its Report in 2005.[47] This document includes the first definition of IG as "the joint development and application by Governments, the private sector and civil society, in their respective roles, of shared principles, norms, rules, decision-making procedures, and programmes that shape the evolution and use of the Internet".[48] This definition addressed all the processes behind the technical and content-related administration of the worldwide electronic network. WGIG presented two other key IG proposals: it drafted a list of urgent IG issues that demanded the prompt attention of the international

40 Comments available at: <http://www.icann.org/en/affirmation/affirmation-reaction.htm> (accessed 11 June 2011).

41 European Union (2009) 'European Commission Welcomes US Move to More Independent, Accountable, International Internet Governance', *EC News IP/09/1397*. <http://ec.europa.eu/information_society/newsroom/cf/itemshortdetail.cfm?item_id=5281>.

42 Although as R. H. Weber rightfully mentions, "Already in the seventies of the last century, a group of block-free countries discussed the idea of a 'New World Information Order' (NWIO) . . . At the same time, the Soviet Union proposed to release a 'Mass Media Declaration' under the auspices of the United Nations Educational, Scientific and Cultural Organization (UNESCO)". R. H. Weber, M. Grosz and R. Weber (2011) *Shaping Internet Governance: Regulatory Challenges*, New York: Springer, p. 25.

43 For a detailed analysis of the process, see e.g. J. Malcolm (2008) *Multi-Stakeholder Governance and the Internet Governance Forum*, Perth: Terminus Press, pp. 322ff.

44 United Nations (2003) *World Summit on the Information Society Declaration of Principles: Building the Information Society: A Global Challenge in the New Millennium*, op. cit. This document was accompanied by the more detailed (2003) *Plan of Action* (Document WSIS-03/GENEVA/DOC/5-E). <http://www.itu.int/wsis/docs/geneva/official/poa.html> (accessed 17 December 2010).

45 United Nations WSIS *Declaration of Principles*, para. 50.

46 Ibid.; the WGIG was to be set up "in an open and inclusive process that ensures a mechanism for the full and active participation of governments, the private sector and civil society from both developing and developed countries, involving relevant intergovernmental and international organizations and forums, to investigate and make proposals for action, as appropriate, on the governance of Internet by 2005".

47 United Nations (2005) *Report of the Working Group on Internet Governance*. <www.wgig.org/docs/WGIGREPORT.pdf> (accessed 17 December 2010).

48 Ibid., para. 10.4.

community[49] and suggested the creation of an international multi-stakeholder discussion forum for debating them.[50] This latter WGIG idea was supported and reaffirmed in the following 2006 WSIS Tunis Agenda,[51] whose signatories asked the UN Secretary-General to create a "new forum for multi-stakeholder policy dialogue – called the Internet Governance Forum (IGF)".[52] The mandate of the Forum was designed, among others,[53] to "discuss public policy issues related to key elements of Internet governance" and to "facilitate discourse between bodies dealing with different cross-cutting international public policies regarding the Internet".[54] The IGF was a result of a crucial compromise[55] and, as such, received no decisional power, just an advisory role to the UN institutions.[56] Nevertheless, it was the first vital step towards creating an international platform of elaborating international law solutions for the global network.[57] The body of work of these UN delegate organizations and the first 5-year term of the IGF, put in the context of the previous achievements of other international law organizations,[58] enable one to identify the basic principles of the international IG regime. This set of rules, together with the organizational

49 Ibid., chapter 3, pp. 5ff.: "(a) Issues relating to infrastructure and the management of critical Internet resources . . .; (b) Issues relating to the use of the Internet, including spam, network security and cybercrime . . .; (c) Issues that are relevant to the Internet but have an impact much wider than the Internet and for which existing organizations are responsible, such as intellectual property rights (IPRs) or international trade; (d) Issues relating to the developmental aspects of Internet governance, in particular capacity-building in developing countries." This catalogue, initially drafted by the WGIG, with time turned into the basis of international IG debates.

50 Ibid., section V.A.1, paras. 40 and 43. The Group proposed that the forum to be "linked to the United Nations" (para. 44) and "be open to all stakeholders from all countries" (para. 46).

51 United Nations (2006) *Report of the Tunis Phase of the World Summit on the Information Society*, WSIS-05/TUNIS/DOC/9(Rev.1)-E. <www.itu.int/wsis/docs2/tunis/off/6rev1.doc> (accessed 17 December 2010), p. 17, para. 72.

52 Ibid.

53 Ibid., paras. 73–74.

54 Ibid., para. 73. This WSIS document also incorporated the WGIG definition of IG (p. 12 para. 34) as well as an elaboration on the WGIG list of key IG issues, including explicitly, Critical Internet Resources (CIRs) management, freedom of Internet access (B3 *Access to Information and Knowledge*), network security (B5 *Building Confidence and Security in the Use of ICTs*), cultural and linguistic diversity (B8 *Cultural Diversity and Identity, Linguistic Diversity and Local Content*), the role of ethics in international Internet Governance (B10 *Ethical Dimensions of the Information Society*) as well as the need for international and regional co-operation (B11).

55 E.g., D. Cogburn 'The US Role in Running the Net', *BBC News* 14 November 2005. <http://news.bbc.co.uk/2/hi/technology/4435352.stm> (accessed 20 December 2010), M. Geist 'Analysis: Net Control Debate Rumbles On', *BBC News*, 17 November 2005. <http://news.bbc.co.uk/2/hi/technology/4446242.stm> (accessed 20 December 2010), J. Twist 'Controversy Blights UN Net Summit', *BBC News*, 18 November 2005. <http://news.bbc.co.uk/2/hi/technology/4450474.stm> (accessed 20 December 2010).

56 *Report of the Tunis Phase of the World Summit*, op. cit., para. 77.

57 For an appraisal of the IGF compromise, see e.g., K. M. Rogers (2006) 'Internet Governance: The United States Won the Battle, But Will the Internet Win the War?' 4(1) *Hertfordshire Law Journal*, pp. 26–35; V. Mayer-Schönberger and M. Ziewitz (2007) 'Jefferson Rebuffed: The United States and the Future of Internet Governance, 8 *Colum. Sci. & Tech. L. Rev*, pp. 184ff. On the genesis and structure of IGF, see generally, Malcolm, op. cit., pp. 321–355.

58 Such as the CoE, IETF, ITU or UNESCO.

framework behind them, allows one to assert that what once was solely a facet of international relations is now becoming a new area of international law with a clear set of principles,[59] its own terminology and discussion fora. International Internet Law (IIL) is being developed not only by international organizations and national governments acting through traditional international law instruments, but also by business and civil society members in a new multi-stakeholder process.

If one looks for an equivalent of the UN General Assembly (being a forum similar to national legislative authorities) for the Internet, we should consider whether IGF may play such a role, engaging all representatives of the multi-stakeholder Internet. The structure of the international Internet law thus starts to resemble the structure of traditional international law. The implementation thereof may prove even simpler than of traditional international law, for it will be possible to not only use the law, but also to execute it through computer code (since in cyberspace, the code is law). The practice has so far highlighted fundamental rules characteristic of this new discipline of international law.

International Internet Law guiding principles

Just as the early 1970s saw the rise of the most recent branch of public international law, international environmental law, so is the early twenty-first century witnessing the rise of IIL. The similarities between those two areas of legal regulation are apparent – just as the natural environment that is equally shared by all states and nations requires universal protection and regulation,[60] so does cyberspace. They both function independently of state borders, which results in the existing jurisdictional struggles.[61] When international cybersecurity is becoming one of the key priorities,[62] it is clear that the only sensible way to regulate human activities online is through international law.

59 On the determining role of principles for the formation of international law see: R. Uerpman-Wittzack (2010) 'Principles of International Internet Law', 11(1) *German Law Journal*, pp. 1245–1247.

60 As K. Wolfke wrote in 1976, "[t]he earth, though one closely interrelated ecosystem, is still politically divided into over 140 sovereign States, on whose consent and active participation the carrying out of the necessary preventive measures depends. Consequently, international law is the only available legal tool for the regulation and, if necessary, enforcement action at the transnational level." K. Wolfke (1976) 'Some Reflections on International Environmental Law-Making and Enforcement', 8 *Polish Yearbook of International Law*, p. 33. Today this very same statement is still true – when it comes to regulating transnational cyberspace.

61 See below.

62 During the 2010 Vilnius IGF Meeting, in response to the growing need for a universal, international solution to cybersecurity challenges, V. Cerf proposed creating a "cyber fire-department", an international organization that would stand guard over international cybersecurity and co-ordinate international efforts in fighting cyber-crime (*Legal Aspects of Internet Governance: International Cooperation on Cyber-Security* (Session 123, IGF 2010, Vilnius, Lithuania, 15 September 2010). A transcript is available at <http://www.afilias.info/webfm_send/138> (accessed 15 December 2010), p. 2. This idea seems to be endorsed through the Dutch initiative of the European Cyber Security Authority (see B. Klaasen (2011) 'The Need for a European Cyber Security Authority' (EuroDIG 2011 workshop proposal). <http://www.guarder.net/eurodig/2011/European_Cybersecurit_Authority_WSProposal.pdf> (accessed 20 December 2010).

So far, the scope of IIL has been set by numerous soft-law documents,[63] few international law treaties,[64] rich scholarly work[65] and an emerging customary framework.[66] Based on these developments, IIL may be defined as the public international law framework for Internet governance, encompassing issues that range from civil law (e.g. protecting personal rights online),[67] through trade law (in respect of e-commerce and international customer protection[68] or trademark protection regulations applied to domain names),[69] administrative law (with e.g. medical services offered through the network, across borders),[70] financial law (with international e-banking and

63 Including the aforementioned WSIS and WGIG documents, numerous UN General Assembly Resolutions have been passed (e.g. Resolution 53/70 on Developments in the Field of Information and Telecommunications in the Context of International Security (1998), UN Doc. A/53/576; Resolution 54/49 on Developments in the Field of Information and Telecommunications in the Context of International Security (1999), UN Doc. A/54/558; Resolution 55/28 on Developments in the Field of Information and Telecommunications (2000), UN Doc. A/55/554; Resolution 56/19 on Developments in the Field of Information and Telecommunications in the Context of International Security (2001), UN Doc. A/55/554; Resolution 57/239 on Creation of a Global Culture of Cybersecurity (2002), UN Doc. A/57/529/Add.3; Resolution 58/199 on Creation of a Global culture of Cybersecurity and the Protection of Critical Information Infrastructures (2003), UN Doc. A/58/481/Add.2) and some fundamental EU documents (e.g. Communication from the Commission to the Council, the European Parliament, the European Economic and Social Committee and the Committee of the Regions (1999) *eEurope 2005: An Information Society for All*, COM (1999) 687; Communication from the Commission to the Council, the European Parliament, the Economic and Social Committee and the Committee of the Regions (1998) *Globalisation and the Information Society: The Need for Strengthened International Coordination*, COM (98)50, Communications to the European Parliament, the Council, the Economic and Social Committee and the Committee of the Regions (1999) *Towards a New Framework for Electronic Communications Infrastructure and Associated Services*, COM (99)539).

64 Including CoE Convention on Cybercrime (2001, ETS No 185), WIPO Copyright Treaty (1996), WIPO Performances and Phonograms Treaty (1996) ("WIPO Internet treaties"). Other important IIL documents include, e.g. United Nations Commission on International Trade Law (1997) Model Law on Electronic Commerce, UN Doc. A/RES/51/162, UNESCO Charter on the Preservation of Digital Heritage, adopted at the 32nd session of the General Conference of UNESCO, 17 October 2003 and the London Action Plan on International Spam Enforcement Cooperation (which was concluded on 11 October 2004 by governments and public agencies from 27 countries).

65 E.g. Uerpman-Wittzack op. cit.; see also (2009) 'Internetvolkerrecht', 47(26) *Archiv des Volkerrechts*, pp. 263–274; S. Hoffer (1998) *World Cyberspace Law*, New York: Juris Publishing, Inc.; A. Segura-Serrano (2006) 'Internet Regulation: A Hard-Law Proposal', op. cit.; see also (2006) 'Internet Regulation and the Role of International Law', in A. von Bogdandy and R. Wolfrum (eds.) 10 *Max Planck Yearbook of United National Law*, Leiden: Koninklijke Brill, pp. 191–272; J. Kurbalija (2005) 'Internet Governance And International Law', in W. J. Drake (ed.) *Reforming Internet Governance: Perspectives from the Working Group on Internet Governance (WGIG)*, New York: United Nations Publications, pp. 105–116. See generally U. Kohl, op. cit.; Malcolm, op. cit., pp. 98–175 and pp. 144ff., and Weber, op. cit., pp. 10–16.

66 Its shape in reference to human rights protection online is being developed by the ground-breaking judicial decisions of the ECHR. See Uerpman-Wittzack (2010) op. cit., pp. 1249–1253.

67 In particular when it comes to protecting privacy online, see below; and for ISP defamation liability see E. M. Barendt (2005), *Freedom of Speech*, 2nd edn., New York: Oxford University Press, pp. 463ff.

68 See generally J. K. Winn (2006) *Consumer Protection in the Age of the Information Economy*, Aldershot: Ashgate Publishing, Ltd.

69 See K. Komaitis, op. cit., who proposes a *sui generis* domain name right.

70 E.g. the use of frequencies allocated by the ITU for "Industrial, Scientific and Medical purposes" by the RFID bands designed for medical purposes ("ISM bands"), such as monitoring a patient's blood pressure and recording the data with a particular medical clinic supervising the treatment. As emphasized

transactions security)[71] and eventually the most difficult questions on criminal law and its international enforcement (starting with cases of teenage hackers testing their skills over a friend's PC and evolving to massive cyberattacks against key state infrastructure).[72] All those issues require an international, basic set of rules that will allow for efficient and flawless international co-operation in all Internet-related matters. The first steps towards such comprehensive regulation have already been taken[73] and in light of the achievements made so far, reaching such an ambitious goal seems possible in a relatively near future. The current evolution of IG enables one to determine a basic set of IIL principles upon which more detailed regulations may be based.

Multi-stakeholderism

The principle of multi-stakeholderism is a direct consequence of the very nature of the World Wide Web. Since the Internet is a global network of peers, its efficient operation requires the equal participation of all stakeholders involved. This principle was first expressed in para. 17 of the 2003 WSIS *Declaration of Principles*, which identified the three groups of stakeholders whose participation is required: "building an inclusive Information Society requires new forms of solidarity, partnership and cooperation among governments and other stakeholders, i.e. the private sector, civil society and international organizations". This idea was further incorporated in the 2005 WSIS Tunis Agenda, according to which the composition of the IGF was originally defined as "a new forum for multi-stakeholder policy dialogue".[74] Consequently, the principle of multi-stakeholderism means the equal involvement of all groups participating in the Internet evolution: the governments (acting on their own behalf or represented through intergovernmental organizations), civil society (representing the users) and the business sector (on behalf, not only of telecommunications, but also every other market segment). This principle gives IG a unique character in the international relations field, one that directly determines any corresponding legal regulation. For the first time it is not only the national authorities that need to find a working, international consensus for their joint co-operation – they need to seek compromise with "the governed" (the civil society and the business sector, who usually play a subordinate role in national legal affairs). Since the Internet is the network of peers, it is only through their common consensus that the network may work flawlessly.[75]

by R. H. Weber, such use of RFIDs requires a global harmonization of telecommunications policies; see: R. H. Weber and R. Weber (2010) *Internet of Things: Legal Perspectives*, New York: Springer, p. 97.

71 See Bank for International Settlements Basel Committee (2000) *Electronic Banking Group Initiatives and White Papers*, Basel: Bank for International Settlements. <http://www.bis.org/publ/bcbs76.htm> (accessed 10 December 2010) and (same author) (2003) *Risk Management Principles for Electronic Banking*, Basel: Bank for International Settlements. <http://www.mobilemoneyexchange.org/Files/86801b83> (accessed 10 December 2010); see also M. Brindle, R. Cox and R. Coleman (2004) *Law of Bank Payments*, London: Sweet & Maxwell, pp. 255ff.

72 See chapter 2.

73 Such as the recent work of the CoE and other initiatives of ITU or WSIS described above.

74 WSIS (2005) *Tunis Agenda*, para. 72.

75 Thus far, a resembling mechanism has been introduced to international law only once, and not in such a broad capacity. The 2001 UNESCO Universal Declaration on Cultural Diversity includes, as its

This principle includes one more element. It requires not only the equal co-operation of all stakeholders, but also an equal representation of all world regions, particularly those less developed. Those states or nations should be represented not only through their governments, but also through their civil society and business sector members.[76] This facet of multi-stakeholderism is supported by the IIL principle of promoting cultural diversity.[77] That multi-stakeholderism is a key principle in IIL can be seen from the criticism of the recent of UNCTAD Commission on Science and Technology for Development (CSTD) decision, where it proposed to form a new Working Group on Improvements to the Internet Governance Forum (a WGIG follow-up) comprised solely of governmental representatives, disregarding other stakeholders.[78] It was criticized[79] on the grounds that such a proposal is clearly contrary to the terms of reference of the CSTD.[80]

Cultural diversity

Cultural diversity has been an expressly defined principle for the international community since at least the 2002 UNESCO Universal Declaration on Cultural Diversity (then considered a counterweight to the WTO globalization).[81] Nowhere is the

signatories, non-state parties (such as non-governmental organizations or national juridical persons); however, they did not participate in the actual drafting of the document and the Declaration itself does not form a legally binding regime. Therefore, IG sets the principle of multi-stakeholderism in a completely new light.

76 This aspect of multi-stakeholderism was emphasized by the WSIS in para. 31 (Part A) of the *Tunis Agenda*, where the signatories commit themselves "to the stability and security of the Internet as a global facility and to ensuring the requisite legitimacy of its governance, based on the full participation of all stakeholders, from both developed and developing countries, within their respective roles and responsibilities".

77 Discussed in more detail in the following paragraph.

78 See United Nations Conference on Trade and Development (UNCTAD) (2010) 'Composition of the Working Group on Internet Governance Agreed' <http://www.unctad.org/Templates/Page.asp?intItemID=5755&lang=1> (accessed 17 December 2010).

79 E.g. M. Mueller (2010) 'The UN Sticks its Head in the Sand', *Internet Governance Project Blog*, 12 December 2010.<http://blog.internetgovernance.org/blog/_archives/2010/12/12/4702148.html> (accessed 15 December 2010). The wave of criticism culminated in an open letter initiated by the Internet Society calling the CSTD to reverse its decision: <http://isoc.org/wp/newsletter/files/2010/12/IGF-Working-Group-Decision1.pdf> (accessed 25 December 2010). The addressee of the letter, F. Riehl, Vice Chair of the CSTD, explained in response that the Working Group formation process had not yet been finished and the Group would eventually meet the multi-stakeholderism criteria: see F. Riehl (2010) *Tentative Road Map of Activities of the CSTD Working Group on IGF*. <http://www.unctad.org/sections/un_cstd/docs/cstd2010d02_en.pdf> (accessed 10 December 2010).

80 United Nations Economic and Social Council (ECOSOC) Resolution 2010/2 on the Assessment of the Progress Made in the Implementation of and Follow-Up to the outcomes of the World Summit on the Information Society, in which ECOSOC "invites the Chair of the Commission on Science and Technology for Development (CSTD) to establish, in an open and inclusive manner, a working group which would seek, compile and review inputs from all Member States and all other stakeholders on improvements to the Internet Governance Forum (IGF), in line with the mandate set out in the *Tunis Agenda*, and which would report to the Commission at its fourteenth session in 2011 with recommendation, as appropriate".

81 See e.g. C. B. Graber (2006) 'The New UNESCO Convention on Cultural Diversity: A Counterbalance to the WTO?' 9(3) *Journal of International Economic Law*, pp. 553–574; M. Hahn (2006), 'A Clash of Cultures? The UNESCO Diversity Convention and International Trade Law', 9(3) *Journal of International Economic Law*, pp. 515–552.

diversity of the world's communities more vivid than in cyberspace – the single shared space where all cultures interact simultaneously at all possible levels.[82] Therefore, all the WSIS documents mention the need to respect and promote cultural diversity online as one of key prerequisites for a successful international IG regime.[83] The obligation of equally promoting and supporting all of the world's cultures online is also repeated in virtually every academic publication on the issue.[84] Cultural diversity is mainly envisaged online through the application of, and modifications to, the Domain Name System (DNS). The key practical application of this principle was the introduction of IDNs[85] in October 2009. Promoting cultural diversity through domain names has already caused some difficult international law questions, resulting in much controversy surrounding some ICANN decisions.[86] It is still unclear whether the registration of a ".gay" gTLD ought to be granted to the LGBT community opting for its registration[87] or who ought to be entitled to register a domain representing the Catholic or Muslim culture.[88] Since the promotion of cultural diversity is a recognized principle of

82 According to statistics, English is still the most popular language of the Internet (with 27.3% of Internet users acknowledging it as their first language); however, the number of Chinese-speaking users has grown almost 13 times over the last decade, with 22.6% of present Internet users recognizing Chinese as their mother-tongue. The third most popular Internet language is Spanish; however, Spanish speakers constitute only 7.8% of all Internet users. See Miniwatts Marketing Group, *Internet World Stats* (last updated 30 July 2010). <http://www.internetworldstats.com/stats.htm> (accessed 17 December 2010).

83 WSIS (2003) *Plan of Action*, section C8 para. 23, WSIS (2003) *Declaration of Principles*, section B8 paras. 52–54 are both entitled 'Cultural Diversity and Identity, Linguistic Diversity and Local Content'. The latter document also includes "promoting cultural diversity" as an explicit principle for IG in its para. 19, entitled 'An Information Society for All: Key Principles'. The obligation to foster and respect cultural diversity is also reaffirmed in section C9 of the WSIS (2005) *Tunis Agenda*; while its section C8, p. 20 delegates the competence for preserving cultural diversity online directly to UNESCO.

84 See e.g. X. Hue (2010) 'Diversity: Achieving an Internet that is Really for All', in W. J. Drake (ed.) *Internet Governance: Creating Opportunities for All*, New York: United Nations, pp. 25–33; J. Kurbalija (2010) *An Introduction to Internet Governance*, Msida: Diplo Foundation, pp. 144–146; K. Cheon (2005) 'Multilingualism and the Domain Name System', in W. J. Drake (ed.) *Reforming Internet Governance: Perspectives from the Working Group on Internet Governance (WGIG)*, New York: United Nations Publications, pp. 67–72; M. C. Kettemann (2008) 'E-Inclusion as a Means to Bridge the Digital Divides: Conceptual Issues and International Approaches', in W. Benedek, V. Bauer and M. Kettemann (eds.) *Internet Governance and the Information Society: Global Perspectives and European Dimensions*, Utrecht: Eleven International Publishing, pp. 51–63.

85 Internationalized Domain Names, a technical standard that enables users to enter and present the domain names in all language-specific scripts other than English (Chinese, Greek, Arabic, Cyrillic etc). See <http://www.icann.org/en/topics/idn/>.

86 Particularly the aforementioned 2005 decision to grant the ".cat" gTLD to the culture of the Spanish region of Catalonia.

87 Lesbian, Gay, Bisexual and Transgender. The ".gay" initiative website, explaining the background of the campaign and its history, can be found at<http://www.dotgay.com/index.html> (accessed 17 December 2010).

88 The current decision-making process at ICANN on the selection of new gTLDs recognizes "national, cultural, geographic and religious sensitivities" as grounds for denying the registration of a new gTLD. This is strongly opposed by civil society, who claim there is no universal standard for "morality and public order" that allows anyone to decide upon the limits of cultural identity protection. See U. Gasser et al. (2010) *Accountability and Transparency at ICANN: An Independent Review*, Mass.: Harvard Law School, Berkman Center for Internet and Society <https://icann.org/en/reviews/affirmation/atrt-review-berkmanfinal-report-20oct10-en.pdf> (accessed 17 December 2010).

public international law, its justification in the online environments needs no further validation; however, its application online will certainly bring new challenges.

Freedom of access

The global character of the network results in one more natural assumption that derives initially from the international community objective of bridging the digital divide.[89] The principle of a worldwide freedom to access the Internet was mentioned by WSIS in all its documents[90] and the fundamental right to Internet access has already found its way into several national legislations.[91] The right to free Internet access is perceived as an emanation of the right to free speech and free communication. Therefore, the practical application of this principle has already come across one important challenge. Since practically no state allows for the freedom of speech to be exercised without any limitations, state authorities also attempt to exercise their legislative restrictions over online forms of expression.[92] Thus, most of them perform some sort of censorship ("Internet filtering" discussed in detail in the previous chapter) for different social, political or security reasons, and this results in the limiting of access to certain Internet content. Presently two polarizing standpoints in the debate over the desired shape of freedom of access may be identified. Most human rights organizations strongly oppose any "Internet filtering" – they believe that real-world problems are only reflected online and it is there that those problems ought to be solved (e.g. blocking access to child pornography will not resolve the actual non-virtual problem

89 The United Nations Information and Communication Technologies Task Force (UN ICT TF) is a multi-stakeholder initiative "to lend a global dimension to the efforts previously made to bridge the global digital divide and to advance digital opportunity for all"; see the UN ICT TF webpage at <http://www.unicttaskforce.org/> (accessed 20 December 2010). This task force was created in November 2001 by the United Nations Secretary General Kofi Annan, as requested by the Economic and Social Council. See generally M. Hilbert (2010) 'The Manifold Definitions of the Digital Divide and Their Diverse Implications for Policy Responsibility', paper delivered at the 38th Research Conference on Communication, Information, and Internet Policy, George Mason University Law School, Arlington. <http://www.tprcweb.com/images/stories/2010%20papers/Hilbert%20manifold%20 Digital%20Divide.pdf> (accessed 20 December 2010).

90 WSIS (2005) *Tunis Agenda* para. 90(n); WSIS (2003) *Declaration of Principles*, section B3 paras. 24–28, p. 4; WSIS (2003) *Plan of Action*, section C2 para. 9, pp. 3–4 and the Constitution of the Digital Solidarity Fund, para. D2, p. 13.

91 Explicitly, in Finland (Communications Market Act 393/2003 and the Decree of the Ministry of Transport and Communications on the Minimum Rate of a Functional Internet Access as a Universal Service 732/2009) and Estonia (Public Information Act, 2000); see generally I. A. M. Hartmann (2010) 'Universal Access Policies and Internet Access as a Fundamental Right: The Constitutional Law Perspective Informed by the Brazilian Case', paper delivered at the Fifth GigaNet Annual Symposium, 13 September 2010, Vilnius, Lithuania, on file with author. See also the decision of the French Constitutional Council from 10 June 2009 (Décision No. 2009-580 DC du 10 Juin 2009 sur la Loi Favorisant la Diffusion et la Protection de la Création sur Internet), in which the court decided that the right of each individual to connect to the Internet incorporates the personal freedom of communication and expression (in the context of the Loi HADOPI sanction, providing a ban on Internet access to copyright infringers).

92 Internet filtering was discussed in detail in the previous chapter.

it constitutes).[93] State authorities present a clearly opposite opinion. They claim that since it is their duty to protect the community, they ought to act online just as they do in "real-life" and disable access to sites regarded as contrary to national policy and law.[94] There is no easy solution to this decades-long debate on legal limitations of free communication; however, the Internet adds a new, global perspective to this old problem – all concurring national regimes suddenly collide in one global cyberspace. Particularly interesting seems to be the international impact of national "filtering" policies and the actual means and ways used to combat online censorship at international (inter-governmental) level.

Openness

The architecture of the global electronic network brings about one more necessary prerequisite for its flawless operation. Since the architecture of the network is decentralized, it not only offers equal access to all users and providers, but it also makes it technically impossible[95] for one entity to control the access of others. This fact results in much online freedom and a difficult challenge for state authorities wishing to limit it. This kind of freedom is a reflection of human rights[96] and is one of the most discussed topics to date. The discussion is intensified by a number of factors. First, it is the effect of the lack of clarity on the actual scope of the present-day human rights catalogue.[97] Regardless, however, of how the particular elements of the human rights catalogue might be defined, their online reflection may be categorized into three groups. The first category may be formed out of those rights, whose application online is limited

93 See J. McNamee (2010) 'ENDitorial: Internet Blocking in Ten Weeks and Counting', 8(18) EDRI-Gram [European Digital Rights Initiative]. <http://www.edri.org/edrigram/number8.18/10-weeks-until-internet-blocking> (accessed 20 December 2010); see also M. L. Mueller (2010) *Networks and States: The Global Politics of Internet Governance*, Cambridge, Mass: MIT Press, pp. 185ff.

94 See e.g. Article 3(2) of the Council Decision 2007/125/JHA of 12 February 2007, Establishing for the Period 2007 to 2013, as Part of General Programme on Security and Safeguarding Liberties, the Specific Programme 'Prevention of and Fight against Crime'.

95 The most efficient filtering regime has been introduced in China, see previous chapter.

96 See e.g. O. Cavalli (2010) 'Openness: Protecting Internet Freedoms', in W. J. Drake (ed.) *Internet Governance: Creating Opportunities for All*, New York: United Nations Publications, pp. 15–25; or J. Kurbalija, op. cit., pp. 133–135.

97 At the present time, the universal human rights catalogue may be defined according to the unbinding 1948 Universal Declaration of Human Rights and the numerous documents following it which drew richly from its ideas (including the two 1966 binding UN human rights covenants: the International Covenant on Civil and Political Rights and the International Covenant on Economic, Social and Cultural Rights). The principles of the Declaration are included in numerous international treaties (e.g. the International Convention on the Elimination of All Forms of Racial Discrimination, the International Convention on the Elimination of Discrimination Against Women, the United Nations Convention on the Rights of the Child, and the United Nations Convention Against Torture). There also exist numerous regional human rights conventions and national human rights standards, much varying when it comes to e.g. the limits of freedom of speech or privacy protection. Because of the global character of cyberspace, all of those different national approaches are now simultaneously confronted in a uniform environment. See generally R. F. Jorgensen (ed.) (2006) *Human Rights in the Global Information Society*, Cambridge, Mass.: MIT Press.

due to the character of the global network and the content of those rights. The right to life, freedom from torture or freedom from slavery or forced labor may not be directly violated online.[98] The second, and largest, group of human rights that might be singled out when looking at the online environment would be formed by those rights that are now well known and exercised; however, their application to the cyber-realm requires certain modifications or amendments. At the top of this list one should place freedom of speech and protection of privacy (with their varying and often contradictory national standards suddenly confronted with the worldwide cyber-arena).[99] Finally, when discussing the shape of the human rights catalogue online, one should mention the third group of human rights: this group is new and consists of the rights that appeared only with the intensifying of online exchange itself. Included in this group would be such rights as the right to virtual personality,[100] the already mentioned right to Internet access, the much discussed right to anonymity,[101] or "the right to be forgotten" mentioned recently by EU Commissioner Viviane Reding.[102] This category is sometimes considered the fourth generation of human rights[103] and is the one that should attract most academic attention, as the formation of this set of principles and their content will allow for the fitting interpretation of the rights included in the largest, second group. Since, as mentioned above, the principle of openness translates into the requirement of human rights protection online, the actual application of the rights will form the content of the IIL "openness" principle. The other side of this problem is the issue of the admissible limits to human rights and the scope of state intervention

98 Promoting genocide or other forms of hate speech might be categorized as falling within the scope of freedom of speech rather than actually directly influencing those rights.

99 This list would also include most of the human rights known and protected today, including the right to a fair trial (for this in relation to ISP liability and personal data protection, see *KU* v. *Finland* (2008) Application No. 2827/02, para. 43 (European Court of Human Rights)) or in relation to the right to property (especially in the aspect of domain name rights), see *Paeffgen GmbH* v. *Germany* (2007) Application Nos. 25379/04, 21688/05, 21722/05 and 21770/05 (European Court of Human Rights)). In the light of recent news, this list could even include the right to marry: see L. Katayama, 'Love in 2-D', *New York Times*, 26 July 2009. <http://www.nytimes.com/2009/07/26/magazine/26FOB-2DLove-t.html> (accessed 26 December 2010).

100 This is expressed in the 2005 revisions, initiated by Jaco Aizenman, to the 1948 Constitution of the Republic of Costa Rica, at Article 24 *bis*. See C.C. Sandi (2005) 'Personalidad Virtual: Necesidad de una Reforma Constitucional', 3 *Revista de Derecho y Tecnologías de la Información*, pp. 1–11.

101 See generally J. Turley (2002) *Registering Publius: The Supreme Court and the Right to Anonymity*, Washington, DC: The Cato Institute, pp. 57–83. In the context of press law and "new media" see *Financial Times Ltd. and others* v. *United Kingdom* (2009) Application No. 821/03 (European Court of Human Rights).

102 Reding, V. (European Commissioner for the Information Society and Media) (2010) 'Building Trust in Europe's Online Single Market', speech at the American Chamber of Commerce, 22 June 2010. <http://europa.eu/rapid/pressReleasesAction.do?reference=SPEECH/10/327> (accessed 20 December 2010).

103 W. Kleinwächter describes the fourth generation of human rights as including the human right to communicate "where communication rights are linked to economic and technical issues of electronic commerce, information security, electronic signature, data protection, intellectual property, frequency allocation, standardization" in his (1998) 'The People's "Right to Communicate" and a "Global Communication Charter": How Does Cyberspace Change Legal Concepts of Human Rights, Access and Participation?' 5(1&2) *Journal of International Communication*, p. 119.

necessary to protect national and community security from attacks and threats initiated or conducted online, as discussed in the previous paragraphs.[104]

IIL international law analogies

Recognizing international Internet law as a part of public international law is favored by more and more courageous references to the concept of the common heritage of mankind, which, in turn, could be applied to cyberspace regulations. The link is made in two ways: by referring to the theory of international spaces or by referring to the international liability regime for trans-boundary harm that is characteristic of international environmental law. Both concepts are discussed in detail below.

The environmental law analogy

International liability is based on numerous multilateral contractual regimes. There is no international, universal standard or a common customary practice. Existing liability regimes usually place the burden of accountability upon private parties – those profiting from the risk-raising activities. Such parties may be held liable should their failure in meeting the existing due diligence standard result in transboundary harm, regardless of their fault. For international risk liability, the due diligence test is of key importance. A state is obliged to provide evidence it has acted in good faith and in accordance with good governance standards in order to free itself from international accountability (responsibility or liability).

Traditionally transboundary harm accountability may arise out of two kinds of situations: accidents or non-accidental (human-caused) actions. In respect of cyberspace, those two categories may be specified as, respectively, technical failures and cybercrimes (cybercrimes may, depending on their scale, be considered acts of cyberterrorism).

In the latter case, a state may be successfully held responsible when it fails to provide due diligence in preventing those criminal and harmful acts from happening.[105] When transboundary harm results from an incidental happening, this situation could be considered grounds for international liability. In the current state of international law, rules governing such liability ought to be embodied in an international law contract.[106] The existing treaties allow three models of international liability (space liability, nuclear liability and maritime oil transport liability) of which one seems applicable to cyberspace.[107]

All of the existing regimes impose the risk liability on private parties profiting from creating the risk. Should such mechanisms be applied to cyberspace, the burden

104 See chapter 2 on network security.

105 See J. Kulesza (2009) 'State Responsibility for Cyberattacks on International Peace and Security', 29 *Polish Yearbook of International Law*, pp. 139–152.

106 See T. Gehring and M. Jachtenfuchs (1993) 'Liability for Transboundary Environmental Damage: Towards a General Liability Regime?' 4 *EJIL*, p. 97.

107 Ibid., pp. 97–104.

of liability may fall onto ISPs. As was the case with the oil industry, assigning such liability ought to result from a community consensus. In the case of the oil tanker liability convention,[108] which followed intense international negotiations that brought no inter-state consensus on shared responsibility for oil-tankers disasters, a community consensus over tanker owners' liability was reached.[109] Their liability is facilitated by a strong insurance background: every tanker owner must insure its actions. Should any regime regulating international liability for transboundary harm inflicted over the Internet be introduced, ISPs would have to take on high insurance costs. Those costs could be reduced should states agree to facilitate ISPs through a joint liability fund, as is the case with nuclear damage liability.[110] In this case an international contract ought to include precise principles for its operation.[111] In the absence of a contractual regime, international liability for transboundary harm in cyberspace may not be evoked.

International spaces analogy

The concept of recognizing cyberspace as the fourth international space[112] is based on the theory of international spaces[113] that combines the priority given to personal jurisdiction and the status of common heritage of mankind (CHMK) granted to elements constituting a particular space. Granting extraterritorial status to cyberspace and submitting it to the active personality principle regime would ensure the foreseeability and harmonization of international practice. Moreover, it introduces balance between possible anarchy and unavoidable worldwide liability of all "netizens".

However, for the international spaces theory to apply to aterritorial cyberspace, a tailored analysis is necessary. The proposals provided so far by the academic community comprise two elements: D. Menthe proposes a direct analogy from international spaces to cyberspace, and proposes specific criteria for determining nationality in cyberspace,[114] while J. Malcolm proposes giving the status of common heritage of mankind to critical web resources.[115]

108 International Convention on Civil Liability for Oil Pollution Damage, Brussels, 29 November 1969, 973 UNTS 3.

109 The consensus is based around a conventional, privately financed voluntary compensation scheme: International Convention on the Establishment of an International Fund for Compensation for Oil Pollution Damage, Brussels, 18 December 1971, 11 ILM 284.

110 Convention on Third Party Liability in the Field of Nuclear Energy, 29 July 1960, 956 UNTS 251.

111 It must be noted that the existing contractual regimes for international liability fail to meet their aims; see T. Gehring and M. Jachtenfuchs, op. cit., p. 93.

112 D. C. Menthe, op. cit.; A. Kamal (2005) *The Law of Cyber-Space*, Geneva: United Nations Institute of Training and Research, pp. 255ff also suggests formulating cyberspace regulations on the basis of those applied to the Law of the Sea; cf. J. Malcolm (2008) 'The Space Law Analogy to Internet Governance', paper delivered at the Giganet Third Annual Symposium, Hyderabad. <http://www.austlii.edu.au/au/journals/JlLawInfoSci/2007/3.html> (accessed 9 March 2009).

113 See generally I. Csabafi (1971) *The Concept of State Jurisdiction in International Space Law*, The Hague: Martinus Nijhoff Publishers, in which the author proposed "designated zones" of functional jurisdiction for outer space.

114 D. C. Menthe, op. cit.

115 J. Malcolm, op. cit.

D. C. Menthe suggests that in cyberspace websites could serve as determinant for nationality. Authors could be held responsible for electronic content according to the laws of their nationality. Links to other websites in cyberspace would be subject to the same jurisdictional analysis. The person creating the link would be subject to his or her legal system regulating the references he or she may make, and the person who opens the link is only a data recipient and is subject to the territorial jurisdiction of the state where he or she stays and to the same laws as his or her fellow nationals. Following such a scheme would guarantee legal certainty to all content and service providers. Unfortunately, the nationality of the author of electronic content seems ill-suited to complex interactions in cyberspace, as it is not applicable in more complex situations that the Internet technically enables (such as sites made for hire, mirroring sites and proxy servers, which would render the determination of the author difficult, if not impossible). This proposal does not provide the clear-cut benefits that would accrue from assuming the theory of the fourth international space, and which may not be gained by applying appropriately modified principles of traditional personal jurisdiction. Moreover, the very nature of the said "spaces" is solidly based on their territorial dimension, and this aspect cannot be ascribed to cyberspace.

J. Malcolm's well-balanced proposal is based on the analysis of space law as compared to cyberspace and Internet governance. He points out key similarities between space law and Internet governance, including the superseding goal of preserving the two spheres for the benefit of mankind and the crucial value of root elements of the network (CIRs) that lies beneath the very idea of CHMK. He also denotes how jurisdictional challenges could be overcome based on the model of international spaces (with the specific role of transnational governance structures). The concept of granting CHMK status to CIRs is attracting forever more academic attention,[116] however, the practical limits for taking that debate to the policy-shaping level lie in the mostly private ownership of CIRs' physical elements (such as the servers of cables). Should those basic legal challenges be overcome (with a system of indemnities to private owners for making their resources a public good), this proposal could be revised.

Cyberspace autonomy

At a time of numerous national attempts to regulate all forms of online activities, an autonomous Internet law, lacking direct links with other regulations, seems unfeasible, but the concept did have prominent pioneers in the early 1990s.[117] Ideas then presented still remain interesting, although ties between "cyber" and "real" law have grown tighter. Nevertheless, it is worth taking a look at key proposals made for a

116 Cf.: A. Segura-Serrano (2006) 'Internet Regulation: A Hard-Law Proposal', op. cit., pp. 192–194; see also A. Segura-Serrano (2006) 'Internet Regulation and the Role of International Law', in A. von Bogdandy and R. Wolfrum (eds.), op. cit., pp. 191–272.

117 See the ground-breaking and still accurate L. Lessig (1999) *Code and Other Laws of Cyberspace*, New York: Basic Books, or an analysis provided by Richard Raysman et al., in (2002) *Emerging Technologies and the Law: Forms and Analysis*, New York: Law Journal Press. For criticism of the autonomous law of cyberspace see F. H. Easterbrook (1996) 'Cyberspace and the Law of the Horse', 1 *University of Chicago Legal Forum*, pp. 207–216.

particular legal regime shaped to fit the specifics of cyberspace, as they still hold some potential for the future regulation of cyberspace.

D. R. Johnson and D. G. Post[118] were the first to openly claim that the principles of territorial jurisdiction are not fit for cyberspace, which requires a different, tailor-made solution. Identifying particular principles and recognizing the legal and practical meaning of electronic boundaries, which could help define, separate and protect particular "areas" of cyberspace, might prove key to establishing an efficient and coherent Internet governance system. The authors suggested identifying an individual set of fundamental rules which could apply to the Internet. Such a code would comprise rules common to all the Internet users within cyber-communities. Cyber-communities with their "netizens" would be a reflection of traditional real-life nations with their citizens[119] – they would be groups of people sharing common principles, goals and interests; however, physically residing in locations distant from one another. The basic set of common principles, shared by all netizens, would constitute a "civic virtue" – the foundation for all cyber-law to follow. It would reflect the decentralized, diverse and complex nature of the Internet, as it reflects the principles common to all cyber-communities.[120]

The authors do not consider democratic norms to be the best alternative to formulating Internet society policies from scratch. According to Johnson and Post, cyber-communities are organized around individual sets of rules and, through internal pressures, exercise their own, restrictive measures (e.g. removing or forcing members who violate the recognized principles to leave). The decentralized approach the authors suggest is to be based on the permission of Internet communities to individually develop, within their own specificity, a set of principles and rules to govern their own "autonomy" in cyberspace.

In their work, Johnson and Post point to the basic guidelines of the new system. This self-regulation mechanism would require legitimacy – the development of a set of principles enabling the repression of violators which would be agreed upon by all the "governed". The second condition would be the internalization of the system by its subjects (they would need to recognize the rules for their own). The authority recognized by the community ought to restrain from exceeding the limit assigned to it and provide for the execution of the rules agreed upon by the group.

The Johnson and Post concept is a milestone on the way to international Internet regulation. Naturally, it was strongly criticized for lacking a sense of physical reality[121] (events in cyberspace are always initiated by specific individuals subject to the laws of the state in which they are present) as well as a social reality. It is hard to imagine groups, such as cyber-communities, so isolated that they do not clash with one another,

118 D. R. Johnson and D. G. Post (1996) 'Law and Borders – the Rise of Law in Cyberspace', 48 *Stanford Law Review*, pp. 1367ff.

119 D. R. Johnson and D. G. Post (1998) 'The New "Civic Virtue" of the Internet: A Complex Systems Model for the Governance of Cyberspace' in C. Firestone (ed.) (1998) *The Emerging Internet (1998 Annual Review of the Institute for Information Studies)*, Washington, DC: The Aspen Institute.

120 Ibid.

121 E.g. A. L. Shapiro (1998), 'The Disappearance of Cyberspace and the Rise of Code', 8 *Seton Hall Constitutional Law Journal*, p. 703.

and at the same time imagine authorities representing such groups to be so morally strong as to resist the temptation to abuse their powers.[122] To implement this concept it would be necessary to guarantee impeccable characters and absolute obedience to the law of cyber-community members who, even though in cyberspace, are still human beings.[123] The idea of "civic virtue" in reference to common cybercrime issues on the one hand, and to Internet censorship on the other, may seem utopian, yet recent concepts pertaining to cyber-community self-organization offer succor; they indicate an underlying economic motive that just might prove that Johnson and Post were right all along and cyber-communities' self-regulation might show us the path for regulating cyberspace.[124]

L. Lessig dedicated his last book, *Remix*, to the hybrid economy, giving it the biased subheading, *Making Art and Commerce Thrive in the Hybrid Economy*. He points to the hybrid economy as a commerce model reflecting the character of mass online interaction and co-operation. He describes it as a mix of elements from commercial economies (the value of which may be denoted in prizes) and sharing economies (like love or friendship, where introducing hard currency deprives them of their essence). As Lessig suggests, communities rely not only on goods that may be estimated with money. Equally important are those elements for which price-offering would be considered inappropriate. To illustrate, offering advice against payment in personal matters may constitute a commercial good; nevertheless, such a relationship would significantly differ from, for example, friendship, the inherent element of which is indeed giving advice in personal endeavors and providing spiritual support. If the sharing relationship was to be violated by money, its nature would change radically.

It was into this dichotomous division between the commercial and sharing economies recognized by social groups that the Internet intervened. Its ideas were noble – at the beginning the Internet was to serve the exchange of knowledge (as it does originate from research and scientific facilities) and was supposed to be free from state or business intervention. However, with time it did gain a dominant commercial character and was subject to massive state regulation, both through legal and extra-legal means. Internet development brought about one more new form of social interaction, never as popular in the "real" world. Successes of such enterprises as media repository Wikimedia or Linux brought non-monetary exchange of goods and services, which on the one hand does rely on altruism, sharing and collaboration, but at the same time flourishes when supported with money.

It was Y. Benkler[125] who noticed that in commercial economies prices are the primary source of information about and incentive for resource allocation. In sharing econo-

122 On the "mapping" of cyber-communities, see K. Bowrey (2005) *Law and Internet Cultures*, Melbourne: Cambridge University Press, pp. 24–31.

123 R. H. Weber points to the problem of "free-riders" not ready to, and unwilling to, collaborate on an equal basis within an egalitarian society. Cf. R. H. Weber, M. Grosz and R. Weber (2011) *Shaping Internet Governance: Regulatory Challenges*, New York: Springer, p. 22.

124 D. G. Post elaborated on his original concept in (2009) *In Search of Jefferson's Moose – Notes on State in Cyberspace*, Oxford: Oxford University Press.

125 Y. Benkler (2004) 'Sharing Nicely: On Shareable Goods and the Emergence of Sharing as a Modality of Economic Production', 114 *Yale Law Journal* p. 273 at pp. 275–358.

mies, non-price-based, social relations play those roles.[126] Benkler provided a detailed description of goods allocated in the sharing economy and values affecting the fact and manner of allocation.[127] In "Wealth of Networks"[128] the author announces a new stage of social development: the era of the network information economy, to be based on peer production, which would generate resources, immeasurable with money, that would dominate the market. The "currency" of such exchange was to be the voluntary contribution of participants in the form of labor and time spent thereon.[129] The author points to actions, already taken by thousands of such volunteers, which contradict the fundamentals of economic knowledge.[130] Lessig also provides a number of examples of such economic "anomalies" comprising the free sharing of resources online which, based on the hybrid economy model, generated considerable monies.[131] The underlying success of such interactions lies in providing users with a free platform for their creativity and allowing them to act. Lessig calls the process the "Lego" mechanism – just as in the case of the Danish bricks, Google services or numerous Wikimedia services are created at the request of users, with their rich participation and adapted to meet their needs, all free of charge. In return, hybrid businesses benefit from the work and ideas of their users, including in income-generating ways. As Lessig rightfully emphasizes, the line between hybrid economies and sharing economies is thin – a transaction primarily effected for altruistic reasons may become such as to derive economic benefit.[132] Lessig and Benkler, when describing examples of this new economic scheme, emphasize that no provisions of law or commercial restrictions will be able to stop them. As Lessig puts it, the "past survives only if it can beat out the future".[133] Therefore, in his opinion, obsessive persistence in applying existing ways and means (be it legal regulations or commercial schemes), which cannot work when confronted with novelty, is unjustified.

The Wikipedia phenomenon, a leading example of the hybrid economy, contributed to the creation of yet another neologism. *Wikinomics*,[134] a book written by D. Tapscott and A. D. Williams, presented yet another economic model allowing for the specificity of what L. Lessig and Y. Benkler called the hybrid economy. The concept presented by Tapscott and Williams is revolutionary, as they attempt to encourage businesses to introduce radical changes in the manner that they play the market. They

126 Ibid., p. 282.

127 Cf. Y. Benkler, op. cit., pp. 321ff.

128 Y. Benkler (2006) *The Wealth of Networks: How Social Production Transforms Markets and Freedom*, New Haven: Yale University Press.

129 Ibid., pp. 43ff.

130 The prime example of this is the Open Source society, see ibid., pp. 59ff (chapter 3, 'Peer Production and Sharing').

131 L. Lessig, *Remix*, op. cit., pp. 161ff.

132 Weblogs serve as a good example. If they enjoy certain popularity, their author may expect offers from companies or producers willing to take advantage of the success of the blog and present their offers to its readers, either by placing advertisements (on which the blogger gains profit), or, (and this is ethically more dubious), by inducing the blogger to positively comment on their products or services in return for providing the blogger with those services free, or providing special additional benefits.

133 L. Lessig, *Remix* op. cit., p. 168.

134 D. Tapscott and A. D. Williams (2008) *Wikinomics: How Mass Collaboration Changes Everything*, New York: Portfolio.

indicate four basic principles of Wikinomics (openness, peering, sharing, and acting globally) as keys to success.[135] The authors also underline the role of the recipients of goods which are produced in Wikinomics, calling them active "prosumers" (as compared with passive consumers).[136] What Lessig called the Lego effect is described here as the effect of active conduct by those to whom goods are addressed, as the Internet provides for an extraordinary chance to listen to and follow their opinions.

Why does the Wiki-economy work? Is it "profitable" to work for no remuneration? In his book "Free", C. Anderson gives a positive answer to this question, for which he provides detailed supporting grounds.[137] Above all, he points to new values that the cyber-communities era has brought about. Recognition, popularity and esteem in cyberspace easily translate into economic value.[138] The best example is the marketing strategy of the book concerned – it has been rendered available free of charge as an audio-book and as an e-book; however, its paper version, as well as individual talks given by Anderson, have brought him revenue. Anderson also suggests that soon multimedia companies will lose the fight for maintaining the current, restrictive copyright structure and it will become essential for the audiovisual industry to find alternative methods of generating profits.

Benkler is also certain about the forthcoming changes in the economic system,[139] including those which are bound to bring about changes in the legal system. As Benkler emphasizes,[140] the purpose of a modern state should be to determine the needs and values key to its society. The author claims that communication is the basic unit of sociological existence.[141] Thus referring to the *jus naturale* system, at a time of the globalization of culture and communication, it is necessary to establish a set of rules and values, common to communities and linked by the electronic network, since it is they who will be subject to state regulation. The increase in peer production offers a unique chance of reassessing the system of principles followed by global society.

This approach suggests an appropriate way to regulate this new economy. If the economic model comprises elements derived from both commercial and sharing economies, than a legal mechanism for its assessment should also envisage the specifics of both the systems. Law has been traditionally used to rule (above all) commercial economies, while sharing economies usually went by without it – it was up to the community itself, its standards and (eventually) ethics, to "regulate" the sharing.[142] If this new economy comprises sharing and money, then both law and ethics must be considered when attempting to ascertain those of its rules upon which any universal standards are to be based. A proposal that combines the two elements is the *jus Internet* concept described below.

135 Ibid., p. 20.
136 Ibid., pp. 124ff.
137 C. Anderson (2009) *Free: The Future of a Radical Price*, New York: Hyperion.
138 Ibid, pp. 180ff.
139 Y. Benkler, *The Wealth of Networks*, op. cit., p. 464
140 Ibid.
141 Ibid., p. 465.
142 One can draw a clear line between love, as an example of a sharing economy, and marriage, as an example of a commercial one.

Attempts to identify moral and legal principles common to all humans have been made on numerous occasions over the centuries. The Roman *jus gentium* referred to values common to all people, to the *jus naturale*. Created in order to enable communities representing numerous and thoroughly varying provinces of the Empire to interact and engage in economic transactions, its content was to reflect the features of human nature, and the human sense of justice and fairness, as the basic common ground for human interactions. The term *jus gentium* was used in the Roman Empire to describe customary regulations on relations between foreigners (non-citizens) and Roman citizens.[143] The principles of *jus gentium* were based on two pillars: trust (*fides*) and equity (*aeguitas*). The content of *jus gentium* norms was derived from two normative systems: *jus naturale* and religious law. That content operated initially as common custom, eventually evolving into binding customary law which was observed by representatives of various cultures and social systems. Although the history of the Roman Empire does not fill one with optimism, the principles of *jus gentium* (law of nations) apply to this day. What we refer to as public international law has originated from *jus gentium* institutions.

Nowadays, consideration of what is fair and just falls within the area of ethics. When applying the lessons learned from the Roman Empire and its multicultural nature to multicultural cyberspace, a similar set of ethically-based rules may be identified and serve as the basis for future legal regulation. By identifying ethical standards, common to all communities (cyber-communities), it might show possible to arrive at a consensus satisfying all concerned – all of the participants of the global electronic exchange. This basic ethical standard might reflect what Johnson and Post once called "civic virtue". Criticism of their concept, however, which focused on the argument of lack of enforcement power in respect of such ethical provisions, would no longer prove accurate in the time of the hybrid economy. Should such a set of ethical rules become recognized and acknowledged by the governed and achieve customary character, the next step would be to ascertain its legally binding power (i.e. to become recognized by national or international courts, as an element of good faith, fairness or equity), just as is the case with customary international law. Therefore *jus Internet* would be the legal, customary regulation of cyber-communities, based on solid, recognized and enforceable ethical rules.

Why should this model of regulation work? Or, rather, why it has worked so far, for the international legal order, originating from *jus gentium* and developed through customary law, is based on such rules. Reasons why states decide to assume international law regulations are varied: they range from natural law, which deems each state equipped with certain "natural" privileges, to the contemporary notion of common interest as the justification for executing international law. In the context of these deliberations, the latter seems most relevant. States observe international law for they have an interest in it: to put it more trivially, it pays off. The *pacta sunt servanda* principle, underlying all international law regulations, provides for the foreseeability of others' actions in the international arena. When a state becomes a member of the

143 Roman citizens' interactions were regulated by the statutory law – *jus civile*.

international community, observing its rules allows it to become a part of the general power guaranteed by compliance with commonly established norms; it may count on the reciprocation of other international actors. Such conduct is driven by the common interests of the global community.

The same mechanisms can be easily identified behind cyber-communities such as e.g. Wikipedia.[144] Their members obey the rules not because they fear sanctions for misconduct, but because they believe that their power is the power of the community of which they are members. Common rules facilitate co-operation and allow foresight of consequences of particular, individual actions. Compliance with common, established rules pays off.

The current challenge is the actual identification of the ethical rules that cyber-communities obey. Elaborating on the fact identified by Johnson and Post (that traditional democracy is not sufficient to meet the challenge of cyberspace), J. Zittrain offers a model for democracy that is modified accordingly. When referring to the Wikipedia phenomenon, he calls its internal organization model "a semiotic democracy".[145] According to him, the decisive element therein is not the majority of votes but the power of the arguments used to support a certain idea or value. Perhaps such a model of identifying rules common to cyber-communities would allow for identification of the *jus Internet* rules.

The proposed *jus Internet* model combines two constitutive elements of the hybrid economy. It proposes eventual customary legal frameworks to meet the economic challenges. At the same time, it offers the flexibility of internal, ethical rules developed by way of semiotic democracy by the cyber-communities themselves. Such rules incorporate the idea of "civic virtue" presented by Johnson and Post, and the commercial element, inherent in a hybrid economy, ensures respect for the rules. Such respect would be based on the concept of common interest known to both international law and self-regulating cyber-communities. Simultaneously, *jus Internet* could serve as a stepping stone to further elaboration of the legal order for cyberspace. Those basic customary law rules, identified as common to all "netizens", combined with the IIL principles described above, might serve as foundations for an international, treaty-based regime for cyberspace (as provided for within an Internet Framework Convention), putting cyberspace next to the open sea, outer space or natural environment, all initially regulated by international custom, and eventually by treaties.

The future of IIL – an Internet Framework Convention

Efficient Internet governance is determined by numerous factors, out of which one is of key importance: the international co-operation of all stakeholders. This key characteristic of IG predetermines the existence and further evolution of IIL. International elaboration of IIL content is currently taking place in multiple international fora, with

144 Cf. J. Zittrain (2008) *The Future of the Internet and How to Stop It*, New Haven: Yale University Press, p. 141.
145 Ibid., p. 147.

the IGF as their original operational model.[146] Criticism of this model of governance centers on its lack of executive power and non-transparent structure,[147] which is the result of IIL being constituted largely of soft law documents. The future of IIL, however, seems to follow the direction of traditional international law. Elaboration of a universal hard-law framework for cyberspace seems to be the background idea behind the recent actions of the CoE,[148] EU[149] and US.[150] Academics have long proposed an international framework convention for the Internet.[151] Such a convention, however, would have to adhere to the specific nature of the medium it would attempt to regulate. It would have to envisage the multi-stakeholder character of IG. Therefore, an Internet Framework Convention would have to: 1) incorporate the IIL principles described above; 2) tackle all the key issues of electronic communications;[152] 3) propose a unique multilateral and multi-stakeholder regime. The possible solution to this last challenge might be the creation of a wide contractual consensus acceptable to all: national authorities, international organizations, industry representatives (national and international juridical persons) and civil society (represented through its societies or other legal forms of incorporation, in accordance with national laws). All of these entities could elaborate on such a consensus within the already-existing forum of the IGF. In order for the consensus to be binding, the convention would have to foresee at least two interrelated responsibility mechanisms. While for states and international organizations the traditional rules for international accountability should suffice, the rules for private law entities (from industry or civil society sectors) would have to differ. They might be based on the current trends in the IT industry, endorsing

146 Including regional IGF initiatives (Asia Pacific Regional IGF (APrIGF), Caribbean Internet Governance Forum, Central Africa IGF, Commonwealth IGF, East Africa IGF (EAIGF), European Dialogue on Internet Governance (EuroDig), Latin America and Caribbean IGF, and the West Africa IGF) and twelve national IGF initiatives. <http://www.intgovforum.org/cms/regional-igfs> (accessed 25 December 2010).

147 J. Malcolm (2008) 'Appraising the Success of the Internet Governance Forum', 8(3) *Internet Governance Project Papers*. <www.internetgovernance.org/pdf/MalcolmIGFReview.pdf> (accessed 25 December 2010).

148 See the CoE sub-groups on new media, covering such issues as new media, public service media governance, cross-border internet, protection neighbouring rights of broadcasting organisations, information society, media diversity and public service media, as detailed on the CoE new media website. <http://www.coe.int/t/dghl/standardsetting/media/> (accessed 25 December 2010).

149 See the comments of Viviane Reding, in *Commissioner Reding's Weekly Videomessage*, 4 May 2009 'The Future of Internet Governance: Towards an Accountable ICANN', op. cit.

150 *Affirmation of Commitments by the United States Department of Commerce and the Internet Corporation for Assigned Names and Numbers*, 30 September 2009, op. cit., with respect to the GAC competence.

151 See e.g., J. Mathiason (2004) 'A Framework Convention: An Institutional Option for Internet Governance', 4(2) *Internet Governance Project Papers*. <www.intgovforum.org/Substantive_1st_IGF/igp-fc.pdf> (accessed 25 December 2010), and A. Segura-Serrano (2006) op. cit.

152 Including the key principles of state responsibility for cyberattacks, with reference to the existing international cybercrime and counter-terrorism agreements; sequence of jurisdictional principles applicable to actions performed over the Internet, preferably with reference to existing e-commerce and private international law standards; reference to existing (both hard- and soft-law) tools for international protection of privacy and the application of human rights online.

self-regulatory privacy protection using peer pressure and consumer choice,[153] rather than traditional contractual risk liability (as is the case with environmental law). Should the convention gather enough industry and civil society representatives, such an ethics-based soft-law approach might be sufficient.

Particular solutions for each issue tackled within the convention might be further developed within Additional Protocols. Their scope could be based on the content of the WGIG Report of 2005. This document specifies social policy issues essential to Internet governance and the implementation of already-existing supervisory mechanisms. The list includes, *inter alia*, the issue of administration of the root zone files and system, Internet stability, security and cybercrime as well as interconnection costs (so far the distribution of such costs is uneven).[154] In its report, WGIG also raised the issue of the allocation of domain names, postulating further development of gTLDs-related policies and procedures. The report also includes concerns pertaining to the protection of intellectual property rights and application of the protection regime to the cyberspace.[155] The Internet Framework Convention should also include provisions regulating the freedom of expression,[156] as well as data protection and privacy rights. The issue of consumer rights protection[157] also requires the attention of international fora, for there are no common standards of consumer protection on the Internet, despite these being essential for the international sale of goods. Problems new to the international community that have arisen by reason of the global network, such as multilingualism,[158] convergence and "next generation networks" (NGNs), as well as e-commerce,[159] should also be identified in the new framework agreement. According to WGIG, developing a common understanding on the respective roles and responsibilities of all stakeholders, from both developed and developing countries, is essential.[160] Depending on the character of the particular issues, those framework legal mechanisms could derive richly from the international law experience (as already mentioned, from environmental law, the human rights regime or the Law of the Sea).

The WGIG Report analyses the role of particular international actors, indicating their respective roles. National governments should establish national, international and regional policies, adopt laws and support community self-regulation by developing international treaties and facilitating benchmarking. It is also necessary for them to provide the legal framework for disputes resolution and arbitration mechanisms. The private sector ought to provide for self-regulation and exchange of best practices, but also engage in developing policy proposals and guidelines, as well as supporting research. Civil society should focus its efforts on raising social

153 Not adhering to the ethical industry standards might result in loss of customers and, eventually, in economic loss.

154 Internet service providers (ISPs) based in countries remote from Internet backbones, thus particularly those in developing countries, must pay the full costs of the international circuits.

155 WGIG (2005) *Report of the Working Group on Internet Governance*, op. cit., para. 22.

156 Ibid., para. 24.

157 Ibid., para. 26.

158 Ibid., para. 27.

159 Ibid., para. 28.

160 Ibid., chapter IV.

awareness and promoting knowledge by actively engaging in democratic processes. It should also promote human rights, sustainable development and social justice, as the counterweight to the already existing industrial or political lobbies.

According to J. Mathiason[161] such a document should be firmly grounded in international law. The convention should, above all, define the term "Internet governance" and the scope of its relevance. It should provide for definitions of key Internet governance related issues, including the definition of the Internet and those entities authorized to exercise governing functions.[162] Above all, however, such a document should name fundamental Internet governance principles. The Framework Convention should incite discussion in those areas where further agreement is required, especially in the context of irreconcilable national legal regulations (e.g. intellectual property rights or freedom of speech protection); its Additional Protocols could provide for detailed norms and obligations of the parties involved (just as the regulations on environmental protection do). Above all, the document should vest power in state parties to the convention to act in the capacity of "supervisors" of the rules, being the essence of Internet governance. Moreover, it is also significant that state parties delegate a part of their competence to civil society organizations and business. The Framework Convention, as such, would not have to include any accountability mechanism, but one which provides for different rights or obligations for each of the three groups of participants (states, business, civil society) ought to be elaborated further upon.

The IIL regime, as presented in this book, could therefore include the following steps: initially the rules recognized in cyberspace ought to be identified. This might be effected not based on a comparison of national legislations, but rather on the compromises of cyber-communities, reached through semiotic democracy mechanisms. Such rules might lead to the second step, the elaboration of customary IIL, recognized by national and international courts within the existing framework of judicial recognition, and from there to the establishment of a contractual framework regime, as was the case with maritime law or environmental law. Such an evolution would provide for the preservation of the unique, global character of the network, the further development of the information society and could prevent the threat of "cyber-Balkanization".

161 Internet Governance Project (2004) *A Framework Convention: An Institutional Option for Internet Governance*. <http://www.intgovforum.org/Substantive_1st_IGF/igp-fc.pdf>. The IGP reiterated, updated and reinforced its proposals (in response to the comments of EU Commissioner V. Reding, referred to above) in its 2009 *Independence and Accountability: the Future of ICANN*, <www.ntia.doc.gov/comments/2009/dnstransition/050.pdf>.

162 A good starting point for discussion about defining the issues is the principle of subsidiarity, which is that international solutions are to be applied only if it is deemed more effective than actions taken within the state, region or local community.

Summary

The commonly-accessible Internet has revolutionized everyday life and affected each aspect of it. Opinions on its negative social impact and on increasing risk related to digitized trade are widespread. The World Wide Web has changed interpersonal relations, the manner in which the exchange of goods and information is effected and created great, new opportunities for interpersonal interactions and free exchange of thoughts. Recent years, however, have brought about real threats to the new medium, a medium which is to revolutionize society to an even greater extent, transforming it into an information society. Consequently, mass commercial and intellectual exchange online have posed new problems and intensified those already existing, so much so that previous mechanisms for resolving these problems have failed. Apart from new problems characteristic of cyberspace and existing in no other field, such as spam or hacking, disputes concerning breach of intellectual property rights and consumer protection have erupted to an extent that is greater than ever before. Questions that have so far been limited to regional or national regulations are now raised in the international arena. Rules were missing, as to which such supranational issues could be resolved. There were also no appropriate international solutions. The consequences of applying the already-existing rules were often quite opposite to those intended: instead of guaranteeing the safe exchange of goods, services or thoughts they rather intensified the chaos and added even greater uncertainty. Answers to questions about the limits of powers of regulating bodies and the competence of state authorities, even though based on commonly known and accepted rules, were rather contradictory. Those limits within which state bodies had hitherto used to resolve disputes proved too narrow and not flexible enough. It turned out to be impossible to apply grounds for exercising jurisdiction over entities operating outside the Internet to those who acted in cyberspace. This often led to powers being exercised with an excessive scope. As a result of the insufficiency of previous legal solutions, they had to be modified, or at least interpreted to guarantee respect for traditional values (such as certainty in legal transactions or respect for civil rights) in cyberspace. The term "cyberspace", native to science fiction literature, has been used in serious studies on the essence of state sovereignty and the limits of state jurisdictional powers. The studies posed rhetorical questions about the essence of cyberspace, and more importantly, about its nature. Questions about the nature and limits of space bring about an avalanche of complex disputes over the international application of legal norms. How to regulate it? Would it be sufficient to modify already existing legal principles or is it necessary to establish new principles adapted to its specificity? The literature on the subject of Internet regulation often mentions the need for international regulation of cyberspace, at least within troublesome areas such as electronic commerce or protection against harmful content. If the Internet poses new risks, it would be reasonable to assume new solutions to the problems it presents. The current state of Internet regulations indicates numerous discrepancies or even conflicts of national rules each of which has advantages yet is also not free from drawbacks. The first possibility for enforcing commonly-established principles for cyberspace would be to involve state bodies. Current practice and insufficient international regulations leave no other possibility of regulating the Internet but to apply national laws enforced abroad. The question whether national laws aimed at regulating the Internet may actually be implemented outside the relevant territorial borders has still not been clearly answered. For those states which prefer a positive answer to this question, a sufficient argument would be that the principles permitting the exercise of the effects jurisdiction can be applied similarly to instances pertaining to the Internet. Enforceability of laws concerning the Internet is still considered on case by case study basis because of the lack of general governing principles. Such a situation leads to the increase in the uncertainty of all entities involved in electronic exchange, even though there are no reasonable grounds supporting the stance that national regulations may be applied in any place in which the Internet may be accessed.

The problem of specifying the limits of state competence in cyberspace has recently gained another international aspect. The problem results from the so-called wave of cyberattacks (attacks, using the Internet, on the key information infrastructure of states). This phenomenon was instituted by the attack of Russian hackers on Estonia in 2007, and its climax was a recent (January 2010) breach into the American resources of Google, most probably initiated from China. This issue might be considered to have risen to the rank of "threat to international peace and security" as per the Charter of the United Nations. The Clinton Doctrine announced by the US Secretary of State immediately after the attacks includes the declaration that the US government will fight against filtering policy.[1] More importantly, however, Clinton compared the attacks on Google servers to international armed attack. This is not the first such analogy invoked by the heads of states. On numerous occasions a threat has been issued of armed (including nuclear) response to the mass cyberattacks on key electronic resources of states.[2] Therefore, there is an urgent need to classify such attacks from the perspective of international law. The law, in its current form, neither allows a cyberattack to be deemed an armed aggression permitting self-defense, nor provides

1 J. Kulesza (2010) 'Amerykańsko-Chiński Spór o Cenzurę w Internecie', 6 *Państwo i Prawo*, pp. 29–41.

2 See S. J. Shackelford (2009) 'From Nuclear War to Net War: Analogizing Cyber Attacks in International Law', 25(3) Berkeley Journal of International Law, pp. 191–250. <http://works.bepress.com/context/scott_shackelford/article/1004/type/native/viewcontent> (accessed 20 December 2010); D. Delibasis (2006) 'State Use of Force in Cyberspace for Self-Defence: A New Challenge for a New Century', (8) *Peace Conflict and Development: An Interdisciplinary Journal*, pp. 13ff. <http://www.peacestudiesjournal.org.uk/dl/Feb%2006%20DELIBASIS.pdf> (accessed 16 February 2011); and D. Delibasis (2007) *The Right to National Self-Defense in Information Warfare Operations*, Bury St Edmunds, UK: Arena Books.

for any protection mechanisms in the event of such attacks. Taking into consideration the fact that key players on the electronic arena are nuclear powers (such as the US, China and Russia), the legal classification of cyberattacks and consequent practical solutions to the problem in question have become a burning issue.

There is a common agreement that not all problems related to the regulation of electronic space may be solved by referring to traditional legal instruments. In some areas closely related to the Internet – and clearly different to that which was previously known as media – it is necessary to put forward specific solutions. If, however, the solution is common to the entire aterritorial cyberspace, one thing is certain: it must correspond to the extraordinary feature thereof, namely it must be transboundary and separated from the territoriality principle that has hitherto been fundamental to legal regulations.

Legislative actions as regards the Internet have been regularly intensified.[3] Until now the main areas of legislative activities have been privacy, data protection, intellectual property protection, tax and cybercrime. Social relations are, however, too complex for legislators to regulate them all. Society undergoes dynamic changes which, in principle, are too rapid for the law to keep up with. This is especially noticeable now, when technological development is being transformed into the social reality much faster than legislators are able to react. Rules of law sometimes even become unnecessary before they are adopted. The risk of creating unnecessary regulations is a serious threat to effective Internet regulation.

Another way in which the international community has attempted to deal with the growing problem of lack of rules governing conduct online, is based on social norms and attempts at self-regulation made by particular groups. Nevertheless, and contrary to legislation, social norms carry no power to secure their exercise with sanctions. They are implemented by the community itself as an effect of pressure exerted by members thereof. At the early stage of the Internet their application was determined by a set of social norms referred to as "netiquette", the main sanctions of which included the pressure of co-users and exclusion from the group. In times when the Internet was used by a relatively small part of society, mainly scientists, establishing and applying customary laws was common. As a result of the expansion of the Internet it has become more and more difficult to implement such principles. However, this type of regulation may still be applied with respect to groups closely integrated and limited in number. In the 1998 White Paper on Internet Governance, as well as a number of other US government documents,[4] self-regulation was proposed as a preferred mechanism of Internet regulation. Self-regulation shares some common features with the abovementioned social principles. The key difference is that, contrary to social norms usually based on a disbursed regulating system, self-regulation, as a rule, is based on a well organized approach. Principles establishing self-regulation

3 This fact is especially noticeable in the case of OECD states, where the sector of information and communication technologies is very wide and strongly affects economic and social relations.

4 United States Department of Commerce, National Telecommunications and Information Administration (1998) *Management of Internet Names and Addresses* ('the White Paper'), Docket Number: 980212036–8146–02.<http://www.ntia.doc.gov/ntiahome/domainname/6_5_98dns.htm> (accessed 14 January 2009).

norms are usually codified. The trend to develop self-regulating norms is still noticeable among Internet service providers. In many states they are under growing pressure exerted by state authorities to implement principles specifying the Internet content control procedures. Internet service providers more often refer to self-regulating norms as a method of imposing certain conduct standards, and consequently, prevent the government from interfering in their activities. While self-regulation may prove a useful tool, it also poses a high risk resulting from possible abuse of freely formulated norms, for instance with respect to the control of accessible content.

In view of the sparse successes of these alternative ways of regulating social behaviors and the radically growing number of users, it is necessary to refer to traditional ways of establishing international norms. Global Internet regulation will require universal consensus that is possible only through a long-lasting negotiation process. Various international law mechanisms may be applied to develop an Internet governance regime. It is worth pointing here to so-called soft law, the role of which has been growing considerably. So far, actions aimed at the harmonization of principles on which electronic activities are based have been taken by a number of expert organizations, whose agendas touched upon the problem of the Internet and its structures only marginally. This led to the situation where the efforts of many fora repeat answers to the same questions, and the process of universal regulation of the medium proceeds at an unsatisfactory pace. At the request of, and on the initiative of, WSIS, the UN Secretary-General established the first international forum that was to become the arena for debates of representatives of all areas of electronic exchange. Within the Internet Governance Forum, key issues concerning international governance of the World Wide Web and the limits of competence of active authorities are to be examined and proposals for change presented. As a result of the efforts of the UN Working Group on Internet Governance, a report was prepared which, apart from proposing structural changes in Internet governance, suggested the development of an international framework of rules for collaboration between state governments and other social representatives in this process. The WGIG also proposed the application of a holistic approach to Internet governance, which should refer not only to technical, but also legal, social, economic and development issues. In order to establish stable rules of collaboration it is necessary to take account of participation of all entities involved in electronic exchange, both horizontally and vertically (from all social groups whose situation will be regulated by international law).

It is beyond any doubt that current modes of Internet governance are bound to fail. Two scenarios are possible. The current World Wide Web governance system will be either particularized into smaller national or regional webs (based on technical and legal principles common to such small communities; such webs, however, will be not directly connected), or democratized and internationalized. In the preferred latter case the interests of all social groups will be represented online, and the basis of electronic exchange will be codified in an agreement incorporating the international consensus – thus laying the foundations for international Internet law. Only the latter solution guarantees further development not only of the Internet, but also the information society that is to form the basis for a global knowledge-based economy. The decision of President Obama in 2009 on internationalization of World Wide Web governance raises hopes for implementation of the more optimistic scenario set out above. The *Affirmation of Commitments*[5] concluded on 1 October 2009 by and between the US Department of Commerce and ICANN introduces international supervision over the Corporation's operations.[6] Following the suggestions of the international community,[7] the position of the GAC has been strengthened: ICANN now reports directly to GAC (and not to the Department of Commerce). Experience will show the effectiveness of this internationalized form of governance. The internationalized formula, along with more effective actions by all IGF stakeholders, could produce a satisfactory solution to the problem of the legal regulation of cyberspace.

The evolution envisaged in this book comprises five steps towards successful, global Internet governance. The initial point ought to be (1) a consensus on the application of jurisdictional principles to cyberspace. (2) Based thereupon, a sequence of Internet Governance principles might be presented. Such principles ought to include (3) particular obligations, the scope of which, to be applicable, ought to be ascertained based on the existing, common practice of the information society, as represented through its cyber-communities. Such a role is ascribed herein to the *jus Internet* concept. Once principles are detailed down to particular norms that might be successfully applied as customary laws, following the path set before by other international law disciplines, such as the Law of the Sea, (4) a Framework Internet Convention may be drafted. Within such a document, those basic principles might be set out, while their elaboration, as based on the customary *jus Internet*, could be (5) put into writing in additional protocols thereto dealing with particular areas of International Internet Law. Such a customary and legal scheme could help preventing the danger of cyber-Balkanization and secure the basic tool for further development of the global information society.

5 ICANN (2009) *Affirmation of Commitments by the United States Department of Commerce and the Internet Corporation for Assigned Names and Numbers,* 30 September 2009. <http://www.icann.org/en/affirmation.htm> (accessed 25 December 2010).

6 See J. Kulesza(2009) 'Internet w Końcu Międzynarodowy', *Stosunki Międzynarodowe*. <http://www.stosunki.pl/?q=node/1200> (accessed 10 January 2010).

7 The last suggestion was made by Viviane Reding (European Commissioner for the Information Society and Media) in (2009) *Commissioner Reding's Weekly Videomessage*, 4 May 2009, 'The Future of Internet Governance: Towards an Accountable ICANN'. <http://ec.europa.eu/commission_barroso/reding/video/text/message_20090504.pdf>.

Bibliography

Journal and news articles, speeches and conference papers

Adelaja, T. (2007) 'AllofMP3 Survives First Test In Court', *Moscow Times,* 16 August 2007. <http://www.themoscowtimes.com/news/article/allofmp3–survives-first-test-in-court/194998.html>

Annan, K. (2004) United Nations Secretary-General (2004) Speech delivered at the Global Internet Governance Forum, New York, March 2004.

Anonymous (2007) 'Apple pays $700,000 for bloggers' legal fees', *MACNN,* 29 January 2007. <http://www.macnn.com/articles/07/01/29/apple.pays.legal.fees/&startNumber=10> (accessed 13 August 2011).

Anonymous (undated) 'Bombs Rain Down on Torrey Canyon', *BBC News*, <http://news.bbc.co.uk/onthisday/hi/dates/stories/march/29/newsid_2819000/2819369.stm> (accessed: 5 February 2011).

Anonymous (2007) 'Estonia Scores World Web First in National Polls', *Information Week*, 28 February 2007. <http://www.informationweek.com/management/showArticle.jhtml?articleID=197700272> (accessed 9 January 2011).

Anonymous (2011) 'EU-Hungary Row over Media Law Cools Down', *BBC News*, 2 February 2011. <http://www.bbc.co.uk/news/world-europe-12343319>.

Anonymous (2010) 'Facebook poza polską jurysdykcją: nie można go ani pozwać, ani skontrolować' ('Facebook Outside Polish Jurisdiction: Cannot be Sued or Controlled'), PAP/Gazeta Prawna, 19 November 2010. <http://prawo.gazetaprawna.pl/artykuly/466155,facebook_poza_polska_jurysdykcja_nie_mozna_go_ani_pozwac_ani_skontrolowac.html> (accessed 25 December 2010).

Anonymous (2009) 'ICANN Be Independent', *The Economist,* 24 September 2009. <http://www.economist.com/businessfinance/PrinterFriendly.cfm?story_id=14517430>

Anonymous (2008) 'Italy Cracks Down on Pirate Bay', New York Times, 14 August 2008. <http://www.nytimes.com/2008/08/14/technology/14iht-webpirate.15301147.html> (accessed 2 February 2011).

Anonymous (2001) 'Supreme People's Court on Stealing State Secrets', Xinhua News Agency, 21 January 2001.

Barlow, J. P. (1996) 'A Declaration of the Independence of Cyberspace', paper published online. <https://projects.eff.org/~barlow/Declaration-Final.html>.

Barnes, D. (1994) 'Coming Jurisdictional Swamp of Global Internetworking', unpublished, Austin, TX: Austin Cyberpunks <http://www.io.com/~cman/swamp.html> (accessed: 29 November 2004).

Barry, C. (2007) 'Italy's High Court Rules that File Downloading not a Crime if not for

Profit', *International Herald Tribune*, 22 January 2007. <http://www.post-gazette.com/pg/07026/756542-96.stm> (accessed 11 February 2011).

Bartsch, K. and Elberling, B. (2003) 'Jus Cogens v. State Immunity, Round Two: The Decision of the European Court of Human Rights in the Kalogeropoulou et al. v. Greece and Germany Decision', 4(5) *German Law Journal*, p. 14 at pp. 477–491. <http://www.germanlawjournal.com/index.php?pageID=11&artID=271> (accessed 29 June 2011).

Barzilai–Nahon, K. and Scholl, H. J. (2007) 'Similarities and Differences of E-Commerce and E-Government: Insights from a Pilot Study', paper given at the 40th Annual Hawaii International Conference on System Sciences (HICSS'07). <http://csdl.computer.org/comp/proceedings/hicss/2007/2755/00/27550092c.pdf> (accessed 4 February 2011).

Bassiouni, M. C. (1996) 'Accountability for International Crimes and Serious Violations of Fundamental Human Rights, International Crimes: Jus Cogens and Obligatio Erga Omnes', 59(4) *Law and Contemporary Problems*, pp. 63–74.

Basu, S. (2008) 'International Taxation of E-Commerce: Persistent Problems and Possible Developments', 1 *Journal of Information, Law & Technology*. <http://www2.warwick.ac.uk/fac/soc/law/elj/jilt/2008_1/basu/> (accessed 4 February 2011).

Baumer, D. L., Earp, J. B. and Poindexter, J. C. (2004) 'Internet Privacy Law: a Comparison between the United States and the European Union', 5(23) *Computers & Security* pp. 400–412.

Bendrath, R. and Hofmann, J. (2005) 'The Return of the State in Cyberspace, Regulation and Legitimacy on the Internet: The Domain Name System and Privacy' paper delivered at the Lucerna conference on *The Internet and the Changing Face of International Relations and Security*, <www.crn.ethz.ch/_docs/BendrathHoffmann_The-Return-of-the-State-in-Cyberspace-final.pdf> (16 February 2011).

Benkler, Y. (2004) 'Sharing Nicely: On Shareable Goods and the Emergence of Sharing as a Modality of Economic Production', 114 *Yale Law Journal*, pp. 273–358.

Birnhack, M. and Elkin-Koren, N. (2011) 'Does Law Matter Online? Empirical Evidence on Privacy Law Compliance', 17 *Michigan Telecommunications & Technology Law Review*, pp. 337–352.

Boister, N. (2003) 'Transnational Criminal Law?' 14(5) *EJIL*, pp. 953–976.

Bos, M. (1993) 'La Competence extraterritoriale des Etats'/The Extraterritorial Jurisdiction of States', 65(1) *Annuaire de l'Institut de Droit International/Yearbook of the Institute of International Law* (Milan Session), p. 39 and pp. 60–125.

Cogburn, D. (2005) 'The US Role in Running the Net', *BBC News*, 14 November 2005. <http://news.bbc.co.uk/2/hi/technology/4435352.stm> (accessed 20 December 2010).

Delibasis, D. (2006) 'State Use of Force in Cyberspace for Self-Defence: A New Challenge for a New Century', (8) *Peace Conflict and Development: An Interdisciplinary Journal*, pp. 13ff. <http://www.peacestudiesjournal.org.uk/dl/Feb%2006%20DELIBASIS.pdf> (accessed 16 February 2011).

Di Leva, C. and Morita, S. (2009) 'Maritime Rights of Coastal States and Climate Change: Should States Adapt to Submerged Boundaries?' 5 *Law and Development Working Paper Series*, New York: The World Bank. <http://siteresources .worldbank.org/INTLAWJUSTICE/Resources/L&D_number5.pdf> (accessed 3 February 2011).

Dickens, R. L. (2007) 'Finding Common Ground in the World of Electronic Contracts: The Consistency of Legal Reasoning in Clickwrap Cases', 11(2) *Marquette Intellectual Property Law Review*, pp. 381–411.

Din, A. M. (1983) 'Stopping the Arms Race in Outer Space', 20(3) *Journal of Peace Research*, pp. 221–225. <http://jpr.sagepub.com/content/20/3/221.full.pdf+html> (accessed 9 February 2011).

Dvorak, J. (2005) 'Creative Commons Humbug', *PC Magazine,* 18 July 2005. <http://www.pcmag.com/article2/0,2817,1838244,00.asp> (accessed 18 December 2010).

Easterbrook, F. H. (1996) 'Cyberspace and the Law of the Horse', 1 *University of Chicago Legal Forum*, pp. 207–216.

EDRI (2009) 'ISPs Asked to Block Child Porn Sites on the Internet', 7(7) *EDRI-Gram.* <http://www.edri.org/edri-gram/number7.7/pornography-blocked-isp> (accessed 29 October 2011).

European Union 'European Commission Welcomes US Move to More Independent, Accountable, International Internet Governance', *EC News IP/09/1397*, September 2009. http://ec.europa.eu/information_society/newsroom/cf/itemshortdetail.cfm?item_id=5281. (accessed 14 January 2011).

Efroni, Z. (2003) 'The Anticybersquatting Consumer Protection Act and the Uniform Dispute Resolution Policy: New Opportunities for International Forum Shopping?' 26 *Columbia Journal of Law & the Arts*, pp. 335–355.

Electronic Frontier Foundation (undated) 'E-Voting'. <http://www.eff.org/Activism/E-voting/> (accessed 23 January 2011).

Elkin-Koren, N. (2005) 'What Contracts Can't Do: The Limits of Private Ordering in Facilitating a Creative Commons', 74(2) *Fordham Law Review,* pp. 375–422.

Evans, R. (2008) 'UN Chief Tells Rights Body Drop Rhetoric, Blocs', Reuters, 12 December 2008. <http://www.reuters.com/article/2008/12/12/us-un-rights-idUSTRE4BB67820081212> (accessed 12 February 2011).

Fairweather, N. B. (1999) 'Surveillance in Employment: The Case of Teleworking', 22(1) *Journal of Business Ethics.*

Fildes, J. (2009) 'US Relaxes Grip on the Internet', *BBC News*, 30 September 2009. <http://news.bbc.co.uk/2/hi/technology/8283310.stm>.

Fisher, K. (2005) 'Schizophrenic on Intellectual Property Laws?' *Ars Technica.* <http://arstechnica.com/news.ars/post/20051222–5827.html> (accessed 5 February 2011).

Fox, W. F. and Murray, M. N. (1997) 'The Sales Tax and Electronic Commerce: So What's New?' 50(3) *National Tax Journal*, pp. 573–592.

Fryer III, W. T. (2008) 'Handling Internet Domain Name Arbitration', 41(1) *The Maryland Bar Journal*, pp. 28–33.

Gehring, T. and Jachtenfuchs, M. (1993) 'Liability for Transboundary Environmental Damage Towards a General Liability Regime?'4 *EJIL,* pp. 92–106.

Geist, M. (2001) 'Is There a There There? Toward Greater Certainty for Internet Jurisdiction', Ottawa: University of Ottawa. <http://arxiv.org/ftp/cs/ papers/0109/0109012.pdf> (accessed 6 February 2007).

Geist, M. (2005) 'Analysis: Net Control Debate Rumbles On', *BBC News*, 17 November 2005. <http://news.bbc.co.uk/2/hi/technology/4446242.stm> (accessed 20 December 2010).

Gerrand, P. (2006) 'A Short History of the Catalan Campaign to Win the .cat Internet Domain, with Implications for Other Minority Languages', 8 *Digithum.* <http://www.uoc.edu/digithum/8/dt/eng/gerrand.pdf> (accessed 17 December 2010).

Goldberg, I., Wagner, D. and Brewer, E. A. (1997) 'Privacy-Enhancing Technologies for the Internet' paper delivered at the 42nd IEEE Spring Computer Society International Conference, San Jose, California. <http://citeseer.ist.psu.edu/rd/35710544%2C54687%2C1%2C0.25%2CDownload/http://coblitz.codeen.org:3125/citeseer.ist.psu.edu/cache/papers/cs/788/http:zSzzSzwww.cs.berkeley.eduzSz%7EdawzSzprivacycompcon97.pdf/goldberg97privacyenhancing.pdf> (accessed 20 January 2011).

Gorman, S. (2010) 'Web Access Is New Clinton Doctrine', *Wall Street Journal*, 21 January 2010.

<http://online.wsj.com/article/SB10001424052748703405704575015461404882830.html> (accessed 21 January 2011).

Graber, C. B. (2006) 'The New UNESCO Convention on Cultural Diversity: A Counterbalance to the WTO?' 9(3) *Journal of International Economic Law*, pp. 553–574.

Gross, D. (2010) 'Aide: Clinton will Address China in Internet Freedom Speech, *CNN*, 21 January 2010. <http://www.allbusiness.com/legal/constitutional-law-freedom-speech/13752059-1.html> (accessed 21 January 2011).

Hahn, M. (2006), 'A Clash of Cultures? The UNESCO Diversity Convention and International Trade Law', 9(3) *Journal of International Economic Law*, pp. 515–552.

Hartmann, I. A. M. (2010) 'Universal Access Policies and Internet Access as a Fundamental Right: The Constitutional Law Perspective Informed by the Brazilian Case', paper delivered at the Fifth GigaNet Annual Symposium, 13 September 2010, Vilnius, Lithuania, on file with author.

Harvey, N. (2010) 'Cyber Warfare: Addressing the Challenge', Chatham House session transcript 9 November 2010. <www.chathamhouse.org.uk/files/17800_091110harvey.pdf> (accessed 25 December 2010).

Hellerstein, W. (2003) 'Jurisdiction to Tax Income and Consumption in the New Economy: A Theoretical and Comparative Perspective', 38 *Georgia Law Review*, pp. 1–70.

Hilbert, M. (2010) 'The Manifold Definitions of the Digital Divide and Their Diverse Implications for Policy Responsibility', paper delivered at the 38th Research Conference on Communication, Information, and Internet Policy, George Mason University Law School, Arlington. <http://www.tprcweb.com/images/stories/2010%20papers/Hilbert%20manifold%20Digital%20Divide.pdf> (accessed 20 December 2010).

Jackson, J. H. (2003) 'Sovereignty-Modern: A New Approach To An Outdated Concept', 97 *US Journal of International Law*, pp. 782–802.

Jarvenpaa, S. L. and Tiller, E. H. (1999) 'Integrating Market, Technology, and Policy Opportunities in E-Business strategy', 8(3) *Journal of Strategic Information Systems*, pp. 235–249. <http://www.reedsresearch.com/SupplyMgt/Jarvenpaa.pdf> (accessed 29 January 2011).

Johnson, D. R. and Post, D. G. (1996) 'Law and Borders – The Rise of Law in Cyberspace', 48 *Stanford Law Review*, pp. 1367–1402. <http://www.cli.org/X0025_LBFIN.html> (accessed 16 February 2011).

Katayama, L. 'Love in 2–D', *New York Times*, 26 July 2009. <http://www.nytimes.com/2009/07/26/magazine/26FOB-2DLove-t.html> (accessed 26 December 2010).

Katsh, M. E. (1996) 'Dispute Resolution In Cyberspace' 28 *Connecticut Law Review*, pp. 953–977. <http://www.umass.edu/legal/articles/uconn.html> (accessed 18 January 2011).

Kish, J. F. (1973) *The Law of International Spaces*, Leiden: Sijthoff.

Klaasen, B. (2010) *The Need for a European Cyber Security Authority* (EuroDIG 2011 workshop proposal).<http://www.guarder.net/eurodig/2011/European_Cybersecurit_Authority_WSProposal.pdf> (accessed 20 December 2010).

Kleinwächter , W. (1998) 'The People's "Right to Communicate" and a "Global Communication Charter": How Does Cyberspace Change Legal Concepts of Human Rights, Access and Participation?' 5(1&2) *Journal of International Communication*.

Kreijen G. (ed.) (2002) *State, Sovereignty and International Governance*, Oxford: Oxford University Press.

Kulesza, J. (2009) 'Internet w Końcu Międzynarodowy', *Stosunki Międzynarodowe*. <http://www.stosunki.pl/?q=node/1200> (accessed 10 January 2010).

Kulesza, J. (2009) 'State Responsibility for Cyberattacks on International Peace and Security', 29 *Polish Yearbook of International Law*, pp. 139–152.

Kulesza, J. (2009) 'Which Legal Standards Should Apply to Web-Logs? The Present Legal Position of Internet Journals in the European *Iuris Prudence* in the Light of the European

Parliament Committee's [sic] on Culture and Education report and Polish Supreme Court decision', 13(3) *Lex Electronica.* <http://www.lex-electronica.org/docs/articles_221.pdf> (accessed 5 February 2011).

Kulesza, J. (2010) 'Amerykańsko-Chiński Spór o Cenzurę w Internecie', 6 *Państwo i Prawo*, pp. 29–41.

Land, M. Beutz (2010) 'Google, China, and Search', 14(25) *ASIL Insights.* <http://www.asil.org/insights100805.cfm> (accessed 16 February 2011).

Lee, T. H. (2004) 'The US Supreme Court as Quasi-International Tribunal: Reclaiming the Court's Original and Exclusive Jurisdiction over Treaty-Based Suits by Foreign States against States', 104(7) *Columbia Law Review.* <http://ssrn.com/abstract=575583> (accessed 4 March 2011).

Liptak, A. (2010) 'When US and European Ideas of Privacy Collide', *New York Times*, 27 February 2010.

Loundy, D. (1997) '"Data Havens" May Protect Online Enterprises' *Chicago Daily Law Bulletin*, 9 January 1997. <http://www.loundy.com/CDLB/Jurisdiction2.html> (accessed 14 January 2011).

MacDonald, R. (2005) 'Challenges and Accomplishments: A Celebration of the Arctic Institute of North America', 58(4) *Infonorth* (Arctic Institute of North America). <http://pubs.aina.ucalgary.ca/arctic/Arctic58–4–440.pdf> (accessed 16 February 2011).

Malcolm, J. (2008) 'Appraising the Success of the Internet Governance Forum', (8)3 *Internet Governance Project Papers.* <www.internetgovernance.org/pdf/MalcolmIGFReview.pdf> (accessed 25 December 2010).

Malcolm, J. (2008) 'The Space Law Analogy to Internet Governance', paper delivered at the Giganet Third Annual Symposium, Hyderabad. <http://www.austlii.edu.au/au/journals/JlLawInfoSci/2007/3.html> (accessed 9 March 2009).

Markoff, J. (2010) 'A Silent Attack, But Not a Subtle One', *New York Times*, 26 September 2010. <http://www.nytimes.com/2010/09/27/technology/27virus.html> (accessed 15 December 2010).

Marsan, C. D. (2004) 'China: ISPs Report Major Growth in 2004', *Network World Fusion*, 20 December 2004. <http://www.nwfusion.com/newsletters/isp/2004/1220isp1.html> (accessed 19 January 2011).

Mathiason, J. (2004) 'A Framework Convention: An Institutional Option for Internet Governance' 4(2) *Internet Governance Project Papers.* <www.intgovforum.org/Substantive_1st_IGF/igp–fc.pdf> (accessed 25 December 2010).

Mathiason, J., et al. (2004) 'Internet Governance: the State of Play', 04(1) *Internet Governance Project Papers.* <http://www.internetgovernance.org/pdf/ig–sop–final.pdf> (accessed 2 January 2011).

Mayer-Schönberger, V. and Ziewitz, M. (2007) 'Jefferson Rebuffed: The United States and the Future of Internet Governance', 8 *Colum. Sci. & Tech. L. Rev*, pp. 184ff.

McNamee, J. (2010) 'ENDitorial: Internet blocking in ten weeks and counting', 8(18) *EDRI-Gram.* <http://www.edri.org/edrigram/number8.18/10–weeks–until–internet–blocking> (accessed 20 December 2010).

Menthe, D. C. (1998) 'Jurisdiction In Cyberspace: A Theory of International Spaces', 4 *Michigan Telecommunications and Technology Law Review*, pp. 69–103. <http://www.mttlr. org/volfour/menthe.pdf> (accessed 9 February 2011).

Middleton, G. (1999) 'Internet Patents', 10 *Journal of Law and Information Science*, pp. 153–167.

Mitrus, L. (2001) 'Telepraca jako nowa forma zatrudnienia', 3 *Transformacje Prawa Prywatnego.*

Mueller, M. (2010) 'Handing Control of the Internet to Governments: Bad Idea', *CBS*

TechNews, 3 February 2010. <http://www.cbsnews.com/8301–501465_162–20030583–501465.html>.

Mueller, M. (2010) 'The UN Sticks its Head in the Sand', *Internet Governance Project Blog*, 12 December 2010. <http://blog.internetgovernance.org/blog/_archives/2010/12/12/4702148.html> (accessed 15 December 2010).

Nanthikesan, S. (2000) 'Trends in Digital Divide', Mass: Harvard Center for Population and Development Studies. <http://hdr.undp.org/en/reports/global/hdr2001/papers/nanthikesan-1.pdf> (accessed 14 February 2011).

Nolan, J. (2008) 'The China Dilemma: Internet Censorship and Corporate Responsibility', 57 *University of New South Wales, Faculty of Law Research Series*. <http://www.austlii.edu.au/au/journals/UNSWLRS/2008/57.html> (accessed 14 January 2011).

Pallas Loren, L. (2007) 'Building a Reliable Semicommons of Creative Works: Enforcement of Creative Commons Licenses and Limited Abandonment of Copyright', 14(2) *George Mason Law Review*, pp. 271–328.

Palzer, C. and Hilger, C. (2001) 'Media Supervision on the Threshold of the 21st Century – Structure and Powers of Regulatory Authorities in the Era of Convergence', 8 *IRIS Legal Observations of the European Audiovisual Laboratory*. <http://www.obs.coe.int/oea_publ/iris/iris_plus/iplus8_2001.pdf.en> (accessed 14 January 2011).

Pasquinelli, M. (2010) 'The Ideology of Free Culture and the Grammar of Sabotage', *Policy Futures In Education* 8(6): 671–682.

Pellet, A. (1992) 'The Opinions of the Badinter Arbitration Committee: a Second Breath for the Self–Determination of Peoples', 3 *EJIL*, pp. 178–185. <http://www.ejil.org/article.php?article=1175&issue=68> (accessed on 14 January 2011).

Perritt, H. H. (2000) 'Dispute Resolution in Cyberspace: Demand for New Forms of ADR' 15(3) *Ohio State Journal on Dispute Resolution*, pp. 675–704. <http://works.bepress.com/henry_perritt/20/> (accessed 19 April 2006).

Perritt, H. H. and Stewart, M. G. (2000) 'ABA Internet Jurisdiction Project', a presentation at the Chicago-Kent College of Law, Illinois Institute of Technology <www.kentlaw.edu/cyberlaw/ottawa3.ppt> (accessed 10 April 2011).

Pletcher, C. (2009) 'Are Publicity Rights Gone in a Flash?: Flickr, Creative Commons, and the Commercial Use of Personal Photographs', 8 *Florida State Business Review*, pp. 129–155.

Podshybykin, L. I. and Leontiew, K. B. (2002) 'Implementation of the Berne Convention in [the] Russian Federation'. <http://www.copyright.ru/publ–412.html> (accessed 11 January 2011).

Privacy International and the GreenNet Educational Trust (PIGNet) 'Silenced, An International Report on Censorship and Control of the Internet.' <http://www.privacyinternational.org/survey/censorship/silenced.pdf> (accessed 15 January 2011).

Raab, C. D. and Bennett, C. J. (2003) 'The Governance of Global Issues: Protecting Privacy In Personal Information', paper presented at the European Consortium For Political Research Workshop on the Governance of Global Issues: Effectiveness, Accountability and Constitutionalization, Edinburgh. <http://www.essex.ac.uk/ECPR/events/jointsessions/paperarchive/edinburgh/ws11/RaabBennett.pdf> (accessed 24 January 2011), p. 6.

Reding, V. (European Commissioner for the Information Society and Media) (2005) 'Open Government and Governance in the On-Line Society', speech delivered in Stockholm, 9 December 2005. <http://ec.europa.eu/information_society/activities/egovernment_research/doc/minconf2005/keynote_speech_%209.12.pdf> (accessed 11 January 2011).

Reding, V. (European Commissioner for the Information Society and Media) (2009) Commissioner Reding's Weekly Videomessage, 4 May 2009, 'The Future of Internet Governance: Towards an Accountable ICANN'. <http://ec.europa.eu/commission_barroso/reding/video/text/message_20090504.pdf>.

Reding, V. (European Commissioner for the Information Society and Media) (2010) 'Building Trust in Europe's Online Single Market', speech at the American Chamber of Commerce, 22 June 2010. <http://europa.eu/rapid/pressReleasesAction.do?reference=SPEECH/10/327> (accessed 20 December 2010).

Reisman, W. M. (1990) 'Sovereignty and Human Rights in Contemporary International Law', 84(4) *The U.S. Journal of International Law*, pp. 866–876.

Reporters without Borders (2009) 'Call for Revision of Repressive Internet Law as it Goes into Effect', 15 July 2009. <http://en.rsf.org/kazakhstan-call-for-revision-of-repressive-15–07–2009,33808>.

Richardson, P. 'Internet Buyers Beware of "Click" Agreements'. <http://www.mbf-law.com/pubs/articles/166.cfm> (accessed 15 January 2011).

Rodan, G. (1996) 'Information Technology and Political Control in Singapore', 26 *Japan Policy Research Institute Working Papers*. <http://www.jpri.org/publications/workingpapers/wp26.html> (accessed 18 January 2011).

Rogers, K. M. (2006) 'Internet Governance: The United States Won the Battle, But Will the Internet Win the War?' 4(1) *Hertfordshire Law Journal*, pp. 26–35.

Rosenne, S. (2001) 'The Perplexities of Modern International Law : General Course on Public International Law', 291 *Recueil des Cours*, pp. 9ff.

Roth, K. (2001) 'The Case For Universal Jurisdiction', *Foreign Affairs,* October 2001. <http://www.foreignaffairs.com/articles/57245/kenneth–roth/the–case–for–universal–jurisdiction> (accessed 7 April 2011).

Rothwell, D. R. (2008) 'The Arctic in International Law: Time for a New Regime?' 8(37) *Australian National University College of Law Research Papers* <http://papers.ssrn.com/sol3/Delivery.cfm/SSRN_ID1317503_code734493.pdf?abstractid=1314546&mirid=5> (accessed 3 February 2011).

Rowland, D. (2006) 'Griping, Bitching and Speaking Your Mind: Defamation and Free Expression on the Internet', 110 *Penn St. L. Rev.*, pp. 519–538.

Sandi, C. C. (2005) 'Personalidad Virtual: Necesidad de una Reforma Constitucional', 3 *Revista de Derecho y Tecnologias de la Información*, pp. 1–11.

Scharf, M. P. (2001) 'The ICC's Jurisdiction over the Nationals of Non-Party States: A Critique of the US Position', 64(1) *Law And Contemporary Problems*, pp. 67–117. <http://www.law.duke.edu/journals/64LCPScharf> (accessed 7 April 2011).

Schmitt, M. N. (1999) 'The Principle of Discrimination in 21st Century Warfare', 2 *Yale Human Rights and Development Law Journal*, pp. 143–182.

Schmitt, M. N. (2001) 'Computer Network Attack: The Normative Software', 4 *Yearbook of International Humanitarian Law*, pp. 53–85.

Segura–Serrano, A. (2006) 'Internet Regulation: A Hard-Law Proposal', 10 *The Jean Monnet Working Papers*. <http://ideas.repec.org/p/erp/jeanmo/p0183.html> (accessed 25 December 2010).

Shackelford, S. J. (2009) 'From Nuclear War to Net War: Analogizing Cyber Attacks in International Law', 25(3) *Berkeley Journal of International Law*, pp. 191–250. <http://works.bepress.com/context/scott_shackelford/article/1004/type/native/viewcontent> (accessed 20 December 2010).

Shapiro, A. L. (1998) 'The Disappearance of Cyberspace and the Rise of Code', 8 *Seton Hall Constitutional Law Journal*, pp. 703–723.

Schatz, G. S. (1996) 'Antarctic Treaty Consultative Parties: Measures Relating to the Furtherance of the Principles and Objectives of the Antarctic Treaty', 35 *ILM*, p. 1165.

Sia, C. L., et al. (2004) 'Effects of Environmental Uncertainty on Organizational Intention to Adopt Distributed Work Arrangements', 51 *Engineering Management*, pp. 253–267.

Simma, B. (1986) 'The Antarctic Treaty as a Treaty Providing for an "Objective Regime"', 19 *Cornell International Law Journal*, pp. 189–198.

Smith, S. (2003) 'From Napster to Kazaa: The Battle over Peer–to–Peer Filesharing goes International', 8 *Duke L. & Tech. Rev.*, pp. 1–8. <http://www.law.duke.edu/journals/dltr/articles/PDF/2003DLTR0008.pdf> (accessed 11 February 2011).

Springer, C. B. (2001) 'Master of the Domain (Name): a History of Domain Name Litigation and the Emergence of the Anticybersquatting Consumer Protection Act and Uniform Dispute Resolution Policy', 17 *Computer & High Technology Law Journal*, pp. 315–365.

Strzelecka, M. (2007) Nadchodzi Epoka Internetu z Otwartą Przyłbicą?' *Gazeta Wyborcza*. <http://gospodarka.gazeta.pl/gospodarka/1,52981,3937067.html> (accessed 6 March 2009).

Struve, C. T. and Wagner, R. P. (2002) 'Realspace Sovereigns in Cyberspace: Problems with the Anticybersquatting Consumer Protection Act', 17(3) *Berkeley Technology Law Journal*, pp. 989–1041.

Thomas, D. A. (2001) 'Current Issues in US State and Federal Taxation of Electronic Commerce', paper delivered at the 16th BILETA Annual Conference, University of Edinburgh. <http://www.bileta.ac.uk/01papers/thomas.html> (accessed 20 January 2011).

Tóth, P. B. (2005) 'Creative Humbug', 2(24) *Indicare Monitor* pp. 8–12. <http://www.indicare.org/tiki–read_article.php?articleId=118> (accessed 18 December 2011).

Turack, D. C. (2002) 'Concept of the Common Heritage of Mankind in International Law', *The Journal of Third World Studies*. <http://www.findarticles.com/p/articles/ mi_qa3821/is_200210/ai_n9115940> (accessed 13 February 2011).

Uerpman-Wittzack, R. (2009) 'Internetvolkerrecht', 47(26) *Archiv des Volkerrechts*, pp. 263–274.

Uerpman-Wittzack, R. (2010) 'Principles of International Internet Law', 11(1) *German Law Journal*, pp. 1245–1263.

United Nations Conference on Trade and Development (UNCTAD) (2010) 'Composition of the Working Group on Internet Governance Agreed', <http://www.unctad.org/Templates/Page.asp?intItemID=5755&lang=1> (accessed 17 December 2010).

van Alstyne, M. and Brynjolfsson, B. (1996) 'Electronic Communities: Global Villages or Cyberbalkanization?', 5 *ICIS 1996 Proceedings Papers*. <http://aisel.aisnet.org/icis1996/5> (accessed 29 January 2009).

Watkins, M. (2005) 'Government Regulation of the Dot-ca. Domain Name Space', 2(1) *University of Ottawa Law & Technology Journal*, pp. 145–172. <http://www.uoltj.ca/articles/vol2.1/2005.2.1.uoltj.Watkins.145–172.pdf> (accessed 29 January 2009).

Weber, R. H. (2009) 'Internet of things – Need for a New Legal Environment?', 25(1) *Computer Law & Security Review*, pp. 522–527.

Weber, R. H. (2010) 'New Sovereignty Concepts in the Age of Internet', 14(8) *Journal of Internet Law*, pp. 12–20.

Wolfke, K. (1976) 'Some Reflections on International Environmental Law-Making and Enforcement', 8 *Polish Yearbook of International Law*, pp. 33–53.

J. Zittrain (2003) 'Be Careful What You Ask For: Reconciling a Global Internet and Local Law', 60 *Harvard Law School Public Law Research Papers*. <http://ssrn.com/abstract_id395300> (accessed 28 December 2006).

Books and reports

Alfredsson, G. and Eide, A. (eds.) (1999) *The Universal Declaration of Human Rights: A Common Standard of Achievement*, The Hague: Martinus Nijhoff Publishers.

Amnesty International (1996) *State Secrets – a Pretext for Repression*, AI INDEX: ASA 17/42/96, section 1.

Anderson, C. (2009) *Free: The Future of a Radical Price*, New York: Hyperion.

APEC Electronic Commerce Steering Group (2004) *Paperless Trading Individual Action Plan* <http://www.apec.org/apec/documents_reports/electronic_commerce_steering_group/2004.MedialibDownload.v1.html?url=/etc/medialib/apec_media_library/downloads/taskforce/ecsg/mtg/2004/pdf.Par.0037.File.v1.1> (accessed 15 January 2011).

Araya, D. (ed.) (2010) *Knowledge and Learning in the Age of Innovation*, Frankfurt: Peter Lang.

Arnold, B. J. and McIntyre, M. J. (2002) *International Tax Primer*, The Hague: Kluwer Law International.

Arzt, G. (1970) *Der Strafrechtliche Schutz der Intimsphäre*, Tübingen: Mohr Siebeck.

Aust, A. (2005) *Handbook of International Law*, 2nd edn., Cambridge: Cambridge University Press.

Bank for International Settlements Basel Committee (2000) *Electronic Banking Group Initiatives and White Papers*, Basel: Bank for International Settlements. <http://www.bis.org/publ/bcbs76.htm> (accessed 10 December 2010).

Bank for International Settlements Basel Committee (2003) *Risk Management Principles for Electronic Banking*, Basel: Bank for International Settlements. <http://www.mobilemoneyexchange.org/Files/86801b83> (accessed 10 December 2010).

Council of Europe Committee of Experts on New Media (MC–NM) (2010) *Report of the Meeting of 25–26 March 2010*, Strasbourg. <http://www.coe.int/t/dghl/standardsetting/media/MC–NM/MC–NM%282010%29006_en%20FIN%20Report%202nd%20meeting.asp#TopOfPage> (accessed 20 December 2010).

Bard, G. M. (1984) *State Immunity: An Analytical and Prognostic View*, The Hague: Martinus Nijhoff Publishers.

Barendt, E. M. (2005) *Freedom of Speech*, 2nd edn., New York: Oxford University Press.

Bassiouni, M. C. (1980) *International Criminal Law: A Draft International Criminal Code*, The Hague: Brill Archive.

Basu, S. (2007) *Global Perspectives on E–Commerce Taxation Law*, Burlington, VT: Ashgate Publishing, Ltd.

Benedek, W., Bauer, V. and Kettemann M. (eds.) (2008) *Internet Governance and the Information Society: Global Perspectives and European Dimensions*, Utrecht: Eleven International Publishing.

Benkler, Y. (2006) *The Wealth of Networks: How Social Production Transforms Markets and Freedom*, New Haven: Yale University Press.

Bennett, C. J. (1992) *Regulating Privacy: Data Protection and Public Policy in Europe and the United States*, New York: Cornell University Press.

Bezzi, M. (ed.) (2010) *Privacy and Identity Management for Life*, New York: Springer.

Bidgoli, H. (2006) *Handbook of Information Security: Threats, Vulnerabilities, Prevention, Detection, and Management*, New York: John Wiley & Sons.

Bowrey, K. (2005) *Law and Internet Cultures*, Melbourne: Cambridge University Press.

Branahl, U. (2009) *Medienrecht: Eine Einführung*, Wiesbaden: VS Verlag.

Brindle, M., Cox, R. and Coleman, R. (2004) *Law of Bank Payments*, London: Sweet & Maxwell.

Brownlie, I. (1966) *Principles of Public International Law*, Oxford: Oxford University Press.

Campbell, D. (2006) *The Internet: Laws and Regulatory Regimes*, Salzburg: Yorkhill Law Publishing.

Carreau, D. (2004) *Droit International*, Paris: Pédone.

Clark, E., et al. (2010) *Cyber Law in Australia*, The Hague: Kluwer Law International.

Commonwealth Centre for Electronic Governance (2002) *International Tracking Survey Report*

No. 1 – E-Government, E-Governance and E-Democracy: A Background Discussion Paper, London: Commonwealth Centre for Electronic Governance. <http://www.electronicgov.net/pubs/research_papers/tracking5/IntlTracking%20Report%20Number%201Jan02.doc> (accessed 4 February 2011).

Cornish, P., et al. (2010) *On Cyber Warfare: A Chatham House Report*, London: Chatham House. <http://www.chathamhouse.org.uk/publications/papers/view/–/id/967/> (accessed 16 February 2011).

Council of Europe (2009) *Internet Governance and Critical Internet Resources*, Strasbourg: Media and Information Society Division, Council of Europe.

Council of Europe (2010) *Interim Report of the Ad Hoc Advisory Group on Cross-Border Internet to the Steering Committee on the Media and New Communication Services, Incorporating Analysis of Proposals for International and Multi-Stakeholder Cooperation on Cross-Border Internet*, Strasbourg, December 2010. <www.coe.int/standardsetting/media–dataprotection/conf–internet–freedom/MC–S–CI/Interim%2520Report.pdf> (accessed 4 February 2011).

Cross, F. B. and Prentice, R. A. (2007) *Law and Corporate Finance*, Cheltenham, UK: Edward Elgar Publishing.

Cryer, R., Friman, H. and Robinson, D. (2010) *An Introduction to International Criminal Law and Procedure*, Cambridge: Cambridge University Press.

Csabafi, I. (1971) *The Concept of State Jurisdiction in International Space Law*, The Hague: Martinus Nijhoff Publishers.

Deibert, R., et al. (eds.) (2008) *Access Denied: The Practice and Policy of Global Internet Filtering*, Cambridge, Mass.: MIT Press.

Deibert, R., et al. (eds.) (2010) *Access Controlled: The Shaping of Power, Rights, and Rule in Cyberspace*, Cambridge, Mass.: MIT Press.

Delibasis, D. (2007) *The Right to National Self-Defense in Information Warfare Operations*, Bury St Edmunds, UK: Arena Books.

Di Martino, V. (2001) *The High Road To Teleworking*, Geneva: ILO. <www.ilo.org/public/english/protection/safework/telework/hrdptl.pdf> (accessed 27 February 2011).

Dinh, N. Q. Daillier, P., and Pellet, A. (1999) *Droit International Public*, 6th edn., Paris: Librairie Generale de Droit et de Jurisprudence.

Donnelly, J. (2003) *Universal Human Rights in Theory and Practice*, New York: Cornell University Press.

Drake W. J. (ed.) (2002) *Internet Governance: Creating Opportunities for All*, New York: United Nations Publishing.

Drake W. J. (ed.) (2005) *Reforming Internet Governance: Perspectives from the Working Group on Internet Governance (WGIG)*, New York: United Nations Publishing.

Dunne, T. (ed.) (1999) *Human Rights in Global Politics*, Cambridge: Cambridge University Press.

Edelman, B. (2003) *Sites Blocked by Internet Filtering Programs*, Harvard, Mass.: Berkman Center for Internet and Society. <http://cyber. law.harvard.edu/people/edelman/mul–v–us/> (accessed 5 January 2011).

Ehlers, D. and Becker, U. (2007) *European Fundamental Rights and Freedoms*, Berlin: Walter de Gruyter.

European Union Commission (1997) *Towards an Information Society Approach: Convergence of the Telecommunications, Media and Information Technology Sector, and the Implications for Regulations*, Commission Green Paper, COM (97) 623.

European Union Commission (2004) *Staff Working Paper: e-Europe 2005 Mid-Term Review*, Background Papers, COM (2004) 108. <http//ec.europa.eu/information_society/eeurope/2005/doc/highlights/whats_new/mtr_wp_isc_version1.41.doc> (accessed 1 June 2011).

European Union Commission (2006) *A Summary of the First Year's Results: The Single European Information Space Achievements May 2005/2006*, Information sheet 7.5. <http://ec.europa.eu/information_society/eeurope/i2010/docs/info_sheets/7–5–i2010–results-en.pdf> (accessed 4 February 2011).

European Union Commission (2009) *Towards a New Framework for Electronic Communications Infrastructure and Associated Services*, COM (99) 539. <http://europa.eu/scadplus/leg/en/lvb/l24216.htm> (accessed 5 February 2011).

European Union Communication from the Commission to the Council, the European Parliament, the European Economic and Social Committee and the Committee of the Regions, *Globalisation and the Information Society: The Need for Strengthened International Coordination*, 4 February 1998, COM (98) 50.

European Union Communication from the Commission to the Council, the European Parliament, the European Economic and Social Committee and the Committee of the Regions, *Towards a New Framework for Electronic Communications Infrastructure and Associated Services*, 10 November 1999, COM (99) 539.

European Union Communication from the Commission to the Council, the European Parliament, the European Economic and Social Committee and the Committee of the Regions (1999) *e-Europe 2005: An Information Society for All*, COM (1999) 687. <http://ec.europa.eu/information_society/eeurope/2002/news_library/documents/eeurope2005/eeurope2005_en.pdf> (accessed 14 January 2011).

European Union Parliament Culture Committee (2007) *Report on Concentration and Pluralism in the Media in the European Union*, Proposal, 2007/2253(INI).

Fandy, M. (2007) *(Un)civil War of Words: Media and Politics in the Arab World*, Westport, Conn.: Greenwood Publishing Group.

Farrell, H. (2002) Negotiating Privacy across Arenas: The EU–US "Safe Harbor". <www.henryfarrell.net/privacy1.pdf> (accessed 18 December 2011). Also in A. Heretier *Common Goods*, see below.

Figliola, P. Moloney, et al. (2010) *US Initiatives to Promote Global Internet Freedom: Issues, Policy, and Technology*, Darby, PA: Diane Publishing Co.

Firestone, C. (ed.) (1998) *The Emerging Internet: 1998 Annual Review of the Institute for Information Studies*, Washington, DC: The Aspen Institute.

France Assemblée Nationale (2003) *Projet de Loi Relatif au Droit d'Auteur et aux Droits Voisins dans la Société de l'Information*, No. 1206. <http://www.assemblee–nationale.fr/12/projets/pl1206.asp> (accessed 5 February 2011).

Gasser, U., et al. (2010) Accountability and Transparency at ICANN: An Independent Review, Mass.: Harvard University Berkman Center for Internet and Society <https://icann.org/en/reviews/affirmation/atrt-review-berkmanfinal-report-20oct10–en.pdf> (accessed 17 December 2010).

Gelbstein, E. and Kurbalija, J. (2005) *Internet Governance: Issues, Actors and Divides*, Msida: Diplo Foundation.

Geist, M. (2006) 'The Law, Borders, and the Internet', BBC News, 24 January 2006. <http://news.bbc.co.uk/2/hi/technology/4641244.stm> (accessed 16 June 2011).

Global Network Initiative (2010) Inaugural Report: Our Work, Our Vision, Our Progress. <http://www.globalnetworkinitiative.org/cms/uploads/1/GNI_annual_report_2010.pdf> (accessed 25 December 2010).

Goldberg, I. A. (2000) *A Pseudonymous Communications Infrastructure for the Internet,* unpublished PhD thesis, University of California At Berkeley. <http://www.cypherpunks.ca/~iang/thesis-final.pdf> (accessed 20 January 2011).

Grotius, H. (1609/2000) *Mare Liberum*, Ontario: Kitchener Batoche Books.

Gutwirth, S., Poullet, Y. and De Hert, P. (2010) *Data Protection in a Profiled World*, New York: Springer Science.

Hall, W. E. (1904) *A Treatise on International Law*, Oxford: Oxford University Press.

Ham, S. and Atkinson, R. D. (2001) *A Third Way Framework for Global E-Commerce*, Washington, DC: Progressive Policy Institute. <http://www.ndol.org/documents/global_ecommerce.pdf> (accessed 29 January 2011).

Henkin, L. (ed.) (1987) *The Foreign Relations Law of the United States: Restatement of the Law*, New York: The American Law Institute.

Heretier, A. (ed.) (2002) *Common Goods: Reinventing European and International Governance*, Boulder, Colorado: Rowman & Littlefield.

Higgins R. (1994) *Problems & Process: International Law and How We Use It*, Oxford: Oxford University Press.

Hillier, T. (1998) *Sourcebook on Public International Law*, London: Routledge.

Hinsley, F. H. (1986) *Sovereignty*, 2nd edn., New York: Cambridge University Press.

Hirst, M. (2003) *Jurisdiction and the Ambit of the Criminal Law*, Oxford: Oxford University Press.

Hoeren, T. (2006) *Internetrecht*, unpublished script available on the Universität Münster website. <http://www.uni–muenster.de/Jura.itm/hoeren/> (accessed 16 February 2011).

Hoffer, S. (1998) *World Cyberspace Law*, New York: Juris Publishing, Inc.

Hornle, J. (2009) *Cross-Border Internet Dispute Resolution*, Cambridge: Cambridge University Press.

Hosein, G. (2000) *A Brief Coverage Of Anonymity And Animosity: The Socio-Technical Network And The Role Of Freedom*, unpublished, London: The London School of Economics and Political Science <http://academic.research.microsoft.com/Publication/4647681/a–brief–coverage–of–anonymity–and–animosity–the–socio–technical–network–and–the–role–of–freedom> (accessed 20 January 2011).

Hromadka, W. and Maschmann, F. (2000) *Arbeitsrecht Band 1: Individualarbeitsrecht*, 3rd edn., New York: Springer.

Human Rights in China (2004) *Who's Who in Labor & State Secrets.* <http://www.hrichina.org/public/contents/article?revision%5fid=18104&item%5fid=18103> (accessed 20 January 2006).

Human Rights Watch (2005) *World Report: China.* <http://hrw.org/english/docs/2005/01/13/china9809.htm> (accessed 19 January 2011).

Ignatieff, M., Gutmann, A. and Appiah, K. A. (eds.) (2003) *Human Rights as Politics and Idolatry*, Princeton, NJ: Princeton University Press.

International Centre for Human Rights and Democratic Development (2001) *Review of China's Internet Regulations and Domestic Legislation.* <http://www.ichrdd.ca/english/commdoc/publications/globalization/legislationInternetChinaEng.pdf> (accessed 16 January 2011).

International Chamber of Commerce (2001) *Jurisdiction and Applicable Law in Electronic Commerce Policy Statement.* <http://www.iccwbo.org/id478/index.html> (accessed 28 January 2011).

Internet Governance Project (2004) *A Framework Convention: An Institutional Option for Internet Governance.* <http://www.intgovforum.org/Substantive_1st_IGF/igp-fc.pdf>.

Internet Governance Project (2009) *Independence and Accountability: The Future of ICANN.* <www.ntia.doc.gov/comments/2009/dnstransition/050.pdf>.

International Labor Organization (2004) World Commission on the Social Dimension of Globalization, *A Fair Globalization: Creating Opportunities For All*, Geneva: ILO. <http://www.ilo.org/public/english/wcsdg/docs/report.pdf> (accessed 14 January 2011).

James, J. (2003) *Cyberpsychology: Principles of Creating Virtual Presence,* unpublished but available at the website of the University of Hawaii. <http://www.soc.hawaii.edu/LEONJ/leonj/leonpsy/cyber.html#forming> (accessed: 16 February 2011).

James, P. (2004) *Is Teleworking Sustainable? – An Analysis of its Economic, Environmental and Social Impact*, Peterborough, UK: SusTel Project. <http://www.sustel.org/documents/Reports/final%20report%20–%20july%202004%20v2.pdf> (accessed 27 February 2011).

Jasentuliyana, N. (1999) *International Space Law and the United Nations*, The Hague: Martinus Nijhoff Publishers.

Jorgensen R. F. (ed.) (2006) *Human Rights in the Global Information Society,* Cambridge, Mass.: MIT Press.

Joyner, C. C. (2005) *International Law in the 21st Century: Rules for Global Governance*, Oxford: Rowman & Littlefield.

Kahin, B, and Nesson, C. R. (eds.) *Borders in Cyberspace: Information Policy and the Global Information Infrastructure*, Cambridge, Mass.: MIT Press.

Kamal, A. (2005) *The Law of Cyber-Space*, Geneva: United Nations Institute of Training and Research.

Katsh, E. E., Katsh, M. E. and Rifkin, J. (2001) *Online Dispute Resolution: Resolving Conflicts in Cyberspace*, New York: Jossey-Bass.

Kelsen, H. (2002) *Principles of International Law*, New Jersey: The Lawbook Exchange, Ltd.

Kirchner, J., Kremp, P. R. and Magotsch, M. (eds.) (2009) *Key Aspects of German Employment and Labour Law*, New York: Springer.

Kohl, U. (2007) *Jurisdiction and the Internet: A Study of Regulatory Competence over Online Activity*, Cambridge: Cambridge University Press.

Komaitis, K. (2010) *The Current State of Domain Name Regulation: Domain Names as Second-Class Citizens in a Mark-Dominated World*, Oxford: Routledge.

Kramer, F. D., Starr, S. H. and Wentz, L. (2009) *Cyberpower and National Security*, Dulles: Potomac Books, Inc.

Kuner, C. (2003 *European Data Privacy Law and Online Business,* Oxford: Oxford University Press.

Kurbalija J. (2010) *An Introduction to Internet Governance*, Msida: Diplo Foundation

Lafferranderie, G. and Crowther D. (eds.) (1997) *Outlook on Space Law Over the Next 30 years: Essays Published for the 30th Anniversary of the Outer Space Treaty*, The Hague: Martinus Nijhoff Publishers.

Lehr, W. (1998) *Understanding Vertical Integration in the Internet*, Cambridge, Mass.: MIT Internet and Telecoms Convergence Consortium. <http://itc.mit.edu/itel/pubs/Lehr. pdf> (accessed 4 February 2011).

Lessig, L. (1999) *Code and Other Laws of Cyberspace*, New York: Basic Books.

Lessig, L. (2004) *Free Culture: How Big Media uses Technology and the Law to Lock Down Culture and Control Creativity*, New York: Penguin.

Lessig, L. (2006) *Code: Version 2.0*, New York: Basic Books.

Lessig, L. (2008) *Remix: Making Art and Culture Thrive in the Hybrid Economy*, London: Bloomsbury Academic.

Macedo, S. (ed.) (2006) *Universal Jurisdiction: National Courts and the Prosecution of Serious Crimes under International Law*, Philadelphia: University of Pennsylvania Press.

Meggs, P. B. and Sergiejew, P. A. (2000) *Intellectual Property*, Budapest: Jurist.

Malcolm, J. (2008) *Multi–Stakeholder Governance and the Internet Governance Forum*, Perth: Terminus Press.

Mann, C. L. (2000) *Transatlantic Issues in Electronic Commerce,* Washington: Institute for International Economics. <http://www.iie.com/publications/wp/00–7.pdf> (accessed 29 January 2011).

Marcella, A. J. and Stucki, C. (2003) *Privacy Handbook: Guidelines, Exposures, Policy Implementation and International Issues*, New York: John Wiley & Sons.

McGoldrick, D., Rowe, P. J. and Donnelly, E. (2004) *The Permanent International Criminal Court: Legal and Policy Issues*, Oxford: Hart Publishing.

Miniwatts Marketing Group (2010) *Internet World Stats* (last updated 30 July 2010). <http://www.internetworldstats.com/stats.htm>.

Møller Johansen, M. (2003) *New Technology and Respect for Privacy/Private Life at the Workplace – the Case of Denmark*, Dublin: European Industrial Relations Observatory. <http://eurofound.europa.eu/eiro/2003/07/word/dk0304103s.doc>) (accessed 29 January 2011).

Mueller, M. L. (2004) *Ruling the Root: Internet Governance and the Taming of Cyberspace*, Cambridge, Mass.: MIT Press.

Mueller, M. L. (2010) *Networks and States: The Global Politics of Internet Governance*, Cambridge, Mass.: MIT Press.

Norris, P. (ed.) (2010) *Public Sentinel: News Media & Governance Reform*, Washington, DC: World Bank Publications.

OpenNet Initiative (2004) *A Starting Point: Legal Implications of Internet Filtering*, Harvard, Mass.: OpenNetInitiative. <http://opennet.net/research/reports>.

OpenNet Initiative (2005) *Internet Filtering in China in 2004–2005*, Harvard, Mass.: OpenNetInitiative. <http://cryptome.org/cn/cn–filter.pdf> (accessed 19 January 2011).

OpenNet Initiative (2005) *Internet Filtering in Singapore in 2004–2005*, Harvard, Mass.: OpenNet Initiative. <www.opennetinitiative.net/singapore/> (accessed 6 January 2011).

Oppenheim, L. (2006) *International Law: A Treatise*, vol. I, New Jersey: The Lawbook Exchange, Ltd.

Owens, J. (2000) *Taxation in the Wired World*, Paris: OECD. <http://ncsi-net.ncsi.iisc.ernet.in/cyberspace/societal-issues/202/202.pdf> (accessed 14 January 2011).

Pattison, J. (2010) *Humanitarian Intervention and the Responsibility to Protect: Who Should Intervene?* Oxford: Oxford University Press.

Personick, S. D. and Patterson C. A. (eds) (2003) *Critical Information Infrastructure Protection and the Law: An Overview of Key Issues*, Washington, DC: The National Academies Press.

Petković, M. and Jonker W. (eds) (2007) *Security, Privacy and Trust in Modern Data Management*, New York: Springer.

Pinto, D. (2003) *E-Commerce and Source-Based Income Taxation*, Amsterdam: International Bureau of Fiscal Documentation (IBFD) Publications BV.

Post, D. G. (2009) *In Search of Jefferson's Moose – Notes on State in Cyberspace*, Oxford: Oxford University Press.

Qin, Z. (2009) *Introduction to E-Commerce*, New York: Springer.

Rahman, S. M. and Raisinghani, M. S. (2000) *Electronic Commerce: Opportunity and Challenges*, Hershey, PA: Idea Group, Inc.

Ramcharan, B. G. (ed.) (1979) *Human Rights: Thirty Years after the Universal Declaration: Commemorative Volume on the Occasion of the Thirtieth Anniversary of the Universal Declaration of Human Rights*, New York: United Nations Publishing.

Raysman, Richard et al. (2002) *Emerging Technologies and the Law: Forms and Analysis*, New York: Law Journal Press.

Reydams, L. (2003) *Universal Jurisdiction: International and Municipal Legal Perspectives*, Oxford: Oxford University Press.

Riehl, F. (2010) *Tentative Road Map of Activities of the CSTD Working Group on IGF*. <http://www.unctad.org/sections/un_cstd/docs/cstd2010d02_en.pdf> (accessed 10 December 2010).

Rosner, N. (2002) *International Jurisdiction in European Union E-Commerce Contracts*, online only at the Law Library Resources Exchange <http://www.llrx.com/features/eu_ecom.htm> (accessed 29 January 2011).

Sharp, W.G. (1999) *CyberSpace and the Use of Force*, Falls Church: Aegis Research Corporation.

Shaw, M. N. (2003) *International Law*, 5th edn., Cambridge: Cambridge University Press.

Singapore Ministry of Information, Communication and the Arts (2003) *Censorship Review Committee: 2003 Report.* <www.mda.gov.sg/wms.file/mobj/mobj.316.Censorship_Review_2003.pdf> (accessed 7 January 2011).

Singapore Media Development Authority *Internet Industry Guide.* <http://www.mda.gov.sg/wms.file/mobj/mobj.496.internet_industry_guide.pdf> (accessed 16 January 2011).

Singapore Media Development Authority *Internet Service Providers.* <http://www.mda.gov.sg/Documents/PDF/licences/mobj.487.ClassLicence.pdf> (accessed 21 May 2011).

Singapore National Computer Board (1992) *IT-2000: A Vision of an Intelligent Island.*

Smith, G. J. H. (2007) *Internet Law and Regulation*, London: Sweet & Maxwell.

Stehn, J. (2002) *Leviathan in Cyberspace: How to Tax E-Commerce*, Kiel: Institut für Weltwirtschaft Kiel.

Sterling, B. (1988) *Islands in the Net*, Southport: Arbor House.

Still, B. (2007) *Handbook of Research on Open Source Software: Technological, Economic, and Social Perspectives*, Hershey, PA: Idea Group, Inc.

Sucharitkul, S. (1976/7) 149 *Académie de Droit International de La Hague Recueil Des Cours* (*Collected Courses)*, The Hague: Martinus Nijhoff Publishers.

Svantesson, D. J. B. (2007) *Private International Law and the Internet*, The Hague: Kluwer Law International.

Tapscott, D. and Williams, A. D. (2008) *Wikinomics: How Mass Collaboration Changes Everything*, New York: Portfolio.

Turley, J. (2002) *Registering Publius: The Supreme Court and the Right to Anonymity*, Washington, DC: The Cato Institute.

United Kingdom House of Commons (1990) *Report of the Committee on Privacy and Related Matters*, Chairman David Calcutt QC, Cmnd. 1102, London: The Stationery Office.

United Kingdom House of Commons' Culture, Media and Sport Committee (2011) *Press Standards, Privacy and Libel: Second Report of Session 2010–2011: Volume 2: Oral and Written Evidence*, London: The Stationery Office.

United Kingdom Britain House of Lords Select Committee (2009) *Surveillance: Citizens and the State*, London: The Stationery Office.

United Nations (2005) Development Programme Report: *International Cooperation at a Crossroads: Aid, Trade and Security in an Unequal World*, New York: United Nations Publishing. <http://hdr.undp.org/reports/global/2005/> (accessed 14 January 2011).

United Nations (2006) *Report of the Tunis Phase of the World Summit on the Information Society*, WSIS-05/TUNIS/DOC/9(Rev.1)-E. <www.itu.int/wsis/docs2/tunis/off/6rev1.doc> (accessed 17 December 2010).

United Nations (2005) *Report of the Working Group on Internet Governance (WGIG).* www.wgig.org/docs/WGIGREPORT.pdf (accessed 17 December 2010).

United Nations (2003) *World Summit on the Information Society Declaration of Principles: Building the Information Society: A Global Challenge in the New Millennium*, WSIS-03/GENEVA/DOC/4–E. <http://www.itu.int/wsis/docs/geneva/official/dop.html> (accessed 17 December 2010).

United Nations (2003) *World Summit on the Information Society Plan of Action,* WSIS–03/GENEVA/DOC/5–E. <http://www.itu.int/wsis/docs/geneva/official/poa.html> (accessed 17 December 2010).

United Nations (2005) *World Summit on the Information Society Tunis Agenda for the Information Society*,

Geneva: ITU. <http://www.itu.int/wsis/docs2/tunis/off/6rev1.html> (accessed 4 January 2011).

United Nations Internet Governance Forum (2010) *Legal Aspects of Internet Governance: International Cooperation on Cyber-Security* (Transcript of session 123, Vilnius, Lithuania, 15 September 2010). <http://www.afilias.info/webfm_send/138> (accessed 15 December 2010).

United States Census Bureau (2006) *Quarterly Retail E-Commerce Sales 1st Quarter 2006*. <http://www.census.gov/mrts/www/data/html/06Q1.html> (accessed 15 January 2011).

United States Department of State (2005) *Singapore: Country Reports on Human Rights Practices – 2004*. <http://www.state.gov/g/drl/rls/hrrpt/2004/41659.htm> (accessed 9 January 2011).

van Schewick, B. (2010) *Internet Architecture and Innovation*, Cambridge, Mass.: MIT Press.

von Bar, C. (2000) *The Common European Law of Torts: Damage and Damages, Liability for and without Personal Misconduct, Causality, and Defenses*, Oxford: Oxford University Press.

von Bogdandy, A. and Wolfrum, R. (eds.) (2006) 10 *Max Planck Yearbook of United National Law*, Leiden: Koninklijke Brill.

Wang, F. F. (2010) *Internet Jurisdiction and Choice of Law: Legal Practices in the EU, US and China*, Cambridge: Cambridge University Press.

Wassenbergh, H. A. (1991) *Principles of Outer Space Law in Hindsight*, The Hague: Martinus Nijhoff Publishers.

Watts, A. (1993) *International Law and the Antarctic Treaty System*, Cambridge: Cambridge University Press.

Weber, R. H., Grosz, M. and Weber, R. (2011) *Shaping Internet Governance: Regulatory Challenges*, New York: Springer.

Weber, R. H. and Weber, R. (2010) *Internet of Things: Legal Perspectives*, New York: Springer.

White House, The (2001) *International Strategy for Cyberspace*. <www.whitehouse.gov/sites/default/files/rss_viewer/international_strategy_for_cyberspace.pdf> (accessed 4 February 2011).

Williams, S. (2002) *Free as in Freedom: Richard Stallman's Crusade for Free Software*, Sebastopol, CA: O'Reilly Media, Inc.

Winn, J. K. (2006) *Consumer Protection in the Age of the Information Economy*, Aldershot: Ashgate Publishing, Ltd.

Wojciechowski, B., (2010) *Philosophical Approach to the Interculturality of Criminal Law*, Frankfurt: Peter Lang.

Wood, A. F. and Smith, M. J. (2005) *Online Communication: Linking Technology, Identity, and Culture*, Oxford: Routledge.

World Trade Organization Ministerial Conference (Second Session, 18–20 May 1998) *Ministerial Declaration on Global Electronic Commerce*, Geneva: WTO. <http://www.wto.org/English/tratop_e/ecom_e/mindecl_e.htm> (accessed 29 January 2011).

World Trade Organization (1998) *Work Programme on Electronic Commerce*, Geneva: WTO. <http://www.wto.org/english/tratop_e/ecom_e/wkprog_e.htm> (accessed 15 January 2011).

Zittrain, J. (2008) *The Future of the Internet and How to Stop It*, New Haven: Yale University Press.

Zittrain, J. and Edelman, B. (2003) *Empirical Analysis of Internet Filtering in China*, unpublished, Mass.: Harvard University Berkman Center for Internet and Society. <http://cyber.law.harvard.edu/filtering/china/> (accessed 21 January 2011).

Cases

3DO Co. v. *PopTop Software, Inc.* (1998) US Dist. LEXIS 21281 (ND Cal.).

A & M Records v. *Napster* (2001) US Court of Appeals for the Ninth Circuit. <http://caselaw.findlaw.com/us–9th–circuit/1047162.html> (accessed 11 February 2011.

Alteen v. *Informix Corporation* (1998) 164 Nfld. and PEIR 301, 507 APR 301).

American Libraries Association v. *Pataki* (1997) 969 F. Supp. 160 (SDNY).

Anthony G. v. *Société Civile des Producteurs Phonographiques* (2005). Decision of 8 December 2005, No. 12 Tribunal de Grande Instance de Paris, 31ème chambre/2, No. d'Affaire: 0504090091. <http://www.audionautes.net/pages/PDF/audionautestgiparis.pdf>.

Apple v. *Does* <http://w2.eff.org/Censorship/Apple_v_Does/memo_of_points.pdf> (accessed 13 August 2011). See *O'Grady*.

Attorney General of Quebec v. *Hyperinfo Canada, Inc.* (2001) No. 550–61–000887–014 (CQ). <http://aix1.uottawa.ca/~geist/hyperinfo.htm> (accessed 4 February 2011).

Attorney General of the State Of New York Internet Bureau, *Assurance of Discontinuance in the matter of Paypal, Inc.*, 16 August 2002. <http://www.oag.state.ny.us/bureaus/internet_bureau/pdfs/paypal.pdf> (accessed 28 February 2011).

Ballard v. *Savage* (1995) 65 F.3d 1495, 1498 (9th Cir.).

Banković et al. v. *Belgium and 16 other NATO Countries* (2001) Application No. 52207/99, Admissibility Decision of 12 December 2001 (European Court of Human Rights).

Bensusan Restaurant Corp. v. *King* (1996) 937 F. Supp. 295 (SDNY), affirmed 126 F. 3d. 25.

Blumenthal v. *Drudge* (1998) 992 F. Supp. 44. <http://legal.web.aol.com/decisions/ dldefam/blumenop.html> (accessed 2 February 2011).

Braintech, Inc. v. *John C. Kostiuk* (1999) BCCA. 0169 (Court of British Columbia). <http://www.courts.gov.bc.ca/jdb-txt/ca/99/01/c99–0169.txt> (accessed 2 February 2011).

Brown v. *Duchesne* (1857) 60 US 183.

Burger King Corp. v. *Rudzewicz* (1985) 471 US 462.

Calder v. *Jones* (1984) 465 US 783.

Castells v. *Spain* (1992) Application No. 11798/85. 24 April 1992 (European Court of Human Rights).

Citizens United v. *Federal Election Commission* (2010) 558 US 08–205.

Commission of the European Communities v. *French Republic* (2005) Case C–59/04, OJ (C 082) (2 April 2005) (Court of Justice of the European Communities), p. 5.

Commission of the European Communities v. *Kingdom of Belgium* (2005) Case C–143/04, OJ (C 006) (8 January 2005) (Court of Justice of the European Communities), p. 20.

Commission of the European Communities v. Kingdom of Spain (2005) Case C–31/04, OJ (C 171) (9 July 2005) (Court of Justice of the European Communities), p. 3.

Commission of the European Communities v. *Kingdom of Sweden* (2005) Case C–91/04, OJ (C 019) (22 January 2005) (Court of Justice of the European Communities), p. 8.

Commission of the European Communities v. *Republic of Finland* (2005)Case C–56/04, OJ (C 31) (5 February 2005) (Court of Justice of the European Communities), pp. 3–4.

Commission of the European Communities v. *United Kingdom of Great Britain and Northern Ireland* (2005) Case C–88/04, OJ (C 045) (19 February 2005) (Court of Justice of the European Communities), p. 11.

CompuServe, Inc, case (German). Amtsgericht München, 8340 Ds. 465 Js 173158/59 and judgment of 17 November 1999, Landgericht München and 20 Ns 465 Js 173158/95 (AG München I). <http://www.netlaw.de/urteile/lgm_12.htm> (accessed 2 February 2011).

CompuServe, Inc. v. *Patterson* (1996) 89 F. 3d 1257.

Coughenour v. *State Auto Property and Casualty Insurance Company* (1995) 62 F.3d 1423.

Curry v. *Audax* (2009) File No. 334492/KG 06–176 SR (Regional Court in Amsterdam). (For an English translation, see <http://mirrors.creativecommons.org/judgements/Curry–Audax–English.pdf> (accessed 18 December 2011)).

Cybersell, Inc. v. *Cybersell, Inc.* (1997) 130 F.3d 414 (9th Cir.).

Décision No. 2009–580 DC du 10 Juin 2009: la Loi Favourisant la Diffusion et la Protection de la Création sur Internet (Paris Conseil Constitutionnel).

Décision No. 2006–540 DC de Juillet 2006 (Paris, Conseil Constitutionnel).

Decision No. 1258 (2009) Romanian Constitutional Court. http://www.ccr.ro/decisions/pdf/ro/2009/D1258_09.pdf>. English translation: <http://www.legi–internet.ro/english/jurisprudenta–it–romania/decizii–it/romanian–constitutional–court–decision–regarding–data–retention.html>.

Decision of the German Constitutional Court (Bundesverfassungsgericht) of 2 March 2010, 1 BvR 256/08, 1 BvR 263/08, 1 BvR 586/08. <http://www.bundesverfassungsgericht.de/entscheidungen/rs20100302_1bvr025608.html> (accessed 18 December 2011).

Dostana Enterprises LLC v. *Federal Express Corporation* (2000) WL 1170134 (SDNY).

Financial Times Ltd. et al. v. *United Kingdom* (2009) Application No. 821/03 (European Court of Human Rights).

France v. *Turkey (the Lotus case)* (1927) PCIJ (Ser. A) No. 10 (PCIJ). <http://www.worldcourts.com/ pcij/eng/decisions/1927.09.07_lotus/> (accessed 2 February 2011).

Goodwin v. *United Kingdom* (1996) 22 EHRR 123 (European Court of Human Rights).

Harrods Limited v. *Sixty Internet Domain Names: Harrodsargentina.com, et al.* (2002) 302 F. 3d 214 (4th Cir.).

Hearst Corp. v. *Goldberger* (1997) WL 97097 (SDNY).

Inset Systems, Inc. v. *Instruction Set, Inc.* (1996) 937 F. Supp. 161 (D. Conn.).

International Shoe Co. v. *Washington* (1945) 326 US 310 (United States Supreme Court).

Italy v. *Drummond et al.* (2010) Tribunale Ordinario di Milano, Sezione 4 Penale, 2 February 2010, Sentenza No. 1972/2010.

Italy v. *Rizzi and Faretti* (2007) East Lombardi Appellate Court (Corte Di Cassazione). Sez. III Penale 149. <http://www.diritto–in–rete.com/sentenza.asp?id=331> (accessed 11 February 2011).

J'Accuse v. *Gen. Communications, et al.* (2001) TGI Paris, No. RG 01/57676. <http://www.juritel.com/Ldj_html–445.html> (accessed 25 June 2011).

Jay D. Sallen v. *Corinthians Licenciamentos Ltd and Desportos Licenciamentos Ltd.* (2001) 273 F.3d 14 (United States Court of Appeals for the First Circuit).

Kenneth M. Zeran v. *America Online Inc.* (1997) US Cert. Pet. 97–1488. <http://laws.findlaw.com/4th/971523p.html> (accessed 2 February 2011).

KU v. *Finland* (2008) Application No. 2827/02 (European Court of Human Rights).

Labor Court Brunswick Case (1999) 3 Ca 370/98 NZA–RR 1999 (German Labor Court/Arbeitsgericht Braunschweig).

La Ligue Contre Le Racisme v. *Yahoo! Inc.*, see Yahoo! Inc.

Lamar v. *US* (1916) 240 US 60. <http://laws.findlaw.com/us/240/60.html> (accessed 5 February 2011).

Lichtenstein v. *Guatemala (the 'Nottebohm' case)* (1955) (International Court of Justice). <http://www.icj–cij.org/icjwww/idecisions/isummaries/ilgsummary550406.htm> (accessed 2 February 2011).

LTU Lufttransportunternehme GmbH & Co. KG v. *Eurocontrol*, case 29–76, [1976] ECR, p. 1541 (Court of Justice of the European Communities).

Maritz, Inc. v. *Cybergold, Inc.* (1996) 947 F. Supp. 1328 (ED Mo.).

Mattel, Inc. v. *Adventure Apparel* (2001) WL 28672 (SDNY).

Mecklermedia Corp. v. *D.C. Congress GmbH* [1997] TLR (Ch.).

MGM Studios, Inc. v. *Grokster, Ltd.* (2005) 545 US 913.

Microsoft Corporation v. *John Does 1–27* (2009) civil action No. 1_10CV156 (LMBIJFA). < www.microsoft.com/presspass/events/rsa/docs/complaint.pdf > (accessed 2 February 2011).

Millennium Enterprises, Inc. v. *Millennium Music LP* (1999) 33 F. Supp. 2d 907 (D. Or.)

Minnesota v. *Granite Gate Resorts, Inc.* (1997) 568 NW 2d 715 (Minn. Ct. App.).

Netherlands v. *USA* (Island of Palmas case) (1928) Permanent Court of Arbitration. The Hague Justice Portal. <http://www.thehaguelegalcapital.nl/eCache/DEF/5/184.html> (accessed 5 February 2011).

Obeschlick v. *Austria (No. 2)* (1997) Application No. 20834/95 (European Court of Human Rights).

O'Grady v. *Superior Court* (2006) 139 Cal.App.4th 1423 (United States Cal.App.).

Paeffgen GmbH v. *Germany* (2007) Application Nos. 25379/04, 21688/05, 21722/05 and 21770/05 (European Court of Human Rights).

Panavision Int'l, L.P. v. *Toeppen* (1998) 141 F.3d 1316 (9th Cir.).

Pebble Beach Company v. *Caddy* (2006) 453 F. 3d 1151 (US Court of Appeals for the Ninth Circuit).

Playboy Enterprises, Inc. v. *Chuckleberry Publishing, Inc.* (1996) 939 F. Supp. 1032 (SDNY).

Reno v. *American Civil Liberties Union* (ACLU) (1997) 521 US 844 (United States Supreme Court).

SACEM, SDRM, SPPF and SCPP v. *Alexis B Juris.com* (2005) Tribunal de Grande Instance Pontoise, 6ème chambre/3. <http://www.juriscom.net/jpt/visu.php?ID=639> (accessed 5 February 2011).

Schooner Exchange, The v. *McFaddon* (1812) 11 US 116.

Schwarzenegger v. *Fred Martin Motor Co.* (2004) 374 F.3d 797, 802 (9th Cir.).

Shevill v. *Presse Alliance SA* (1995) case 68/93, [1995] ECR 1–415 (Court of Justice of the European Communities).

Sociedad General de Autores y Editores (SGAE) v. *Fernández* (2005) Procedimiento Ordinario 761/2005, File No. 15/2.006 (Court of First Instance No. 6, Badajoz, Spain). <www.extremaduracreativa.org/sentencia1.pdf> (accessed 18 December 2011)

United States v. *Aluminium Corporation of America* (1945) 148 F. 2d 416. <http://hubcap.clemson.edu/~sauerr/classes/425/cases/alcoa.pdf> (accessed 5 January 2011).

United States v. *Swiss American Bank, Ltd.* (2001) 274 F.3d 610, 623–24 (1st Cir.).

United States v. *Thomas* (1996) 74 F.3d 701 (6th Cir.).

United States v. *Yunis* (1991) 924 F. 2d 1086. <http://www.tkb.org/documents/Cases/87–CR-0377–Indictment.pdf> (accessed 12 February 2011).

Universal Music Australia Pty, Ltd. v. *Sharman License Holdings. Ltd.* [2005] FCA 1242 (Federal Court of Australia). <http://www.austlii.edu.au/au/cases/cth/federal_ct/2004/934.html> (accessed 11 February 2011).

Vereniging Buma and Stichting Stemra v. *Kazaa B.V.* (2006) Supreme Court of the Netherlands (Hoge Raad der Nederlanden) C02/186HR JMH/AT. For an English translation, see Mudd Law Offices. <http://www.muddlawoffices.com/RIAA/cases/Netherlands.pdf> (accessed 11 February 2011).

Vereniging Weekblad 'Bluf!' v. *The Netherlands* (1995) Application No. 16616/90, 20 EHRR 189 (European Court of Human Rights).

Yahoo! Inc. v. *La Ligue Contre Le Racisme et l'Antisémitisme (The League Against Racism and Antisemitism (LICRA))* (2006) 433 F.3d 1199 (United States Court of Appeals for the Ninth Circuit). For the original French decision, see decision of the regional court in Paris of 20 November 2000, No. RG 00/05308. <http://www.eff.org/legal/Jurisdiction_and_sovereignty/LICRA_v_Yahoo/20001120_fr_int_ruling.en.pdf> (accessed 16 January 2011). For the regional US decision, successfully appealed, see (2006) WL 60670 (9th Cir.) <http://www.ca9.uscourts.gov/ca9/newopinions.nsf/3DF703F416DC0608882570F40006DDCF/$file/0117424.pdf?openelement> (accessed 16 June 2006).

Zippo Manufacturing Co. v. *Zippo Dot Com, Inc.* (1997) 952 F. Supp. 1119 (ED Penn.).

Domestic constitutions, legislation and legislative codes

China: Provisions on the Administration of the Protection of Secrets on Internationally Networked Computer Information Systems. An English translation is available at <http://www.cecc.gov/pages/virtualAcad/exp/expsecurity.php> (accessed 16 January 2011).

China: Computer Information Network and Internet Security, Protection and Management Regulations, 1997. For an English translation, see <http://www.asianlii.org/cn/legis/cen/laws/cinaispamr904> (accessed 13 January 2011).

China: Congressional-Executive Commission decision on Provisions on the Administration of Internet Electronic Messaging Services, 27 October 2000. An English translation can be found at <http://www.cecc.gov/pages/virtualAcad/index.phpd?showsingle=1568> (accessed 13 January 2011).

China: Interim Provisions on the Administration of Internet Publication, 2002. <http://www.cecc.gov/pages/virtualAcad/index.phpd?showsingle=1563> (accessed 19 January 2010). An English translation is available at <http://www.cecc.gov/pages/virtualAcad/index.phpd?showsingle=1563> (accessed 19 January 2010).

China: Law of the People's Republic of China on Protection of State Secrets, 1988. For an English translation see <http://www.cecc.gov/pages/newLaws/protectSecretsENG.php> (accessed 8 January 2011).

China: Public Pledge of Self-Regulation and Professional Ethics for China Internet Industry, 2002. An English translation can be found at <http://www.isc.org.cn/20020417/ca102762.htm> (accessed 16 January 2011).

China: State Council Order No 291 of 11 October 2000 (Telecommunications Regulations). An English translation can be found at <http://tradeinservices.mofcom.gov.cn/en/b/2000–09–25/18619.shtml> (accessed 6 January 2011).

State Council Order No 292 of 25 September 2000 (Administrative Measures for Managing Internet Information Systems). An English translation can be found at <http://www.chinaitlaw.org/?p1=print&p2=050306173518> (accessed 13 January 2011).

China: State Security Law, 1993. An English translation can be found at <http://www.cecc.gov/pages/virtualAcad/exp/explaws.php> (accessed 19 January 2011).

Constitution of the Republic of Costa Rica, 1949.

Estonia: Public Information Act, 2000, RT1 I 2000, 92, 597.

Finland: Act on Blocking Child Pornography ('Laki Lapsipornografian Levittämisen Estotoimista'), 2006, 1.12.2006/1068 (Finland). <http://www.finlex.fi/fi/laki/ajantasa/2006/20061068> (accessed 13 February 2011).

Finland: Communications Market Act, 2003, FINLEX 393/2003. <www.finlex.fi/en/laki/kaannokset/2003/en20030393.pdf > (accessed 13 February 2011).

Finland: Decree of the Ministry of Transport and Communications on the Minimum Rate of a Functional Internet Access as a Universal Service, 2009, FINLEX 732/2009. <www.finlex.fi/fi/laki/kaannokset/2009/en20090732.pdf> (accessed: 13 February 2011).

France: Loi No. 2011–669 du 12 Juin 2009 Favorisant la Diffusion et la Protection de la Création sur Internet ('La Loi Hadopi'), NOR: MCCX0811238L, ORF No. 0135, 13 Juin 2009, p. 9666.

France: Loi No. 2006–961 du 1er Août 2006 Relative au Droit D'Auteur et aux Droits Voisins dans la Société de L'information (DADVSI), NOR: MCCX0300082L. *http://www.legifrance.gouv.fr/WAspad/UnTexteDeJorf?numjo=MCCX0300082L* (accessed 5 February 2011).

Germany: Copyright Law (*Gesetz über Urheberrecht und verwandte Schutzrechte – Urheberrechtsgesetz*), 1965 as amended (uniform text: BGBl I S 2349).

Germany: Penal Code (Strafgesetzbuch) 1998, BGBl. I S. 3322.

India: Communications Convergence Bill No. 89 of 2001. <http://www.dot.gov.in/Acts/CCBill_of_pages_41.doc> (accessed 5 January 2011).

Poland: Polish Institute of National Remembrance Act, 1998, 155(1016) Dz. U. [Journal of Laws].

Russia: Civil Code.

Russia: Federation Law on Copyright and Neighboring Rights, 1993, Зкон РФ N5351–1. An English translation is available at <http://en.wikisource.org/wiki/Russian_Federation._Law_on_Copyright_and_Neighboring_Rights>.

Singapore: Broadcasting Act, 1994. An English translation is available at Singapore Statutes Online. <http://statutes.agc.gov.sg/non_version/cgi–bin/cgi_retrieve.pl?&actno=Reved–297&date=latest&method=part> (accessed 16 January 2011).

Singapore: Computer Misuse Act, 1993. An English translation is available at Singapore Statutes Online. <http://statutes.agc.gov.sg/non_version/cgi–bin/cgi_retrieve.pl?actno=REVED–50A&doctitle=COMPUTER%20MISUSE%20ACT%0A&date=latest&method=part> (accessed 7 June 2011).

Singapore: Defamation Act, 1965. An English translation is available at Singapore Statutes Online. <http://statutes.agc.gov.sg/non_version/cgi–bin/cgi_retrieve.pl?actno=REVED–75&doctitle=DEFAMATION%20ACT%0A&date=latest&method=part&sl=1> (accessed 13 January 2011).

Singapore: Media Development Authority of Singapore Act.

Singapore Media Development Authority *Internet Code of Practice*. <http://www.mda.gov.sg/wms.file/mobj/mobj.497.internet_code.pdf> (accessed 16 January 2011). This document has the force of law.

Spain: Ley Orgánica del Poder Judicial, 1985, 6/1985. <http://noticias.juridicas.com/base_datos/Admin/lo6–1985.html> (accessed 19 January 2011).

United Kingdom: Channel Tunnel Act 1987, c. 53.

United Kingdom: Regulation of Investigatory Powers Act (RIPA), 2000.

United States: Alien Tort Claims Act, 1982, 28 USC § 1350.

United States: Anticybersquatting Consumer Protection Act (ACPA), 1999.

United States: Antiterrorism and Effective Death Penalty Act (AEDPA), 28 USC § 2254 (1996). This was an amendment to the Alien Torts Act. <http://usinfo.state.gov/usa/infousa/laws/majorlaw/s735.htm> (accessed 4 March 2011).

United States: California Corporations Code § 5000.

United States: Can-Spam Act (2010) 15 USC §§ 7701–7713.

United States: Children's Internet Protection Act, 2000, 17 USC § 1701.

United States: Code of Federal Regulations (US), Title 16.

United States Commission on Uniform State Laws (1962) model statute, The Uniform Interstate and International Procedure Act (UIIPA).

United States: Communications Decency Act (CDA), 1997, 47 USC § 151.

United States: Computer Fraud and Abuse Act, 1986, 18 USC § 1030.

United States: Digital Millennium Copyright Act (DMCA), 1998, 17 USC § 1201

United States: Electronic Communications Privacy Act (ECPA), 1986, 18 USC §§ 2510–2522.

United States: Global Internet Freedom Act, H.r. 2216. <http://www.govtrack.us/congress/billtext.xpd?bill=h109–2216> (accessed 5 January 2011). (Not yet passed.)

United States: Illinois 'long-arm' statute, 1955, 735 ILCS 5/2–209.

United States: Internet Tax Freedom Act, 1998, 47 USC §151.

United States: Lanham Act, 1946, 15 USC § 1125, Subchapter III.

United States: Omnibus Appropriations Act, 1998.

United States: Protecting Cyberspace as a National Asset [draft] Act, § 3480.

United States: Uniform Interstate and International Procedure Act [adopted model law], 1962.

United States: Uniting and Strengthening America by Providing Appropriate Tools Required to Intercept and Obstruct Terrorism Act (USA PATRIOT Act), 2001, HR 3162.

International legal and quasi-legal documents

Agreement between the Parties to the North Atlantic Treaty Organization regarding the Status of their Forces, London, 9 June 1951.

Agreement on the Status of the North Atlantic Treaty Organization, National Representatives and International Staff, Ottawa, 20 September 1951. <http://www.nato.int/docu/basictxt/b510920a.htm> (accessed 13 January 2011).

Antarctic Treaty, Washington, 1959, 402 UNTS 71.

Charter of the United Nations, San Francisco, 1945.

Convention for the Conservation of Antarctic Seals, 1972.

Convention for the Protection of Literary and Artistic Works, Berne, 9 September1886 ('the Berne Convention'). <http://www.wipo.int/treaties/en/ip/berne/trtdocs_wo001.html> (accessed 19 January 2011).

Convention for the Suppression of Unlawful Acts Against the Safety of Civil Aviation (Sabotage), Montreal, 23 September 1971 ('the Montreal Convention'), 24 UST 564.

Convention for the Suppression of Unlawful Seizure of Aircraft (Hijacking), The Hague, 16 December 1970 ('the Hague Convention'), 22 UST 1641.

Convention on International Liability for Damage Caused by Space Objects, London, Moscow and Washington, 29 March 1972 ('the Liability Convention'), 961 UNTS 187.

Convention on Jurisdiction and the Enforcement of Judgments in Civil and Commercial Matters, Brussels, 27 September 1968, OJ (C 27) (26 January 1978).

Convention on Jurisdiction and the Enforcement of Judgments in Civil and Commercial Matters, Lugano, 16 September 1988 ('the Lugano Convention'), OJ (L 319) (25 November 1988), pp. 9–48.

Convention on Mutual Administrative Assistance in Tax Matters, Council of Europe, Strasbourg, 25 January 1988, CETS No. 127.

Convention on Offenses and Certain Other Acts Committed on Board Aircraft, Tokyo, 14 September 1963 ('the Tokyo Convention'), 704 UNTS 220.

Convention on Registration of Objects Launched into Outer Space ('the Registration Convention'), New York, 12 November 1974, 1023 UNTS 15.

Convention on the High Seas, Geneva, 1958, UNTS 450 UNTS 11 (No. 6465).

Convention on the Law Applicable to Contractual Obligations, Rome, 1980, OJ (C 27) (26 January 1998), pp. 34–52.

Convention on the Law of the Sea, Montego Bay, 10 December 1982, 1833 UNTS 397.

Convention on the Law of Treaties, Vienna, 1969, 1155 UNTS 331, 8 ILM 679.

Convention on the Prevention and Punishment of the Crime of Genocide, Paris, 1948, 78 UNTS 277.

Convention on the Regulation of Antarctic Mineral Resource Activities, Wellington, 2 June 1988, 27 ILM. 868.

Convention on the Safety of United Nations and Associated Personnel, 9 September 1994, GA Res., UN Doc. A/RES/49/59.

Convention on Third Party Liability in the Field of Nuclear Energy, Paris, 1960, 956 UNTS 251.

Convention Relating to Intervention on the High Seas in Cases of Oil Pollution Casualties, Brussels, 29 November 1969, in force 6 May 1975, 9 ILM.

Council of Europe Additional Protocol to the Convention on Cybercrime, Concerning the Criminalization of Acts of a Racist and Xenophobic Nature Committed Through Computer Systems, Strasbourg, 28 January 2003. <http://conventions.coe.int/Treaty/en/Treaties/Html/189.htm> (accessed 11 January 2011).

Council of Europe Convention for the Protection of Individuals with Regard to Automatic Processing of Personal Data, Strasbourg, 28 January 1981, ETS No. 108.

Council of Europe Convention on Cybercrime, Budapest, 23 November 2001, Europ. T. S. No. 185. For the Explanatory Report, see <http://conventions.coe.int/Treaty/EN/Reports/Html/185.htm> (accessed 16 January 2011).

Council Of Europe Convention on the Legal Status of Migrant Workers, Strasbourg, 24 November 1977, Europ. T. S. No. 93.

Council of Europe Declaration on Freedom of Communication on the Internet, 28 May 2003. <http://www.coe.int/t/informationsociety/documents/Freedom%20of%20communication%20on%20the%20Internet_en.pdf> (accessed 13 February 2011).

Covenant of the League of Nations, Paris, 1924.

European Convention for the Protection of Human Rights and Fundamental Freedoms, Rome, 4 November 1950 (entered into force 3 September 1953).

European Union Commission Recommendation of 12 May 2009 on the Implementation of Privacy and Data Protection Principles in Applications supported by Radio-Frequency Identification, SEC (2009), pp. 585–586.

European Union Council Decision 2007/125/JHA of 12 February 2007, Establishing for the Period 2007 to 2013, as Part of General Programme on Security and Safeguarding Liberties, the Specific Programme 'Prevention of and Fight against Crime'.

European Union Directive 1989/552/EEC of the European Parliament and of the Council of 3 October 1989 on the Coordination of Certain Provisions laid down by Law, Regulation or Administrative Action in Member States concerning the Pursuit of Television Broadcasting Activities, OJ (L 298) (17 October 1989), pp. 23–30.

European Union Directive 1995/46/EC of the European Parliament and of the Council of 24 October 1995 on the Protection of Individuals with Regard to the Processing of Personal Data and on the Free Movement of such Data, OJ (L 281), (23 November 1995), pp. 31–50.

European Union Directive 1999/93/EC of the European Parliament and of the Council of 13 December 1999 on a Community Framework for Electronic Signatures, OJ (L 013) (19 January 2000), pp. 12–20.

European Union Directive 2000/31/EC of the European Parliament and of the Council of 8 June 2000 on Certain Legal Aspects of Information Society Services, in Particular Electronic Commerce, in the Internal Market ('the Directive on Electronic Commerce'), OJ (L 178) (17 July 2000), pp. 1–16.

European Union Directive 2002/19/EC of the European Parliament and of the Council of 7 March 2002 on Access to, and Interconnection of, Electronic Communications Networks and Associated Facilities ('the Access Directive'), OJ (L 108) (24 April 2002), pp. 21–32.

European Union Directive 2002/20/EC of the European Parliament and of the Council of 7 March 2002 on the Authorization of Electronic Communications Networks and Services ('the Authorization Directive'), OJ (L 108) (24 April 2002), pp. 21–31.

European Union Directive 2002/21/EC of the European Parliament and of the Council of 7 March 2002 on a Common Regulatory Framework for Electronic Communications Networks and Services ('the Framework Directive'), OJ (L 108) (24 April 2002), pp. 33–50.

European Union Directive 2002/22/EC of the European Parliament and of the Council of 7 March 2002 on Universal Service and Users' Rights relating to Electronic Communications Networks and Services ('the Universal Service Directive'), OJ (L 108), 24 April 2002, pp. 51–77.

European Union Directive 2002/58/EC of the European Parliament and of the Council of 12 July 2002 Concerning the Processing of Personal Data and the Protection of Privacy in the Electronic Communications Sector ('the Directive on Privacy and Electronic Communications'), OJ (L 201/37) (31 July 2002), pp. 37–47.

European Union Directive 2006/24/EC of the European Parliament and of the Council of 15 March 2006 on the Retention of Data Generated or Processed in Connection with the Provision of Publicly Available Electronic Communications Services or of Public Communications Networks and Amending Directive 2002/58/EC, OJ (L 105) (13 April 2006), p. 54–63.

European Union Directive 2007/65/EC of the European Parliament and of the Council of 11 December 2007 amending Council Directive 89/552/EEC on the Coordination of Certain Provisions laid down by Law, Regulation or Administrative Action in Member States concerning the Pursuit of Television Broadcasting Activities, OJ (L 332) (18 December 2007), pp. 27–45.

European Union Regulation 44/2001 of the Council 22 December 2000 on Jurisdiction and the Recognition and Enforcement of Judgments in Civil and Commercial Matters, OJ (L 012) (16 January 2001), pp. 1–23.

European Union Regulation 1882/2003 of the European Parliament and of the Council of 29 September 2003, OJ (L 284) (31 October 2003), pp. 1–53.

European Union Regulation 864/2007 of the European Parliament and of the Council of 11 July 2007 on the Law Applicable to Non-Contractual Obligations (Rome II), OJ (L 199) (31 July 2007), pp. 40–49.

Hague Conference on Private International Law (2005) Draft Convention on Jurisdiction and Foreign Judgments in Civil and Commercial Matters, The Hague.

International Convention for the Protection of Industrial Property, Paris, 1883.

International Convention on Civil Liability for Oil Pollution Damage, Brussels, 1969, 973 UNTS 3.

International Convention on the Establishment of an International Fund for Compensation for Oil Pollution Damage, Brussels, 1971, 11 ILM 284.

International Law Commission's Draft Articles on Prevention of Transboundary Harm from Hazardous Activities

International Maritime Organization Convention for the Suppression of Unlawful Acts against the Safety of Maritime Navigation ('the Maritime Terrorism Convention'), Rome, 10 March 1988, 1678 UNTS 201.

London Action Plan on International Spam Enforcement Cooperation, London, 2004. <http://www.londonactionplan.com/> (accessed 15 January 2011).

Protocol between the Government of the United Kingdom of Great Britain and Northern Ireland and the Government of the French Republic Concerning Frontier Controls and Policing, Cooperation in Criminal Justice, Public Safety and Mutual Assistance relating to the Channel Fixed Link, Sangatte, 25 November 1991, 1747 UNTS 109. <http://www.cps.gov.uk/legal/section2/chapter_f.html> (accessed 4 March 2011).

Protocol on Environmental Protection to the Antarctic Treaty, Madrid, 1991 ('the Madrid Protocol'). <http://www.antarctica.ac.uk/About_Antarctica/Treaty/ protocol.html> (accessed 14 February 2011).

Rome Statute of the International Criminal Court, Rome, 17 July 1988, 2187 UNTS 90.

Treaty Banning Nuclear Weapon Tests in the Atmosphere, in Outer Space and Under Water, Moscow, 5 August 1963, 480 UNTS 43.

Treaty on Principles Governing the Activities of States in the Exploration and Use of Outer Space, including the Moon and Other Celestial Bodies, New York, 27 January 1967, 610 UNTS 205.

United Nations UNESCO Charter on the Preservation of Digital Heritage, Paris, 2003. <http://portal.unesco.org/en/ev.php–URL_ID=17721&URL_DO=DO_TOPIC&URL_SECTION=201.html>.

United Nations UNESCO Universal Declaration on Cultural Diversity, Paris, 2001.

United Nations Commission on International Trade Law (UNCITRAL) Law Model Law on Electronic Commerce, 1997, U. N. Doc. A/RES/51/162.

United Nations Commission on International Trade Law (UNCITRAL) Draft Uniform Rules on Electronic Signatures, New York, February 2000. UN Doc. A/CN.9/WG.IV/WP.84. <http://www.un.or.at/uncitral/english/sessions/wg_ec/wp-77.htm> (accessed 28 January 2011).

United Nations Commission on International Trade Law (UNCITRAL) Model Law on Electronic Commerce, New York, 1996. For its adoption by the UN Commission on International Trade Law, see New York, 16 December 1996, UN Doc. A/RES/51/162. For the related GA Resolution, see <http://www.jus.uio.no/lm/un.electronic.commerce.model.law.1996/> (accessed 14 January 2011).

United Nations Draft Code Against the Peace and Security of Mankind, 1991, UN Doc. A/46/10.

United Nations Economic and Social Council (ECOSOC) Resolution 2010/2 on the Assessment of the Progress Made in the Implementation of and Follow-Up to the outcomes of the World Summit on the Information Society.

United Nations International Covenant on Civil and Political Rights, 1966, UN Doc. A/6316, 999 UNTS 171, entered into force on 23 March 1976.

United Nations International Covenant on Economic, Social and Cultural Rights, 1966, U.N. Doc. A/6316.

United Nations Resolution 53/70 on Developments in the Field of Information and Telecommunications in the Context of International Security, 1998, U.N. Doc. A/53/576.

United Nations Resolution 54/49 on Developments in the Field of Information and Telecommunications in the Context of International Security, 1999, U.N. Doc. A/54/558.

United Nations Resolution 55/28 on Developments in the Field of Information and Telecommunications, 2000, U.N. Doc. A/55/554.

United Nations Resolution 56/19 on Developments in the Field of Information and Telecommunications in the context of international security, 2001, U.N. Doc. A/55/554.

United Nations Resolution 57/239 on Creation of a Global Culture of Cybersecurity, 2002, U.N. Doc. A/57/529/Add.3.

United Nations Resolution 58/199 on Creation of a Global Culture of Cybersecurity and the Protection of Critical Information Infrastructures, 2003, U.N. Doc. A/58/481/Add.2.

United Nations Resolution of the 12th session of the Human Rights Council, 2 October 2009, 'Freedom of Opinion and Expression', UN Doc. A/HRC/RES/12/16.

Universal Copyright Convention, Geneva, 1952, as revised in Paris, 1971, 943 UNTS 178.

Universal Declaration of Human Rights, 1948, G.A. res. 217A (III), U.N. Doc A/810 at 71.

WIPO Copyright Treaty, 1996.

WIPO Draft Revised Trademark Law Treaty, 2004, SCT/12/2. <www.wipo.int/edocs/mdocs/sct/en/sct_12/sct_12_2.pdf> (accessed 25 June 2011).

WIPO Performances and Phonograms Treaty, 1996.

WIPO Protocol Relating to the Madrid Agreement Concerning the International Registration of Marks, Madrid, 1989. <http://www.wipo.int/madrid/en/legal_texts/trtdocs_wo016.html> (accessed 14 February 2011).

World Trade Organization Agreement on Trade-Related Aspects of Intellectual Property Rights, Marrakesh, 15 April 1994.

ICANN, IANA and IETF documents in chronological order

Internet Engineering Task Force (IETF) (1994) *IETF Standard RFC 1591 Domain Name System Structure and Delegation.* <http://www.isi.edu/in–notes/rfc1591.txt> (accessed 1 January 2009).

ICANN (1998) *Memorandum of Understanding Between the US Department of Commerce and Internet Corporation for Assigned Names and Numbers.* <http://www.ntia.doc.gov/ntiahome/domainname/icann–memorandum.htm> (accessed 16 January 2009).

ICANN (1999) *Internet Co-ordination Policy: Internet Domain Name System Structure and Delegation (ccTLD Administration and Delegation).* <http://www.icann.org/en/icp/icp–1.htm> (accessed 26 June 2011).

ICANN (1999) *Uniform Domain Name Dispute Resolution Policy* (UDRP). <http://www.icann.org/en/udrp/udrp.htm>

ICANN (2000) *March 2000 ICANN Meeting in Cairo: ccTLD Delegation and Administration Policies.* <www.icann.org/cairo2000/cctld–topic.htm> (accessed 1 January 2009).

ICANN (2000) *Yokohama Meeting Topic: ccTLD Delegation and Administration Policies.* <www.icann.org/yokohama/cctld–topic.htm> (accessed 1 January 2009).

Twomey, P. (2000) *Letter from GAC Chairman Paul Twomey Transmitting GAC Views on ccTLD Delegation and Administration Principles.* <www.icann.org/committees/gac/twomey–letter–23feb00.htm> (accessed 1 January 2009).

ICANN GAC (2000) *Principles for Delegation and Administration of ccTLDs Presented by Governmental Advisory Committee.* <http://www.isi.edu/in–notes/rfc1591.txt> (accessed 1 January 2009).

ICANN Assistance Group on Proposed Implementation of an At-Large Advisory Committee (2002) Report to the Evolution and Reform Committee. <http://www.icann.org/en/committees/evol-reform/alacag-report-19aug02.htm>. (accessed 1 January 2009).

IANA (2002) *ccTLD Redelegation Step-by-Step Overview.* <www.iana.org/cctld/redelegation–overview–19jun02.htm> (accessed 1 January 2009).

ICANN (2004) *ccTLDs .ht Registry Decision.* <http://www.iana.org/reports/2004/ht–report–13jan04.html>.

Stuart Lynn, M. (2004) *President's Report: ICANN - The Case for Reform.* <www.icann.org/general/lynn–reform–proposal–24feb02.html> (accessed 1 January 2009)

ICANN (2007) Issues Paper: Selection of IDN ccTLDs Associated with the ISO 3166–1 Two Letter Codes.

ICANN (2007) *DNS Attack Factsheet 1.1*, California: ICANN. <http://www.icann.org/en/announcements/announcement–08mar07.htm> (accessed 25 December 2010).

ICANN (2009) *Affirmation of Commitments by the United States Department of Commerce and the Internet Corporation for Assigned Names and Numbers,* 30 September 2009. <http://www.icann.org/en/affirmation.htm> (accessed 25 December 2010).

ICANN (2011) GNSO Council Resolution, 3 February 2011. <http://gnso.icann.org/mailing–lists/archives/council/msg10635.html> (accessed 15 June 2011).

Organization for economic co-operation and development documents in chronological order

Organization for Economic Co-operation and Development (1980) *Guidelines on the Protection of Privacy and Transborder Flows of Personal Data*, Paris: OECD Publishing. <http://www.oecd.org/document/18/0,2340,en_2649_34255_1815186_1_1_1_1,00.html> (accessed 9 January 2011).

Organization for Economic Co-operation and Development (1985) *Declaration on Transborder Data Flows*, Paris: OECD Publishing. <http://www.oecd.org/document/60/0,2340,en_2649_34225_2373500_1_1_1_1,00.html> (accessed 9 January 2011).

Organization for Economic Co-operation and Development (1998) *Electronic Commerce: Taxation Framework Conditions* ('the Ottawa Principles'). <http://www.oecd.org/dataoecd/46/3/1923256.pdf> (accessed 14 January 2011).

Organization for Economic Co-operation and Development (1998) *Ministerial Declaration on the Protection of Privacy on Global Networks.* <http://www.oecd.org/dataoecd/39/13/1840065.pdf> (accessed 9 January 2011).

Organization for Economic Co-operation and Development (1999) *Recommendation Concerning Guidelines for Consumer Protection in the Context of Electronic Commerce.* <www.oecd.org/dataoecd/18/13/34023235.pdf> (accessed 9 January 2011).

Organization for Economic Co-operation and Development (2003) *Privacy Online: OECD Guidance on Policy and Practice*, Paris: OECD Publishing.

Organization for Economic Co-operation and Development (2003) *Guidelines for Protecting Consumers from Fraudulent and Deceptive Commercial Practices Across Borders.* <http://www.oecd.org/dataoecd/15/51/34011414.pdf> (accessed 9 January 2011).

Organization for Economic Co-operation and Development (2003) *Promise and Problems of E–Democracy,* Paris: OECD. <http://www.oecd.org/dataoecd/9/11/35176328.pdf> (accessed 4 February 2011).

Organization for Economic Co-operation and Development (2004) Minutes of the Electronic Commerce Steering Group Meeting, Santiago, Chile, 26–27 February 2004.

Organization for Economic Co-operation and Development Directorate for Science, Technology and Industry, Committee for Information, Computer and Communications Policy (2005) *Guide To Measuring The Information Society* Paris: OECD. <http://www.olis.oecd.org/olis/2005doc.nsf/0/49b3a67e2dbbab51c12570b300392351/DocPDFEng/0.A6?OpenElement&FieldElemFormat=gif> (accessed 7 February 2011).

Software licenses

CeCILL (2005) Free Software License Agreement Version 2.0. <http://www.cecill.info/licences/Licence_CeCILL_V2–en.html CeCILL> (accessed 13 January 2011).

GNU (2007), General Public License Version 3. <http://www.gnu.org/licenses/gpl.html> (accessed 18 December 2011).

University of California (1998) Berkeley Software Distribution License.

Miscellaneous

G7 (2000) Summary of the First Meeting of the G8 Digital Opportunity Taskforce (the Dot Force,), 30 November 2000). <http://www.g7.utoronto.ca/dot_force/summary–nov–00.html> (accessed 28 February 2011).

Stanford Draft Convention on Protection from Cyber Crimes and Terrorism, (2000) IWAR. <http://www.iwar.org.uk/law/resources/cybercrime/stanford/cisac–draft.htm> (accessed 13 January 2011).

United States Department of Commerce, National Telecommunications and Information Administration (1998) *Management of Internet Names and Addresses* ('the White Paper'), Docket Number: 980212036–8146–02.<http://www.ntia.doc.gov/ntiahome/domainname/6_5_98dns.htm> (accessed 14 January 2009).

Index

Milton Keynes UK
Ingram Content Group UK Ltd.
UKHW040100071024
449327UK00019B/696